THE NEW CAMBRIDGE SHAKESPEARE

GENERAL EDITOR
Brian Gibbons

ASSOCIATE GENERAL EDITOR
A. R. Braunmuller, *University of California, Los Angeles*

From the publication of the first volumes in 1984 the General Editor of the New Cambridge Shakespeare was Philip Brockbank and the Associate General Editors were Brian Gibbons and Robin Hood. From 1990 to 1994 the General Editor was Brian Gibbons and the Associate General Editors were A. R. Braunmuller and Robin Hood.

ROMEO AND JULIET

Professor Evans helps the reader to visualise the stage action of *Romeo and Juliet*, a vital element in the play's significance and useful to students approaching it for the first time. The history of the play in the theatre is accompanied by illustrations of notable productions from the eighteenth century onwards. A lucid commentary alerts the reader to the difficulties of language, thought and staging.

For this updated edition Thomas Moisan has added a new section to the Introduction which takes account of the number of important professional theatre productions and the large output of scholarly criticism on the play which have appeared in recent years. The Reading List has also been revised and augmented.

THE NEW CAMBRIDGE SHAKESPEARE

All's Well That Ends Well, edited by Russell Fraser
Antony and Cleopatra, edited by David Bevington
As You Like It, edited by Michael Hattaway
The Comedy of Errors, edited by T. S. Dorsch
Coriolanus, edited by Lee Bliss
Cymbeline, edited by Martin Butler
Hamlet, edited by Philip Edwards
Julius Caesar, edited by Marvin Spevack
King Edward III, edited by Giorgio Melchiori
The First Part of King Henry IV, edited by Herbert Weil and Judith Weil
The Second Part of King Henry IV, edited by Giorgio Melchiori
King Henry V, edited by Andrew Gurr
The First Part of King Henry VI, edited by Michael Hattaway
The Second Part of King Henry VI, edited by Michael Hattaway
The Third Part of King Henry VI, edited by Michael Hattaway
King Henry VIII, edited by John Margeson
King John, edited by L. A. Beaurline
The Tragedy of King Lear, edited by Jay L. Halio
King Richard II, edited by Andrew Gurr
King Richard III, edited by Janis Lull
Love's Labour's Lost, edited by William C. Carroll
Macbeth, edited by A. R. Braunmuller
Measure for Measure, edited by Brian Gibbons
The Merchant of Venice, edited by M. M. Mahood
The Merry Wives of Windsor, edited by David Crane
A Midsummer Night's Dream, edited by R. A. Foakes
Much Ado About Nothing, edited by F. H. Mares
Othello, edited by Norman Sanders
Pericles, edited by Doreen DelVecchio and Antony Hammond
The Poems, edited by John Roe
Romeo and Juliet, edited by G. Blakemore Evans
The Sonnets, edited by G. Blakemore Evans
The Taming of the Shrew, edited by Ann Thompson
The Tempest, edited by David Lindley
Timon of Athens, edited by Karl Klein
Titus Andronicus, edited by Alan Hughes
Troilus and Cressida, edited by Anthony B. Dawson
Twelfth Night, edited by Elizabeth Story Donno
The Two Gentlemen of Verona, edited by Kurt Schlueter
The Two Noble Kinsmen, edited by Robert Kean Turner and Patricia Tatspaugh
The Winter's Tale, edited by Susan Snyder and Deborah T. Curren-Aquino

THE EARLY QUARTOS
The First Quarto of Hamlet, edited by Kathleen O. Irace
The First Quarto of King Henry V, edited by Andrew Gurr
The First Quarto of King Lear, edited by Jay L. Halio
The First Quarto of King Richard III, edited by Peter Davison
The First Quarto of Othello, edited by Scott McMillin
The First Quarto of Romeo and Juliet, edited by Lukas Erne
The Taming of a Shrew: The 1594 Quarto, edited by Stephen Roy Miller

ROMEO AND JULIET

Updated edition

Edited by
G. BLAKEMORE EVANS

CAMBRIDGE
UNIVERSITY PRESS

CAMBRIDGE
UNIVERSITY PRESS

University Printing House, Cambridge CB2 8BS, United Kingdom

One Liberty Plaza, 20th Floor, New York, NY 10006, USA

477 Williamstown Road, Port Melbourne, VIC 3207, Australia

314-321, 3rd Floor, Plot 3, Splendor Forum, Jasola District Centre, New Delhi - 110025, India

79 Anson Road, #06-04/06, Singapore 079906

Cambridge University Press is part of the University of Cambridge.

It furthers the University's mission by disseminating knowledge in the pursuit of education, learning and research at the highest international levels of excellence.

www.cambridge.org
Information on this title: www.cambridge.org/9780521532532

First published 1984
Reprinted 1986, 1988, 1989, 1992, 1994, 1996, 1997 (with revisions), 1998, 2000
Updated edition 2003
19th printing 2018

A catalogue record for this publication is available from the British Library

Library of Congress Cataloging Card Number: 83–7776

ISBN 978-0-521-82546-7 Hardback
ISBN 978-0-521-53253-2 Paperback

CONTENTS

ILLUSTRATIONS

PREFACE

Anyone who undertakes to edit *Romeo and Juliet* today owes a heavy debt to the whole editorial tradition, both textual and critical, especially to the work of Theobald, Capell, W. A. Wright, Dowden, Kittredge, Dover Wilson, G. I. Duthie, Richard Hosley and George W. Williams. I have tried as fully as possible to acknowledge this debt. But I must add a particular word of thanks to Professor Brian Gibbons, an Associate General Editor of this series, whose own Arden edition of *Romeo and Juliet* appeared in 1980, shortly after my work was under way, and to Professor Philip Brockbank, the General Editor. Their example and careful criticism, as well as their patience, though sorely tried, have been a source of great comfort and support.

I am, of course, deeply indebted to other friends and colleagues – to Dr Marie Edel, Professors John Klause, Richard Marius, Charles Shattuck and John H. Smith, all of whom read substantial parts of the manuscript and offered much helpful criticism, and to Professors Henry Hatfield, Albert Lord, Harry Levin, Marvin Spevack, Donald Stone and John Tobin, each of whom assisted me with information when I most needed it. My special thanks must also go to Miss Anne Macaulay, my secretary, and to my former student, Dr Kevin Cope, who checked the text and textual collations.

The Houghton Library and the Harvard Theatre Collection have been unfailingly helpful and have generously granted me permission to draw on some of their riches for most of the photographic illustrations. I am particularly grateful to Dr Jeanne Newlin, Curator of the Theatre Collection, and Miss Sandra LaFleur for their aid in assembling these illustrations. I also wish to thank Miss Sarah Stanton, Mr Michael Black, and, especially, Mr Paul Chipchase of the Cambridge University Press for their continual good offices in wrestling with a large and intractable manuscript and reducing it to something resembling form and substance. Some welcome financial aid was granted to me by the Harvard Graduate Society and the Hyder E. Rollins Memorial Fund.

Finally, as always, my deepest debt, and most lasting, is to my wife, whose support and companionship continue to be a 'bounty as boundless as the sea'.

G. B. E.

Harvard University

ABBREVIATIONS AND CONVENTIONS

1. Shakespeare's plays

The abbreviated titles of Shakespeare's plays have been modified from those used in the *Harvard Concordance to Shakespeare*. All quotations and line references to plays other than *Romeo and Juliet* are to G. Blakemore Evans (ed.), *The Riverside Shakespeare*, 1974, on which the *Concordance* is based.

Ado	*Much Ado about Nothing*
Ant.	*Antony and Cleopatra*
AWW	*All's Well That Ends Well*
AYLI	*As You Like It*
Cor.	*Coriolanus*
Cym.	*Cymbeline*
Err.	*The Comedy of Errors*
Ham.	*Hamlet*
1H4	*The First Part of King Henry the Fourth*
2H4	*The Second Part of King Henry the Fourth*
H5	*King Henry the Fifth*
1H6	*The First Part of King Henry the Sixth*
2H6	*The Second Part of King Henry the Sixth*
3H6	*The Third Part of King Henry the Sixth*
H8	*King Henry the Eighth*
JC	*Julius Caesar*
John	*King John*
LLL	*Love's Labour's Lost*
Lear	*King Lear*
Mac.	*Macbeth*
MM	*Measure for Measure*
MND	*A Midsummer Night's Dream*
MV	*The Merchant of Venice*
Oth.	*Othello*
Per.	*Pericles*
R2	*King Richard the Second*
R3	*King Richard the Third*
Rom.	*Romeo and Juliet*
Shr.	*The Taming of the Shrew*
STM	*Sir Thomas More*
Temp.	*The Tempest*
TGV	*The Two Gentlemen of Verona*
Tim.	*Timon of Athens*
Tit.	*Titus Andronicus*
TN	*Twelfth Night*
TNK	*The Two Noble Kinsmen*

Tro.	*Troilus and Cressida*
Wiv.	*The Merry Wives of Windsor*
WT	*The Winter's Tale*

2. Editions

Alexander	*Works*, ed. Peter Alexander, 1951
Bevington	*Works*, ed. David Bevington, 1980
Boswell	*Works*, ed. James Boswell, 1821
Bryant	*Romeo and Juliet* (Signet), ed. J. A. Bryant, 1964
Cam.	*Works* (Cambridge), ed. W. G. Clark, John Glover and W. A. Wright, 1863–6
Cam.²	*Works* (Cambridge), ed. W. A. Wright, 1891–3
Capell	*Works*, ed. Edward Capell, [1768]
Collier	*Works*, ed. John P. Collier, 1842–4
Collier²	*Works*, 2nd edn, 1853
Cowden Clarke	*Works*, ed. Charles and Mary Cowden Clarke, 1864–8
Craig	*Works* (Oxford), ed. W. J. Craig, 1891
Crofts	*Romeo and Juliet* (Warwick), ed. J. E. Crofts, 1936
Daniel	*Romeo and Juliet*, ed. P. A. Daniel, 1875
Deighton	*Romeo and Juliet*, ed. K. Deighton, 1893
Delius	*Werke*, ed. Nicolaus Delius, 1854–60
Dowden	*Romeo and Juliet* (Arden), ed. E. Dowden, 1900
Durham	*Romeo and Juliet* (Yale), ed. W. H. Durham, 1917
Dyce	*Works*, ed. Alexander Dyce, 1857
Dyce²	*Works*, 2nd edn, 1864–7
F	First Folio, *Works*, 1623
F2	Second Folio, *Works*, 1632
F3	Third Folio, *Works*, 1664
F4	Fourth Folio, *Works*, 1685
Furness	*Romeo and Juliet* (Variorum), ed. H. H. Furness, 1871
Gibbons	*Romeo and Juliet* (Arden), ed. Brian Gibbons, 1980
Globe	*Works*, ed. W. G. Clark and W. A. Wright, 1864
Hankins	*Romeo and Juliet* (Pelican), ed. J. E. Hankins, 1960
Hanmer	*Works*, ed. Thomas Hanmer, 1743–4
Hazlitt	*Works*, ed. William Hazlitt, 1852
Hoppe	*Romeo and Juliet*, ed. H. R. Hoppe, 1947
Hosley	*Romeo and Juliet* (New Yale), ed. Richard Hosley, 1954
Houghton	*Romeo and Juliet* (New Clarendon), ed. R. E. C. Houghton, 1947
Hudson	*Works*, ed. Henry Hudson, 1851–6
Johnson	*Works*, ed. Samuel Johnson, 1765
Keightley	*Works*, ed. Thomas Keightley, 1864
Kittredge	*Romeo and Juliet*, ed. G. L. Kittredge, 1940
Knight	*Works*, ed. Charles Knight, 1838–43
Malone	*Works*, ed. Edmond Malone, 1790
Mommsen	*Romeo und Julia*, ed. Tycho Mommsen, 1859
Munro	*Works* (London), ed. John Munro, 1958
NS	*Romeo and Juliet* (New Shakespeare), ed. J. Dover Wilson and G. I. Duthie, 1955
Neilson	*Works*, ed. W. A. Neilson, 1906

Pope	*Works*, ed. Alexander Pope, 1723–5
Pope[2]	*Works*, 2nd edn, 1728
Q1	First quarto, *Romeo and Juliet*, 1597
Q2	Second quarto, *Romeo and Juliet*, 1599
Q3	Third quarto, *Romeo and Juliet*, 1609
Q4	Fourth quarto, *Romeo and Juliet*, n.d. [*c.* 1622]
Q5	Fifth quarto, *Romeo and Juliet*, 1637
Rann	*Works*, ed. Joseph Rann, 1768–[94]
Ridley	*Romeo and Juliet* (New Temple), ed. M. R. Ridley, 1935
Riverside	*The Riverside Shakespeare*, textual ed. G. Blakemore Evans, 1974
Rolfe	*Romeo and Juliet*, ed. W. J. Rolfe, 1879
Rowe	*Works*, ed. Nicholas Rowe, 1709
Rowe[2]	*Works*, 2nd edn, 1709
Rowe[3]	*Works*, 3rd edn, 1714
Singer	*Works*, ed. S. W. Singer, 1826
Singer[2]	*Works*, 2nd edn, 1855–6
Sisson	*Works*, ed. C. J. Sisson, 1954
Spencer	*Romeo and Juliet* (New Penguin), ed. T. J. B. Spencer, 1967
Spevack	*Romeo and Juliet* (Blackfriars), ed. Marvin Spevack, 1970
Staunton	*Works*, ed. Howard Staunton, 1858–60
Steevens	*Works*, ed. George Steevens, 1773 (with Johnson), 1778, 1793
Theobald	*Works*, ed. Lewis Theobald, 1733
Theobald[2]	*Works*, 2nd edn, 1740
Ulrici	*Romeo and Juliet*, ed. H. Ulrici, 1853
Warburton	*Works*, ed. William Warburton, 1747
White	*Works*, ed. Richard Grant White, 1857–66
Williams	*Romeo and Juliet*, ed. G. W. Williams, 1964

3. Other works, periodicals, general references

Abbott	E. A. Abbott, *A Shakespearian Grammar*, 1869 (references are to numbered paragraphs)
Allen	*see* Furness
AN&Q	*American Notes and Queries*
Bailey	Samuel Bailey, *see* Cam.[2]
Becket	Andrew Becket, *see* Cam.[2]
Brooke	Arthur Brooke, *The Tragicall Historye of Romeus and Juliet* (1562)
Bulloch	John Bulloch, *Studies on the Text of Shakespeare*, 1878
Bullough	Geoffrey Bullough, *Narrative and Dramatic Sources of Shakespeare*, I, 1957
Burton	Robert Burton, *The Anatomy of Melancholy*, ed. A. R. Shilleto, 3 vols., 1896
Capell	Edward Capell, *Notes and Various Readings to Shakespeare*, II, 1780
Carr	*see* Cam.[2]
Chambers	E. K. Chambers, *The Elizabethan Stage*, 4 vols., 1923
Chapman	George Chapman, *Comedies*, ed. Allan Holaday *et al.*, 1970; *Tragedies*, ed. T. M. Parrott, 1910
Chaucer	Geoffrey Chaucer, *Works*, ed. F. N. Robinson, 2nd edn, 1957
Collier MS.	in Perkins's Second Folio (1632), Huntington Library
conj.	conjecture

Cotgrave	Randle Cotgrave, *A Dictionarie of the French and English Tongues* (1611)
Crow	John Crow, 'Editing and emending', *Essays and Studies*, 1955
Daniel	Samuel Daniel, *Poems and 'A Defence of Ryme'*, ed. A. C. Sprague, 1930
Daniel, P. A.	P. A. Daniel, *Notes and Conjectural Emendations...in Shakespeare's Plays*, 1870
Dekker	Thomas Dekker, *Dramatic Works*, ed. Fredson Bowers, 4 vols., 1953–61
Drayton	Michael Drayton, *Works*, ed. J. W. Hebel, 5 vols., 1931–41
Douai MS.	MS. of *Romeo and Juliet* (1694) in Douai Public Library
Duthie	*see* NS
ELN	*English Language Notes*
Farmer	Richard Farmer, *see* Cam.²
Fleay	F. G. Fleay, *see* Cam.²
Franz	Wilhelm Franz, *Die Sprache Shakespeares*, 1939 (4th edn of *Shakespeare-grammatik*)
G	Geneva translation of the Bible (1560)
Gascoigne	George Gascoigne, *The Posies* (1575), ed. J. W. Cunliffe, 1907
Golding	Arthur Golding, *The .xv. Bookes of P. Ovidius Naso, entytuled Metamorphosis* (1567), ed. W. H. D. Rouse, 1904
Greene	Robert Greene, *Works*, ed. A. B. Grosart, 15 vols., 1881–6
Greg	W. W. Greg, *Principles of Emendation in Shakespeare* (British Academy Lecture), 1928
Hazlitt	W. C. Hazlitt, *see* Cam.²
Heath	Benjamin Heath, *Revisal of Shakespeare's Text*, 1765
Hoppe	H. R. Hoppe, *The Bad Quarto of 'Romeo and Juliet'*, 1948
Jackson	Zachary Jackson, *see* Cam.²
JEGP	*Journal of English and Germanic Philology*
Jonson	Ben Jonson, *Works*, ed. C. H. Herford and Percy Simpson, 11 vols., 1925–52
Kellner	Leon Kellner, *Restoring Shakespeare*, 1925
Kermode	Frank Kermode, *see* Riverside
Kinnear	B. G. Kinnear, *Cruces Shakespearianae*, 1883
KJ	King James translation of the Bible (1611)
Kyd	Thomas Kyd, *Works*, ed. F. S. Boas, 1901
Lettsom	W. N. Lettsom, *see* Cam.²
Lyly	John Lyly, *Works*, ed. R. W. Bond, 3 vols., 1902
Mahood	M. M. Mahood, *Shakespeare's Wordplay*, 1957
Marlowe	Christopher Marlowe, *Works*, ed. Fredson Bowers, 2 vols., 1973
Mason	J. Monk Mason, *Comments on...Shakespeare's Plays*, rev. edn, 1807
Mitford	John Mitford, *see* Cam.²
MLN	*Modern Language Notes*
MLR	*Modern Language Review*
Montemayor	Jorge de Montemayor, *Diana*, trans. Bartholomew Yong (1598), ed. J. M. Kennedy, 1968
MP	*Modern Philology*
MSR	Malone Society Reprints
Muir	Kenneth Muir, *The Sources of Shakespeare's Plays*, rev. edn, 1977
Nares	Robert Nares, *A Glossary...of Words*, ed. J. O. Halliwell and Thomas Wright, 2 vols., 1882
Nashe	Thomas Nashe, *Works*, ed. R. B. McKerrow, 5 vols., 1904–10, rev. F. P. Wilson, 1958

N&Q	*Notes and Queries*
OED	*Oxford English Dictionary*
Otway	Thomas Otway, *Caius Marius* (1680), in *Works*, ed. J. C. Gosh, 2 vols., 1932
Painter	William Painter, 'Rhomeo and Julietta', ed. P. A. Daniel, 1875
Partridge	Eric Partridge, *Shakespeare's Bawdy*, rev. edn, 1968
PBSA	*Papers of the Bibliographical Society of America*
PMLA	*Publications of the Modern Language Association of America*
PQ	*Philological Quarterly*
RES	*Review of English Studies*
Ritson	Joseph Ritson, *Remarks, Critical and Illustrative . . . on the Last Edition of Shakespeare*, 1778
SB	*Studies in Bibliography*
Schmidt	Alexander Schmidt, *Shakespeare-Lexicon*, rev. Gregor Sarrazin, 2 vols., 1902
SD	stage direction
Seymour	E. H. Seymour, *Remarks . . . upon the Plays of Shakespeare*, II, 1805
SH	speech heading
Shirley	James Shirley, *Works*, ed. Alexander Dyce, 6 vols., 1833
Sidney	Philip Sidney, *Poems*, ed. W. A. Ringler, 1962
Singer MSS.	S. W. Singer, *see* Cam.²
Sisson, *New Readings*	C. J. Sisson, *New Readings in Shakespeare*, II, 1956
Smith	C. G. Smith, *Shakespeare's Proverb Lore*, 1963
Spenser	Edmund Spenser, *Works* (Variorum), ed. Edwin Greenlaw *et al.*, 8 vols. 1932–49
SQ	*Shakespeare Quarterly*
S.St.	*Shakespeare Studies*
S.Sur.	*Shakespeare Survey*
subst.	substantively
Tilley	M. P. Tilley, *A Dictionary of the Proverbs in England in the Sixteenth and Seventeenth Centuries*, 1950 (references are to numbered proverbs)
Tyrwhitt	Thomas Tyrwhitt, *Observations and Conjectures upon Some Passages of Shakespeare*, 1766
Upton	John Upton, *Critical Observations on Shakespeare*, 1746
Walker	Alice Walker, *see* NS
Walker, *Critical Examination*	W. S. Walker, *Critical Examination of the Text of Shakespeare*, III, 1860
Webster	John Webster, *Works*, ed. F. L. Lucas, 4 vols., 1928
Wilson	Dover Wilson, *see* NS

INTRODUCTION

The date

The date of composition for *Romeo and Juliet* is uncertain, and dates ranging from 1591 to 1596 have been proposed. A terminal date is set by the publication of the first quarto (Q1) in 1597,[1] but a *terminus a quo* is more difficult to establish, since much of the external and internal evidence is ambiguous.

External evidence, though meagre, seems to point to a later rather than an earlier date. On the strength of Q1's reference to performance by 'the L. of *Hunsdon* his Servants', Malone confidently dated the play (in Boswell, 1821) as first produced between 22 July 1596 and 17 March 1597, the only period when Shakespeare's company could properly have been called Lord Hunsdon's.[2] But the reference may be only a publisher's device to capitalise on the most recent performances and does not prove that the play was not acted earlier when Shakespeare's company was known as the Lord Chamberlain's Men.

Although two probable echoes of *Romeo and Juliet* may be found in works appearing in 1597, no direct allusions to the play appear until 1598.[3] In that year, Francis Meres included it among Shakespeare's tragedies in his *Palladis Tamia* (1598) and John Marston commented on it in his *Scourge of Villanie* (1598). The Meres reference for the first time affirms Shakespeare's authorship, but throws no light on the dating problem. Marston's reference, however, is perhaps more significant than has been allowed. In Satire XI ('Humours'), seven lines after an echo of *Romeo and Juliet* (1.5.25: 'A hall, a hall') and a reference to Will Kemp, who acted Peter, Marston continues (lines 37–48):

> *Luscus* what's playd to day? faith now I know
> I set thy lips abroach, from whence doth flow
> Naught but pure *Iuliat* and *Romio*.
> Say, who acts best? *Drusus* [? Burbage], or *Roscio* [? Alleyn]?
> Now I have him, that nere of ought did speake
> But when of playes or Plaiers he did treate.
> H'ath made a common-place booke out of plaies,
> And speaks in print, at least what ere he sayes

---

[1] See Textual Analysis, pp. 222–4 below.   [2] See Textual Analysis, p. 223.

[3] See Commentary, 2.2.33–42. A sudden rash of echoes from *Rom.*, mostly unnoticed, appeared in four plays written in 1598 (Porter's *Two Angry Women of Abingdon*, Haughton's *Englishmen for My Money* and Munday and Chettle's *Downfall of Robert Earl of Huntingdon* and *Death of Robert Earl of Huntingdon*); these echoes are noted in the Commentary. From 1598 to 1642 allusions to (or lines and passages imitated from) *Rom.* are outnumbered only by those to *Ham.*, *Venus and Adonis* and *1H4* (see *Shakespeare's Centurie of Prayse*, ed. L. T. Smith, 1879, and *Some 300 Fresh Allusions to Shakespere*, ed. F. J. Furnivall, 1886).

Is warranted by Curtaine *plaudeties*,
If ere you heard him courting *Lesbias* eyes;
Say (Curteous Sir) speakes he not movingly
From out some new pathetique Tragedie?[1]

Apart from attesting to the popularity of *Romeo and Juliet* on the stage in 1598, Marston here appears to be linking it with 'some new pathetique Tragedie', which Luscus pilfers in wooing his lady. No other known play which might have been considered 'new' in 1598 fits the description so well,[2] and this suggests that *Romeo and Juliet* was comparatively new in 1598.

Internal evidence for dating rests on (a) possible references to topical events and conditions; (b) Shakespeare's apparent dependence on datable published (and unpublished) works by other writers; and (c) the interrelations between *Romeo and Juliet* and Shakespeare's other plays and poems written before 1597.

Of the topical events to which the play may be thought to refer, the most discussed has been the earthquake recalled by the Nurse in 1.3.24–36. She twice insists that this had occurred eleven years earlier on the day Juliet was weaned, just before her third birthday. Thomas Tyrwhitt was the first to suggest that Shakespeare was referring to an actual earth tremor which was felt strongly in England on 6 April 1580, and he extrapolated a date of composition, at least for this part of the play, between 7 April and the middle of July 1591, because, as the Nurse tells us, Juliet was born on Lammas Eve (31 July) and her fourteenth birthday is now only 'A fortnight and odd days' away.[3] Other earthquakes have been canvassed since Tyrwhitt wrote. Sidney Thomas[4] has called attention to another 'terrible earthquake' on 1 March 1584/5, alluded to in William Covell's *Polimanteia*, published in 1595, a book perhaps known to Shakespeare since Covell makes an appreciative sidenote reference to '*All praise worthy. Lucrecia Sweet Shakspeare*' (sig. R2ᵛ). The allusion, made by an interlocutor called 'England', who includes the 1584/5 earthquake among 'Threatnings of God against my subjects lives', seems definitely to imply that this earthquake had been felt in England. If this is the Nurse's earthquake, a date for the play of 1595/6 might be indicated. Similar speculative computations, however, can be made on the basis of landslips at Blackmore, Dorset, on 13 January 1583, and at Mottingham, Kent, just eight miles from London, on 4 August 1585.[5] In other words, the supposed earthquake clue, even if it represents anything more significant than an imaginative detail thrown in for dramatic effect, can be adjusted to fit almost any year between 1591 and 1596.[6]

---

[1] *The Poems of John Marston*, ed. Arnold Davenport, 1961, p. 168.
[2] This interpretation finds some support in *The Return from Parnassus, Part I* (performed between Christmas 1598 and Christmas 1601 at St John's College, Cambridge), where, in a passage apparently inspired by Marston, as Davenport points out (*Poems of Marston*, p. 359), Gullio, accused in his wooing of speaking 'nothing but pure Shakspeare', lets go with a version of *Rom.* 2.4.35–7.
[3] Cited in Furness, p. 43.
[4] 'The earthquake in *Romeo and Juliet*', *MLN* 64 (1949), 417–19.
[5] Sarah Dodson, 'Notes on the earthquake in *Romeo and Juliet*', *MLN* 65 (1950), 144.
[6] Joseph Hunter (1845; cited in Furness, p. 44) calls attention to a severe earthquake near Verona in 1570, another warning against interpreting the Nurse's reference too literally.

Two other possible topical references have been noted. In 1.4.82–8 Mercutio describes the soldier's dream of 'cutting foreign throats, / Of breaches, ambuscadoes, Spanish blades, / Of healths five fathom deep'. It has been suggested that Shakespeare is here glancing at the Cadiz expedition of June 1596.[1] An examination of the phases of the moon and their relation to when Monday, the day after the Capulets' feast, fell on 12 or 14 July (o.s.) in the 1590s (i.e. 'A fortnight and odd days' before Lammas-tide) shows that the only Monday which fits the phases of the moon 'described' in the 'balcony scene' (2.2) is 12 July 1596. This date, like that of the Cadiz expedition, may be linked with Malone's hypothesis that Romeo and Juliet was first performed between 23 July 1596 and the following April,[2] but neither is much more than suggestive.

More solid evidence begins to emerge when we turn to literary influences. Two works have frequently been cited as having influenced Romeo and Juliet: Samuel Daniel's Complaint of Rosamond (1592) and John Eliot's Ortho-epia Gallica (1593). Since Daniel's Complaint has left its mark throughout the play[3] and furnishes one of its recurring images (Death as Juliet's lover and husband), Shakespeare's indebtedness to it seems to rule out any date earlier than 1592;[4] and the influence of Eliot's Ortho-epia, though confined to a single passage (3.5.1–7, 22), may fairly be taken as advancing the date another year, to 1593. Recently, however, J. J. M. Tobin has suggested Shakespeare's use of a third work, Thomas Nashe's Have with You to Saffron-Walden. Although this was not published until after September 1596, parts of it must have been written before the end of 1595, and there is evidence that the last three-quarters, at least, circulated in manuscript among friends in May–June 1596, some three months before publication.[5] Tobin's evidence is of two kinds: (1) passages from which Shakespeare may have taken hints for the presentation of certain characters;[6] and (2) nine words or phrases scattered throughout Romeo and Juliet, which occur nowhere else in Shakespeare's work but which are to be found also in Have with You to Saffron-Walden – most of them employed there by Nashe for the first time in his own writing.[7] The nature and number of the parallels suggested are

---

[1] R. W. Babcock, 'Romeo and Juliet, I.iv.86: an emendation', PQ 8 (1929), 407–8.

[2] J. W. Draper, 'The date of Romeo and Juliet', RES 25 (1949), 55–7.

[3] See Commentary, 1.1.206–7, 209–11; 1.4.109; 3.2.5; 5.1.61; 5.3.92–115.

[4] Against this statement must be set the possibility that Shakespeare was able to read Daniel's poem, as he did some other works, before publication.

[5] Nashe, Works, IV, 302. There is a reference to projected publication in Hilary Term (23 Jan. to 12 Feb.), but Hilary Term of what year is uncertain (see Nashe, Works, III, 133, and IV, 369). Nashe complains in the dedication to The Terrors of the Night (1594) that the 'Coppie [of his MS.] progressed from one scriveners shop to another, and at length grew so common, that it was readie to bee hung out for one of their signes, like a paire of indentures' (Works, I, 341).

[6] 'Nashe and the texture of Romeo and Juliet', Aligarh Journal of English Studies 5 (1980), 162–74. Tobin notes some suggestive hints in Saffron-Walden for the language and characters of Mercutio, Benvolio, the Nurse and the Capulet servants (1.1), and a reference to the 1580 earthquake (Nashe, Works, III, 69–70).

[7] 'Nashe and Romeo and Juliet', N&Q 27 (1980), 161–2. To these may be added the quite rare word 'coying' (2.2.101; Nashe, Works, III, 116). Tobin argues for adopting Q1's 'fantasticoes' for Q2's 'phantacies' (2.4.25) (see supplementary note) because it appears in Saffron-Walden (Nashe, Works, III, 31).

more than usually persuasive. Shakespeare's fascination with Nashe's rich, innovative and free-wheeling vocabulary is well attested[1] and is evidenced elsewhere in *Romeo and Juliet* by similar echoes from earlier works by Nashe.[2] It may be argued that Nashe, not Shakespeare, is the borrower, but a fair analysis of the evidence makes this view highly unlikely. If then we are willing to admit the probable influence of *Have with You to Saffron-Walden*, we may postulate a date of composition for substantial parts of *Romeo and Juliet* between May–June 1596 and the end of the year. This agrees well enough with some of the other external and internal evidence and is not ruled out by any definite evidence to the contrary.

How does this late date for *Romeo and Juliet* fit into the generally accepted chronology of Shakespeare's plays during the 1590s, particularly those most often associated with *Romeo and Juliet*: *The Two Gentlemen of Verona* (1594), *Love's Labour's Lost* (1594–5, revised 1597), and *A Midsummer Night's Dream* (1595–6)? Although Meres (in *Palladis Tamia*) sets a terminal date of 1598 for these plays, including *Romeo*, the several dates assigned above are provisional, the problems involved being similar to those encountered with *Romeo*. But these three plays and *Romeo*, and, in certain respects, *Richard II*,[3] constitute a group which shares a common lyrical quality, evidenced by the high frequency of rhyme, a fondness (sometimes excessive and self-conscious) for the figures of rhetoric, a central concern with the vicissitudes of love and the materials of romance (characteristics that link the group to the poems and *Sonnets*), and a unity of comic tone, particularly, except perhaps in the *Dream*, in what may be called low comedy. In addition, various kinds of connections, thematic, rhetorical and verbal, echo and re-echo from play to play within the group. An examination of some of these echoes may help to place *Romeo* in relation to the other plays in this group.

Two Gentlemen, like *Romeo*, draws upon Brooke's *Romeus and Juliet* (1562), particularly for aspects of the Valentine–Silvia plot, and is generally thought of as Shakespeare's earliest essay in romantic comedy; the question is, *how* early. Considering the usually assigned date of 1594 too late, Clifford Leech has argued for a preliminary and partial draft as early as 1592, reworked and completed in late 1593.[4] That the play was written earlier than *Romeo* is suggested by its groping and uncertain quality in style and structure and by what seems to be Shakespeare's merely general memory of Brooke's poem, drawing on plot situations more than on exact verbal echoes. This kind of indebtedness would be less likely had Shakespeare already written *Romeo*. An earlier date is also suggested by the connections between 3.1 of *Two Gentlemen* (particularly Valentine's lament on his banishment, lines 170–87), *2 Henry VI* 3.2.300–412 (Suffolk's parting from Queen Margaret following his banishment), and

---

[1] See Rupert Taylor, *The Date of 'Love's Labour's Lost'*, 1932 (Taylor does not allow for a later revision of the play); John Dover Wilson (ed.), *1H4*, 1946, pp. 191–6; G. B. Evans (ed.), 'Variorum "Supplement" to *1 Henry IV*', 1956, p. 53; G. B. Evans, *N&Q* 204 (1959), 250; J. J. M. Tobin, *English Studies* 61 (1980), 318–28, and *ELN* 18 (1980), 172–5.

[2] See Commentary, 4.5.96 (and supplementary note) and 99.

[3] Harold Brooks (ed.), *MND*, 1979, pp. xlv–li, examines in detail the rhetorical devices common to that play, *R2*, and *Rom*. *Rom.* also shows two interesting links with *John*; see Commentary, 1.3.82–95, 98.

[4] Leech (ed.), *TGV*, 1969, pp. xxii–xxxv.

3 Henry VI 5.4.37–8, a scene in which Shakespeare draws directly on both Brooke's *Romeus* and *2 Henry VI*.[1] The comparable passage in *Romeo* (3.3.12–70), in which, at Lawrence's cell, Romeo bewails his sentence of banishment, reads like an expanded version of Valentine's lament in *Two Gentlemen* but lacks any obvious verbal connections with *2* and *3 Henry VI*. That the direction of influence thus runs from *Two Gentlemen* to *Romeo* and not the other way is suggested by the close verbal links throughout 3.1 of *Two Gentlemen* and the admittedly earlier Henry VI plays, usually dated 1590–1, and by the absence of such early echoes from the Henry plays in *Romeo*.

Love's Labour's Lost, like *Two Gentlemen*, is a thesis play in the earlier tradition of Lyly's comedies. In both plays Shakespeare's involvement with character fails to break through the formal restraints of the overriding thesis. Such is not the case with the later comedies beginning with *The Merchant of Venice* (1596–7); and the slightly earlier *Midsummer Night's Dream* (1595–6), though strongly driven by an underlying theme, wears its thesis with a difference and a new complexity. Thus the intention and tone of *Love's Labour's Lost* associate it with Shakespeare's earlier work in comedy, and a date of 1594–5 in its unrevised form, following immediately after *Two Gentlemen*, is widely accepted. Assessment of the notable verbal connections between *Romeo* (particularly in 2.4) and *Love's Labour's Lost* is complicated, however, by a revision of the latter sometime between July–September and Christmas of 1597,[2] probably for a court performance. Hence, the cluster of close verbal echoes between *Love's Labour's Lost* and 2.4 of *Romeo*,[3] a scene which also contains several connections with Nashe's *Have with You to Saffron-Walden* (1596),[4] may in fact be derived from *Romeo* rather than from the first version of *Love's Labour's Lost*.

The position of the last of the group, *A Midsummer Night's Dream*, is open to greater question, though its most recent editor, Harold Brooks,[5] favours the view that *Romeo* is probably the earlier. He points out that Mercutio's Queen Mab speech seems more like an anticipation of the fairy world of the *Dream* than a recollection, and that the earlier parts of the *Dream* contain what seem to be echoes of *Romeo*, echoes that grow less obvious as the play progresses. C. L. Barber[6] has also noticed that the original casting (later altered) of the *Pyramus and Thisbe* play in 1.2, with its careful assignment of roles to Thisbe's mother and father and Pyramus's father, seems to look back to the Romeo and Juliet story rather than to Shakespeare's principal source for the Pyramus story in Golding's translation (1567) of Ovid's *Metamorphoses*. Another small clue, which does not seem to have been noticed, appears in 5.1.148–9: 'And Thisbe, tarrying in mulberry shade, / His dagger drew, and died.' In the play which follows, Thisbe, as in Ovid, kills herself with Pyramus's sword and no dagger is mentioned, but Quince's prologue lines exactly describe the death of Juliet in both Brooke (2772) and Shakespeare. Though not conclusive, the directional evidence is suggestive.

[1] A. S. Cairncross (ed.), *3H6*, 1964, seems first to have called attention to Shakespeare's direct use of Brooke's *Romeus* in this early play.

[2] See Richard David (ed.), *LLL*, rev. edn, 1956, pp. xxvi–xxxii. The probability of the July–September limit is indicated by Shakespeare's use of John Gerard's *Herbal* (1597).

[3] See Commentary, 2.4.13–14, 15, 22–3, 25, 53.

[4] See Commentary, 2.4.18, 25, 26, 56.   [5] Brooks, *MND*, pp. xliii–xlv.

[6] *Shakespeare's Festive Comedy*, 1959, p. 152 n. 25.

Brooks's conclusion on the dating of the *Dream*, which he admits must remain hypothetical, is that it was probably written 'between autumn 1594 and spring 1596'.[1] In view of the tendency of our discussion to place *Romeo* late in 1596, such a date for the *Dream* would make *Romeo* the later play, a conclusion Brooks himself would query. Brooks's 'spring of 1596' arises from connecting the composition of the *Dream* with the bad weather of 1594, supposedly referred to in 2.1.88–114, and with the wedding on 19 February 1596 of Elizabeth Carey and Thomas Berkeley, but Sidney Thomas[2] has suggested that the weather described in the *Dream* fits the winter and spring of 1596 much more closely than that of 1594 and that we should therefore seriously consider the wedding involved to be that of Lady Elizabeth and Lady Katherine Somerset to Henry Guildford and William Petre on 18 November 1596, an occasion for which Spenser wrote his *Prothalamion*. As a double wedding this has some possible relevance to the doubling of the young lovers in the *Dream* (for which there is no definite suggestion in the sources); and its date is just late enough to allow *Romeo* to be considered the earlier play. Such an argument is, of course, just as hypothetical as Brooks's.

A date for *Romeo* later than May 1596 raises no serious difficulties in the usually accepted chronological order, except perhaps with *Romeo* and the *Dream*. Various kinds of evidence appear to favour such a date and even the publication of Q1 so soon afterwards, though unusual, may be paralleled by the appearance of the 'bad' quarto of *Henry V* (composed in 1599) in 1600. The strongest evidence is the proposed influence of Nashe's *Have with You to Saffron-Walden*. Accept it, and the case for the composition or completion of *Romeo* in the latter half of 1596 is strong. Deny it, and the other evidence pointing to such a late date is either weak or ambiguous and would not seriously stand against a date as early as 1594. There the matter must rest until, if ever, new and conclusive evidence is discovered.

Sources and structure

The general type of story represented by *Romeo and Juliet* has its roots in folklore and mythology. Best described as a separation-romance, it shows obvious analogies with the stories of Hero and Leander, Pyramus and Thisbe, Tristan and Isolde, and with later medieval works like *Floris and Blanchefleur* and Chaucer's *Troilus and Criseyde*.[3] Chaucer's poem leaves its mark strongly on Shakespeare's principal source for the play, Arthur Brooke's *Romeus and Juliet*, and, independently perhaps, on Shakespeare's play itself.

The earlier history of the Romeo and Juliet story has been treated in detail by a number of critics,[4] but since there is no persuasive evidence that Shakespeare knew

---

[1] Brooks, *MND*, p. lvii.

[2] 'The bad weather in *A Midsummer Night's Dream*', *MLN* 64 (1949), 319–22.

[3] See J. J. Munro (ed.), *Brooke's 'Romeus and Juliet'*, 1908, pp. i–xxi; Stith Thompson (ed.), *Motif-Index of Folk-Literature*, 6 vols., rev. edn, 1955, D 1364.7, K 1348, N 343, T 211.3.

[4] See Munro, *Romeus*, pp. xxv–lii; H. B. Charlton, 'France as chaperone of Romeo and Juliet', *Studies in French Language and Literature Presented to M. K. Pope*, 1939, pp. 43–59; Olin H. Moore, *The Legend of Romeo and Juliet*, 1950; Bullough, I, 269–76.

the Italian or French versions at first hand,[1] we may limit our discussion to the two
English versions:[2] Arthur Brooke's long poem, *The Tragicall Historye of Romeus and
Juliet* (1562); and William Painter's 'Rhomeo and Julietta' included in volume II
(1567) of his widely known *Palace of Pleasure*, a collection of prose translations from
classical sources and from Italian and French *novelle*.[3] Both Brooke and Painter used
a French version of the story by Pierre Boaistuau, published in volume I of François
de Belleforest's *Histoires Tragiques* (1559),[4] which in turn was based primarily on
Matteo Bandello's 'Romeo e Giulietta' (1554) and, in some details, on Luigi da Porto's
Giuletta e Romeo (about 1530), the immediate source of Bandello's version and the
first to lay the action in Verona and to give the names Romeo and Juliet to the
protagonists.[5]

Shakespeare worked directly with Brooke's *Romeus*, for verbal echoes resound
throughout the play; that he knew Painter's prose version is highly probable, but,
except for four or five suggestive and scattered details,[6] Painter's influence remains
shadowy, though we may surmise that at least Shakespeare's use of 'Romeo' (instead
of Brooke's 'Romeus') was due to Painter's title.[7] It is not surprising that Shakespeare
concentrated his attention on Brooke. Painter's translation of Boaistuau's version is
close and generally accurate, but Brooke's much longer verse narrative, 3020 lines in
poulter's measure,[8] gives essentially everything in Boaistuau (and hence in Painter),
and makes substantial additions and slighter alterations that considerably enhance the
dramatic potentialities of the story.[9] The more important additions are the Nurse's
interview with Romeo following the lovers' first meeting (631–73), the consequent

[1] Moore, *Legend* (pp. 111–18, 138), argues for direct influence from Luigi da Porto's *Giuletta e Romeo*
(*c*. 1530), but the evidence is tenuous and has received little notice; see, however, Muir, p. 38. Muir
(p. 39, following Charlton, 'France as chaperone', p. 50) notes that Shakespeare may have taken one
detail directly from Boaistuau (Romeo's attending the Capulet feast in the hope of seeing Rosaline)
which is omitted by Bandello, Painter and Brooke; but it is also omitted by Boaistuau. It is Da Porto
who includes such a motive for Romeo. The proposed influence of Luigi Groto's *La Hadriana* (1578)
and Lope de Vega's *Castelvines y Monteses* (not published until 1647) is now generally discounted.

[2] Brooke in 'To the Reader' reports that he had recently seen a play on the Romeo and Juliet story
(see the excerpts from Brooke in the Appendix, p. 229–63 below). Formerly, many of Brooke's
differences from Boaistuau, as well as Shakespeare's deviations from Brooke, were attributed to it. Recent
criticism, however, barely mentions it (Muir, p. 38; Bullough, p. 275). The anonymous Latin tragedy
Romeus et Julietta, preserved in the British Library (Sloane MS. 1775), is later than Shakespeare's
play, probably early-seventeenth-century.

[3] The text of Painter's translation here used is that edited by P. A. Daniel (New Shakespeare Society,
Ser. III, No. 1, 1875). Bullough does not include Painter. Painter appears to have made some slight
use of Brooke's poem (Daniel, *Rhomeo*, p. xxi).

[4] *Histoires tragiques, extraites des œuvres italiennes de Bandel* (1559), Histoire troisieme. The edition here
used was published at Turin in 1570.

[5] Following Da Porto, Bandello arranges the death scene so that Juliet awakes just after Romeo takes
the poison and the lovers are allowed a few moments of recognition and reunion before Romeo dies.
This handling of the situation influenced later adaptations of *Rom.* (see below, pp. 34–8).

[6] See Commentary, 1.1.93; 3.1.55–8, 61–5; 4.1.105; 4.5.104; 5.1.59.

[7] Brooke uses the form 'Romeo' once (253) as a rhyme for 'Mercutio'.

[8] Rhymed couplets, a six-stress line followed by a seven-stress line, the first line breaking three and three
and the second line breaking four and three (and so printed in the three sixteenth-century editions of
Brooke's poem).

[9] Brooke owes the inspiration for several of his additions and other changes to the influence of Chaucer's
Troilus and Criseyde. See Munro, *Romeus* (pp. lii–liv and Appendix II), for an analysis of his borrowings.

report to Juliet of the Nurse's arrangements for the marriage (674–704), Romeo's long and highly emotional interview with the Friar after Tybalt's death (1257–1510), the account of Romeo's sorrow in exile in Mantua (1740–80), and the Nurse's cross advice urging Juliet to marry Paris while she maintains a liaison with Romeo (2295–2312). In all of these additions, except the description of Romeo's sorrow in exile, Shakespeare found viable dramatic material, which he put to memorable use in parts of 2.4, 2.5, 3.3 and 3.5. Brooke also sometimes converts narrative statement in Boaistuau into direct speech, expands speeches already present, or adds extra bits of short dialogue (apart from the larger additions already noticed), which give the poem more life and movement. Finally, Brooke occasionally showed some flair for inventing new detail in description and character, particularly in his presentation of the Nurse, who under his hand emerges as the only character Shakespeare inherited from the source story that offered more than a romance stereotype. Despite Brooke's virtues, however, the poem is pedestrian, long-winded, overdecorated with 'poetic' common-places, and written in a lumbering pseudo-high style. The miracle is what Shakespeare was able to make from it.

Shakespeare's treatment of Brooke's poem has been discussed many times.[1] To convert it into a play, Brooke's leisurely narrative required tightening, focusing, and restructuring. The story as it existed in Brooke and in Painter already offered both a public and a private dimension: the blood-feud with its larger social implications in the life of a city state and the intimate, private love of two young people tragically caught in the web of a world inimical to their private vision. But unlike Brooke, Shakespeare establishes this important underlying duality in the first scene, opening with the cautious sparring of the Capulet and Montague servants – a comic beginning that quickly turns serious as they are joined first by Benvolio (a Montague), then by Tybalt (a Capulet), followed immediately by Officers of the Watch, Capulet and his wife, Montague and his wife, and finally by the Prince as the voice of authority. The play, then, begins on a note of threat and public discord, resolved for the moment by an imposed and uneasy truce. In contrast, Brooke, though mentioning the Capulet–Montague feud early in the poem (25–50) and suggesting that it is still smouldering, only allows it to erupt in violence after Romeus and Juliet's marriage (955–1034), thus losing the immediate potential conflict which Shakespeare sets up between the public and private worlds of the play.

The formal, almost mechanical patterning of the first scene (through line 94)[2] is essentially repeated twice more, at the crisis (3.1) and at the end (5.3), both scenes more formally patterned and concentrated than in Brooke (959–1046; 2809–3020), in each of which the outer world of the feud impinges on the inner world of Romeo and Juliet. This formality may be seen as Shakespeare's mode of distinguishing and

---

[1] Daniel, *Rhomeo*, pp. xii–xviii; Munro, *Romeus*, Appendix 1 (a detailed comparison of the poem and the play); R. A. Law, 'On Shakespeare's changes of his source material in *Romeo and Juliet*', *University of Texas Bulletin, Studies in English*, 1929, pp. 86–102; Moore, *Legend*, pp. 111–18; Bullough, 1, 274–83; Muir, pp. 40–2.

[2] G. K. Hunter ('Shakespeare's earliest tragedies: *Titus Andronicus* and *Romeo and Juliet*', *S.Sur.* 27 (1974), 3–4) compares the similarly patterned structure of the opening scene of *Titus Andronicus*.

distancing the public from the private voice, the characters here speaking less as individuals and more as spokesmen for the contending parties and the arbitration of law, a role from which the Prince never escapes. With the exit of the Prince in 1.1, however, the tone changes and we begin to hear the voice of personal involvement and concern in Romeo's parents and his friend Benvolio, as, ironically, they worry over the problem of Romeo's apparently anti-social behaviour. At this point the play moves onto a different level, one that sounds the note of personal emotion and establishes the emergence of individual character, catching us up into the smaller, more intimate and intense sphere of human relations. These dual modes, the public and the private, interrelated but carefully distinguished, set up the larger dimensions of the play, in which the concerns of individual lives (their love and hate, joy and grief) will be played out against the muted but inescapable demands of convention and society – 'Here's much to do with hate, but more with love' (1.1.166).

Other structural departures from Brooke's narrative are equally significant. Tybalt and Paris appear in Brooke only when events demand them. Tybalt is unheard of until he is needed as the ringleader of the Capulet faction in the street brawl, which breaks out some months after Romeus and Juliet have been secretly married (955–1034), and he no sooner appears than he is slain by Romeus. Shakespeare, however, introduces Tybalt in the first scene in his self-appointed role as leader of the younger Capulets and then underscores this by showing him as a troublemaker at the Capulet feast (1.5), a further foreshadowing of Tybalt's later decisive function that finds no place in Brooke. Shakespeare can thus draw on an already sharply defined character at the moment of crisis in 3.1, creating a sense of Tybalt's apparently strong personal hostility to Romeo and achieving a dramatically effective cause-and-effect relationship. In the same way, Shakespeare introduces Paris in 1.2, even before Romeo first meets Juliet, in order to suggest the potential conflict of a rival suitor and to lay the grounds for Capulet's later ill-advised, if well-intentioned, insistence on Juliet's immediate marriage with him. Brooke again delays any mention of Paris (1881 ff.) until the plot demands an eligible husband for Juliet to cure her seeming grief over Tybalt's death. As the final block in this expository structure Shakespeare also shows us Juliet with her mother and the Nurse in 1.3, when the marriage with Paris is first broached, a scene that again advances Brooke's narrative scheme, in which we learn nothing of any of these characters until after the beginning of the Capulet feast. With the opening of 1.4 and the sudden and unprepared appearance of Mercutio as one of the masking party, all the major characters, except Friar Lawrence, have been introduced and the lines of possible tension and future conflict suggested.

After 1.4, with a firmly established series of expository scenes behind him, Shakespeare essentially follows Brooke's narrative order, with one significant exception. Whereas Brooke describes first the consummation of Romeo and Juliet's marriage (827–918), followed by the killing of Tybalt a month or two later, with the resulting sentence of banishment (949–1046), and then the lovers' last night together (1527–1728), Shakespeare telescopes these meetings, reducing the lovers' period of happiness to a single night *after* the fateful killing of Tybalt. Not only does this heighten the sense of the overwhelming pressure of events and increase the emotional tension by forcing the lovers to consummate their marriage under the shadow of immediate separation,[1] but, as Mark Rose notes,[2] it enables Shakespeare structurally to balance 'the two lovers' scenes [2.2 and 3.5] one on either side of the centerpiece [3.1]'. Even in this single example, we can glimpse how Shakespeare, by a slight rearrangement of Brooke, concentrates the time-scheme, establishes firmly the relations of the key points in the play's structure, and achieves a more powerful emotional impact.

This brings us to a consideration of the larger implications of Shakespeare's use of time in the play. Brooke's story develops slowly over a period of at least nine months.[3] After Romeus first meets Juliet at Capulet's Christmas feast, 'a weeke or two' (461) passes before he is able to speak to her again, and, after their secret marriage, they continue to meet clandestinely each night for 'a month or twayne' (949) before the fight with Tybalt.[4] But for Shakespeare time does not 'amble withal'. He turns it into a powerful dramatic instrument. Instead of Brooke's months, Shakespeare, setting the season around the middle of July, two weeks before Lammas-tide (1.3.15–16), packs the dramatic action into four days and nights (Sunday through Wednesday), ending early on the morning of the fifth day (Thursday):

Day I   Sunday: 1.1–2.2 (from shortly before 9 a.m. to just before dawn of Monday)
Day II   Monday: 2.3–3.4 (from dawn to bedtime)
Day III Tuesday: 3.5–4.3 (from dawn to after bedtime)
Day IV   Wednesday: 4.4–5.2 (from early morning to very late Wednesday evening)
Day V   Thursday: 5.3 (from very late Wednesday night to early Thursday morning)[5]

An intense and driving tension is thus set up that results in our heightened understanding of and sympathy for the headlong actions of the lovers. The audience, like Romeo and Juliet, is swept along by the apparently overwhelming rush and pressure of events, even though some of those events are, in fact, not beyond the lovers' rational control. Shakespeare achieves part of this effect not by ignoring actual (or clock) time, but by stressing it. The play is unusually full, perhaps more so than any other Shakespearean play, of words like *time, day, night, today, tomorrow, years, hours, minutes* and specific days of the week, giving us a sense of events moving steadily and inexorably in a tight temporal framework. But Shakespeare can also, when he wishes, concentrate and speed the action by annihilating time in favour of what

[1] Muir, p. 40.
[2] *Shakespearean Design*, 1972, p. 149.
[3] Munro, *Romeus*, p. 132. Brooke's story begins shortly before Christmas and seems to end sometime after 10 September (Brooke, 2072).
[4] These vague time references are generally typical of Brooke; unlike Painter (p. 127), who follows Boaistuau, Brooke gives no specific length of time for the working of the potion.
[5] Although Shakespeare carefully reinforces (with frequent temporal signposts) the time-scheme outlined above, he appears to trip himself when the Friar tells Juliet that the potion will take forty-two hours (4.1.105) to run its course. Since she drinks the potion shortly before 3 o'clock on Wednesday morning (4.4.4) and awakens shortly before dawn on Thursday (5.3), the time elapsed is around twenty-seven hours, not forty-two. If, on the other hand, Shakespeare inadvertently thought of the play as ending on the early morning of the sixth day (Friday), the forty-two hour period is not long enough.

Granville-Barker calls 'tempo'. Thus in 4.2, though Juliet has only just returned from her morning shrift at Friar Lawrence's cell, we are told a few lines later by Lady Capulet that 'It is now near night', so late in fact that they cannot be prepared for the wedding feast now suddenly arranged for the next day (Wednesday).[1] The device here serves, by abridging a period of 'dead' time, to advance the immediate movement toward the moment, earlier prepared for in 4.1, when Juliet must drink the Friar's potion.

Apart from Brooke (and perhaps Painter) a number of other, comparatively minor influences on *Romeo and Juliet* have been pointed out, some of them already discussed in the section on dating: Samuel Daniel's *Complaint of Rosamond* (1592), John Eliot's *Ortho-epia Gallica* (1593), Sidney's *Astrophil and Stella* (1591), several works by Thomas Nashe, notably *Have with You to Saffron-Walden* (1596), and Bartholomew Yong's translation of Montemayor's *Diana* and Gil Polo's *Enamoured Diana* (1598, but available to Shakespeare in manuscript several years earlier). There are also links with other Shakespearean plays, particularly *Two Gentlemen*, *Love's Labour's Lost*, and *Midsummer Night's Dream*. Except for Daniel, and possibly Sidney and Nashe, none of these minor non-Shakespearean sources did more than contribute a passing phrase or image, but one aspect of the play, its debt to the sonnet tradition and to Shakespeare's own *Sonnets*, warrants further comment.[2]

Coleridge, forgetting or not knowing Brooke's *Romeus*, particularly praises Shakespeare for opening the play with a Romeo who is already 'love-bewildered'.[3] Brooke, of course, also devotes a number of lines (53–100) to Romeus's unrequited love for an unnamed lady: 'In sighs, in teares, in plainte, in care, in sorow and unrest, / He mones the daye, he wakes the long and wery night' (92–3). But Coleridge is quite correct in one important respect. Even though Brooke may have furnished the hint, the development of the idea is very much Shakespeare's own. It is Shakespeare, not Brooke, who first introduces us to a Romeo who is undergoing all the delicious pangs and enjoyed agonies of a young man fashionably 'in love' or, as Coleridge puts it, 'in love only with his own idea'.[4] To present this kind of bloodless figment of the mind, Shakespeare turns to the conventional language of earlier courtly love as it had developed in the sonnet tradition from Petrarch and other continental practitioners to Wyatt, Surrey, Watson, Sidney and Spenser. As practised by most sonnet writers (Watson is the perfect example) it is a language compounded of hyperbole, more or less witty conceits, word-play, oxymorons and endless repetition, usually focused on the versifier's unrequited love (real or imagined) for a disdainful or otherwise unattainable mistress. A Sidney, Spenser or Shakespeare (in his own sonnets) could, and usually did, rise above the conventional techniques of the sonnet tradition, but they were conscious of its dangers and limitations, and Shakespeare, before he wrote *Romeo*, had already exposed its hollowness in *Love's Labour's Lost*, where the four would-be lovers are finally forced to abjure

---

[1] There is no sudden change in the day set for the wedding in Brooke; see Commentary, 4.2.24.
[2] See Gibbons (pp. 42–52) for an excellent discussion of the influence of the sonnet tradition on *Rom.*, particularly that of Sidney's *Astrophil and Stella*.
[3] *Lectures and Notes on Shakespeare*, ed. T. Ashe, 1885, p. 323.   [4] *Ibid.*, p. 98.

> Taffata phrases, silken terms precise,
> Three-pil'd hyperboles, spruce affection,
> Figures pedantical...

and express their wooing minds 'In russet yeas and honest kersey noes' (5.2.406–13). When, therefore, Romeo appears in 1.1, lamenting the cruel day and longing for night and darkness, he is unconsciously 'playing' the conventional role. His first substantial speech puts the authentic verbal seal on this role:

> Here's much to do with hate, but more with love:
> Why then, O brawling love, O loving hate,
> O any thing of nothing first create!
> O heavy lightness, serious vanity,
> Misshapen chaos of well-seeming forms,
> Feather of lead, bright smoke, cold fire, sick health,
> Still-waking sleep, that is not what it is! (1.1.166–72)

As Mercutio later says (2.4.34–5), Romeo is 'for the numbers that Petrarch flowed in'. Thus Shakespeare employs Romeo's role as the lover in love with love (hence largely with himself) as a clearly realised foil to set off the new Romeo who begins to emerge after he meets Juliet and who loses his heart in a real love, the kind of love that is beyond the posturing of what may be expressed through the facile medium of mere sonnetese. But Shakespeare goes beyond this simple contrast, using Romeo's verbal acrobatics to foreshadow one of the central themes of the play – the ambiguous and frighteningly fragile nature of love itself, 'A choking gall, and a preserving sweet' (185).[1] Shakespeare's preoccupation with the ambiguous and unseizable qualities of love may be traced too in the constant, almost frenetic word-play and punning – both serious and comic – that characterises this play, and in Friar Lawrence's remarks on the ambivalence of good and evil:

> For nought so vile, that on the earth doth live,
> But to the earth some special good doth give;
> Nor ought so good but, strained from that fair use,
> Revolts from true birth, stumbling on abuse.
> Virtue itself turns vice, being misapplied,
> And vice sometime by action dignified. (2.3.17–22)

Nor is it accidental that sonnet form, tone and situation seem so strongly marked and dominant in the first part of the play. The sonnet choruses to Act 1 preside over a structure that seems to reflect a typical sonnet situation (a cold-hearted lady rejects her suitor; a family feud separates two lovers). Thus it is fitting that Romeo and Juliet first address each other in a highly patterned and figurative sonnet in antiphonal form. But after the balcony scene, in which Romeo still from time to time speaks in sonnet clichés, the impact and operation of the sonnet tradition fade,[2] replaced by sterner realities, symbolised in part by Friar Lawrence; mere talk (the essence of the sonnet tradition) becomes action, and life, with its attendant death, takes over from literature.

Finally, we may notice Shakespeare's debt to Chaucer, which, in *Romeo and Juliet*,

---

[1] Lines 181–5 foreshadow the four stages of Romeo's love; see Commentary, 1.1.181–5.
[2] The first two acts, for example, contain many echoes of Shakespeare's own sonnets, as the Commentary shows; such echoes become rarer in the last three acts.

may be considered large or small[1] depending on the extent to which we are willing to allow direct influence from *Troilus and Criseyde*. The evidence for such influence remains suggestive rather than substantive and is complicated by Brooke's own considerable borrowings from Chaucer's poem in his *Romeus*, a debt that tends to confuse the actual genesis of points in common between Chaucer and Shakespeare, and by the lack of identifiable verbal echoes of Chaucer's *Troilus*.[2] Nevertheless, recent critics,[3] recognising that Shakespeare had already shown some knowledge of Chaucer's works before he composed *Romeo*,[4] feel that the two stories naturally invited comparison (as Brooke had recognised) and call attention to certain thematic, psychological and tonal affinities, lacking in Brooke's treatment, that seem to link Shakespeare's play with Chaucer's great poem. Among these we may note the interplay (not always clearly realised) of Fate (or Fortune) and free will (a tension in *Romeo* that will have to be considered in some detail later); the infusion of comedy which enables both writers 'to maintain a comic or affirmative tone much of the time', allowing us to forget for the moment the tragic outcome announced at the beginning of *Troilus* and by the opening Chorus in Shakespeare; and the presentation of Criseyde and Juliet as psychologically mature compared with Troilus and Romeo.[5]

The tragic pattern

Critical opinion of *Romeo and Juliet* has ranged from simple adulation to measured disapproval, raising a number of interrelated and vexing questions. Two may be considered here. Is *Romeo and Juliet* in the usually accepted sense a successful tragedy or an experiment that fails to come off? Is the play a tragedy of Fate or a tragedy of character? Or is it both? That is, does Shakespeare succeed here in creating the paradox that has long been felt to lie at the heart of great tragedy, the mysterious interaction and fusion of Fate and free will?

Some critics, of whom the most influential is H. B. Charlton,[6] admit the powerfully

---

[1] See Commentary, 1.4.70–88 and 5.1.1–9.

[2] Even when Shakespeare used Chaucer's poem in his own *Tro.* (1601–2) there are very few verbal echoes.

[3] J. W. Hales ('Chaucer and Shakespeare', *Quarterly Review* 134 (1873), 225–55) began the study of Shakespeare's debt to Chaucer. For more recent criticism see N. Coghill, 'Shakespeare's reading in Chaucer', in *Elizabethan and Jacobean Studies Presented to F. P. Wilson*, ed. H. Davis and H. Gardner, 1959, pp. 86–99; Ann Thompson, *Shakespeare's Chaucer*, 1978; Thomas Moisan, 'Chaucer's Pandarus and the sententious Friar Lawrence', *Arkansas Philological Association* 8 (1982), 38–48.

[4] Shakespeare shows a knowledge of Chaucer (*The Legend of Good Women*) as early as *Lucrece* (1593–4).

[5] Thompson, *Shakespeare's Chaucer*, pp. 99–103.

[6] *Shakespearian Tragedy*, 1948, pp. 49–63. Charlton (pp. 53–4) attributes Shakespeare's use of Fate to the influence of Brooke's *Romeus*, but it should be pointed out that, though Brooke sprinkles references to Fortune liberally (some forty times) and refers very occasionally and off-handedly to Fate (e.g. 859, 936, 1574, 1328, 1753, the last two being the stars), a reader gets very little sense in his poem of any significant operation of the kind of Fate Charlton is talking about in relation to *Rom.* In Brooke, Fortune is simply the inconstant goddess, who raises a man one day, casts him down the next, and may be expected to raise him again in the future (a continuing cyclical pattern; see Brooke 935–46, 1391–1412, particularly), and Brooke (2872–4) declares, through the Friar, that man has freedom of choice. His indiscriminate approach may be gathered from 1752–4: '...out aloude he cryes / Against the restles starres, in rolling skyes that raunge, / Against the fatall sisters three, and Fortune full of chaunge'. For Brooke (935–8), Fate seems in general to represent man's enthralment to an inconstant Fortune. G. I. Duthie (NS, 1955) essentially accepts Charlton's view of the play.

moving quality of the love story, but find the play a failed tragedy, an experiment which does not quite succeed, or which, so far as it succeeds at all, does so, in Charlton's words, 'by a trick'. He considers the feud as 'a bribe' used by Shakespeare 'to exonerate himself from all complicity in their [the lovers'] murder...disown[ing] responsibility and throw[ing] it on Destiny, Fate...the feud [being] the means by which Fate acts' (p. 52). But neither Fate nor feud, he finds, is strongly enough handled by Shakespeare to carry the weight of the tragedy, and Shakespeare's 'achievement is due to the magic of [his] poetic genius and to the intermittent force of his dramatic power rather than to his grasp of the foundations of tragedy' (p. 62).

An older and more popular view, most recently supported by Bertrand Evans,[1] treats the play as a pure tragedy of Fate, in which not only every action of Romeo and Juliet themselves but every action of all the other characters is dictated by the Prologue's reference to 'star-crossed lovers' and 'death-marked love'. If this seems simplistic, it is no more so than the opposite extreme embraced by, among others, Franklin M. Dickey and W. H. Auden.[2] Essentially sidestepping the Prologue and later suggestions of Fate (or Fortune) in the play, or subsuming Fate under Divine Providence, they find Romeo and Juliet basically free agents, who, in pursuing their love blindly and recklessly, become moral exempla of excessive passion (they die 'For doting, not for loving') and are condignly punished (Auden declares both Romeo and Juliet to be damned) for trespassing beyond the temperate married love sanctioned by church and state.

More recently, John Lawlor[3] has examined *Romeo and Juliet* in the light of medieval conceptions of tragedy (which he distinguishes by the spelling *tragedie*), of which, of course, Chaucer's *Troilus and Criseyde* is the supreme example in English. 'Its central truth is that Fortune knows nothing of human deserving. But her activities are not, in the end, inscrutable; for those who are minded to learn, a greater good is in prospect' (p. 124); and 'Where such tragedy [i.e. the Greek form, found in Shakespeare's later tragedies] returns us to the real world, *tragedie* takes us beyond it' (p. 125), where 'Death has no final power over the lovers' (p. 127). Lawlor thus sees the play as one which 'does not minimize, much less cancel, Fortune's power, but which denies her an entire victory' (p. 127). Choosing to die for their love, Romeo and Juliet may be seen as shaking off the yoke of inauspicious stars in an assertion of personal will and sealing a triumphant and dateless bargain to eternity.

Another medieval concept, that 'sexual love is a manifestation of the all-pervading love of God, through which the universe is governed', has been brought to bear on the play by Paul Siegel.[4] In this view, the love of Romeo and Juliet serves Divine

---

[1] *Shakespeare's Tragic Practice*, 1979, pp. 22–51. P. N. Siegel (*SQ* 12 (1961), 371) offers a useful list of those critics who see the play as a tragedy of Fate and those who discuss it as a tragedy of character.

[2] Franklin M. Dickey, *Not Wisely But Too Well: Shakespeare's Love Tragedies*, 1957, pp. 63–117. Dickey makes 'fortune the agent of divine justice without absolving anyone from his responsibility for the tragic conclusion' (p. 64). W. H. Auden, in *The Laurel Shakespeare*, Gen. Ed. Francis Fergusson, 1958, pp. 21–39, gives a table listing all the wrong choices (and their consequences) made by each of the characters.

[3] '*Romeo and Juliet*', in *Early Shakespeare*, ed. J. R. Brown and B. Harris, 1961, pp. 123–43. See also Lawlor's *The Tragic Sense in Shakespeare*, 1960, pp. 74–87.

[4] 'Christianity and the religion of love in *Romeo and Juliet*', *SQ* 12 (1961), 371–92.

Providence as part of the cosmic love through which the universe is nurtured by God, and their death converts the evil and hate of the world into the social harmony of love in the 'death' of the feud (pp. 383–92). Like Lawlor, Siegel finds the lovers entering triumphantly upon a new and better existence, adding, however, specific reference to the medieval and Renaissance conception of the 'paradise of lovers' (pp. 384–6), a commonplace of courtly love literature, given contemporary expression in Spenser's garden of the Temple of Venus (*Faerie Queene*, x).

Finally, T. J. Cribb has sought to find the 'ordering principle' in *Romeo and Juliet* by suggesting that we should see the play as a dramatic expression of the neo-Platonic concept of love as it was interpreted by Ficino, Pico della Mirandola and Leone Ebreo, a revaluation in which passional love, 'love of another, not for another, *eros* not *caritas*', is a new key element.[1] He believes, for example, that the sense of 'awe and amazement' in Romeo's 'sun' and 'angel' images in his opening soliloquy in 2.2 are intelligible only in the context of neo-Platonic thought, and he sees the death of the lovers, in these somewhat intellectualised terms, as a triumphant affirmation of love achieved through a victory over hate, the opposing principle, represented for Cribb in the centrally important role of Tybalt. Tybalt thus becomes 'an agent not merely of the stars, but of the metaphysical paradoxes which present the lovers both as star-crossed by "misadventur'd pittious overthrowes" (Prologue, 7) and as heroes of love who triumph over the stars through love itself'. His argument, therefore, views the play 'at a poetic level' and he is refreshingly honest in admitting that such a reading 'may not be fully appreciable on the stage' and that 'in this play poet and playwright are not perfectly united'.

These are, in brief, the principal more recent approaches to *Romeo and Juliet*. That any of them solves all the problems of the play may be doubted. They are after all simply ways of looking at (or ignoring) some of these problems in an attempt to explain the one incontrovertible fact – the universal appeal which the play has exercised on generations of readers and theatre-goers. One of the principal stumbling blocks to seeing the play as an organic whole is, as we have already noted, the confusion which many critics see in Shakespeare's treatment of the concepts of Fate and free will. Virgil Whitaker's statement may be taken as typical:

The metaphysics of the play is not particularly sophisticated, and it is nowhere clear whether the stars symbolize blind fate or chance or whether they indicate, as in *Julius Caesar* and other later plays, the operation of natural forces which may be resisted or modified by human will.[2]

---

[1] 'The unity of *Romeo and Juliet*', *S.Sur.* 34 (1981), 93–104.

[2] *The Mirror up to Nature: The Technique of Shakespeare's Tragedies*, 1965, p. 111. Samuel Daniel in *The Complaint of Rosamond* (1592), a poem which influenced Shakespeare's play, states the conventional paradox (lines 407–13):

> These presidents presented to my view,
> Wherein the presage of my fall was showne:
> Might have fore-warn'd me well what would ensue,
> And others harmes have made me shunne mine owne;
> But fate is not prevented though fore-knowne.
> For that must hap decreed by heavenly powers,
> Who worke our fall, yet make the fault still ours.

Compare *Rom.* 5.3.153–4, 260–1, where Shakespeare suggests the working of God's providence.

The comment is a fair one, but what is not generally asked is what the effect on the play would have been if Shakespeare had decided to concentrate on only one or the other (as some critics, in fact, believe he essentially did). May it not perhaps be argued that his handling of these two paradoxically opposed concepts, confused though it may be, is nevertheless an effective cause of *Romeo and Juliet*'s success as a tragedy? By thus playing, occasionally a bit fast and loose perhaps, with the dual ideas of Fate and free will, does he not achieve an otherwise unobtainable effect in the final impact? Emphasising at strategic moments the overshadowing of Fate (or Fortune or Chance), he softens the moral implications of the headlong and self-willed career of the lovers so that we are not in danger of applying a simple moral yardstick to their actions, of measuring them, in fact, by the harshly Protestant tone of Brooke's address 'To the Reader':

And to this ende (good Reader) is this tragicall matter written, to describe unto thee a coople of unfortunate lovers, thralling themselves to unhonest desire, neglecting the authoritie and advise of parents and frendes, conferring their principall counsels with dronken gossyppes, and superstitious friers...attemptyng all adventures of peryll, for thattaynyng of their wished lust...abusyng the honorable name of lawefull mariage, to cloke the shame of stolne contractes, finallye, by all meanes of unhonest lyfe, hastyng to most unhappye deathe.

On the other hand, by employing Friar Lawrence as the voice of Christian morality, a kind of muted but sufficiently stated undersong counselling temperance and reason, which the lovers generally choose to ignore, Shakespeare significantly humanises the situation and escapes from presenting the unbearable spectacle of two young people, helpless puppets, driven to an early death as sacrifices to the President of the Immortals for his 'sport', mere means to an end, however laudable in one sense (the resolving of the feud) that end may be.

By thus juxtaposing the concepts of Fate and free will, and by the intermittent but powerful play of irony that results, Shakespeare may be seen as attempting to ensure a humanely tempered reaction to his story of young and tragic love. That he juxtaposes these concepts instead of fusing them, as he is able to do in his later major tragedies, may indeed be recognised as a sign of immaturity and inexperience, but it should also be admitted that the play succeeds because of, not despite, what critics have described as Shakespeare's 'confusion'.

Language, style and imagery

Language, style and imagery in *Romeo and Juliet* interact on many levels. We have earlier commented on the public and private voices established in the first scene, but the private voice, particularly, has a variety of tones of its own: the 'low' bawdy word-play of the servants set against the 'high' bawdy wit games of Mercutio and Benvolio (into which Romeo is briefly drawn); the oxymoron and hyperbole of sonnet love counterpointed and balanced by the obscenely physical extremes of Mercutio and the Nurse; the conventionally mannered language of adult society in Capulet and Lady Capulet played off against the earthy amoral prattle of the Nurse and complemented by the *gravitas* of Friar Lawrence's moral pronouncements; all these are brilliantly set off by the free and natural outpouring of feeling that, in intimate moments, pulses in the language (and imagery) of Romeo and Juliet. Except for this last, which expresses the private world of the lovers, language in the play shows many faces: intentionally ambiguous and quibbling, broodingly foreshadowing, brutally threatening, sexually suggestive; it is often the language of rhetorical artifice and role-playing, of social convention and moral statement, of wit and some wisdom.

Stylistically, *Romeo and Juliet* comes at a point in Shakespeare's development when he is beginning to break away from the conventional and rhetorically bound use of language and figure,[1] of images 'used for their own sakes', of the overextended conceit with its 'vain pleasure taken in painting every detail',[2] and is discovering, fitfully, a dramatic language which, though it continues to use the figures, uses them directly and integrally, so that language and imagery not only describe character but through organic metaphor become the expression of character itself.

Among the all too frequent examples of the early conventional style,[3] we may notice Lady Capulet's praise of Paris (1.3.81–95), Capulet's description of Juliet in tears (3.5.126–37), Juliet's reaction first to what she interprets as news of Romeo's death (3.2.43–51) and then to the discovery that Tybalt, not Romeo, is dead (3.2.73–85). Each of these passages shows self-indulgence, embroidering and spinning out the central conceit to a point where it becomes an ornamental set-piece calculated to display the writer's wit rather than a character's feeling. It has been suggested that this style is properly characteristic of Juliet's parents,[4] but the same saving argument can scarcely be made for Juliet's outbursts in 3.2,[5] which are separated by only a few lines from one of the most famous speeches in the play ('Gallop apace, you fiery-footed steeds'), Juliet's personal epithalamium, a speech in which Shakespeare writes with an immediacy of feeling and a perfect projection of the dramatic moment. Art here becomes nature, and what Juliet says realises essentially what she is. This is the new style, and we find it most notably in the earlier window scene (2.2), particularly when Juliet speaks; later, in the dawn parting of the lovers (3.5); and finally, in Romeo's last speech in 5.3.[6]

Where the new style emerges most successfully, Shakespeare is writing with little or no direct dependence on Brooke, and this tends to be especially true when he is concerned with the lovers either singly or when alone together. Usually at these

---

[1] For Shakespeare's use of various rhetorical figures in *Rom.*, see Sister Miriam Joseph, *Shakespeare's Use of the Arts of Language*, 1947; Harry Levin, 'Form and formality in *Romeo and Juliet*', in *Shakespeare and the Revolution of the Times*, 1976, pp. 103–20; Brooks, *MND*, pp. xlv–xlviii.

[2] W. H. Clemen, *The Development of Shakespeare's Imagery* 1951, pp. 38, 63. See also Madeleine Doran, *Shakespeare's Dramatic Language* 1976, pp. 10–13.

[3] On the set lamentations following the discovery of Juliet's supposed death, see Commentary, 4.5.43–64, and supplementary note.   [4] Clemen, *Development*, p. 64.

[5] Mahood (p. 70) excuses 3.2.43–51: 'this is one of Shakespeare's first attempts to reveal a profound disturbance of mind by the use of quibbles'; and (p. 107) she defends 3.2.73–85: 'When Juliet feels at one with Romeo, her intonations are genuine; when she feels at odds with him, they should be unconvincing.'

[6] As Levin ('Form and formality', p. 114) notes, however, 'The naturalness of their diction is artfully gained...through a running critique of artificiality.'

moments Shakespeare translates the love theme into a poetic world totally out of Brooke's sphere and far beyond the emotional bounds of the traditional story. At one of these moments, however, Shakespeare remains Brooke's prisoner: Juliet's dramatically important soliloquy before drinking the sleeping potion (4.3). The speech is a pastiche of bits and pieces rearranged from lines 2337–2400 of Brooke's poem, and, although Shakespeare concentrates the material and makes some incidental additions (the dagger, the passing suspicion of the Friar's motives, the substitution of 'spirits' for Brooke's 'serpentes odious, / And other beastes and wormes', the fear of madness and of dashing out her brains with a kinsman's bone), neither the additional material nor the speech as a whole rises imaginatively or emotionally much beyond Brooke's merely competent level. Somehow the moment failed to involve Shakespeare creatively.

Shakespeare's use of imagery in *Romeo and Juliet* has received considerable attention, especially, of course, since Caroline Spurgeon's pioneer study in 1936.[1] As usual in Shakespeare, images from nature and animals are among the most frequent, but his use of personification is unusually high (perhaps in part under the influence of Brooke, who often uses the figure). Particularly important are the fire/light images:

> There can be no question, I think, that Shakespeare saw the story, in its swift and tragic beauty, as an almost blinding flash of light, suddenly ignited, and as swiftly quenched.[2]

As Friar Lawrence warns (2.6.9–11):

> These violent delights have violent ends,
> And in their triumph die like fire and powder,
> Which as they kiss consume.

Shakespeare may have found some suggestion for his fire imagery in Brooke,[3] who, as Miss Spurgeon notes, describes the feud, in well-worn metaphor, as a 'little sparke' flashing into 'flame' (35–6, 49–50, 956–8, 978) and the love of Romeus and Juliet as 'quick sparks and glowing furious gleade', which 'set on fyre, eche feling parte' (303–5). We may, indeed, compare one of Brooke's comments (209–10) with Shakespeare's lines above:

> This sodain kindled fyre [of love] in time is wox so great:
> That onely death, and both theyr blouds might quench the fiery heate.

The light image, in its associations with fire and its opposite, darkness, is further extended by the frequent references to sun, moon, stars, day, night, heaven and lightning, a running series of iterative images which emphasises both the intensity and glory of love and its terrible brevity – 'So quick bright things come to confusion' (*MND* 1.1.149).[4] Night and darkness as sympathetic to love, and day and light as

---

[1] *Shakespeare's Imagery and What It Tells Us*, 1936. Spurgeon (pp. 364–7) gives 'A detailed analysis of the subject-matter of the images' in *Rom*. Imagery study may be said to begin with Walter Whiter's *A Specimen of a Commentary on Shakspeare*, 1794 (see Commentary, 5.3.111–18). See also: Clemen, *Development*; E. A. Armstrong, *Shakespeare's Imagination*, 1946, rev. edn, 1963.

[2] Spurgeon, *Shakespeare's Imagery*, p. 312.

[3] He could have found it in Painter or a dozen other places, if he needed to find it anywhere.

[4] Mahood (p. 65) calls attention to the 'play's central paradox of love's strength and fragility'.

inimical to it, are foreshadowed in the first scene when we are told how Romeo steals 'Away from light', 'locks fair daylight out' and 'makes himself an artificial night' (128–31). At the same time, the lover's view is contrasted with conventional praise of day and light by Benvolio's reference to 'the worshipped sun' (109), by Montague's 'all-cheering sun' (125), and by his ill-fated hope that Romeo might 'dedicate his beauty to the sun' (144). Like much else in this opening scene (an important measure of Shakespeare's mastery), Romeo's histrionics and conventional attitude to day/light and night/darkness set up the terms in which, ironically, something of the truth of real love, once it strikes Romeo, will be played out – 'then turn tears to fires' (1.2.89).

When Romeo first sees Juliet, she appears to him 'As a rich jewel in an Ethiop's ear', a brilliance that 'teach[es] the torches to burn bright' (1.5.43–5). It is through this special quality of light in darkness that we now, through Romeo's eyes, experience Juliet. In the garden scene (2.2) Romeo's first two speeches are suffused with Juliet as light: she is the 'fair sun' that in the dark of night makes the pale moon envious; 'Two of the fairest stars in all the heaven' court her eyes, which 'stream so bright / That birds would sing and think it were not night' (15–22); she is one of those 'Earth-treading stars that make dark heaven light' described by Capulet earlier (1.2.25), and a 'bright angel' 'glorious to this night' (26–7), this 'blessèd, blessèd night' (139) as it is perceived by Romeo, while word-play on 'good night, good night' runs like a refrain through the last third of the scene. The following scenes, through 3.1, are daylight scenes and the light/dark imagery does not appear again until the opening of 3.2 (Juliet's epithalamium), where the sun ('Phoebus') is banished and 'love-performing', 'gentle', 'loving' night summoned to comfort and conceal the lovers, who can 'see to do their amorous rites / By [the light of] their own beauties' (8–9). The light imagery now embraces Romeo, who becomes, first, Juliet's 'day in night' shining like 'new snow upon a raven's back' (17–19), then, a constellation of 'little stars' that puts 'the garish sun' to shame (21–5). This sense of night and darkness as the ally of love is further developed in the dawn-parting scene (3.5). It is the invasion of day (light) with its 'envious streaks...in yonder east' (7–8) that parts the lovers:

> ROMEO More light and light, more dark and dark our woes!...
> JULIET Then, window, let day in, and let life out.   (36, 41)[1]

Indeed, Shakespeare seems to reverse our normal expectations. Night and darkness, usually associated with evil and death, take on the qualities of light and life, while day, usually identified with light and life, assumes the aspect of darkness and death. Thus, even though he plays continually on the conventional association of night and death ('The horrible conceit of death and night' as Juliet terms it, 4.3.37), linked closely with the concept of the stars as the supposed arbiters of Fate[2] (as in the

---

[1] Romeo and Juliet are also parted by dawn in 2.2 and 5.3, though in this last scene the parting becomes a final reunion.

[2] In the orthodox religious view of the period the stars could 'influence though not directly determine [man's] choice' (D. L. Peterson, 'Romeo and Juliet and the art of moral navigation', in Pacific Coast Studies in Shakespeare, ed. W. F. McNeir and T. N. Greenfield, 1966, p. 35).

'star-crossed lovers' and 'death-marked love' of the Prologue and in Romeo's premonition of 'untimely death' 'yet hanging in the stars' 1.4.111, 107), yet at the end we are made to feel that the lovers defy Fate ('Is it e'en so? then I defy you, stars!', 5.1.24) and, 'shak[ing] the yoke of inauspicious stars' (5.3.111), usurp death's role 'in a triumphant grave', 'a feasting presence full of light' (5.3.83, 86).

The most powerful evocation of death (often personified) is, of course, as Juliet's surrogate husband. The image begins in 1.5.133–4 when Juliet says, 'If he be marrièd, / My grave is like to be my wedding bed'; it is repeated by Juliet in 3.2.136–7, 'I'll to my wedding bed, / And death, not Romeo, take my maidenhead!'; echoed by Lady Capulet, 'I would the fool were married to her grave'(3.5.140); stated as the theme of Capulet's lament at the discovery of Juliet's 'death' (4.5.38–9), 'Death is my son-in-law, Death is my heir, / My daughter he hath wedded'; and it finally becomes, with powerful dramatic irony, the central driving image in Romeo's soliloquy over the supposedly dead Juliet in 5.3.88–120. This speech, in its intimate evocation of powerful feeling, in the effortless way it brings to a final focus all the leading images and themes in the play (light in darkness, the stars (as Fate), the sea/wreck, womb–tomb, and life-as-journey[1] images, night, death, life, and love, the 'love in death' of 4.5.58), and in its mature denial of hate and triumphant affirmation of love – a love that embraces not Juliet alone, but Paris and Tybalt[2] – crystallises the tragic moment with a strength and emotional immediacy new in Shakespeare.

The characters

Shakespeare inherited from Brooke not only his story, but all his principal characters apart from Mercutio; by way of Brooke, he was drawing on Italian romance as seen by French eyes.[3] The inhabitants of this romance world are rarely more than stock figures on which to hang stories of love intrigue and attendant cuckoldry, double dealing, witty escapes, disguising and mistaken identity – what Painter calls 'the thousand thousand slippery sleightes of Love's gallantise'.[4] Usually such tales end happily, if not exactly morally (love as a topic being considered essentially the proper province of comedy), but occasionally, as in the stories of Tancred and Gismunda or the Duchess of Malfi, the love sport turns deadly serious and tragedy results. Even so, the characters involved remain largely flat, conventional figures, constitutionally given to argumentative, motive-probing discussions and long-winded complaints.

Such – with the partial exception of the Nurse – are the generic types Shakespeare encountered in Brooke or Painter. In the case of some of the supporting characters Shakespeare was content simply to sharpen the stereotype. Neither the Prince nor the Montague and Capulet parents emerge as much more. In Capulet, for example, both the considerate and loving father of 1.2 and the tyrannical autocrat of 3.5 are

---

[1] On the life-as-journey image in *Rom.*, see W. C. Carroll, '"We were born to die": *Romeo and Juliet*', *Comparative Drama* 15 (1981), 54–71.

[2] The reference to Tybalt was suggested to Shakespeare by Brooke (2660–70).

[3] See Charlton, 'France as chaperone', pp. 43–59.

[4] *The Palace of Pleasure*, ed. J. Jacobs, 1890, III, 28.

already fully sketched by Brooke; only Capulet's reminiscences of vanished youth (1.5) and the occasional comic moment really distinguish Shakespeare's portrait. In the same way, Tybalt and Paris remain as they are in Brooke: Tybalt as the *agent provocateur*, a figure of inherited hate with a mistaken sense of honour, Paris as the young gallant, well-born, rich and honourably in love, who finds himself cast through no fault of his own as Romeo's rival – though Shakespeare extends these roles by introducing them early and inventing the death of Paris in the final scene. There Shakespeare bestows a pathetic integrity on Paris and allows him a noble gesture as he dies protecting, as he believes, his lady's body from desecration at the hands of a marauding enemy. The slaying of Paris has raised some critical questions, but there is a mysterious rightness in it that validates Paris's love and allows him, in company with Romeo, to be joined with Juliet in the silent communion and consummation of death.

Apart from this sudden illumination of Paris's character, Shakespeare's imaginative involvement with the minor supporting characters is fitful. Even Capulet, Lady Capulet and Benvolio, all of whom have comparatively large roles (50, 45, and 63 speeches), are little more than conventional sketches of well-meaning but self-centred parents and the male confidant and friend, who, after 1.1, surprisingly ceases to share Romeo's confidences and becomes merely a reporter of action and a sounding-board for Mercutio's wit, disappearing suddenly from the play in 3.1.[1] But on the three principal supporting characters, Mercutio, the Nurse and Friar Lawrence, Shakespeare has lavished memorable attention.

Brooke says little of Mercutio except for his reputation as a courtier 'highly had in pryce', 'coorteous of his speche, and pleasant of devise':

> Even as a Lyon would emong the lambes be bolde:
> Such was emong the bashfull maydes, Mercutio to beholde.   (Brooke, 255–8)

The Mercutio we know is wholly Shakespeare's invention – perhaps, indeed, an invention that only occurred to him after he had blocked out the major lines of the play. His appearance in 1.4 is rather sudden and one is given the impression that, along with Romeo and Benvolio, he is gate-crashing Capulet's feast, although he is named, along with a brother called Valentine, in the Clown's list of invited guests in 1.2. He dominates 1.4, particularly with his set-piece on Queen Mab, a brilliant *tour de force* of doubtful dramatic or thematic relevance, and then fades into complete silence at the feast (1.5), surely a strange fate for such a compulsive talker. It is almost as if Shakespeare had planned or even written 1.5 before he thought of creating Mercutio.[2]

---

[1] Benvolio's original function was suggested by an unnamed older friend in Brooke (101–40), who counsels Romeus to throw off his unrequited passion for a likewise unnamed lady (Shakespeare's Rosaline) and to haunt social gatherings where he may find a suitable substitute. Romeus accepts his advice and the friend is never heard of again. Q1 introduces a reference in 5.3 to Benvolio's recent death (see collation 5.3.211).

[2] 1.5 is curious in two other respects. In 1.2 Capulet specially invites Paris to attend his feast that evening in order to compare Juliet with other young marriageable girls, but Paris does not come. Again in 1.2, Romeo is urged by Benvolio to attend this same feast because the 'fair Rosaline' is among those invited; like Paris, Rosaline does not appear.

Dryden, in what appears to be the earliest critical comment on *Romeo and Juliet*, singles Mercutio out as Shakespeare's most successful attempt to portray a 'fine gentleman':

Shakespeare showed the best of his skill in his Mercutio; and he [Shakespeare] said himself, that he was forced to kill him in the third act, to prevent being killed by him. But, for my part, I cannot find he was so dangerous a person: I see nothing in him but what was so exceeding harmless, that he might have lived to the end of the play, and died in his bed, without offence to any man.[1]

Since by 'fine gentleman' Dryden meant a Restoration rake like Etherege's Dorimant, his grudging praise of Mercutio may be interpreted as unintentionally complimentary. Dr Johnson puts Dryden firmly in his place:

Mercutio's wit, gaiety and courage, will always procure him friends that wish him a longer life; but his death is not precipitated, he has lived out the time allotted him in the construction of the play; nor do I doubt the ability of Shakespeare to have continued his existence, though some of his sallies are perhaps out of the reach of Dryden...[2]

Here, for the first time, we encounter a hint of one of Mercutio's principal dramatic functions: his role as a foil. Representing one extreme through his continual, witty insistence on the purely physical side of love, Mercutio contrasts with and comments on Romeo's equally extreme position as conventional lover in the sonnet tradition and emphasises Romeo's later more mature understanding that love is not either body or spirit but a fusion of both, the 'subtle knot that makes us man'. Once Romeo has outgrown Rosaline, Mercutio's function on one level has been outworn, but Shakespeare does not waste his creation wantonly. In inventing the accidental death of Mercutio, a character whose irrepressible high spirits and 'sure wit' have won our hearts, Shakespeare has also set up a situation that gains our understanding and sympathy for Romeo, who blames himself for his friend's death, and softens the impact of his slaying of Tybalt. Lacking a Mercutio at this point, Brooke's handling of Romeus is different. After a vain attempt to stop the growing street brawl, Romeus is attacked mercilessly by Tybalt. Instead of attempting to defend himself, Romeus loses his control, and, turning on Tybalt with the ferocity of a wounded boar or a lion bereft of its whelps (as Brooke puts it), kills him without scruple.

Mercutio is also the source or provoker of much of the word-play, witty as well as bawdy, with which the comic levels of the play abound. It is, as Mahood points out, 'one of Shakespeare's most punning plays'.[3] Falstaff, indeed, defines Mercutio's way with language when he characterises 'excellent wit' as 'apprehensive, quick, forgetive, full of nimble, fiery, and delectable shapes' (*2 Henry IV* 4.3.99–100). Words are Mercutio's 'whirlwind passion': he is 'A gentleman...that loves to hear himself talk, and will speak more in a minute than he will stand to in a month' (2.4.123–4). But although words are his only true love, his sense of their ambiguity – a sense which complements Friar Lawrence's belief in the alternative possibilities for good or evil

[1] *Defence of the Epilogue* (1672) in *Essays of John Dryden*, ed. W. P. Ker, 1901, I, 174.
[2] *Johnson on Shakespeare*, ed. Arthur Sherbo, in *The Yale Johnson*, 13 vols., 1958– , VIII, 1968, 956–7.
[3] Mahood, p. 56. Miss Mahood adds: 'a conservative count yields a hundred and seventy-five quibbles'.

in all levels of God's creation – not only provides an intellectual tension and drive in the first half of the play but obliges us to realise that under the airy speculations of romantic love lies a hard core of physical and inescapable reality.

With his usual incisiveness Dr Johnson catches the Nurse as it were in full flight:

[She] is one of the characters in which the Author delighted: he has, with great subtilty of distinction, drawn her at once loquacious and secret, obsequious and insolent, trusty and dishonest.[1]

But if we allow for the difference between genius and talent, much the same characterisation might be given of Shakespeare's original in Brooke.[2] There is in both the same moral obtuseness, garrulousness, appetite for secrecy, opportunism and pleasure in the physical aspects of love (693–704, 890–900), all softened by a real if sentimental affection for her 'nurce childe'. To these traits Brooke adds a touch of venality (627–8, 667–73) which Shakespeare wisely omits. Shakespeare, of course, extends and lovingly elaborates Brooke's portrait, giving the Nurse an animal vitality (comparable to Mercutio's) through her continual, in part unconscious (unlike Mercutio's) obsession with sexuality. Her function thus parallels Mercutio's in certain ways, but, more important, as nurse–confidante and co-conspirator, she complements, on a serio-comic level, the role of Friar Lawrence, the spiritual counsellor and friend to both Romeo and Juliet.[3]

Juliet's final assessment of the Nurse ('Ancient damnation!', 3.5.235) implies perhaps a harsher and more general condemnation than her character as a whole warrants, but it reaches out beyond her and underscores the vital difference between complete commitment to an ideal and the easy opportunism that governs the world surrounding Romeo and Juliet, a world in which the Nurse is happily and thoughtlessly at home.

Critical reaction to Friar Lawrence ranges from the uneasily ambiguous to the downright hostile. The reasons for this confused response lie partly in the inherited story-line and partly in Shakespeare's treatment of the character. In following Brooke, Shakespeare is twice seemingly content to make Friar Lawrence a victim of the plot: first when, under the pressure of Juliet's impending marriage to Paris, he fails to reveal the prior marriage of Romeo and Juliet and tries to cover up the situation by the questionable subterfuge of the sleeping potion; and second when, in the final scene, he turns tail and attempts to run away, abandoning Juliet in her moment of supreme need. The second action is the more obviously damaging, since it seems to undercut at a single stroke all our former sympathy for Friar Lawrence, who, like Romeo and Juliet, had been perceived as caught in a tangled web of 'accidental judgments' and 'purposes mistook/Fall'n on th'inventors' heads' (*Hamlet* 5.2.382–5). It would probably be too much to suggest that Shakespeare saw in this action a lurking weakness in the Friar's character. It seems more likely that Shakespeare was concentrating at this point on what may have appeared to him a dramatic necessity:

---

[1] *Johnson on Shakespeare*, p. 957.
[2] Brooke considerably enlarged and improved the portrait of the Nurse that he found in Boaistuau. Some credit, therefore, belongs to Brooke's feeling for the character.
[3] On this point see H. C. Goddard, *The Meaning of Shakespeare*, 1951, pp. 120–4.

the symbolic isolation of Juliet at the moment she joins Romeo in death, recalling and focusing for us her earlier moments of isolation when she is deserted by her parents and the Nurse (3.5) and her declaration before drinking the sleeping potion, 'My dismal scene I needs must act alone' (4.3.19). Even the Friar, as spectator, would have violated the privacy of her union with Romeo and death. This may not entirely excuse sacrificing Friar Lawrence, but it at least suggests that Shakespeare was not blindly following his source without dramatic and thematic considerations.

The first instance, Friar Lawrence's recourse to the sleeping potion subterfuge, is, of course, in a different category; it is a 'given', something that could not be altered without a radical change in the whole story. But Shakespeare by his earlier presentation of the Friar's character gives it perhaps a deeper significance than it has in Brooke.

Friar Lawrence is first introduced in 2.3 as a choral voice through whom Shakespeare explains the potentiality for either good or evil inherent in all created things, including man, an explanation, as R. M. Frye points out, that expresses an orthodox Christian view which could have been shared by Catholics and Protestants.[1] His first interview with Romeo immediately follows, in which he emerges as a kindly 'father surrogate', admonitory but indulgent, showing a playfully humorous understanding of Romeo's excess in 'doting' on Rosaline, and an immediate if unthinking willingness to perform the marriage. This, to be sure, he couples with a single brief warning,[2] a warning repeated several times in later scenes, not to allow a similar excess to govern his newly declared love for Juliet ('Wisely and slow, they stumble that run fast', 94), a warning which ominously echoes his earlier choral lines:

> Nor ought so good but, strained from that fair use,
> Revolts from true birth, stumbling on abuse.   (19–20)

His intentions are good, but his action is precipitate, without any consideration of the dangers involved in Romeo's clandestine marriage.[3] When events get out of hand Friar Lawrence is pushed, to some extent out of a dangerous personal involvement,[4] into proposing the subterfuge of the sleeping potion to Juliet (4.1). In a sense, then, what began as a potential work of 'grace' – to heal the feud by a marriage between the families – is twisted instead, by the Friar's choice of 'desperate' means, into something verging on a work of 'rude will' ('Virtue itself turns vice, being misapplied', 2.3.21). Ironically, Friar Lawrence illustrates through his own actions the moral

---

[1] *Shakespeare and Christian Doctrine*, 1963, pp. 216–19.

[2] Garrick (1748) was concerned by the Friar's failure to be more strongly admonitory at this point and, omitting lines 66–84, composed an eight-line speech to make good what he considered a deficiency.

[3] Brooke's Friar, who is pictured, approvingly, as a kind of White Magician (569–72), is more cautious; he warns Romeus of 'A thousand daungers like to come' and 'readeth him refrayne: / Perhaps he shalbe bet advisde within a weeke or twayne' (598–600); he has to be talked into performing the marriage. Shakespeare's Friar is thus more immediately generous and co-operative, but less thoughtful and provident.

[4] Juliet's passing suspicion (4.3.24–9; not in Brooke) that Friar Lawrence may have given her a poison instead of a sleeping potion suggests that she recognises the personal dangers inherent in the Friar's position.

dangers inherent in man's dual nature that he had warned against in his opening choral speech:

> Two such oppos̀ed kings encamp them still
> In man as well as herbs, grace and rude will;
> And where the worser is predominant,
> Full soon the canker death eats up that plant.   (2.3.27–30)

Shakespeare thus creates a character in which the Friar's function as orthodox moral commentator – an emphasis which is not in Brooke – seems to be at odds with aspects of his character and actions as a man. The ambiguity of the critical response to Friar Lawrence, therefore, is not surprising or entirely unjustified. As we suggested earlier, Shakespeare wanted the moral voice, insistently but quietly implying man's freedom to choose 'grace' or 'rude will', to offset the dehumanising effect of his pervasive and strong emphasis on the operation of Fate. But he also wanted a fallibly human Friar Lawrence, who would not, by a too marked moral contrast, endanger our sympathy with the actions of the young lovers. In this way, although he may not be entirely successful in fusing Friar Lawrence's dual function (as chorus and as a character in the plot), Shakespeare achieves an effect, analogous to his handling of Fate and free will, which he feels to be necessary in balancing our reactions to the central characters, Romeo and Juliet.

The special quality of the love that is finally expressed through Romeo and Juliet is, of course, Shakespeare's supreme achievement in this play. Drayton, in 1597, in a poem that appears to show some knowledge of *Romeo and Juliet*,[1] seems to catch much of its essence:

> True love is simple, like his mother Truth,
> Kindlie affection, youth to love with youth.

Here, with almost critical precision, are all but one of the special qualities we associate with the lovers and their love: simplicity, truth, natural passion, youth and mutuality. Absolute commitment, the one quality lacking in Drayton's definition, is the theme of Shakespeare's Sonnet 116, parts of which seem to bear directly on this, the central focus of the play, in its celebrated definition of love:

> O no, it is an ever-fixed mark
> That looks on tempests and is never shaken;
> It is the star to every wand'ring bark,
> Whose worth's unknown, although his highth be taken...
> Love alters not with his [Time's] brief hours and weeks,
> But bears it out even to the edge of doom.

Juliet gives complete expression to her character as well as to her conception of love when she says to Romeo about her love:

> But to be frank and give it thee again,
> And yet I wish but for the thing I have:
> My bounty is as boundless as the sea,

---

[1] See Commentary, 2.2.33–42.

> My love as deep; the more I give to thee
> The more I have, for both are infinite. $(2.2.131-5)^1$

And Romeo, though the inner security of his love matures more slowly, captures the same sense of selfless giving when, in a speech strongly marked by tragic foreshadowing, he cries out:

> Amen, amen! but come what sorrow can,
> It cannot countervail the exchange of joy
> That one short minute gives me in her sight.
> Do thou but close our hands with holy words,
> Then love-devouring Death do what he dare,
> It is enough I may but call her mine. $(2.6.3-8)$

In 2.3.91–2, Friar Lawrence expresses his hope that

> ...this alliance may so happy prove
> To turn your households' rancour to pure love.

He is speaking, of course, of 'pure love' in its social sense, but it is surely an irony that the 'pure love' of Romeo and Juliet, warmly human and alive, which does indeed bring to the Montagues and Capulets a 'glooming peace', only achieves its final public symbolic expression in the cold and lifeless 'pure gold' of a funeral monument.

But Romeo and Juliet are more than static evocations of the spirit of ideal love. Here, for essentially the first time in his career as a dramatist, Shakespeare undertakes to present something like developing characters – the growth from thoughtless adolescence to the inescapable and painful realities of maturity.[2] The bare story-line for such character development was ready to hand in Brooke, but Brooke gives us little sense that the lovers have grown in self-knowledge or in awareness of the heavy responsibilities that such understanding entails. Shakespeare accomplishes this movement in part by establishing what may be called two early points of contrast. In 1.3 Juliet is introduced as a demure, almost tongue-tied girl of barely fourteen, properly dutiful in the presence of such authorities as her mother and the Nurse (she manages only six-and-a-half lines in a scene of over a hundred).[3] Shakespeare thus emphasises her extreme youth and her almost cloistered dependence, in contrast to Brooke's Juliet, who is sixteen and appears for the first time in the context of the Capulet feast, where she receives the attentions of both Mercutio and Romeo with aplomb, and in her handling of the situation is described by Brooke (350) as 'the yong and wyly dame'. So too Romeo, whatever his age may be,[4] is presented (1.1) by Shakespeare as more boyish in his solemn vapourings about unrequited love than Brooke's Romeus, who having been repulsed by an unnamed lady (Shakespeare's

---

[1] T. S. Eliot (*On Poetry and Poets*, 1957, pp. 94–5) describes lines 133–5 as 'the dominant phrase of the whole duet', a duet in which 'Juliet's voice...has the leading part.'

[2] On the maturation theme, see Marjorie Garber, *Coming of Age in Shakespeare*, 1981, pp. 165–70.

[3] In only one speech does a flash of the later Juliet appear: 'And stint thou too, I pray thee, Nurse, say I' (59).

[4] Neither Brooke nor Shakespeare gives Romeo's age, though Painter (p. 97), following Boaistuau, makes him 'of the age of .20. or .21. yeares'. Shakespeare's Romeo seems somewhat younger than this.

Rosaline) takes his friend's advice[1] to forget her (141–50) and for three months surveys the field 'where Ladies wont to meete', judging 'them all with unallured eye', determined that 'his savage heart [should] lyke all indifferently'. Not so Romeo, who only agrees to attend the Capulet banquet in the hope of being able to feast his eyes on Rosaline.

Critics have often pointed out that Juliet is a stronger personality than Romeo and that she wins through to an almost frightening maturity more quickly. We sense this in her poised and playfully serious exchange with Romeo at their first meeting (1.5) and it is underscored in the famous window scene (2.2), where she shows herself more thoughtful, prudent and realistic than Romeo, though no less deeply engaged, in sensing the tragic threat involved in such 'sudden haste':

> Although I joy in thee,
> I have no joy of this contract tonight,
> It is too rash, too unadvised, too sudden,
> Too like the lightning, which doth cease to be
> Ere one can say 'It lightens'.
>
> (2.2.116–20)

But the threat, though recognised, does not deter Juliet, nor does Shakespeare make us feel that it should, any more than Friar Lawrence's wise cautions to Romeo cause us emotionally to question the essential rightness of the lovers' headlong commitment – though they make us aware of what sound doctrine and reason dictate. Juliet accepts complete responsibility for her actions by the end of 3.5. Repudiated by her father and mother and betrayed by the Nurse's amoral advice, isolated, that is, from her immediate family, Juliet is able to say:

> I'll to the Friar to know his remedy;
> If all else fail, myself have power to die.

All that follows grows out of the absolute commitment expressed in that last line – no weakening or turning back.

Romeo's final commitment, though no less absolute, is achieved only after he believes Juliet to be dead (5.1.24): 'Is it e'en so? then I defy you, stars!' This is a new note in Romeo, particularly when we recall his hysterical performance as late as 3.3, the scene in Friar Lawrence's cell, in which, consumed with self-pity, he tries to stab himself rather than face banishment deprived of Juliet.[2] His attempted suicide here is an important index of his comparative immaturity, a moment in the scene that owes nothing to Brooke. The implied commitment of such an action – to die for love – disguises nothing more than a selfish and thoughtless emotional reaction, without any real consideration for Juliet's feelings or the difficulty of her position.

---

[1] Brooke's Romeus also listens to reason following the slaying of Tybalt, when the Friar lectures him on the conduct befitting a man (1349–1482); only then does the Friar suggest a last visit to Juliet that night. Romeo is only restored to something like rationality by Friar Lawrence's promise of a visit to Juliet.

[2] The Friar's 'Hold thy desperate hand!' (3.3.108) surely warrants the inclusion of the Q1 SD: *He offers to stab himself, and Nurse snatches the dagger away*, even though the Nurse's role in the action may reflect an added piece of stage business. Capell, indeed, assigns the seizing of the dagger to the Friar, following the end of 108.

Through this scene, and particularly through this moment, Shakespeare sets up a startling point of contrast with the Romeo we encounter in the last act. After disappearing from the play for the whole of the fourth act (some 400 lines),[1] Romeo in 5.1 suddenly faces a situation, the report of Juliet's death, that might be expected, for anything we have seen to the contrary, to produce a repetition of the emotional debauchery of 3.3. Instead, Romeo meets the news with control, quiet resolution and unhesitating commitment ('Well, Juliet, I will lie with thee tonight'). With Juliet dead, as he believes, there is nothing left worth living for, and we can now accept his determination to die for love as the supreme expression of a commitment that, like Juliet's, 'is as boundless as the sea'.

Romeo and Juliet in the theatre

I

How *Romeo and Juliet* was presented on the Elizabethan stage can only be conjectured from what we know generally of the earlier theatres (the Theatre, the Curtain, the Swan) and contemporary stage conventions and, more specifically, from the text and stage directions in Q1 (1597) and Q2 (1599). No other records exist, not even the date of a performance before the Restoration. We learn from the title pages of Q1 and Q2 that the play was acted by Shakespeare's company, and Marston's reference in *The Scourge of Villanie* (1598) to 'Curtaine *plaudeties*', in close proximity to a direct reference to *Romeo and Juliet*, seems to link the play with performance at the Curtain, where Shakespeare's company is believed to have acted from October 1597 until the Globe was ready in 1599.[2] Earlier performances would presumably have been given at the Theatre, which was pulled down in December 1598 to furnish materials for the Globe. Q2 further corroborates the connection with Shakespeare's company by assigning Will Kemp, a shareholder and the principal comedian of the company until 1598/9, to the role of Peter in 4.5, and it is generally assumed that Richard Burbage, the company's leading actor (in 1596 he was about twenty-eight) created Romeo, playing to the Juliet of Master Robert Goffe, who appears to have acted leading-lady roles in most of Shakespeare's earlier plays.[3] Considering the demands of a large cast and the relative size of the company (then about twelve), a good deal of doubling would have been required.[4]

Ironically, we know rather more about the stage fortunes of *Romeo and Juliet* on the Continent than in England for this early period. A German version (or versions) of Shakespeare's play was part of the repertory of groups known as *Englischen Comoedianten*, who toured Europe during the later sixteenth century and the first half

[1] As with Hamlet, Shakespeare allows the change in Romeo to take place behind the scenes.
[2] Chambers, II, 402–3.
[3] A reference to Burbage as Romeo in one of the elegies on the death of Burbage (May 1619) is now considered a forged interpolation by J. P. Collier (see Chambers, II, 309). T. W. Baldwin (*The Organization and Personnel of the Shakespearean Company*, 1927, Chart II, following p. 228) assigns Romeo to Burbage and suggests which roles other principal members of the company played.
[4] Giorgio Melchiori ('Peter, Balthasar, and Shakespeare's art of doubling', *MLR* 78 (1983), 777–92) suggests that the roles of the Clown and Peter were doubled (by Kemp) and that a single actor played Paris and Balthasar.

of the seventeenth performing English plays in German or Dutch versions. A *Romeo and Juliet* was performed at Nördlingen in 1604, a play of the same name was twice performed at Dresden in 1626 as part of the repertory of John Green, and a *Romeo and Juliet* was again put on at Dresden in 1646 and 1678.[1] It is unlikely that the extant *Tragaedia von Romeo und Julietta* (text and translation in Cohn) is exactly the same play as those acted at Nördlingen and Dresden, but it is generally representative of the 'quality' of the earlier seventeenth-century German adaptations of Shakespeare.

As a 'literary' text, deriving from Shakespeare's 'foul papers',[2] Q2 contains stage directions that are sometimes confused and often uninformative about details of staging or action. Q1, however, as a 'bad' quarto or memorial reconstruction, based on what the reporter(s) could recall of an earlier production, contains a substantial number of stage directions which arise from visual recollection of staging and business caught from actual performance. Since they often throw valuable light on particular moments in the play, many of these Q1 directions have been adopted in recent editions, as they are in the present text.[3] Two examples will suggest their usefulness. At 1.5.120 Capulet urges his masked guests to stay longer, but then at line 123, without explanation in Q2, changes his mind and bids them 'good night'. Q1, however, explains the change by the direction *They whisper in his ear* following line 121. Again, in 3.5, after Juliet has pretended to accept the Nurse's wicked advice to marry Paris and forget Romeo (230–3), Q1 adds the direction *She looks after Nurse* as she speaks the words 'Ancient damnation! O most wicked fiend!' This 'look' suggests not only the direction in which she points these epithets but the vehemence of her delivery, and captures an important dramatic moment of high tension.

Most of the action in the play occurs on the main stage, with probable use in 4.3–5 and the final scene (5.3) of the discovery space at the rear (formerly, and perhaps more accurately, called the inner stage) for Juliet's bed and the Capulet tomb. Twice, however, action is called for *above* or *aloft*. In 2.2, the so-called balcony or window scene, Juliet is clearly stationed above, although none of the early texts (Q1–4, F) gives her an entry or indicates her position. Taking his cue from line 2 ('what light through yonder window breaks?'), Rowe (1709) placed Juliet *above at her window*;[4] Capell later (1768), however, simply entered her *above*. The difference is significant for the staging, since *at her window* may be taken as placing Juliet at one of the tiring-house windows, to right or left of the upper stage, while Capell's *above* implies the use of the upper stage or 'terras'. The present edition, despite Q1's opening stage direction (*at the window*)[5] for 3.5 (discussed below), accepts the central upper stage setting, allowing

---

[1] See Albert Cohn, *Shakespeare in Germany in the Sixteenth and Seventeenth Centuries*, 1865, pp. cxv–cxvi, cxviii–cxix; Chambers, II, 283; Willem Schrickx, 'English actors at the courts of Wolfenbüttel, Brussels and Graz', *S.Sur.* 33 (1980), 153–68.   [2] See Textual Analysis, pp. 224–5 below.

[3] See, for example, the stage directions at 1.5.121; 2.4.133; 3.1.81; 3.2.31; 3.3.108; 3.3.162; 3.4.11; 3.5.0 SD, 36, 42, 67, 159, 235; 4.2.20; 4.3.58; 4.5.95; 5.1.11; 5.3.0 SD, 11, 21, 48, 70, 139, 146. A few Q1 stage directions do not seem applicable to the Q2 text; see, for example, the collation at 1.1.52–71; 2.6.15 SD; 4.5.43–64 (the last two are discussed in the Commentary).

[4] Compare Brooke (467–8).

[5] It may be argued that Q1 here reflects the limitations of the kind of stage on which it was acted and that a regular upper stage was not available. My discussion of the staging generally accepts Richard Hosley's argument for three acting areas: (1) the 'main stage'; (2) the 'upper stage'; (3) the 'discovery space' (see his 'The use of the upper stage in *Romeo and Juliet*', *SQ* 5 (1954), 371–9).

the window to be a part of the imaginative word-picture conjured up by Romeo (i.e. *Juliet appears aloft as at a window*). This accords with the implications of Q2's direction *aloft* for 3.5 and improves the sight lines for part of the audience in this important scene.

Several other scenes require special comment.

1.4–5: Like many other Elizabethan and Jacobean plays, *Romeo and Juliet* offers examples of continuous scenes which begin in one location and change location during the course of the scene. Thus 1.4–5, although here, as is customary, separately numbered for the convenience of general reference (following eighteenth- and nineteenth-century usage), are actually a single continuous scene, during which the stage is never cleared. It begins, judging by indications in the dialogue (33–4), outside the Capulet house; then, without an exit by Romeo, Benvolio, Mercutio and the other Maskers (*They march about the stage [and stand to one side]*), the locale becomes first an inner room in Capulet's house as the Servingmen *come forth with napkins*, talking about removing the 'join-stools', the 'court-cupboard' and the 'plate' (all probably imaginary), and then, as Capulet and the guests enter and the Servingmen stand aside, the 'great chamber', which, according to the First and Fourth Servingmen (12–14), the servants were being called upon to attend in at the opening of 1.5. The exact staging is further complicated by Capulet's order (26) to 'turn the tables up', implying that they had been eating in the 'great chamber' itself.

2.1–2: The same metamorphosis happens in what is here designated as 2.1 and 2.2, the lane outside Capulet's orchard becoming the orchard itself after the exit of Mercutio and Benvolio (the early texts give Romeo no exit after line 2 of 2.1 or re-entry before line 1 of 2.2). The staging problem, however, concerns the presence or absence on stage of a wall, which, Benvolio claims (2.1.5), Romeo leaps over after line 2 ('He ran this way and leapt this orchard wall'). The early texts offer no help and Capell was the first to imply an actual wall (*leaps the Wall*), and later editors – with the apparent exception of Grant White (1861) – followed suit until the edition by Richard Hosley in 1954. It is now generally felt that a wall dividing the stage and running from near the front to the back would seriously interfere with the sight lines of a large part of the audience, particularly those on the lower levels of the theatre, during one of the most important scenes of the play (2.2), and that to provide one would be to insist upon the kind of unnecessary realism that the conventions of Elizabethan staging did not demand. A low fence-like wall would be merely ridiculous.[1] A satisfactory solution allows the main stage to represent first (2.1) the lane outside Capulet's orchard. Romeo enters, speaks his two lines and withdraws, perhaps behind one of the pillars supporting the 'heavens' (the canopy above the upper stage area, projecting over half or more of the main stage), while Benvolio and Mercutio enter and discuss his disappearance.[2] They then exit and Romeo advances again, his first line rhyming with the last line of 2.1 and showing that he has been eavesdropping; at which point the locale automatically becomes Capulet's orchard (2.2).

---

[1] See Gibbons for an excellent note on the staging here. Harold Brooks, *MND*, p. xliv, still favours the use of a property wall.

[2] Leaping the wall was suggested by Brooke (830): 'So light he wox, he lept the wall', but Shakespeare may have forgotten this detail when, at line 30, Benvolio says 'Come, he hath hid himself among these trees', a line favouring the absence of a wall.

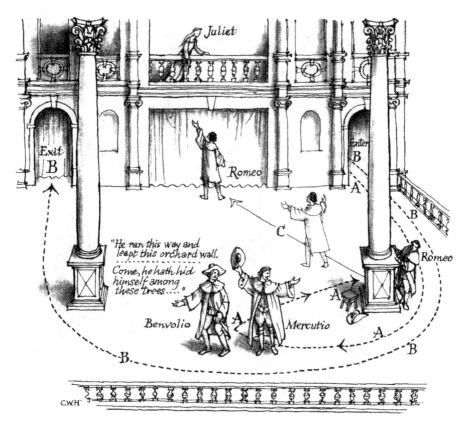

1   The staging of the orchard scene, Act 2, Scene 1, by C. Walter Hodges. A–A shows the path of Romeo outside the 'orchard', turning back to concealment behind 'wall'; B–B shows the path of Benvolio and Mercutio outside the 'orchard', going 'about the stage'; C shows Romeo within the 'orchard'. The three men are shown still in masquing dress, as 'pilgrims'. It is here supposed that, to simulate climbing the wall, Romeo might climb over the plinth of the pillar, perhaps helped by a convenient stool. In doing so he has dropped his pilgrim's hat, which is seen by Benvolio and Mercutio

3.5: This is another scene that changes locale (after 64, first part), though for four lines (64, second part, to 67) it seems to combine both locations on different stage levels. The scene begins *aloft* [*as at the window*] (i.e. on the upper stage), as Romeo and Juliet bid farewell with the unwelcome coming of dawn. The detailed location (*at the window*) is from Q1. At this point the main stage represents, as in 2.2, the Capulet orchard, to which Romeo descends (by the ladder of cords) after line 42 (*He goeth down*, Q1). With Lady Capulet's entrance (64), however, the main stage becomes Juliet's bedchamber, and Juliet, after a three-line speech (65–7) from above, enters below after line 67, 'her bedroom on her back, as it were'.[1] Again, the stage direction is from Q1 (*She goeth down from the window*). A rather awkward arrangement, but, as Granville-Barker points out, 'Capulet's outburst could have been effectively played nowhere but on the lower stage.'

[1] H. Granville-Barker, *Prefaces to Shakespeare*, 1951, II, 325 n. 22.

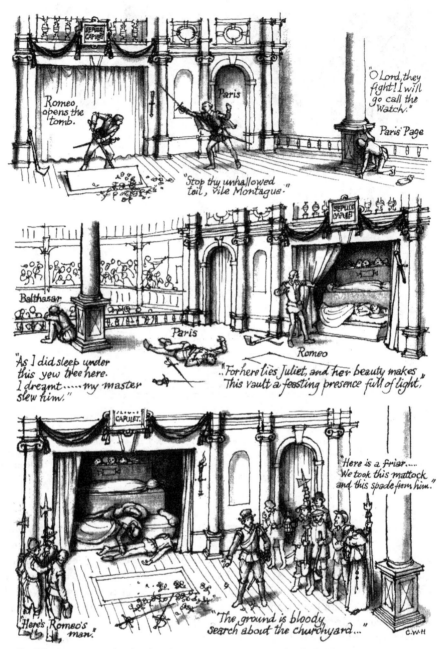

2 Possible ways to stage the churchyard sequence, Act 5, Scene 3, by C. Walter Hodges

4.3–5: In Elizabethan terms these three scenes represent one continuous scene. 4.3 represents Juliet's bedchamber, the focus of action shifting, after the exit of Lady Capulet and the Nurse, to the rear of the stage, where Juliet's bed has been set up in the discovery space, the curtains of which would be open at the beginning of the scene. After Juliet drinks the potion, *She falls upon her bed, within the curtains* (from Q1), that is, she lies down on the bed, drawing the curtains as she does so.[1] 4.4 then follows, returning the focus to the main stage (now another room in Capulet's house), thus for the time being neutralising the rear stage area. With Capulet's exit (4.4.28), however, the focus shifts again to the rear of the stage (Juliet's bedchamber) as the Nurse, who has re-entered at line 24, tries to awaken Juliet (4.5), opening the curtains and displaying the supposedly dead Juliet lying on her bed. With the entry of the other characters, the scene then expands from the rear area to embrace the whole stage, until line 95, at which point the curtains are closed (from Q1) as all but the Nurse and the Musicians go off. The closing of the curtains on the discovery area seems to signal the end of the setting as Juliet's bedchamber and the exchanges which follow, between the Musicians and the Nurse and the Musicians and Peter (96–138), appear to take place on the front main stage, essentially divorced from any intimate association with earlier locations.

5.3: The only staging problem raised by this final scene concerns the location of the Capulet burial monument. The simplest and most probable solution, as in 4.3–5, is to postulate the use of the discovery space, centre rear, below the upper stage. Whether something more realistic than the usual traverse curtains (used, we have argued, in 4.3–5) was employed for the doors of the monument which Romeo breaks open with his mattock and wrenching iron after line 48 (*Romeo opens the tomb*, Q1) must remain conjectural, but the introduction of framed wooden doors, slipped across the discovery space during 5.2 (on the main front stage), would not present any special difficulty. C. Walter Hodges's drawing (illustration 2) offers a different approach (suggested by Brooke's poem) to the opening of the tomb.

II

The first recorded performance of *Romeo and Juliet* in England occurred not long after the Restoration. In December 1660 *Romeo and Juliet* was allotted to the Duke's Company (Sir William Davenant's) and a revival took place on 1 March 1662, a performance that left Pepys much dissatisfied:

...and thence to the Opera and there saw *Romeo and Julett*, the first time it was ever acted. But it is the play of itself the worst that ever I heard in my life, and the worst acted that ever I saw these people do; and I am resolved to go no more to see the first time of acting, for they were all of them out more or less [i.e. did not know their lines].[2]

---

[1] Hosley ('The use of the upper stage', p. 378) accepts the use of the discovery space for Juliet's bed, but later admits the possibility of a bed 'thrust out' on the main stage (see his review of A. M. Nagler, *Shakespeare's Stage*, 1958, in *Comparative Literature* 12 (1960), 66). Williams (p. 147), denying the existence of an inner stage (and presumably a discovery space) on the shaky evidence of the Swan drawing (about 1596), postulates, following Nagler, 'a "pavilion" or "tent"', a curtained structure large enough to represent or contain a bed', set up on the rear of the main stage. This structure remains in place through 5.1 and 5.2 and serves as the tomb in 5.3: 'By a common symbolic transfer involving simultaneous settings, Juliet's marriage bed in fact becomes her tomb.'

[2] *The Diary of Samuel Pepys*, ed. R. Latham and W. Matthews, III, 1970, 39.

A short time later – exactly when is not known – the play was transformed into a tragi-comedy by James Howard, and, according to John Downes, 'when the Tragedy was Reviv'd again, 'twas Play'd Alternately, Tragical one Day, and Tragicomical another; for several Days together'.[1] Downes gives us part of the 1662 cast, among whom Henry Harris played Romeo, Thomas Betterton Mercutio, and Mrs Saunderson Juliet, probably the first woman to play the role. He also recounts an amusing anecdote, which may perhaps have contributed to Pepys's dissatisfaction with this performance:

There being a Fight and Scuffle in this play, between the House of *Capulet*, and the House of *Paris*; Mrs. *Holden* Acting his Wife, enter'd in a *Hurry*, Crying, O my dear *Count*! She inadvertently left out, O, in the pronuntiation of the Word *Count*! giving it a Vehement Accent, put the House into such a Laughter, that *London* Bridge at low-water was silence to it.[2]

No further record of a performance of Shakespeare's play occurs until 1744, but in October 1679 the Duke's Company produced Thomas Otway's *Caius Marius*, an adaptation of *Romeo and Juliet* given a Roman republican setting with Restoration political overtones. Critics have nothing kind to say about Otway's adaptation,[3] but the play held the stage for over sixty years, during which *Romeo and Juliet* went unacted.[4] Otway made one influential change in the last scene: following Bandello, he allowed Lavinia (Juliet) to awake just after Marius Jr (Romeo) takes the poison, a situation to which he contributes some flat, bathetic dialogue between the two before Marius dies. A short passage, the equivalent of Shakespeare's 3.5.6–11, may be quoted as fairly representative of the sort of revision Shakespeare's verse suffered in the process of 'refinement' at the hands, not only of Otway, but of Davenant, Dryden, Tate and other seventeenth- and eighteenth-century 'improvers':

Oh! 'twas the Lark, the Herald of the Morn,
No Nightingale. Look, Love, what envious Streaks
Of Light embroider all the cloudy East.

[1] John Downes, *Roscius Anglicanus*, 1708, ed. Montague Summers, n.d., p. 22.

[2] Downes is obviously confused: for 'House of *Capulet*' read 'House of *Montague*' and for 'House of *Paris*' read 'House of *Capulet*'. Summers (p. 180) suggests that the slip may be connected with 1.3.72 instead of 1.1.

[3] See, for example, Hazelton Spencer, *Shakespeare Improved*, 1927, pp. 292–8; Francis Gentleman, *The Dramatic Censor*, 2 vols., 1770, I, 171. Gentleman (in Bell's *Shakespeare*, 1773, II, 89) also throws light on the character of Mercutio as it was conceived from Otway through the latter part of the eighteenth century: 'As to *Mercutio*, we are rather at a loss to determine upon his requisites; by critics and actors of late, he has been depicted a vacant, swaggering blade; *Otway*...has metamorphos'd him into a snarling cynic. Now, if we may judge by the outlines and dialogue, it seems no hard matter to decide, that there is more pleasantry in the former style of acting; but that *Otway*'s conception of him is more consistent with nature and *Shakespeare*.'

[4] On the public stage. An acting text was prepared at the English College at Douai in 1694 and presumably performed there. Some 971 lines were cut, leaving a play of about 2004 lines, some 50 lines shorter than Garrick's 1750 acting version (see G. B. Evans, *PQ* 41 (1962), 170–1). The playing time for the Garrick–Kemble text was two hours and fifty-eight minutes (William Oxberry's acting edition, 1819). *Rom.* may have been acted, fourteen years earlier than the London revival, in New York at the Revenge Meeting-house in 1730; if so, it was the first of Shakespeare's plays to be performed in America (see *Bulletin of the New York Public Library* 40 (1935), 494).

3 David Garrick and Miss Bellamy as Romeo and Juliet. From an engraving by R. S. Ravenet (1753) after a painting by Benjamin Wilson

> Night's Candles are burnt out, and jocund Day
> Upon the Mountain-tops sits gaily drest,
> Whilst all the Birds bring Musick to his Levy.
> I must be gone and live, or stay and dy. (4.6–12)

In 1744 Shakespeare's play, though with many infusions from Otway, was revived in an adaptation by Theophilus Cibber at the Little Haymarket. After ten performances, in which Cibber himself played Romeo and his daughter, Jane, then not quite fifteen, played Juliet,[1] the Licensing Act of 1737 was invoked under pressure from rival theatrical interests and Cibber's company was forbidden to perform. Since Cibber's revival had attracted some attention, David Garrick undertook a revival of *Romeo and Juliet* at Drury Lane in 1748 and prepared an acting version which, with minor deletions, held the stage for the remainder of the century; it had received more than 450 performances by 1800, and between 1750 and 1800 proved the most popular of Shakespeare's plays.[2] Very slightly modified by J. P. Kemble (about 1803), Garrick's version continued to be acted down to the middle of the nineteenth century.

[1] *Romeo and Juliet, A Tragedy, Revis'd, and Alter'd from Shakespear*, By Mr Theophilus Cibber, 1748, p. 73.
[2] C. B. Hogan, *Shakespeare in the Theatre, 1701–1800*, 2 vols., 1952–7, II, 716–17.

Though Dr Johnson remarked acidly of Garrick that 'he too altered Shakespeare', it must be remembered to his credit that Garrick jettisoned most of the remnants of Otway's *Caius Marius* which Cibber had allowed to stand – though he followed Otway and Cibber in omitting Romeo's earlier love for Rosaline, which, Garrick declares, was considered by many as 'a Blemish in his Character'.[1] Romeo's love for Juliet is first revealed before the Capulet feast in his conversation (1.1) with Benvolio (accompanied in Garrick's version by Mercutio). This part of 1.1, however, considerably cut and joined with the Queen Mab speech from 1.4, is moved to follow Shakespeare's 1.2,[2] itself reduced to 22 of the opening 23 lines, and is followed in turn by 1.3, the conversation between Lady Capulet, the Nurse and Juliet (now aged almost eighteen), and 1.5 (Capulet's feast), which Garrick begins with line 16, in this way cutting the low comedy of the servants, as he did everywhere else except in 1.1. Beginning with the second act, however, Garrick follows Shakespeare's scene sequence exactly, still, of course, cutting a good deal; the chorus-like lamentations over the supposedly dead Juliet in 4.5, for example, are reduced almost to nothing, and the dialogue of Peter and the Musicians at the conclusion of the same scene is completely excised. He always kept in mind, too, his grand 'Design...to clear the Original as much as possible, from the Jingle and Quibble which were always thought a great Objection to performing it'.[3] Mercutio is no longer allowed to die 'a grave man'. In the final tomb scene (5.3), dutifully following Otway and Cibber, Garrick awakes Juliet before Romeo dies and gives the lovers, with occasional echoes from Otway, some 65 lines of sentimental rapture, heavily punctuated with breathless dashes, a 'catastrophe...so much improved, that to it we impute a great part of the success which has attended this tragedy of late years'.[4] He then cuts the Friar's recital from 41 lines to 23, reduces lines 270–94 to 3 by the Prince, and concludes the play with Capulet's and Montague's speeches of reconciliation (296–304) and an essentially new final speech by the Prince:

> A gloomy peace this morning with it brings,
> Let Romeo's man and let the boy attend us:
> We'll hence and farther scan these sad disasters:
> Well may you mourn, my Lords, (now wise too late)
> These tragic issues of your mutual hate:
> From private feuds, what dire misfortunes flow;
> Whate'er the cause, the sure effect is WOE.[5]

[1] From the Advertisement to Garrick's 1750 text (Tonson). Garrick originally (1748) retained Romeo's earlier love for Rosaline. See G. W. Stone, '*Romeo and Juliet*: the source of its modern stage career', in *Shakespeare 400*, ed. J. G. McManaway, 1964, pp. 191–206, for a full account of Garrick's version.

[2] As G. C. D. Odell points out (*Shakespeare – From Betterton to Irving*, 2 vols., 1920, I, 342), this telescoping of two scenes makes nonsense of the time-scheme, since it opens with Benvolio's reference to 9 o'clock in the morning (1.1.152) and ends with his fear (1.4.105) that they will 'come too late' for Capulet's feast that evening! No effort to correct this time botch was made as long as the Garrick–Kemble text was used.   [3] From Garrick's Advertisement.

[4] From Francis Gentleman's Introduction to Bell's *Shakespeare*, 8 vols., 1773, II, 83. Thomas Davies (*Memoirs of the Life of David Garrick*, 2 vols., 1808, I, 154) describes it as 'a scene...written with a spirit not unworthy of Shakespeare himself'.

[5] By 1773 (Bell's *Shakespeare*) the Friar is reduced to five lines and the speeches of Capulet and Montague

AT THE

TheatreRoyal in *Drury-Lane*,

This prefent *Tuefday*, being the 16th of *November*, 1756

Will be prefented a P L A Y, call'd

RO MEO and *JULIET*.

Romeo by Mr. GARRICK,

Efcalus by Mr. B R A N S B Y,

Capulet by Mr. BERRY,

Paris by Mr. J E F F E R S O N,
Benvolio by Mr. U S H E R,
Mountague by Mr. B U R T O N,
Tibalt by Mr. B L A K E S,

Fryar *Lawrence* by Mr. HAVARD,

Mercutio by Mr. WOODWARD,

Lady *Capulet* by Mrs. PRITCHARD,

Nurfe by Mrs. M A C K L I N,

Juliet by Mifs PRITCHARD.

With the A D D I T I O N A L S C E N E Reprefenting

TheFuneral PROCESSION

To the MONUMENT of the *CAPULETS*.

The V O C A L P A R T S by
Mr. *Beard*, Mr. *Champnefs* and *Others*.
In Act I. a *Mafquerade Dance* proper to the Play.
To which will be added a F A R C E, call'd

The A N A T O M I S T.

Monf. *Le Medecin* by Mr. B L A K E S,
Crifpin by Mr. Y A T E S,
Beatrice by Mrs. B E N N E T.

Boxes 5s. Pit 3s. Firft Gallery 2s. Upper Gallery 1s.
Places for the Boxes to be had of Mr. V A R N E Y, at the Stage-
door of the *Theatre*.
† *No Perfons to be admitted behind the Scenes, nor any Money to be returned
after the* Curtain *is drawn up*. *Vivat* R E X.

To-morrow, the MOURNING BRIDE. *Ofmyn* by Mr. MOSSOP,
(*Being the* Firft *Time of his appearing in that Character.*)

4 Drury Lane playbill of *Romeo and Juliet* for 16 November 1756: Garrick as Romeo, Miss Pritchard as Juliet, Henry Woodward as Mercutio. Note the attention given to Garrick's added scene of Juliet's funeral and the Act 1 'Masquerade Dance'

Later, as happy afterthoughts, Garrick turned 1.5 into a lavish 'Masquerade Dance' and added, at the opening of the fifth act, a funeral procession in a church for Juliet's burial, replete with dirge (music by William Boyce). This scene, which persisted as late as 1845, was deplored as 'absurd and truly ridiculous' by the judicious,[1] but was esteemed as a great attraction by both Drury Lane and Covent Garden, which vied with each other in the splendour of its staging.

Garrick did not himself play in the 1748 revival but assumed the role of Romeo only after Spranger Barry moved over to Covent Garden in 1750, when he became Garrick's principal competitor in the role for the next eight years.[2] During a twelve-day run in 1750, 'spectators preferring Barry's seductive scenes in the first three acts at Covent Garden nipped over to see Garrick's more tragic presentation of the star-crossed lovers in the last two acts at Drury Lane',[3] and an anonymous lady is reported to have said: 'Had I been Juliet to Garrick's Romeo, – so ardent and impassioned was he, I should have expected that he would have *come up* to me in the balcony; but had I been Juliet to Barry's Romeo, so tender, so eloquent, and so seductive was he, I should certainly have *gone down* to him!'[4] Although Romeo remained as the principal starring role until the second half of the nineteenth century, the eighteenth produced a number of famous Juliets (Susannah Cibber, Anne Bellamy, Hannah Pritchard). The great Sarah Siddons, however, 'The Tragic Muse', appears to have essayed Juliet only once, with her brother J. P. Kemble as Romeo, in 1789.

The first four decades of the nineteenth century did little towards freeing Shakespeare's text of *Romeo and Juliet* from Garrick's 'improvements'. Moreover the spirit of Mrs Grundy was abroad, in the shape of Thomas Bowdler, whose *Family Shakespeare* (completed 1818; twenty plays in 1807) was dedicated to removing 'words and expressions which are of such a nature as to raise a blush on the cheek of modesty' (Preface, 1807). J. P. Kemble's acting text (1811), though not too much affected by 'bowdlerisation', nevertheless alters 'By Jesu, a very good blade! a very tall man! a very good whore!' (2.4.26–7) to '*Ma foi*, a very good blade! – a very tall man! – a very fine wench!', though he retains 'A bawd, a bawd, a bawd!' in 107 and Rosaline's 'quivering thigh' in 2.1.19. Unlike Garrick, however, he cut the following line ('And the demesnes that there adjacent lie'). All these passages were too much for Bowdler, who even alters 'a white wench's black eye' (2.4.13–14) to 'a white girl's black eye', though he retains 'kitchen wench' in 35, presumably as a proper social distinction. However, by the time of French's ubiquitous acting text (undated, but after 1847),

---

are cut completely – a truncated conclusion that persists in Kemble. In later versions (Mary Anderson's, 1884, and Maude Adams's, 1899) the final scene concludes with Juliet's last line (170); Henry Irving (1882) retains lines 305–6 and 309–10.
[1] Quoted from a contemporary account by Odell, *Betterton to Irving*, I, 420.
[2] Garrick played the role of Mercutio only once (Hogan, *Shakespeare in the Theatre*, II, 586). Gentleman (*Dramatic Censor*, I, 180) relates a piece of stage business in 2.4: 'stage policy, to please the upper regions, generally presents Peter as bearing an enormous fan before his mistress; skipping also and grinning like a baboon; the beating which he gets for not resenting Mercutio's raillery, is a very mean, pantomimical, yet sure motive for laughter'. He also reports that Mercutio's death (3.1) 'commonly proves a very laughable incident' (p. 181).
[3] *The London Stage*, Part 4, 1962, ed. G. W. Stone, p. xxx.
[4] John Doran, *Annals of the English Stage*, 1888, II, 123.

5 Spranger Barry and Miss Nossiter as Romeo and Juliet. From an engraving by William Elliott (*c.* 1753) after a painting by R. Pyle

6 Charlotte Cushman in her 'breeches role' as Romeo, with her sister Susan as Juliet. From an engraving (1858) published by Johnson, Fry and Company, New York

the passages retained by Kemble (except his chastened form of 2.4.26–7) are gone until the twentieth century.[1]

Despite the popularity of his long-lived acting version of *Romeo and Juliet*, Kemble himself was not successful as Romeo ('Youthful love... was never well expressed by Kemble: the thoughtful strength of his features was at variance with juvenile passion').[2] His near contemporary, Edmund Kean, was no more fortunate a few years later.[3]

[1] Compare Gentleman's outraged comment (*Dramatic Censor*, I, 175) on the immorality of the Nurse's speeches (1.3.17–58), speeches severely curtailed in the Victorian period.
[2] James Boaden, *Memoirs of the Life of John Philip Kemble*, 2 vols., 1825, I, 256.
[3] See William Hazlitt's famous review of Kean's debut as Romeo (*Works*, ed. P. P. Howe, 21 vols., 1930–4, V, 208–11).

The year 1845 was important for *Romeo and Juliet*. In that year, for the first time since 1679, the play was performed at the Haymarket Theatre using Shakespeare's original text – heavily cut, of course. Only a few years earlier (1838), the famous actor–manager William Charles Macready, who had made his debut in 1810 as Romeo, had staged a highly successful revival of the play at Covent Garden; Juliet was played by the talented Helen Faucit, but Macready, because of his age and somewhat to his own disgust, subordinated himself in the role of Friar Lawrence.[1] However, despite his efforts to restore Shakespeare's text in other plays, and his interest in historical settings and costumes, Macready was here content to repeat the conventional Garrick–Kemble version essentially unchanged. Credit for the restoration of the 'true text' belongs to Charlotte Cushman,[2] an American actress who, during an English tour in 1845, insisted personally on discarding all the Garrick flummery, reinstating the original order of the opening scenes (including Romeo's early love for Rosaline) and dropping the funeral procession and the dialogue between Romeo and Juliet in the tomb scene. She herself played Romeo to her younger sister Susan Cushman's Juliet.[3] This extension of the conventional breeches role was daring by the standards of the English stage, but apart from a little grumbling about the impropriety of a female Romeo (*The Athenaeum*, 3 January 1846), the reviews were generally ecstatic, sympathetic to the departure from the Garrick tradition and warmly receptive to the performance of the Cushman sisters. Despite its caveat, *The Athenaeum* declared Charlotte Cushman's Romeo to be 'one of the most extraordinary pieces of acting, perhaps, ever exhibited by a woman' and *The Spectator* (3 January 1846) hailed her as 'the best Romeo that has appeared on the stage these thirty years'. Even if we allow for a grain or two of sentimental hyperbole, it is not surprising that the production was a long-term success, receiving some eighty-four performances in the 1845–6 season.[4] Almost immediately (16 September 1846) Samuel Phelps followed suit with another restored revival at Sadler's Wells.

The tyranny of the Garrick–Kemble version was now finally broken, and, although it continued to be used in minor or amateur productions, none of the major revivals (Edwin Booth's, 1868; Henry Irving's, 1882; Mary Anderson's, 1884; Maude Adams's, 1899) ever reverted to it, except that Mary Anderson retained Garrick's funeral procession at the beginning of Act 5 (minus the dismal dirge). But old allegiances die hard, and Fanny Kemble, the daughter of Charles Kemble and niece of J. P. Kemble and Mrs Siddons, still preferred the Garrick–Kemble text as late as 1879: 'I have played both; my father has played both; and I *know* which is best for the stage.'[5]

Before we turn briefly to the stage history of *Romeo and Juliet* in the present century, something must be said about the use of scenery and costuming before 1900. Prior

---

[1] See Alan S. Downer, *The Eminent Tragedian William Charles Macready*, 1966, p. 241.
[2] George Vandenhoff (*Leaves from an Actor's Notebook*, 1860, p. 60) claims that, as manager, Madame Vestris first restored Shakespeare's text at Covent Garden about 1840 (see Odell, *Betterton to Irving*, II, 191), but his claim remains otherwise unsupported.
[3] Cushman's text may be consulted in T. H. Lacy's acting edition (*c.* 1855).
[4] Odell, *Betterton to Irving*, II, 271–2.
[5] Reported by Clifford Harrison, *Stray Records*, 1893, p. 132.

7 Artist's impression of the last scene of Henry Irving's production at the Lyceum in 1882, with Irving as Romeo and Ellen Terry as Juliet. Moonlight from the churchyard above, where the first part of the scene was staged on a separate set, shines down the steps into the vault where Romeo has dragged Paris's body for the final action

to the Restoration and the introduction of the proscenium stage, scenery in the ordinarily accepted sense was not called for and costuming would have been that of more or less fashionable contemporary dress. What we know of scenery and costuming before and around the middle of the nineteenth century is dependent on acting texts and stray illustrations, some of which can be misleading. Until the fourth or fifth decade of the nineteenth century, the scenery used seems to have been, as with most of Shakespeare's plays, largely made up of wing-and-shutter 'stock scenes' (i.e. scenes used from play to play for recurring indoor and outdoor locations). Although *Romeo and Juliet* does not appear to have been performed by the Dublin Smock Alley company in the seventeenth century, the kind and variety of scenes there employed repeatedly during the 1670s and 1680s in other Shakespearean productions would be typical for the Restoration and, in great part, for the eighteenth century: 'Antichamber', 'bed chamber', 'Church', 'Court', 'Grove', 'Towne', 'Wood'.[1] Neither Garrick's version nor Kemble's, both of which drew their scene notations from Rowe

---

[1] *Shakespearean Prompt-Books of the Seventeenth Century*, ed. G. B. Evans, Vol. I, Part i (1960), 23–4. Garrick sets his 1.4 in '*A Wood near* Verona'.

and Pope, suggests that any special attempt was made to mount the play with more than stock scenes; even Garrick's conversion of Capulet's feast (1.5) into a 'Masquerade Dance' and his inserted funeral procession in a 'church' after Juliet's 'death' seem to have depended largely on numbers and lavish (if not historically accurate) costuming.

So far as *Romeo and Juliet* was concerned, the rage for historical accuracy in setting and costume seems to have arrived later than it did for most of Shakespeare's plays. The histories especially, under leading actor–managers such as Charles Kemble, William Charles Macready, Samuel Phelps and particularly Charles Kean, were produced from the 1820s on with meticulous and nigglingly learned attention to antiquarian detail.[1] Garrick and Barry, for example, played Romeo in typical mid-eighteenth-century dress (knee-length coat over a long waistcoat, knee-breeches, tye-wig, and (certainly in Barry's case) a three-cornered cocked hat).[2] Juliet's costume may have been somewhat less obviously contemporary but seems to have consisted of a low-cut tight bodice and a full, ballooning, possibly hooped petticoat, her head crowned in some cases by a high coiffure. By the end of the eighteenth century at the latest, however, costuming had become more or less Renaissance, though it was not until about 1840 that Macready commissioned Colonel C. H. Smith to sketch costumes for the play representing life in Verona about the year 1200 for a performance that never materialised.[3] But the seed had been sown and it flowered, some years later, in the following typical statement by Henry L. Hinton, prefaced to Edwin Booth's 1868 acting text (p. vi):

As…it would be quite absurd at the present day to array the characters of Shakespeare in the costume of his own period, we are left in this matter to the exercise of our own judgment; and good taste, as well as modern realism, demands that we aim at historical accuracy of costume, allowing only such modifications as the exigencies of the play may imperatively demand.

From what follows under 'Scenery' it is clear that some considerable attempt was also made to reproduce aspects of Verona (the Piazza dell' Erbe, for example, or, in Mary Anderson's 1884 production, the Piazza Dante) as they might have appeared in the fourteenth century, and that interiors were presented from early paintings as 'a true copy of the "still life" of the times'.

This stifling mid–century insistence on historical accuracy continued more or less unabated through at least the first decade of the twentieth century, particularly under such famous actor–managers as Henry Irving, who produced his *Romeo and Juliet* in 1882,[4] and Herbert Beerbohm Tree, whose production appeared, lavishly staged,

[1] The kinds of settings being designed during these years may be judged by the reproductions of the scenes (and costumes) designed for Macready's *King John* in 1842 and for Kean's in 1858 (see *William Charles Macready's 'King John'*, ed. C. H. Shattuck, 1962).

[2] See illustration 3 above, Garrick and Miss Bellamy in the tomb scene, and illustration 5, Barry and Miss Nossiter in the balcony scene. A print of Henry Woodward as Mercutio (1753) shows him as an eighteenth-century blade, cocked hat and all.

[3] Downer, *Macready*, p. 235. Smith's costume designs (sixteen figures) are in the University of Illinois Library (see *The Shakespeare Promptbooks*, ed. C. H. Shattuck, 1965, No. 19).

[4] Like some earlier famous actors, Irving, despite having Ellen Terry as his Juliet, received unfavourable notices. Henry James's comment is typical: 'I had never thought of *Romeo and Juliet* as a dull drama;

in 1913. But winds of change were blowing; William Poel, who wished to return to Elizabethan staging and costuming, and Harley Granville-Barker, who put into practice some of Poel's antiquarian ideas (in particular by restoring as far as possible the full texts of Shakespeare's plays), were the leading innovators. Granville-Barker's scene settings were strongly influenced by Gordon Craig's atmospheric and symbolic theories, and with his productions of *The Winter's Tale* (1912) and *A Midsummer Night's Dream* (1914) what has been called the modern approach to staging Shakespeare was under way.[1]

III

There is comparatively little that can usefully be said, given the limitations of space in a short survey, about the many and often idiosyncratic revivals of *Romeo and Juliet* staged over the past sixty years. Although the movement begun by Poel, Granville-Barker and Craig has had some salutary effects, too often the play is still over-produced, over-directed and over-decorated in the Kean–Irving pictorial tradition. As Alan Downer remarked in 1955, 'The modern producer nods respectfully in the direction of William Poel and Adolf Appia, but he sits at the feet of Henry Irving and Beerbohm Tree.'[2] And Irving had described *Romeo and Juliet* as 'a dramatic poem rather than a drama', a play 'that proceeds from picture to picture', thus turning Shakespeare's lines into a mere adjunct of the scene.[3]

It is true, indeed, that Shakespeare's text is now more generally honoured, with less juggling of scene sequence to accommodate the stage sets, and some reduction of the heavy cutting which had been necessary in nineteenth-century stage versions to allow for the excessive time required to 'change scenes'. But the old game still goes on and many examples could be cited. A 1919 revival, in which Ellen Terry played the Nurse, cut the whole of 3.2 with its famous opening ('Gallop apace, you fiery-footed steeds') and ended the play with Juliet's suicide,[4] and Peter Brook's 1947 Stratford production omitted all of 4.1 (Juliet's visit to Friar Lawrence), apparently to avoid a scene change, and again concluded with Juliet's death and a short choral comment borrowed from the Prince's final lines.[5] In most of Shakespeare's plays, judicious cutting is of course necessary, as even the Elizabethans recognised, but these are examples not of cutting but of amputation. To bring the curtain down on Juliet's death, an ending dear to the Victorians, borders on the melodramatic and sacrifices

but Mr Irving has succeeded in making it so…The Play is not acted, it is costumed…obstructed, interrupted; its passionate rapidity is chopped up into little tableaus' (E. J. West, 'Irving in Shakespeare: interpretation or creation?', *SQ* 6 (1955), 419). The production used some nineteen different stage settings.

[1] See C. H. Shattuck, 'Shakespeare's plays in performance from 1660 to the present' (in Riverside, p. 1812).

[2] 'A comparison of two stagings: Stratford-upon-Avon and London', *SQ* 6 (1955), 429.

[3] Quoted in West, 'Irving in Shakespeare', p. 419.

[4] William Archer, 'On "cutting" Shakespeare', *Fortnightly Review* 111 (1919), 965. Archer offers some generally sound advice on cutting, with special reference to *Rom.* (pp. 969–71).

[5] H. S. Bennett and George Rylands, 'Stratford productions', *S.Sur.* 1 (1948), 110. Franco Zeffirelli's 1960 Old Vic stage production omitted 120 lines following Juliet's death, concluding with the last 20 lines (291–310); his film version (1968) reduced the final scene further by deleting the death of Paris.

8 *Romeo and Juliet* at Stratford-upon-Avon, 1954. Directed by Glen Byam Shaw: Laurence Harvey as Romeo, Zena Walker as Juliet. Photograph by Angus McBean

Shakespeare's finely held balance between the personal tragedy of the lovers and the larger social implications of the feud. It shrinks the play and destroys what Milton described as the final effect of great tragedy – 'calm of mind, all passion spent'.

One aspect of the text that in more recent years has received a resounding endorsement is Shakespeare's forthright bawdy, of which *Romeo and Juliet* has an ample share. William Archer, writing in 1919, still endorsed the Victorian view, but he foresaw the day when the 'purists' (as he ironically called them) would have their way.[1] They have, and the bawdy is now played to the hilt, a development the 'nut-cracking Elizabethans' would surely have applauded. But what would they (or Shakespeare) have thought of Mercutio in Terry Hands's 1973 Stratford production, where he was presented as an aggressive homosexual? In order to underline the 'ploy', Mercutio was introduced in 1.4 clasping a life-size female doll, which in 2.1 he obscenely dismembers to illustrate his conjuration 'by Rosaline's bright eyes'.[2] Such character perversion, all too common today in Shakespeare productions generally, is nothing more than a meretricious attempt, at whatever drastic cost to the integrity of the play, to make Shakespeare 'our contemporary'; only if the friendship of Romeo,

[1] Archer, 'On "cutting" Shakespeare', p. 969.
[2] Peter Thomson, 'Shakespeare straight and crooked', *S.Sur.* 27 (1974), 151. Hands may have taken a hint from Zeffirelli's presentation of Mercutio, who, Zeffirelli considers, is Shakespeare's self-portrait (Shattuck, 'Plays in performance', p. 1824).

9 John Stride and Joanna Dunham in Franco Zeffirelli's production at the Old Vic, 1960

Benvolio and Mercutio can be given an exciting nuance of homosexuality does the play become relevant for a modern audience – so runs the directors' justification.

Some advance has been achieved in disencumbering the play of the nineteenth-century emphasis, so destructive of imaginative response, on historically accurate settings; the 'picture spectacle' has to some extent been subordinated and the audience's attention directed instead to the swift interplay of language and action. This advance is, of course, particularly noticeable when *Romeo and Juliet* is acted (as at Stratford, Ontario, in 1960) on a stage modelled in many respects after the Elizabethan pattern, with permanent playing areas, stripped of scenery in the usual sense and allowing for a continuous flow of action either on the main thrust stage or above (or in combination). Much the same effect, however, may be achieved on a proscenium stage, as in Glen Byam Shaw's 1954 Stratford revival, which used a single starkly conceived set with a 'wide balcony almost spanning the stage... flanked on either side by squat, square towers, the whole being of that palest pink or "natural wood" colour that characterizes the views, in miniature, of Florence or Bergamo or Verona'.[1] This kind of single permanent set for *Romeo and Juliet*, essentially only a more localised adaptation of the unlocalised Elizabethan 'scene', first gained wide critical praise in John Gielgud's memorable and influential 1935 production at the New Theatre, a production in which Gielgud and Laurence Olivier alternated as Romeo and Mercutio to Peggy Ashcroft's Juliet and Edith Evans's Nurse.[2]

In 1960 Franco Zeffirelli directed a revival of *Romeo and Juliet* at the Old Vic which, through his later popular film version (1968), has done much to determine the general public's conception of how the play should be staged and acted. In several respects this may be considered unfortunate. Zeffirelli cuts Shakespeare's text very heavily to accommodate a typically cinematic emphasis on noisy mass action scenes and spectacle, very much in Irving's manner, with gorgeously lavish colour shots of Verona, thus dissipating, as in a kind of brilliant void, the concentration and paradoxical intimacy that dialogue written for the stage requires even in the midst of surrounding confusion. And, although the film is full of an almost frenetic energy, exciting to watch and to a limited extent moving (particularly if you are coming to the play for the first time),[3] it is narrowly conceived and reductionist: 'In many ways, this film is a "youth movie" of the 1960's which glorifies the young and caricatures the old, a Renaissance *Graduate*.[4] Zeffirelli's Old Vic Romeo (played by John Stride) broke with the tradition of an ideally brooding or poetic figure[5] and presented himself as just another thoughtless teenager in love, one of the gang, who might have felt comfortably at home in Leonard Bernstein's *West Side Story* (1957), itself a musical adaptation of the Romeo and Juliet story set in New York's Spanish Harlem. Thus,

[1] Richard David, 'Stratford 1954', *SQ* 5 (1954), 388.

[2] See a photograph of the balcony scene in *S.Sur.* 2 (1949), Plate VI.

[3] Zeffirelli's film is much more successful in this respect than George Cukor's Hollywood version (1936), which is a conventionally staid and rather stolid production, apart from John Barrymore's somewhat outrageous Mercutio. Cukor, however, deserves credit for preserving most of the text intact.

[4] Jack J. Jorgens, *Shakespeare on Film*, 1977, p. 86.

[5] John R. Brown, 'S. Franco Zeffirelli's *Romeo and Juliet*', *S.Sur.* 15 (1962), 147–8 (an account of the stage version).

although Romeo and Juliet acted and spoke with an immediacy and unrhetorical naturalness that communicated itself easily to a modern (and particularly to a young) audience, the larger aspects of their love, its developing maturity and final dignity, were diminished by a simplistic emphasis on adolescence.' Shakespeare aimed at more than a final sweet sadness.

Jorgens, *Shakespeare on Film*, pp. 86–91. See also Shattuck, 'Plays in performance', p. 1824, and a remark by Judi Dench, who, as well as Joanna Dunham, played Juliet in Zeffirelli's Old Vic production, in interview with G. Lloyd Evans (*S.Sur.* 27 (1974), 138) that she felt on looking back that Zeffirelli 'forgot the poetry'.

Recent Developments in Criticism and Production, by Thomas Moisan

Romeo and Juliet and Recent Criticism:

Recent years have seen shifts in the kinds of questions *Romeo and Juliet* provokes. Where once critics debated whether the play can *really* be called a tragedy, they now ask from where it derives its unquestionably tragic power and enduring appeal.[1] And where once they debated whether the play was an 'experimental' tragedy or tragedy of character or fate, and whether Romeo and Juliet were endowed with Aristotelian tragic flaws or were 'Fortune's fool[s]' (3.1.127),[2] they have increasingly read the play in more communal terms and seen *Romeo and Juliet* as no less a tragedy for being as much about the 'two households, both alike in dignity, / in fair Verona' (1.1.1–2), and about the violence those households beget, as about the eponymous offspring of those households.[3] Readings still strive to identify tragedy with personal responsibility and locate the moment in the play when through a character's wilfully destructive and self-destructive act the play turns irreversibly tragic;[4] others analyse the complex interaction of the individual with societal and cultural forces, and define tragic character by what Susan Snyder has called 'the dual meaning of *subject*, the 'autonomous' agent who is formed by and in a social formation to which he is subjected'.[5] Indeed, some studies advertise their anthropological orientations in their very titles, Coppélia Kahn's 'Coming of Age in Verona', for instance, or Marjorie Garber's *Coming of Age in Shakespeare*.[6]

Gender and Romeo and Juliet

At the same time, a wealth of recent feminist criticism including Kahn's has reminded us in various ways that *Romeo and Juliet* is not simply about coming of age in Verona, but coming of age as male and female in Verona. In some readings, of course, this interest in theoretical approaches to gender has coincided with the more traditional

---

[1] See, for example, Joan Ozark Holmer, '"Myself Condemned and Myself Excused": Tragic Effects in *Romeo and Juliet*', *Studies in Philology* (1991), p. 345.

[2] The label 'experimental' comes from H. B. Charlton, '*Romeo and Juliet* as an Experimental Tragedy', *Proceedings of the British Academy*, 25 (1939), 143–85.

   On the relationship of the tragedy of the play to such adventitious devices as the persistent misdirection of messages, see David Lucking's comment in '"That Which We Call a Name": The Balcony Scene in *Romeo and Juliet*', *English* 44 (1995), p. 6. Note the variation introduced in Baz Luhrmann's film, *William Shakespeare's Romeo + Juliet*, in which Friar John's undelivered message for Romeo from Friar Lawrence turns into an undeliverable express mail document.

[3] For a discussion of the developments in tragic theory that have had an impact upon the study of *Romeo and Juliet*, see John Drakakis, ed., *Shakespearean Tragedy*, 1992, pp. 2–3, 20–37.

[4] Holmer, '"Myself Condemned and Myself Excused"', pp. 358–9.

[5] 'Ideology and Feud in *Romeo and Juliet*', *S.Sur.* 49 (1996), p. 90; see also Lloyd Davis's contention in '"Death-marked love": Desire and Presence in *Romeo and Juliet*', *S.Sur.* 49 (1996), p. 65, that the depiction of desire in *Romeo and Juliet* is integral to the representation of subjectivity emergent in the early modern period.

[6] 'Coming of Age in Verona', *The Woman's Part: Feminist Criticism of Shakespeare*, ed. Carolyn Ruth Swift Lenz, Gayle Greene and Carol Thomas Neely, 1980, pp. 171–93; *Coming of Age in Shakespeare*, 1981, esp. 165–73.

49

tack of reading Romeo and Juliet as figures in whom we recognise traits we associate with modern adolescents.¹ Thus, Edward Snow declares that Romeo's language is abstract, Juliet's concrete; she is always here while he seeks to be elsewhere; she is an 'I', a centred self, he a self-disintegrating, self-distancing 'Other', a figure, as Kent Cartwright puts it, of 'extraordinary betwixt-and-betweenness'.² Radically differentiated in the life of their love, they remain no less so in their apprehensions of their deaths, their separations in death a sign of the tragic separateness 'that in spite of their fit assigns them separate meanings and separate destinations'.³

For Snow, however, profound gender differenences are symptoms of Romeo and Juliet's tragedy, not its cause; its cause lies in a much more conventionally romantic and externalised opposition, one 'between the imaginative vision its protagonists bear witness to in love and the truth of a world whose order must be enforced at passion's expense'.⁴ For other critics gender is less sign than instrument, less an intrinsic badge than a set of social prescriptions whose imposition *is* truth and order in Verona. According to such critics what Romeo and Juliet are for each other is inherently inimical to what they must be, as male and female, to be, as Mercutio tells Romeo, 'sociable' in Verona (2.4.73). What defines society's expectations of them as male and female and brings those expectations into fatal conflict with their love is, of course, the feud: to participate in the feud is to choose death; to be masculine is to participate in the feud.⁵ At the same time, the violence through which men in the play define themselves as men has inevitable consequences for their attitudes towards and relationships with women. That Shakespeare wastes no time in making the connection is evident in the grumbling-to-rumbling dialogue with which the play begins, where the serving men Samson and Gregory are led by a chain of puns and free association from assertions of self-esteem to fantasies about women to fantasies about violence towards women to violence itself (1.1.1–28). And while the serving men joke about the 'civil' violence they will do to maidens' 'heads', it is the fear of violence women can do to masculinity that operates tragically upon Romeo's mind when he blames Juliet for the disastrously pacific role he played in Tybalt and Mercutio's duel – and then proceeds to violence of his own: 'O sweet Juliet, / Thy beauty hath made me effeminate, / And in my temper softened valour's steel' (3.1.104–6).⁶

¹ See Irene Dash, *Wooing, Wedding, and Power: Women in Shakespeare's Plays*, 1981, pp. 88, 100, and Angela Pitt, *Shakespeare's Women*, 1981, pp. 45–7. On the fidelity of its representation of adolescence, see Jill Levenson, *The Oxford Shakespeare Romeo and Juliet*, ed. Levenson, 2000, p. 17.

² 'Language and Sexual Difference in *Romeo and Juliet*', 1985; rpt *Romeo and Juliet: Critical Essays*, ed. John F. Andrews, 1993, pp. 373–82; Cartwright, *Shakespearean Tragedy and Its Double: The Rhythms of Audience Response*, 1991, p. 82.

³ Ibid., p. 396.

⁴ Snow, 'Language and Sexual Difference', p. 371.

⁵ For Madelon Gohlke [Sprengnether], '"I wooed thee with my sword": Shakespeare's Tragic Paradigms', *The Woman's Part*, p. 152, '[t]o participate in the masculine ethic of this play is to participate in the feud'; see also Kahn, 'Coming of Age in Verona', p. 171.

⁶ See Snow, 'Language and Sexual Difference,' p. 393. See also Janet Adelman, 'Male Bonding in Shakespeare's Comedies', *Shakespeare's Rough Magic: Renaissance Essays in Honor of C.L. Barber*, ed. Peter Erickson and Kahn, 1985, p. 81.

The notion that the play celebrates and privileges heterosexual love has been challenged in studies that call attention to the representation in the play of homosocial bonds and to the complication in the play of male sexual identity.[1] And no figure has come to embody that challenge more than Mercutio, whose 'profoundly homoerotic' representation, Dympna C. Callaghan contends, would only have underscored for the audience the erotic ambiguities routinely emitted by the all-male casting and boy actresses of a contemporary Elizabethan production of the play.[2] For Joseph A. Porter, in the most exhaustive study of the character to date, Mercutio is not a secondary figure but a dominant presence, whose 'immanence' permeates the audience's awareness both before his first entrance and well after his final exit;[3] taking issue with those who see male friendship as merely a bump in the road to 'normal' sexual development, or would make Mercutio the incarnation of all that is misogynist or violently self-destructive in Verona, Porter argues that Shakespeare's Mercutio, true to his classical forebear, is a 'mercurial' and priapic figure who imbues the play with a phallic consciousness and offers Romeo the alternative of masculine friendship and a 'warning away from love to the fellowship of men'.[4] Read this way Mercutio becomes integral to the tragedy of *Romeo and Juliet* and not, as he has often been taken to be, the brilliant comedian upon whose removal the survival of the play *as* tragedy depends.

'... wherefore art thou Romeo?'

Yet, as Juliet's plaintive and often misunderstood question implies, the tragedy of Romeo and Juliet may not just be about growing up male and female in Verona, but about growing up as a Montague and a Capulet, son and daughter in warring households. And, indeed, critics who make this point have found a purple passage in the cherished balcony dialogue of 2.2, where the urgency in Juliet's questioning why Romeo is Romeo and a Montague is matched only by Romeo's ardour in vowing to be neither. As Catherine Belsey has remarked, though Juliet attempts to separate Romeo himself from the names of Romeo and Montague, even as 'a rose / By other name would smell as sweet' (2.2.43–4), the severance cannot be complete.[5] Or as Jacques Derrida puts it, in probing the tragic paradox in Juliet's invocation of Romeo's name, 'Romeo would not be what he is, a stranger to this name, without this name.'[6]

[1] See Jonathan Goldberg, 'Romeo and Juliet's *Open Rs*', *Queering the Renaissance*, ed. Goldberg, 1994, pp. 218–35; and Robert Appelbaum, '"Standing to the wall": The Pressures of Masculinity in *Romeo and Juliet*', *SQ* 48 (1997), pp. 251–72.

[2] 'The Ideology of Romantic Love: The Case of *Romeo and Juliet*', Callaghan, Lorraine Helms and Jyotsna Singh, *The Wayward Sisters: Shakespeare and Feminist Politics*, 1994, p. 61.

[3] *Shakespeare's Mercutio: His History and Drama*, 1988, pp. 116–18.

[4] Ibid., pp. 114, 150–1; in *Shakespearean Films / Shakespearean Directors*, 1990, p. 159, Peter Donaldson, limiting his remarks to the representation of Mercutio in Franco Zeffirelli's film, takes issue with Porter and sees Mercutio as 'more confused and troubled' than he is for Porter and also 'deeply implicated in the misogyny and disavowals that structure the social world of the play'.

[5] 'The Name of the Rose in *Romeo and Juliet*', *Critical Essays on Shakespeare's Romeo and Juliet*, ed. Porter, 1997, pp. 70, 79.

[6] 'Aphorism Countertime' (1986); rpt in *Acts of Literature*, ed. Derek Attridge, 1992, p. 427.

Hence, fathers, both biological fathers, Capulet and Montague, and the political and spiritual fathers, Escalus and Friar Lawrence respectively, loom as significant and problematic.[1] And of these the most complex is, of course, Capulet, a figure whose mixture of comedic traits and tragic destructiveness makes him a microcosm of his play; bearing a resemblance to the comically conventional obstructionist fathers we encounter in 'lighter' works such as *A Midsummer Night's Dream* or the various renderings of the story of Pyramus and Thisbe, he is a figure whose emotional volatility and irascible assertion of authority are instrumental in destroying the daughter he initially calls 'the hopeful lady of my earth' (1.2.15), and in vitiating the very nuptial decorums his position as patriarch would ordain him to uphold.[2]

Death

References to death commence with the Prologue (5–6)[3] and recur throughout.[4] An anxiety over death is conspicuous in the elaborate and devious rhetorical strategies characters employ to cope with and evade it,[5] and so inheres in the imagery and incident of the play as to turn *Romeo and Juliet*, for one critic, into an evocation of medieval allegory, a meditation on life as journey culminating in the inexorable *memento mori* of the tomb, with death incarnated in the ultimate *coup de théâtre* of having the bodies of the lovers left visible on stage, a lingering expression of that 'horrible conceit' Juliet so dreads of 'death and night' (4.3.37).[6]

Yet it is not only the horrible conceit of death and night that has drawn critical scrutiny, but the more horrible conceit linking death and desire. In part this linkage is conventional: an early modern play so rich in wordplay and so concerned with sexual consummation could hardly resist the famliiar Elizabethan pun coupling death and coition. For Julia Kristeva, in whose Freudian reading there's much to do with love in *Romeo and Juliet*, but more, perhaps, with hate, death arrives in time to save 'the pure couple' from the corruption their passion will inexorably endure, a strong hint of which Kristeva hears in the violence with which Juliet's remarkable epithalamic apostrophe to Night at the outset of 3.2 culminates, with Juliet's call upon Night to '[t]ake' Romeo, 'when I shall die . . . and cut him out in little stars' (3.2.21–2).[7]

---

[1] Indeed, for James L. Calderwood, *Shakespeare and the Denial of Death*, 1987, p. 109, the fact that Friar Lawrence, *exemplum* of 'spiritual sterility', emerges at all as a father figure to Romeo and Juliet is in itself symptomatic of a tragic dysfunction in the natural patriarchal order. Niky Rathbone, *S.Sur.* 53 (2000), p. 282, cites a recent production that makes the theme of 'inadequate parenting' a central conceit.

[2] On the ritual disorder and 'broken' nuptial rites Capulet's behaviour is instrumental in bringing about, see Naomi Conn Liebler, *Shakespeare's Festive Tragedy*, 1995, p. 150.

[3] See Davis, '"Death-marked love"', p. 59.

[4] See G. Blakemore Evans's Introduction to this edition, pp. 16–20.

[5] Thomas Moisan, 'Rhetoric and the Rehearsal of Death: The "Lamentations" Scene in *Romeo and Juliet*', *SQ* 34 (1983), 389–404.

[6] William Carroll, '"We were born to die": *Romeo and Juliet*', *Comparative Drama* 15 (1981), pp. 57, 69; for a view less uncompromisingly severe, see Brian Gibbons, 'Introduction', *The Arden Shakespeare Romeo and Juliet*, ed. Gibbons, 1980, p. 76.

[7] *Tales of Love*, trans. Leon S. Roudiez, 1987, pp. 212, 214, 217; see also Jonathan Dollimore, *Death, Desire, and Loss in Western Culture*, 1998, pp. 111–13.

Festival and Black Funeral

While the ubiquity of death in *Romeo and Juliet* obviously deepens our sense of the play as tragedy, it also throws into sharper relief the elements of characterisation and structure that make the play resemble comedy. While some critics have sought to show how the tragedy of *Romeo and Juliet* could embody comic elements and structures and still be tragedy,[1] others have given new life to the old doubts about *Romeo and Juliet*'s genre, suggesting that it may be a generic hybrid, a kind of tragic-comedy.[2] Because of its mixture of elements comic and tragic, and the omnipresence in it of death, a number of critics of *Romeo and Juliet* have invoked Mikhail Bakhtin and his notion of the carnivalesque. In doing so, of course, they have merely taken the bait provided by Bakhtin himself who professed to see 'many' aspects of the carnivalesque in Shakespeare's plays, specifically, 'images of the material bodily lower stratum, of ambivalent obscenities, and of popular banquet scenes'.[3] Such images critics have found abundantly strewn throughout *Romeo and Juliet*, memorably in the Nurse's highly iterative, 'non-linear' monologue of 1.3, which interweaves corporeal references to nurturing and weaning, death and copulation, embodying the Bakhtinian carnivalesque in both its themes and form.[4] And though the 'death-marked' ending of *Romeo and Juliet* would seem at odds with the regenerative promise intrinsic to the Bakhtinian carnivalesque,[5] for Cartwright it is this very dissonance that makes *Romeo and Juliet* theatrically satisfying drama, conditioning and guiding the audience's response.[6]

'In fair Verona where we set our scene': the Text In its Time

Yet in following the audience's interaction with *Romeo and Juliet*, we feel increasingly primed to ask, 'which audience?' Historicism has alerted us to the distinction between what an early modern play may mean for 'us' and what it meant for 'them', the original audience. And though our Prologue and Chorus may pointedly inform us that it is in fair Verona that Shakespeare has set his scene, and though the sources would suggest a late medieval setting, historicist readings of *Romeo and Juliet* have more often looked at the concerns of Elizabethan England, sometimes audible in single words or phrases: an anxiety over the emerging and economically destabilising coal

---

[1] Gibbons, 'Introduction', pp. 72–80; Snyder, *The Comic Matrix of Shakespeare's Tragedies*, 1979; Martha Tuck Rozett, 'The Comic Structures of Tragic Endings: The Suicide Scenes in *Romeo and Juliet* and *Antony and Cleopatra*', *SQ* 36 (1985), pp. 153–8.

[2] Levenson, *The Oxford Shakespeare Romeo and Juliet*, pp. 50–2; Douglas Bruster, 'Teaching the Tragicomedy of *Romeo and Juliet*', *Approaches to Teaching Romeo and Juliet*, ed. Maurice Hunt, 2000, pp. 59–68.

[3] *Rabelais and his World*, trans. Hélène Iswolsky, 1984, p. 275.

[4] For Snow, 'Language and Sexual Difference', p. 388, the Nurse's monologue in 1.3 anticipates the 'eventfulness' of Juliet's life as a woman and 'weaves [it] into a matrix of primary female experience (birth, lactation, weaning, marriage, maidenheads and their loss)'.

[5] See Ronald Knowles, 'Carnival and Death in *Romeo and Juliet*', *Shakespeare and Carnival After Bakhtin*, ed. Knowles, 1998, p. 58.

[6] *Shakespearean Tragedy*, p. 44.

industry can be heard in the 'coals' that Sampson opens Act One by declaring he won't 'carry' (1.1.1);[1] contemporary fears about thievery resonate, we're told, in the willingness of the desperate Juliet to 'walk in thievish ways' rather than marry Paris (3).[2] And to a broad array of contemporary materials have critics turned to explain problematic moments and characters more familiarly viewed in the context of literary and theatrical conventions, such as the catastrophic duels of 3.1,[3] the legally muddied state of affairs at the end of the play, where some are to 'be pardoned and some punished',[4] or the problematic behaviours of characters such as Friar Lawrence, the Apothecary and the Nurse.[5] Indeed, in Gail Kern Paster's analysis of the Nurse's rich monologue in 1.3 the literary carnivalesque merges with the material conditions of the day, as recollections of death, copulation and regeneration give voice simultaneously to contemporary medical ideas and cultural anxieties concerning sex, childbirth, and infant-feeding and weaning, with the Nurse's jarring juxtaposition with Lady Capulet a comically dramatic clash of contemporary notions of motherhood and femininity.[6]

Yet to hear the concerns of the age echoed in the lines and action of *Romeo and Juliet* is not automatically to understand the attitude of the play towards those concerns and how the echoing of those concerns affects our sense of the meaning of the play. The effect of the so-called 'new historicism', so prominent in the study of Shakespeare in recent years, has been to intensify our sense of the shadowy and complex relationship between a work of art and the socio-political orb it represents. Michel Foucault's work, for example, on the relationship of cultural production to prevailing power structures, has been particularly influential in recent discussions of *Romeo and Juliet* and in the debate over how the play would have been perceived in its own times. How dangerous, how transgressive, was the 'young affection' that is its central fable? Does desire, in the form of Romeo and Juliet's stolen relationship, subvert the patriarchy that impedes it, or does it somehow promote the interests of that obstructionist patriarchy? The testimony of early modern history is not transparent; can we be so sure that Shakespeare's audience would have read, for example, the struggle of wills between Capulet and Juliet as 'we' do and sided with Juliet and not, as David Lindley has suggested, seen the tragic ending as 'vindication of the attitude which sees young, romantic love as excessive and dangerous in its self-preoccupation'?[7] Can we be sure that Shakespeare's audience would not, in other words, have read the play as

---

[1] Nathaniel Wallace, 'Cultural Tropology in *Romeo and Juliet*', *Studies in Philology* 88 (1991), p. 333.

[2] Heather Dubrow, *Shakespeare and Domestic Loss: Forms of Deprivation, Mourning, and Recuperation*, 1999, pp. 21–2.

[3] Holmer, '"Draw, if you be men": Saviolo's Significance for *Romeo and Juliet*', *SQ* 45 (1994): 163–89 ; Levenson, '"*Alla stoccado* carries it away": Codes of Violence in *Romeo and Juliet*', *Shakespeare's Romeo and Juliet*, ed. Halio, 83–96.

[4] Natalie Zemon Davis, *Fiction in the Archives: Pardon Tales and Their Tellers in Sixteenth-Century France*, 1987, pp. 74–6.

[5] Dorothea Kehler, 'Teaching *Romeo and Juliet* Historically', *Approaches to Teaching Shakespeare's Romeo and Juliet*, 78–84.

[6] *The Body Embarrassed: Drama and the Disciplines of Shame in Early Modern England*, 1993, pp. 225, 231.

[7] *The Trials of Frances Howard*, 1993, p. 40.

Brooke offered it, as a story of a 'couple of unfortunate lovers, thralling themselves to unfortunate desire'?[1]

The Text in Our Times

Concerned as we are with what *Romeo and Juliet means*, a number of critics in recent years have been reminding us that we cannnot take for granted what it *says*. Spurred by a questioning of the assumptions and practices that have governed the editing of Shakespearean texts in general, various critics have challenged the judgements that have given us the text of *Romeo and Juliet* recognisable in most modern editions of the play.[2] Challenged, for example, has been the well-established position that the second published version of the play (1599), the Second Quarto, is the 'good' quarto, more authoritative and likely to give us the words Shakespeare meant us to hear and read, than the earlier and shorter version, the First Quarto (1597). For the most part the scepticism in this challenge is posed as a corrective, an attempt to get the words of *Romeo and Juliet* right by questioning why we have favoured certain textual versions of the play and marginalised others.[3] Yet this questioning has fed a more radical scepticism, one that not only impugns the authority of some of the most familiar and cherished lines in the play – for instance, 'what's in a name?' – but demands we reconsider the assumption that there *is* a one true text capable of being made right and asks us to look at the early printed versions of the play as scripts keyed to particular performances with no special claim to authority or finality.[4]

Romeo and Juliet *in Recent Stage and Film Productions*

Indeed, it is for this openness, and for its capacity to re- and outlive and stage infinite variations upon its protagonists' story, that Derrida has described *Romeo and Juliet* as an 'anthology' or 'palimpsest' or 'open theater of narratives',[5] terms that come very much to mind when we consider the experience of the play in recent years on the stage. Derrida's piece on *Romeo and Juliet*, '*L'aphorisme à contretemps*', was occasioned

---

[1] Arthur Brooke, 'To the Reader', *The Tragicall Historye of Romeus and Juliet*, Evans, Appendix, p. 215. For a pointed illustration of the strong differences of opinion these questions have provoked about the ideological agenda and uses of Shakespeare's play, see Callaghan, 'The Ideology of Romantic Love', pp. 59–60, 72–86, for whom 'desire' in the play is but a cultural construction and ideological tool serving the interests of 'the state', and Kiernan Ryan, *Shakespeare*, 2nd edn, 1995, pp. 75–86, for whom *Romeo and Juliet* is no tool of power but a humanist challenge to it, with Callaghan's position, p. 86, that of 'the crude radical critic'.

[2] For accounts of the arguments influential in producing the most familiar texts of the play, see Evans, this edn, pp. 208–14, and Gibbons, 'Introduction', pp. 1–24.

[3] For example, Jay Halio, 'Handy-Dandy: Q1/Q2 *Romeo and Juliet*', *Shakespeare's Romeo and Juliet*, ed. Halio, pp. 125–34; David Farley-Hills, 'The "Bad" Quarto of *Romeo and Juliet*', *S.Sur.* 49 (1996), 27–44; 'Random Cloud' [aka Randall McLeod], 'The Marriage of Good and Bad Quartos,' *SQ* 33 (1982), 421–31; David Scott Kastan, *Shakespeare and the Book*, 2001, pp. 40–9.

[4] '"What? in a names that which we call a Rose", The Desired Texts of *Romeo and Juliet*', *Crisis in Editing: Texts of the English Renaissance*, ed. Randall McLeod, 1994, pp. 177–85.

[5] P. 433.

by a production of the play in Paris in 1985 by Daniel Mesguich, and essay and play could not have been better matched. With much to do with Shakespeare, but as much, perhaps, with Pirandello, Mesguich's production enveloped Romeo and Juliet's story in a densely packed literary and dramatic context of 'misadventured' love. Scripted and designed as a palimpsest, its central space, according to Marvin Carlson, presented 'a huge labyrinth, an enormous library with corridors filled with hundreds of books', one of which, falling, by chance or destiny, to the stage floor, was picked up by the knockabout servants Abraham and Gregory who read out of it the verbal byplay that produces the opening events of the play. The masked ball was attended by figures dressed as notably unhappy lovers – Juliet, for example, as Nina from *The Seagull* – who acted out scenes conspicuous for their display of sexual anxieties, the scene where Gloucester woos Anne from *Richard III*, for instance, the scene in Gertrude's 'closet' from *Hamlet*. And after their deaths, Romeo and Juliet were led off into the stacks by ghostly literary figures to assume their life in death in what was literally an 'open theater of narratives'.[1]

And even productions of *Romeo and Juliet* that advertise their intertextuality a little less exuberantly are almost bound, according to Stanley Wells, to bear resonances of previous productions and be measured by the expectations both director and audience bring to the new production from their experience,[2] and Wells's point is underscored in stagings of recent years. Hence, even in a production as ferociously modern as Michael Bogdanov's Royal Shakespeare Company production of 1986 – replete with a red sportscar on stage – the past was not permitted to be forgotten, either by involving it in a head-on collision with the present, as when Romeo took a lethal injection only to have Juliet complain moments later that he had 'left no friendly drop / To help me after' (5.3.163–4),[3] or by gently letting it insinuate itself upon the ears, as when, according to Wells, the dying sounds of motorcycle engines on which the revellers left the Capulets' ball in Bogdanov's production recalled the music from the corresponding moment in Berlioz's *Romeo and Juliet*.[4] And even when a director professes to banish the past the effect may only be praetoritive; in a production of 1995 directed by Neil Bartlett that sought to create a *Romeo and Juliet* fresh and 'stripped', in the words of Peter Holland's review, 'to its essentials', the audience was given opening music quoting well-known musical adaptations of Shakespeare by Tchaikovsky, Prokofiev and Bernstein, 'as if to summon them up', Holland remarks, 'and then firmly discard them' – while also, one could as easily say, reminding the audience of what they weren't supposed to hear![5]

No director has had a greater influence upon the theatrical representation of *Romeo and Juliet* in recent years than Franco Zeffirelli, particularly through his film (1968) and its naturalistic insistence upon, not simply the youth, but adolescent youth of the

---

[1] 'Daniel Mesguich and intertextual Shakespeare', *Foreign Shakespeare: Contemporary Performance*, ed. Dennis Kennedy, 1993, pp. 218–19.

[2] 'The Challenges of *Romeo and Juliet*', *S.Sur.* 49 (1996), pp. 3–4.

[3] *Looking at Shakespeare: A Visual History of Twentieth-Century Performance*, 1993, p. 297.

[4] P. 4.

[5] 'Shakespeare Performances in England: A Couple of *Romeo and Juliets*', *S.Sur.* 49 (1996), p. 240.

protagonists, an influence all the more evident, however, when acknowledged in parody. One recent American staging of 2.5, for example, had Juliet, played as a modern American secondary school student and attired in familiar schoolgirl uniform of white blouse and plaid skirt, trying to divert herself while waiting for the Nurse to bring word of her mission to Romeo by watching a video with music that evoked the major theme of Nino Rota's lush score to Zeffirelli's film.[1] Emulating Zeffirelli in the age of its Romeo and Juliet, it departed from Zeffirelli and earlier youthfully oriented productions in modernising the play and, in doing so, it merely followed a trend in late twentieth-century production.[2] The trend toward physically credible and socially recognisable representations of the lovers suggests an attempt to have it both ways, tapping into the complex feelings adults and pre-adults are supposed to have for the spectacle of vibrantly loving and poignantly dying youth, while deepening the audience's involvement in the lovers' tragedy by setting young love against the backdrop of recognisable and recent civil wars such as the war in Bosnia, with its conflict between Christian and Muslim.[3]

Yet in underscoring the youth of the protagonists, recent productions have also focused on the representation in the play of desire, and particularly on the representation of desire as transgressive. To complicate the love of Romeo and Juliet, productions have paid more attention to the homosocial behaviours on display in Verona and in particular, following the strong hints provided in Zeffirelli's film,[4] they have explored the potential in Mercutio as a homosexual lover to Romeo and rival to Juliet. Thus, in Michael Boyd's production for the RSC in 2000 Mercutio was a suitor for Romeo's affection both before and *after* his death, literally haunting in death the relationship from which he had been excluded in life, according to Michael Dobson, a 'malevolent shade' who is on hand when Juliet ingests the Friar's potion, puts the Apothecary's poison in Romeo's hands, and even delivers Friar John's distressing news to Friar Lawrence.[5] Another production in this spirit, though not a production of the play *per se*, was Joe Calarco's *Shakespeare's R&J*, a four-character play that opened in New York in 1998,[6] in which four students from a Catholic boys' secondary

[1] *Romeo and Juliet*, dir. Joe Banno, Folger Elizabethan Theatre, Nov. 14, 1997–Dec. 14, 1997. An accent on youth was evident in the casting, particularly of Juliet, in the 1978 version of the play directed by Alvin Rakoff for the BBC; according to Susan Willis, *The BBC Shakespeare Plays: Making the Televised Canon*, 1991, pp. 16, 197, this had mixed results. Noting a 1996 production at Magdalene College, Oxford, Niky Rathbone, *S.Sur.* 51 (1996), p. 266, comments, with presumably unintended ambiguity, that '[i]n an otherwise professional production, the actress playing Juliet was a thirteen-year-old'.

[2] A trend sufficiently widespread as to encompass a Japanese *Romeo and Juliet* in the 1970s that was staged, Andrea Nouryer tells us, in 'Shakespeare and the Japanese Stage', *Foreign Shakespeare*, p. 261, 'as a contemporary Japanese love story between two ordinary young people' to the accompaniment of music by Elton John.

[3] Aubrey Mellor, director of a production of *Romeo and Juliet* in Brisbane, 1993, discusses present-day Bosnia as a parallel to feuding Verona, cited in Davis, '"Death-Marked Love"', p. 60.

[4] See Jack Jorgens, *Shakespeare on Film*, 1977; Porter, *Shakespeare's Mercutio*, pp. 190–3; and Donaldson, *Shakespearean Films*, pp. 156–60; also, Evans, this edn, p. 45, on Terry Hands's 1973 staging.

[5] 'Shakespeare Performances in England, 2000', *S.Sur.* 54 (2001), pp. 256–7.

[6] The play was also directed by Joel Sass and staged by the Mary Worth Theater in Minneapolis at the meeting of the Shakespeare Association of America in March, 2002; observations about the play draw upon both the New York and Minneapolis productions.

10   Two students play the parts of Romeo and Juliet in Joe Calarco's all male *Shakespeare's R&J*, in The Mary Worth Theatre Company's production directed by Joel Sass, Minneapolis, 2002. Photo by Christine Rosholt, courtesy of Mary Worth Theatre

school find diversion from their rote recitals of prayers and Latin conjugations – including, predictably, *amo, amas, amat* – by secretly performing *Romeo and Juliet*, with two of the four coming to assume the parts of the two lovers. Proceeding from the now familiar trope linking the ethos of the single-sex religious school to sexual repression, *Shakespeare's R&J* draws upon the status *Romeo and Juliet* enjoys as the Shakespearean school play of choice only to make subversive use of the play to explore uncomfortable emotions. 'I wanted the play to be dangerous', Calarco has claimed, 'to be about the forbidden'.[1] 'Forbidden', of course, in offering the possibility that the emotions on display, particularly between the actors playing Romeo and Juliet, include homoerotic feelings hitherto repressed, though on this point the play maintains an unresolved tension. The audience is not permitted to forget that all of the actors before it are male; unlike their counterparts playing female parts on the Elizabethan stage, here all of the actors remain in their schoolboy uniforms, and thus we cannot even pretend that we are being asked by the use of gender-appropriate costumes to fantasise gender diversity; but on the other hand, the actors move seamlessly into their theatrical identities and stay there, so that we are not given an opportunity to learn whether what they have expressed on stage is what they really are and feel, or are merely the actions a man may play. 'Forbidden', also, in that the experience the students enact is stolen from their daily lives in school, even as Romeo and Juliet's love is necessarily stolen from the world of Verona. To dramatise these tensions, the play draws upon a relentless physicality from the players – even the kissing, Calarco insisted, was to be violent[2] – and upon the sense of claustrophobia and isolation produced by the dark, barren and confined set, and thus keeps the focus intensively on the two lovers, its violent delights yielding violent ends.

In appropriating *Romeo and Juliet*, Calarco cut the text extensively – and on this point could be said simply to have followed recent convention.[3] Bogdanov's production, for instance, performed radical surgery in reducing the last one hundred and forty lines of the play to eight, while producing a thematically devastating but virtually mute closing photo-op, and we find extensive cutting for the sake of economy and linguistic de-obfuscation in other productions as well.[4] The frequency with which the play continues to be staged and its appropriation in a wide array of forms and media that vary wildly in their view of the integrity of its text – be they plays or big-budget movies, successful operas and ballets or a long-running Broadway show, or even, as

---

[1] Quoted by Rachel Shteir, 'Making Juliet One of the Guys in a Macho Verona', *New York Times* (14 June 1998), p. 6.

[2] P. 25.

[3] For example, Calarco symbolically represents or excises the 'lamentations' scene, Romeo's dialogue with the Apothecary, Paris's presence in the tomb, Friar Lawrence's final effort at an expository account of events, and Escalus's 'glooming peace' speech.

[4] On the ending of Bogdanov's production, see Barbara Hodgdon, 'Absent Bodies, Present Voices: Performance Work and the Close of Romeo and Juliet's Golden Story', 1989; rpt *Romeo and Juliet: Critical Essays*, ed. Andrews, pp. 252–4; in 'A Couple of *Romeo and Juliets*', Holland, pp. 240–2, reports that the programme to a production directed by Adrian Noble for the RSC in 1995 mentions that about 564 lines have been cut, while in Bartlett's production the same year, the director attempted to fit the lines of Q2 into the much more compact Q1, cutting or representing through stage action any language whose 'beauty' did not offset the difficulty posed by its datedness.

Stephen M. Buhler has shown, *Romeo and Juliet*'s 'crossover' popularity across a broad spectrum of 'pop' and 'post-pop' music, from Peggy Lee to hip hop[1] – attest resoundingly to the enduring reach of *Romeo and Juliet* and the cultural superstardom of its author.

Such celebrity has its price. Given their adaptive appeal, there lurks a fear that *Romeo and Juliet* and its author might morph out of existence – indeed, that the recent two-hour theatrical spoof, *The Reduced Shakespeare Co. presents The Compleat Works of Wllm Shkspr (abridged)*, may have been on to something in making *Romeo and Juliet* only the most prominent among a set of thirty-eight miniatures.[2] And where once the burning question of *Romeo and Juliet* was, 'is it a tragedy?' now we hear with increasing urgency, 'is it Shakespeare?'[3]

Or, at least, is it a 'Shakespeare film'? This variation on the question hovers over discussions of the recent, much discussed and commercially successful, adaptation of *Romeo and Juliet* into film, Baz Luhrmann's *William Shakespeare's Romeo + Juliet* (1996). To be sure, Luhrmann's film follows the play reasonably closely in plot and language – its ending, for example, no more radically abbreviated than that in Bogdanov's production – and, starting with its very title, overlooks no opportunity to associate itself with Shakespeare and images and references Shakespearean. Yet it can invoke these connections with mordant detachment. While stopping short of the travesty of the play we find in, as Barbara Hodgdon calls it, the 'slasher-porn' film *Tromeo and Juliet* released shortly afterward (1997),[4] the *mise en scène* of Luhrmann's film could easily be taken for virtual Shakespeare. Situating *Romeo and Juliet* in something like a Shakespeare theme park, the film transforms Verona into the sun-drenched seaside dystopia of Verona Beach, where unsavoury establishments bear names taken from other plays in the canon: the 'Merchant of Verona Beach' loan company, 'Mistress Quickly's' massage parlour.

Nor are allusions to Shakespeare the only vein of reference tapped in Verona Beach; indeed, to attend to all of the signs and sounds emitted from this visually and aurally congested text is to run the risk of a semiotic overdose.[5] For one thing, the film frequently and self-consciously reminds us that it *is* a film. As critics have noted, Luhrmann's film incorporates visual references to a wide array of celluloid *auteurs* and styles.[6] Moreover, unlike Zeffirelli, who deliberately chose for his title characters

[1] 'Reviving Juliet, Repackaging Romeo: Transformations of Character in Pop and Post-Pop Music', *Shakespeare After Mass Media*, ed. Richard Burt, 2002, 243–64.

[2] In their text of this burlesque, 1994, pp. 9–25, Jess Borgeson, Adam Long and Daniel Singer allot a disproportionately significant fraction of their 'reduced' time to *Romeo and Juliet*, including a mock scholarly note on the Balcony scene and the misunderstood line, 'wherefore art thou Romeo?', p. 16.

[3] Consider the variations on the 'Is-it-Shakespeare?' question articulated in Rex Gibson, '"O, What Learning Is": Pedagogy and the Afterlife of *Romeo and Juliet*', *S.Sur.* 49 (1996), pp. 149–50.

[4] '*William Shakespeare's Romeo + Juliet*: Everything's Nice in America?' *S.Sur.* 52 (1999), p. 90.

[5] Or what Hodgdon, 'Everything's Nice in America?', p. 90, calls 'a semiotician's dream', adding the benediction, 'If this be postmodernism, give me excess of it.'

[6] See Hodgdon, 'Everything's Nice in America?' p. 90, Levenson, *The Oxford Shakespeare Romeo and Juliet*, p. 95, and Denise Albanese, 'The Shakespeare Film and the Americanization of Culture', *Marxist Shakespeares*, ed. Jean E. Howard and Scott Cutler Shershow, 2001, pp. 216, 222; to these one might add Hitchcock's *The Birds*, its bird-induced conflagration at a filling station pyrotechnically recalled by Luhrmann in the feud-induced conflagration at the convenience store at the outset.

11   *Liebestod* in Verona Beach. Leonardo DiCaprio and Claire Danes as Romeo and Juliet in their final encounter in Baz Luhrmann's 1996 film, *William Shakespeare's Romeo + Juliet*. Photo courtesy of Photofest.

young actors who were screen 'unknowns',[1] in Claire Danes and Leonardo DiCaprio – even the pre-*Titanic* DiCaprio – Luhrmann chose young actors already known, particularly by the young audience for whom the film was marketed, and with established *personae*, indeed, in DiCaprio's case, a *persona* with a complex, to use Hodgdon's epithet, 'polysexual' appeal, part James Dean, part Aryan Michael Jackson.[2]

Nor is Hollywood the far horizon of the film's cultural reach. For the fair Verona Beach where *William Shakespeare's Romeo + Juliet* lays its scene is a densely packed cultural site that challenges the very efforts at decoding it that it invites. With its tall buildings and strip shopping centres – and a bit of Australian outback for Mantua – Verona Beach is indeterminate but not entirely unrecognisable, perhaps a place in the United States with a strong Latino presence, Florida, southern California, but not entirely dissociable, however, from Mexico City where the film was actually made, its exploitation of the realities of the 'global economy' making it a participant in the very capitalism it slickly sends up.[3] With its mix of Anglo, Latino and African characters, Verona Beach is ethnically and racially complex but neither harmonious nor divided along precisely drawn racial lines, the signals in its casting of African Americans, for

[1] See Levenson, *Shakespeare in Performance: Romeo and Juliet*, 1987, p. 105.

[2] 'Everything's Nice in America?' p. 93; on the breadth of DiCaprio's sexual appeal see Gary Taylor, 'Shakespeare Performed: Theatrical Proximities: The Stratford Festival, 1998', *SQ* 50 (1999), p. 350, on DiCaprio and Danes as 'teen idols'; and Albanese, 'Shakespeare Film', p. 225 n. 6, on DiCaprio as a 'gay icon'.

[3] Albanese, 'Shakespeare Film', pp. 217–18, or what on p. 223 she dubs 'neocolonial outsourcing'.

example, teasingly enigmatic.[1] Finally, in the degree to which Verona Beach visually defines itself as a place driven simultaneously by God and the Mammon of capitalism and consumption, the film seems to offer religion as one more commodity. With the high tower of a cathedral topped by, as if to honour both God and Fellini, a huge statue of Christ, the impulses of devotion and consumption seem to converge in a glut of religious *objets* – the garishly opulent sea of candles and blue neon lights inundating the church that holds the Capulets' tomb, the crucifixes which, as Peter Donaldson notes, adorn everything from the backs of car seats to the back of Friar Lawrence.[2]

In so visually and semiotically rich a film, in so complex a vision of American and postmodern culture, what role is there for Shakespeare's *Romeo and Juliet* to play beyond that of narrative fodder? Denise Albanese argues that Luhrmann's *Romeo + Juliet* keeps Shakespeare's *Romeo and Juliet* in our consciousness, but only through a species of alienation, through juxtapositions that remind us of the 'correct' Shakespearean detail and reading even as it is being visually displaced by Luhrmann's version, as, for example, when the camera shows us 'gun' when what we hear or remember from the text is 'sword'.[3] Others, making no claims about 'reverence', nonetheless do see a critical engagement between the film and the play. For Hodgdon, for example, a hint of that engagement lies in the analogy established early in the film between Luhrmann's deployment of MTV and Shakespeare's use of soliloquies as devices for exploring 'emotions and interior states of mind'.[4] And a stronger hint of it arrives at the end, when Luhrmann's film eliminates any tonal distance it has maintained between itself and its Shakespearean fable to embrace the death of the lovers as both a romantic and horrific event. Philip Armstrong has commented on the 'absolute privacy' the film confers upon the lovers in the final scene in the church that is Juliet's tomb.[5] It is in this 'absolute privacy' and the absolute rupture it implies between the lovers and the social order that the film engages Shakespeare's play most deeply. Hodgdon has argued that the way in which Luhrmann's film ends reveals a deep ambivalence: from images in the church of romantic excess, the film peremptorily changes its mode to social realism to show the bodies being put onto an ambulance; the falloff from the private splendour of Romeo and Juliet's love to the tawdry glare of Verona Beach cannot but underscore the failures of the latter, and to the degree to which the culture represented in Verona Beach reflects our own, its failures are a comment on us.[6] In *Romeo and Juliet* Luhrmann's film of *William Shakespeare's Romeo + Juliet* found a correlative for its own ambivalence, and in this way helps keep Shakespeare's play, like its author, our contemporary.

[1] African-Americans embody a number of authoritative voices in the film, but they are voices in various ways detached or incapable of altering events; so too, in casting Mercutio with an African-American and playing him as the sexually ambiguous, drag performer of the Capulets' ball, the film seems both to mock cultural stereotypes linking 'black' with 'exotic' while pandering to them. See also Albanese, 'Shakespeare Film', p. 216.

[2] '"All which it inherit": Shakespeare, Globes, and Global Media', *S.Sur.* 52 (1999), p. 199.

[3] Pp. 220, 222.

[4] 'Everything's Nice in America?', p. 96.

[5] *Shakespeare in Psychoanalysis*, 2001, p. 217.

[6] 'Everything's Nice in America?', p. 98.

NOTE ON THE TEXT

The copy-text for this edition is the second quarto of 1599 (Q2). All substantive and semi-substantive emendations of and additions to Q2 are recorded in the collation. In the format of the collations, the authority for this edition's reading follows immediately after the square bracket enclosing the quotation from the text. Other readings, if any, follow in chronological order. Emendations of Q2 accidentals (i.e. spelling and punctuation) have not been recorded unless the change significantly affects meaning. The collation also records all substantive and semi-substantive variants between Q2 and Q3 (1609), Q4 (*c.* 1622), F (First Folio, 1623), with the following exceptions: (1) obvious typographical errors, unless they explain how later textual variants arose; (2) isolated variants in Q3 and Q4 that do not become part of the later textual tradition: (3) variants in the accidentals that do not affect meaning. The later seventeenth-century texts (F2, 1632; Q5, 1637; F3, 1664; F4, 1685) are recorded only when they furnish an emendation to Q2 or offer readings of special interest for the later history of the text. Q1 (1597), as a 'bad' quarto or memorially reported text, often uniquely variant and roughly one-third shorter than Q2–4, F, offers a special problem. Since, however, Q1 has played an important role in editorial decisions about the text, from Pope's edition (1724) to the present time, it is desirable to give as much information about its readings as may be possible within the limitations imposed by a single collation based on Q2–4, F. The following information, therefore, has been included: (1) Q1 omissions in relation to Q2–4, F of more than a single line; (2) Q1 passages that offer a telescoped or radically different version of two or more lines in Q2–4, F; (3) Q1 variant stage directions or speech headings; (4) Q1 variants (if any) of all Q2–4, F readings here recorded; (5) Q1 readings adopted by editors from Pope on; (6) occasional Q1 unique readings of special interest. The absence of Q1 among the sigla in any reading or passage indicates the omission of that reading or passage in Q1. An asterisk in the lemma of a note in the Commentary is used to call attention to a word or phrase that has been emended in the text; the collation should be consulted for further information. See the Textual Analysis, pp. 206–12 below, for a detailed discussion of the provenance of, and relations between, Q1, Q2 and F.

Romeo and Juliet

LIST OF CHARACTERS

CHORUS
ESCALES, *Prince of Verona*
PARIS, *a young nobleman, kinsman to the Prince*
MONTAGUE } *heads of two houses at variance with each other*
CAPULET
COUSIN CAPULET, *kinsman to Capulet*
ROMEO, *son to Montague*
MERCUTIO, *kinsman to the Prince, and friend to Romeo*
BENVOLIO, *nephew to Montague, and friend to Romeo*
TYBALT, *nephew to Lady Capulet*
PETRUCHIO, *a (mute) follower of Tybalt*
FRIAR LAWRENCE } *Franciscans*
FRIAR JOHN
BALTHASAR, *servant to Romeo*
ABRAM, *servant to Montague*
SAMPSON
GREGORY } *servants to Capulet*
CLOWN
PETER, *servant to Juliet's Nurse*
PAGE *to Paris*
APOTHECARY
Three MUSICIANS

LADY MONTAGUE, *wife to Montague*
LADY CAPULET, *wife to Capulet*
JULIET, *daughter to Capulet*
NURSE *to Juliet*

GENTLEMEN *and* GENTLEWOMEN, MASKERS, TORCH-BEARERS, OFFICERS *of the Watch,*
    other CITIZENS, SERVINGMEN *and* ATTENDANTS

SCENE: *Verona, Mantua*

Note

The List of Characters was first given in published form by Rowe (1709), although an earlier list appears in the Douai MS. (1694).

66

THE TRAGEDY OF ROMEO AND JULIET

THE PROLOGUE

[*Enter*] CHORUS.

Two households, both alike in dignity,
In fair Verona (where we lay our scene),
From ancient grudge break to new mutiny,
Where civil blood makes civil hands unclean.
From forth the fatal loins of these two foes   5
A pair of star-crossed lovers take their life;
Whose misadventured piteous overthrows
Doth with their death bury their parents' strife.
The fearful passage of their death-marked love,
And the continuance of their parents' rage,   10
Which but their children's end nought could remove,
Is now the two hours' traffic of our stage;

immediately introduces the end

love is not w/o consequences

Title] F; The Most Excellent and lamentable Tragedie, of Romeo and *Iuliet. Newly corrected, augmented, and amended*: As it hath been sundry times publiquely acted, by the right Honourable the Lord Chamberlaine his Seruants. Q2 *(title page)*; An Excellent conceited Tragedie of Romeo and Iuliet, As it hath been often (with great applause) plaid publiquely, by the right Honourable the L. of *Hunsdon* his Seruants. Q1 *(title page)* The Prologue] *not in* F 0 SD *Enter* CHORUS.] Capell; Corus. Q2; Chorus. Q3–4; *not in* Q1 2] *Pope; (In faire* Verona…*Scene)* Q2–4, Q1 7 misaduentured] Q2–4; misaduentures, Q1 8–11] Q2–4; *(Through the continuing of their Fathers strife, / And death-markt passage of their Parents rage)* Q1 8 Doth] Q2–4; Do *Rowe* 10 rage,] Q4; rage: Q2–3; rage) Q1

THE PROLOGUE Cast as a 'Shakespearean' sonnet, this prologue–chorus serves as what was called 'The Argument of the Tragedie' (*Gorboduc* (1561)), usually prefixed to both tragedies and comedies written under classical or neo-classical influence (George Gascoigne, in *Supposes* (1566), describes it as 'The Prologue or Argument'). The verse form was probably suggested by Brooke's 'Argument', in Italian sonnet form.

1 **dignity** social status. Compare Brooke (25–6).

3 **ancient grudge** longstanding feud. Gascoigne uses this phrase in the same context (see 1.1.0 SD.2 n.); Brooke has 'sparke of grudge' (36).

4 **civil blood…unclean** i.e. the blood of citizens soils the hands of fellow citizens (perhaps with ironic play on 'civil'; compare Munday, *Downfall of…Huntingdon* (1598; MSR, 763–4)).

6 **star-crossed** thwarted by the influence of a malignant star. Compare 'death-marked' (9) and

1.4.106–11, 5.1.24, 5.3.111; also *Lear* 1.2.124–5: 'by an enforc'd obedience of planetary influence'. See suppl. note.

7 **misadventured** unlucky, unfortunate. *OED* records no other example and its uniqueness raises the possibility that Q1 '*misadventures*,' may be correct.

8 **Doth** Southern form of third per. pl., still common in Elizabethan English (Abbott 334).

9 **fearful passage…death-marked** Mahood (p. 56) recalls the 'ever-fixed mark' of *Sonnets* 116 and the 'sea-mark' of Othello's 'utmost sail' (5.2.268), and suggests that 'death-marked' may mean not only 'foredoomed' but 'with death as their objective', and that 'fearful' means either 'fearsome' or 'frightened'.

12 **two hours' traffic** The conventional time designated for a performance (see *H8*, Prologue, 12–13; *TNK*, Prologue, 27–9; Robert Tailor, *The Hogge Hath Lost His Pearl* (1614), Epilogue, 16).

67

The which if you with patient ears attend,
What here shall miss, our toil shall strive to mend.   [*Exit*]

[*handwritten note: Addresses audience directly*]

[**1.1**] *Enter* SAMPSON *and* GREGORY, *with swords and bucklers, of the house of Capulet.*

SAMPSON Gregory, on my word, we'll not carry coals.
GREGORY No, for then we should be colliers.
SAMPSON I mean, and we be in choler, we'll draw.
GREGORY Ay, while you live, draw your neck out of collar.
SAMPSON I strike quickly, being moved.   5
GREGORY But thou art not quickly moved to strike.
SAMPSON A dog of the house of Montague moves me.
GREGORY To move is to stir, and to be valiant is to stand: therefore
      if thou art moved thou runn'st away.
SAMPSON A dog of that house shall move me to stand: I will take the   10
      wall of any man or maid of Montague's.

[*handwritten note: est. form conflict FIRST*]

14 SD] *Capell; no* SD, Q2–4, Q1   **Act 1, Scene 1**   1.1] *Actus Primus. Scæna Prima.* F; *not in* Q2–4, Q1   Location] *Capell (after Rowe)*   0 SD.1–2] Q2–4, F; *Enter 2. Seruing-men of the* Capolets. Q1   1 on] Q2–4; A F; of Q1; o' *Capell*   2 SH GREGORY] Q2–4; *2* Q1 *(throughout scene)*   3 SH SAMPSON] Q2–4, F; *1* Q1 *(throughout scene)*   3 and] Q2–4; if F; If Q1   4 Ay] *Rowe*; I Q2–4, F *(not hereafter recorded unless ambiguous)*; Euer Q1   4 collar] F, Q1; choller Q2–3; Coller Q4   5 quickly,] F; quickly Q2–4, Q1   7 Montague] *Theobald (from Brooke)*; *Mountague* Q2–4, F *(the spelling in* Q2 *throughout, except* Montague *at* 2.2.98*);* the Mountagues Q1   8–9 To...away.] *As prose*, Q1, *Pope; two lines, ending* stand / ...away Q2–4, F   8 stand] Q2–4, F; stand to it Q1   10–11 A...Montague's.] *As prose, Pope; two lines, ending* stand / ...Mountagues Q2–4, F; There's not a man of them I meete, but Ile take the wall of. Q1

14 miss prove inadequate in the performance. Compare Q1 '*here we want*'.

14 mend improve (in the future). Compare *MND* 5.1.429–30.

Act 1, Scene 1
Location Verona. A public place.

0 SD.1 swords and bucklers 'Heavy swords and small shields were the ordinary weapons of servants; gentlemen wore rapier and dagger' (Kittredge).

0 SD.2 house of Capulet The followers of Capulet and Montague may have been distinguished by 'tokens' worn in their hats. See George Gascoigne, 'A devise of a Maske for the right honorable Viscount Mountacute' (*The Posies* (1575), p. 83): 'he shewed in his hat, / This token which the *Mountacutes* dyd beare alwaies, for that / They covet to be knowne from *Capels* where they passe / For auncient grutch which long ago, twene these two houses was'. See supplementary note.

1 carry coals submit passively to indignity or insult. Proverbial (Tilley T513, N69).

2 colliers (1) coal carriers; (2) term of abuse

(from the dirtiness of the trade and the reputation of colliers for cheating).

3 and if.

3 in...draw draw (our swords) in anger (with play, in 4, on 'draw...collar' = slip out of the hangman's noose).

4 while you live i.e. under any circumstance (with play on being 'dead' once hanged).

5–10 moved...stand to be moved = (1) to react emotionally, (2) to be forced to retreat; to stand = (1) to take a firm and courageous position under threat of attack, (2) to have an erection (25). Quibbles like these and the similar ones at lines 3–4 above are the stock-in-trade of servants or servant-clowns in Elizabethan drama. Compare Feste as Olivia's 'corrupter of words', *TN* 3.1.36.

10–11 take the wall assert social position or physical superiority. City streets, lacking pavements and slanted to a kennel (or channel) running down the centre, were the dumping grounds for refuse; the wall-side was therefore cleaner and safer and was claimed by people of rank or by anyone (like Sampson) who wanted to pick a fight.

GREGORY That shows thee a weak slave, for the weakest goes to the
wall.

SAMPSON 'Tis true, and therefore women being the weaker vessels are
ever thrust to the wall: therefore I will push Montague's men from   15
the wall, and thrust his maids to the wall.

GREGORY The quarrel is between our masters, and us their men.

SAMPSON 'Tis all one, I will show myself a tyrant: when I have fought
with the men, I will be civil with the maids; I will cut off their
heads.   20

GREGORY The heads of the maids?

SAMPSON Ay, the heads of the maids, or their maidenheads, take it in
what sense thou wilt.

GREGORY They must take it in sense that feel it.

SAMPSON Me they shall feel while I am able to stand, and 'tis known   25
I am a pretty piece of flesh.

GREGORY 'Tis well thou art not fish; if thou hadst, thou hadst been
poor-John. Draw thy tool, here comes of the house of Montagues.

Enter two other SERVINGMEN, [*one being* ABRAM].

SAMPSON My naked weapon is out. Quarrel, I will back thee.

GREGORY How, turn thy back and run?   30

14 'Tis true] Q2–4; True F; Thats true Q1   17] *not in* Q1   18 tyrant:] F; tyrant, Q2–4, Q1   19 civil] Q2–3, F; cruell
Q4   19 I will] Q2–4; and F, Q1   21 maids?] F, Q1; maids. Q2–4   22 their] Q2–4, F; the Q1, *Warburton*   24 in] Q4,
Q1; *not in* Q2–3, F   28 comes of] Q2–4, F; comes two of Q1   28 house of Montagues] Q2–4; House of the *Mountagues*
F; two of the *Mountagues* Q1   28 SD *one being* ABRAM] *Name supplied from following speech headings in* Q2–4, F; *Enter
two Seruingmen of the* Mountagues. Q1 (*Rowe introduced* Balthasar *as the second servingman*)   29–30] *not in* Q1

12–13 weakest...wall In a fight the weakest
were driven up against the wall (Tilley W15, W185);
but here used with some suggestion that cowards
may seek the wall as a safer place.

14 weaker vessels Compare 1 Pet. 3.7 (G):
'Likewise ye housbands, dwel with them as men of
knowledge, giving honour unto the woman, as unto
the weaker vessel.' Shakespeare here begins a series
of bawdy *doubles entendres* carried on (15–29) in
'thrust', 'cut...heads', 'maidenheads', 'take it in
sense', 'stand', 'piece of flesh', 'fish', 'tool' and
'naked weapon'. See Partridge, and
E. A. M. Coleman, *The Dramatic Use of Bawdy in
Shakespeare*, 1974, for comment on these and other
sexual puns.

17 quarrel...men i.e. we have no quarrel with
women (Montagues or not).

19 civil Most eds. emend to 'cruel' (Q4),
explaining 'civil' as a minim misprint (NS), but
'civil' may here be intended ironically, the

paradoxical civility proper to Sampson in his role
as 'tyrant' (Dowden).

24 They...it i.e. those that feel it (sexual
intercourse) must experience it as physical sensation;
perhaps with play on 'incense' = set on fire.

27 fish With play on 'woman' or 'prostitute'
(slang).

28 poor-John salted hake; cheap, lenten fare
suggestive of sexual passivity, popularly associated
with women ('weaker vessels', 'fish').

28 comes of the house A partitive genitive
(*OED* Of *prep*. XIII 45); Williams compares *Ham.*
3.2.40–1 ('there be of them that will themselves
laugh') and Num. 13.21, 24 (G; 13.20, 23 KJ). Until
recently most eds., since Malone, have inserted Q1
'two' after 'comes', an easier reading. Ulrici
suggests that the Q2 reading expresses contempt.

28 SD The identity of the second servingman is
not known; Rowe suggested Balthasar, Romeo's
servant, and has been followed by many eds.

SAMPSON Fear me not.

GREGORY No, marry, I fear thee!

SAMPSON Let us take the law of our sides, let them begin.

GREGORY I will frown as I pass by, and let them take it as they list.

SAMPSON Nay, as they dare. I will bite my thumb at them, which is   35
disgrace to them if they bear it.

ABRAM Do you bite your thumb at us, sir?

SAMPSON I do bite my thumb, sir.

ABRAM Do you bite your thumb at us, sir?

SAMPSON [*Aside to Gregory*] Is the law of our side if I say ay?   40

GREGORY [*Aside to Sampson*] No.

SAMPSON No, sir, I do not bite my thumb at you, sir, but I bite my
thumb, sir.

GREGORY Do you quarrel, sir?

ABRAM Quarrel, sir? No, sir.   45

SAMPSON But if you do, sir, I am for you. I serve as good a man as
you.

ABRAM No better.

SAMPSON Well, sir.

Enter BENVOLIO.

GREGORY [*Aside to Sampson*] Say 'better', here comes one of my   50
master's kinsmen.

SAMPSON Yes, better, sir.

ABRAM You lie.

SAMPSON Draw, if you be men. Gregory, remember thy washing blow.

They fight.

32 thee!] Q5; thee. Q2–4, F; thee, Q1   36 disgrace] Q2, Q1; a disgrace Q3–4, F   37 SH ABRAM] Q2–4, F; *1 Moun*: Q1
39 SH ABRAM] Q2–4, F; *2 Moun*: Q1 *(reading,* I but i'st at vs?*)*   40 SD] Capell; no SD, Q2–4, F, Q1   41 SD] Capell; no
SD, Q2–4, F, Q1   44–9] *not in* Q1   45 sir?] F; sir, Q2–4   46 But if] Q2–4; If F   48 better.] Q2–4; better? F
50 SD] Capell; no SD, Q2–4, F, Q1   52–71] *not in* Q1, *which substitutes a* SD: *They draw, to them enters* Tybalt, *they
fight, to them the Prince, old* Mountague, *and his wife, old* Capulet *and his wife, and other Citizens and part them.*
52 sir] Q2–4; *not in* F   54 washing] Q2–3, F; swashing Q4, *Pope*

31 **Fear me not** i.e. don't worry about my
support (backing). Gregory (32) pretends to take the
words literally: 'Don't be afraid of me.'

32 **marry** indeed. (Weakened form of an oath
using the name of the Virgin Mary.)

33 **law of our sides** Compare Porter, *Two
Angry Women* (1598; MSR, 1877–8).

34 **list** wish, please.

35 **bite...at** A provocative, probably obscene
gesture. Cotgrave (1611, sig. 3K1): 'faire la
nique...*to threaten or defie, by putting the thumbe*

*naile into the mouth, and with a jerke (from the upper
teeth) make it to knacke*'. There seems to have been
some contemporary confusion between this phrase
and 'to give the fico (or fig)'; see Cotgrave (sig.
2N3ᵛ) and Thomas Lodge, *Wits Miserie* (1596, sig.
D4): 'Contempt...giving me the Fico with his
thombe in his mouth' (*OED* Fico 3).

50 **one** i.e. Tybalt, who is seen approaching.

54 **washing** slashing with great force (*OED*,
which cites 'washing blow' in Arthur Golding's
translation (1567) of Ovid's *Metamorphoses* V, 252).

BENVOLIO Part, fools!   55
    Put up your swords, you know not what you do.
               [*Beats down their swords.*]

                Enter TYBALT.

TYBALT What, art thou drawn among these heartless hinds?
    Turn thee, Benvolio, look upon thy death.
BENVOLIO I do but keep the peace. Put up thy sword,
    Or manage it to part these men with me.   60
TYBALT What, drawn and talk of peace? I hate the word,
    As I hate hell, all Montagues, and thee.
    Have at thee, coward.
              [*They fight.*]

    Enter [*several of both houses, who join the fray, and*] *three or four*
    Citizens [*as* OFFICERS *of the Watch,*] *with clubs or partisans.*

OFFICERS Clubs, bills, and partisans! Strike! Beat them down!
    Down with the Capulets! Down with the Montagues!   65

    Enter old CAPULET *in his gown, and his wife* [LADY CAPULET].

CAPULET What noise is this? Give me my long sword, ho!
LADY CAPULET A crutch, a crutch! why call you for a sword?
CAPULET My sword, I say! old Montague is come,
    And flourishes his blade in spite of me.

    Enter old MONTAGUE *and his wife* [LADY MONTAGUE].

MONTAGUE Thou villain Capulet! – Hold me not, let me go.   70
LADY MONTAGUE Thou shalt not stir one foot to seek a foe.

55–6 Part...do.] *As verse, Capell; as prose,* Q2–4, F   56 SD] *Capell; no* SD, Q2–4, F, Q1   61 drawn] Q2–4; draw, F
63 SD.1] *Malone; Fight.* F; *no* SD, Q2–4; *see above, 52–71, for* Q1   63 SD.2 *several...and*] *Capell* (*subst.*)   63 SD.3
as...Watch] *This edn*   63 SD.3 *or partisans*] Q5; *or partysons* Q2–4; *not in* F   64 SH OFFICERS] *This edn; Offi.* Q2–4,
F; *Cit. / Steevens;* 1. *Cit. / Malone; First Off. / Cam.; Citizens. / Cowden Clarke*   65] *Assigned to / Citizens. / conj.*
Cam.   67 SH LADY CAPULET] *Rowe; Wife.* Q2–4, F   67 crutch, a crutch] F; crowch, a crowch Q2–4   70 Capulet!
– Hold] *Rowe* (*subst., after* F Capulet. Hold); *Capulet, hold* Q2–4   71 SH LADY MONTAGUE] *Rowe; M. Wife.* 2.
Q2–4; 2. *Wife* F   71 one] Q2–4; a F

---

57 **heartless hinds** cowardly menials (with play
on 'hart' = male deer and 'hind' = female deer –
weaklings without a stag to lead them). Tybalt
suggests that Benvolio is demeaned by his
willingness to fight servants.

60 **manage** handle, wield (with suggestion of
proper control).

63 **Have at thee** A common formula, warning
of immediate attack.

63 SD.2–3 **Enter...partisans** See supplementary note.

64 **Clubs...partisans** Weapons (the last two,
long staves with a curved blade or axe-head on the

end, forms of the halberd), here transferred as a
rallying cry to those carrying them. 'Clubs' in this
sense had long been used to incite violence by
London apprentices; 'bills' were regularly associated
with constables (i.e. officers) of the watch (*OED*).

65 SD **gown** dressing-gown (Capulet has been
aroused from sleep).

66 **long sword** An old fashioned, heavy, often
two-handed, sword. The comic treatment of both
Old Capulet and Old Montague here underlines the
'age' and futility of the feud; compare 80–5.

69 **in spite of** out of spite for.

Enter PRINCE ESCALES *with his train.*

PRINCE Rebellious subjects, enemies to peace,
       Profaners of this neighbour-stainèd steel –
       Will they not hear? – What ho, you men, you beasts!
       That quench the fire of your pernicious rage   75
       With purple fountains issuing from your veins:
       On pain of torture, from those bloody hands
       Throw your mistempered weapons to the ground,
       And hear the sentence of your movèd prince.
       Three civil brawls, bred of an airy word,   80
       By thee, old Capulet, and Montague,
       Have thrice disturbed the quiet of our streets,
       And made Verona's ancient citizens
       Cast by their grave beseeming ornaments
       To wield old partisans, in hands as old,   85
       Cankered with peace, to part your cankered hate;
       If ever you disturb our streets again,
       Your lives shall pay the forfeit of the peace.
       For this time all the rest depart away:
       You, Capulet, shall go along with me,   90
       And, Montague, come you this afternoon,
       To know our farther pleasure in this case,
       To old Free-town, our common judgement-place.
       Once more, on pain of death, all men depart.
       Exeunt [all but Montague, Lady Montague, and Benvolio]

71 SD ESCALES] *This edn;* Eskales Q2–4, F; *the Prince* Q1; ESCALUS *Cam. (from Brooke)*   73–6] *not in* Q1
77 torture,...hands] F, Q1; torture...hands, Q2–3; torture,...hands, Q4   78 mistempered] F (mistemper'd); mistempered Q2–4, Q1   80 brawls] Q2–4, Q1; Broyles F   83–6] *not in* Q1   83 Verona's] Q3–4, F; *Neronas* Q2
92 case,] Q1; case: Q2–4, F   94 SD *all...Benvolio*] *Hudson (after Rowe)*

73 **Profaners...steel** Those who desecrate the purity of steel with the blood of neighbours. Compare Prologue, 4.

77 **On...torture** i.e. failure to obey will be punished by torture.

78 **mistempered** (1) figuratively, tempered (= made hard and resilient) in hot blood instead of icy water; (2) ill-tempered, angry.

80 **Three civil brawls** Shakespeare's detail; Brooke suggests repeated outbreaks.

80 **airy** empty, vain. Compare Brooke (37): 'first hatchd of trifling stryfe'.

84 **grave beseeming ornaments** accessories proper to the dignity of age. Lady Capulet has sarcastically suggested a 'crutch' (67).

86 **Cankered...cankered** rusted, corroded (from disuse)...malignant, diseased.

88 **Your...peace** i.e. you will pay with your lives for any further breach of the peace.

93 **old Free-town** Brooke's translation (1974, 2258) of Boaistuau's 'Villefranche' (Bandello, 'Villa franca'; Painter, 'Villafranco'); in all these it is a castle, apparently outside Verona, belonging to Capulet. Shakespeare's designation of Free-town as 'our common judgement-place' and the use of 'old' to describe it may have arisen from confusion with 'the olde castel of *Verona*' (Boaistuau, 'le chasteau vieux de Veronne') mentioned by Painter (p. 111) but not by Brooke.

MONTAGUE Who set this ancient quarrel new abroach? 95
     Speak, nephew, were you by when it began?
BENVOLIO Here were the servants of your adversary,
     And yours, close fighting ere I did approach:
     I drew to part them; in the instant came
     The fiery Tybalt, with his sword prepared, 100
     Which, as he breathed defiance to my ears,
     He swung about his head and cut the winds,
     Who, nothing hurt withal, hissed him in scorn;
     While we were interchanging thrusts and blows,
     Came more and more, and fought on part and part, 105
     Till the Prince came, who parted either part.
LADY MONTAGUE O where is Romeo? saw you him today?
     Right glad I am he was not at this fray.
BENVOLIO Madam, an hour before the worshipped sun
     Peered forth the golden window of the east, 110
     A troubled mind drive me to walk abroad,
     Where underneath the grove of sycamore,
     That westward rooteth from this city side,
     So early walking did I see your son;
     Towards him I made, but he was ware of me, 115
     And stole into the covert of the wood;
     I, measuring his affections by my own,
     Which then most sought where most might not be found,

95 SH MONTAGUE] Q2–4, F; M: *wife*. Q1, Rowe 99–106] *not in* Q1 102 swung] *Pope*; swoong Q2; swong Q3–4, F
107 SH LADY MONTAGUE] *Rowe*; *Wife*. Q2–4, F, Q1 108 I am] Q2, Q1; am I Q3–4, F 110 Peered forth] Q2–4, F; Peept
through Q1, *Pope*; Peer'd through *Theobald* 111 drive…abroad] Q2; drave…abroad Q3–4, F; drew me from companie
Q1, *Pope*; drew…abroad *Theobald* 112 sycamore] F, Q1; Syramour Q2–4 113 this city] Q2–4, F; the Citties Q1,
Malone; the City *Theobald*; this city' *Capell*; the city' *Steevens* 118] Q5; Which…sought,…found: Q2–4, F; That
most are busied when th'are most alone, Q1, *Pope (both omitting 119)*

95 **new abroach** newly afoot (literally, tapped or pierced and set running afresh).

100 **prepared** already drawn. Compare *Lear* 2.1.51.

103 **nothing hurt withal** not a bit injured thereby. Compare *Ham.* 1.1.145, 'the air, invulnerable'; *Mac.* 5.8.9, 'intrenchant air'.

105 **on…part** on one side and the other.

106 **either part** both parties.

109 **worshipped** honoured, revered.

110 **golden…east** Compare Porter, *Two Angry Women* (1598; MSR, 2660): 'Open the christall windowes of the East.'

111 **drive** drove (archaic form of preterite, pronounced *driv*; used in Spenser, Beaumont's *Bonduca* and Lodge's *Rosalynde* (New Variorum *AYLI*, 1977, p. 419).

111 **abroad** from home.

112 **sycamore** A tree associated with dejected lovers. Compare *Oth.* 4.3.40; *LLL* 5.2.89.

113 **this city side** the side of this city. An unusual locution; Q1 'the Cities side' is easier, but not, therefore, right.

115 **ware** aware (perhaps with suggestion of 'wary' (Kermode)).

116 **covert** shelter, hiding place (the implied secretiveness links with 'stole').

117–21 **I…me** i.e. taking my cue from my own feelings ('A troubled mind' (111)), which at that moment most desired a place where I could be solitary ('most' = all others except myself), even my melancholy self being one more person than I could bear, I followed my mood in not pursuing Romeo's and was happy to avoid him who was happy to avoid me. See supplementary note.

Being one too many by my weary self,
Pursued my humour, not pursuing his,   120
And gladly shunned who gladly fled from me.

MONTAGUE Many a morning hath he there been seen,
With tears augmenting the fresh morning's dew,
Adding to clouds more clouds with his deep sighs,
But all so soon as the all-cheering sun   125
Should in the farthest east begin to draw
The shady curtains from Aurora's bed,
Away from light steals home my heavy son,
And private in his chamber pens himself,
Shuts up his windows, locks fair daylight out,   130
And makes himself an artificial night:
Black and portentous must this humour prove,
Unless good counsel may the cause remove.

BENVOLIO My noble uncle, do you know the cause?
MONTAGUE I neither know it, nor can learn of him.   135
BENVOLIO Have you importuned him by any means?
MONTAGUE Both by myself and many other friends,
But he, his own affections' counsellor,
Is to himself (I will not say how true)
But to himself so secret and so close,   140
So far from sounding and discovery,
As is the bud bit with an envious worm

---

120 Pursued] *Capell* (Persu'd); Pursued Q2–4, F, Q1   120 humour] Q2, Q4; honour Q3, F, Q1   121–31] *not in* Q1
121 shunned] F (shunn'd); shunned Q2–4   132 portentous] F2; portendous Q2–3, F *(variant form)*; protendous Q4;
portentious Q1   135 learn] Q2–4, F, Q1; learn it *Rowe*   136–46] *not in* Q1   137 other] Q2–4; others F   138 his] Q3–4,
F; is Q2

122–31 These lines describe the typical anti-social attitude proper to the inamorato, who obviously gets a measure of enjoyment by playing the role of the rejected lover in the sonnet tradition. See supplementary note.

127 **Aurora** Goddess of the dawn.

128 **son** With play on 'sun' (125); the sun rises, while Montague's 'son' sets (seeking darkness).

130 **windows** shutters.

132 **Black** Malignant, baneful (with reference to black bile, the 'humour' proper to melancholy; see 'humour' (132)).

132 **humour** inclination, mood (but the connection with the melancholy humour, associated with madness, is indicated by 'heavy' (128) and 'Black'). For the faculty psychology deriving from the doctrine of the four humours, see J. W. Draper, *The Humours and Shakespeare's Characters*, 1945.

136 **by any means** in every possible way.

138 **his...counsellor** the (only) confidant of his own feelings.

139 **true** i.e. wise in the counsel he gives himself.

141 **sounding** investigation by cautious or indirect questioning (*OED vbl sb*[2] 1b and Sound *v*[2] 6b); this passage, however, is the only instance of such figurative use before 1856 and 'sounding' may here more literally have its nautical sense of 'probing to ascertain the depth or bottom'.

141 **discovery** laying open to view, exposure.

142–4 **As...sun** The simile comparing Romeo in his secretive humour to a bud devoured from within (and secretly) by a malicious ('envious') cankerworm, causing it to die before it blossoms (compare *Ham.* 1.3.39–40; *Sonnets* 1.11), is introduced without clear transition. Johnson suspected the omission of some lines that 'lamented the danger that Romeo will die of his melancholy, before his virtues or abilities are known to the world'.

Ere he can spread his sweet leaves to the air,
Or dedicate his beauty to the sun.
Could we but learn from whence his sorrows grow,   145
We would as willingly give cure as know.

Enter ROMEO.

BENVOLIO See where he comes. So please you step aside,
   I'll know his grievance or be much denied.
MONTAGUE I would thou wert so happy by thy stay
   To hear true shrift. Come, madam, let's away.   150

Exeunt [Montague and Lady Montague]

BENVOLIO Good morrow, cousin.
ROMEO   Is the day so young?
BENVOLIO But new struck nine.
ROMEO   Ay me, sad hours seem long.
   Was that my father that went hence so fast?
BENVOLIO It was. What sadness lengthens Romeo's hours?
ROMEO Not having that, which, having, makes them short.   155
BENVOLIO In love?
ROMEO Out –
BENVOLIO Of love?
ROMEO Out of her favour where I am in love.
BENVOLIO Alas that Love, so gentle in his view,   *foreshadow* 160
   Should be so tyrannous and rough in proof!
ROMEO Alas that Love, whose view is muffled still,
   Should, without eyes, see pathways to his will!
   Where shall we dine? O me! what fray was here?
   Yet tell me not, for I have heard it all: 165
   Here's much to do with hate, but more with love:

---

144 sun] *Pope² (conj. Theobald)*; same Q2–4, F   150 SD *Montague and Lady Montague*] *Capell*   152 struck] *Rowe*; strooke Q2–4, F; stroke Q1 *(variant forms)*   156, 158 love?] Q5, *Rowe*; loue. Q2–4, F, Q1   157 Out –] *Rowe*; Out. Q2–4, F, Q1   164 O me!] Q2–4, F; Gods me, Q1

144 **sun** Q2 'same' (= the air) makes sense but sounds flat; Theobald's conjecture is imaginatively superior; 'same' is an easy minim misreading of 'sunne' in Secretary hand.   150 **shrift** confession.
   151–9 See supplementary note.
   151 **Is…young?** Compare Brooke (93): 'He mones the daye, he wakes the long and wery night.'
   155 **that** i.e. the reciprocation of his love.
   160 **view** appearance (i.e. the boy Cupid; compare 202).
   161 **rough in proof** harsh in actual experience.
   162 **whose…still** whose vision is always ('still') blindfolded. Compare 1.4.4; 2.4.15.

163 **Should…will** Should, though blindfolded, nevertheless be able to see to impose his will (upon us as lovers). NS suggests verbal influence from Brooke (129–30).
   164 **Where…dine?** 'A lover, of course, could not seriously think of his dinner. Romeo wishes to turn aside Benvolio's inquiries' (Dowden).
   165 **heard it all** i.e. it's an old story to me (and I don't want to hear the details).
   166 **Here's…love** 'Here's a great disturbance on account of the feud – "but," Romeo adds with a sigh, "my unhappy love causes me even more disturbance than that"' (Kittredge). On

Why then, O brawling love, O loving hate,
O any thing of nothing first create!
O heavy lightness, serious vanity,
Misshapen chaos of well-seeming forms,   170
Feather of lead, bright smoke, cold fire, sick health,
Still-waking sleep, that is not what it is!
This love feel I, that feel no love in this.
Dost thou not laugh?

BENVOLIO   No, coz, I rather weep.

ROMEO Good heart, at what?

BENVOLIO   At thy good heart's oppression.   175

ROMEO Why, such is love's transgression:
Griefs of mine own lie heavy in my breast,
Which thou wilt propagate to have it pressed
With more of thine; this love that thou hast shown
Doth add more grief to too much of mine own.   180
Love is a smoke made with the fume of sighs,
Being purged, a fire sparkling in lovers' eyes,
Being vexed, a sea nourished with loving tears.
What is it else? a madness most discreet,
A choking gall, and a preserving sweet.   185
Farewell, my coz.

BENVOLIO   Soft, I will go along;

168 create!] Q1; created: Q2–4, F   170 well-seeming] Q4 *(hyphen, F3)*; welseeing Q2–3, F; best seeming Q1
172 Still-waking] F2; Still waking Q2–4, F, Q1   174 Dost] Q5; Doest Q2–4, F, Q1   178 propagate] Q3–4, F, Q1; propogate
Q2 *(a possible, if erroneous, form; compare Per. 1.2.73)*   178 it] Q2–4, F; them Q1, *Pope*   181 made] Q2–4, F; raisde Q1,
Pope   182 purged] Q2–4, F, Q1; urg'd *conj. Johnson*; puff'd *Collier MS.*   183 loving] Q2–4, F; a louers Q1; lovers
(= lovers') *Pope*   184 madness] Q4, Q1; madnesse, Q2–3, F

Shakespeare's use of what may be termed 'son-netese' for characterising Romeo's 'love' for Rosaline and for foreshadowing the ambiguous nature of love, see above, pp. 11–12. See supplementary note.

168 *create created (see Abbott 342); from Q1. Q2 'created', while grammatically acceptable, is metrically harsh and thwarts the rhyme with 'hate'.

172 Still-waking Ever wakeful.

173 This...this I suffer this kind of love ('that is not what it is' (172)) but can find no happiness ('love') in it (since, as we learn shortly, his lady spurns him). Compare 214–15.

174 coz cousin.

176–80 Romeo wittily retorts Benvolio's concern (or love, i.e. Benvolio's figurative weeping for him (174)) by claiming that, ironically, he is only increasing the weight of Romeo's love-grief by making him suffer added grief for Benvolio's apparent grief for him. 'oppression' (= being

weighed down with sorrow) is picked up by 'pressed' (178), which, with 'breast' (177) and 'propagate' (178), images the birth of new grief in sexual terms.

176 love's transgression the way love oversteps its proper bounds; hence, love's sin. Compare Tilley L508.

181–5 These lines ironically describe the present stage and foreshadow the three later stages of Romeo's love: (1) his professed love for Rosaline ('smoke' and 'sighs'); (2) his new love for Juliet (the 'smoke' cleared away ('purged'), a mutual 'fire' burns in the lovers' eyes'); (3) his love threatened ('vexed') by banishment and inundated by the tears of love; (4) his love, turned to desperation ('a discreet madness'), finds death ('a choking gall') and finally immortality ('a preserving sweet').

185 gall bitterness.

186 Soft Stay, stop (in modern idiom, 'Hold it!').

And if you leave me so, you do me wrong.
ROMEO Tut, I have lost myself, I am not here,
        This is not Romeo, he's some other where.
BENVOLIO Tell me in sadness, who is that you love?   190
ROMEO What, shall I groan and tell thee?
BENVOLIO   Groan? why, no;
        But sadly tell me, who?
ROMEO Bid a sick man in sadness make his will –
        A word ill urged to one that is so ill:
        In sadness, cousin, I do love a woman.   195
BENVOLIO I aimed so near, when I supposed you loved.
ROMEO A right good mark-man! and she's fair I love.
BENVOLIO A right fair mark, fair coz, is soonest hit.
ROMEO Well, in that hit you miss: she'll not be hit
        With Cupid's arrow, she hath Dian's wit;   200
        And in strong proof of chastity well armed,
        From Love's weak childish bow she lives uncharmed.
        She will not stay the siege of loving terms,
        Nor bide th'encounter of assailing eyes,
        Nor ope her lap to saint-seducing gold.   205
        O, she is rich in beauty, only poor

---

188 ROMEO Tut] But Q2 *(catchword)*, F3; Tut Q3 *(catchword)*   188 lost] Q2–4, F, Q1; left *Daniel (conj. Allen)*
190 who is that] Q2–4, F; whome she is Q1; who she is *Pope*; who 'tis *Singer²*; who is't that *Daniel*
191–2 Groan...who?] *As Hanmer; one line*, Q2–4, F; Why no, but sadly tell me who. Q1   191 Groan?]F3; Grone, Q2–4, F
193 Bid... make] Q4, Q1; A sicke man in sadnesse makes Q2–3, F; A sicke man in good sadnesse makes F2
194 A] Q2–4, F; Ah Q1, *Malone;* O, F2   197 mark-man] Q4, Q1; mark man Q2–3, F; marks-man F3   199 Well,] Q4;
Well Q2–3, F; But Q1, *Pope*   202 uncharmed] Q2–4, F; vnharm'd Q1, *Pope*   204 bide] Q2–4; bid F; Q1 *omits 204*
204 eyes,] Q5; eies. Q2–4, F; Q1 *omits 204*   205 ope] Q2–4, Q1; open F   205 saint-seducing] Q3, F; sainct seducing
Q2, Q4; Saint seducing Q1   206 rich in beauty,] Q3–4, F, Q1; rich, in bewtie Q2

---

187 **And if** If.
190 **sadness** seriousness (without witty sparring); compare 'sadly' (192). Romeo, however, continues to play with words: 'groan' (191), 'sick man' and 'sadness' (= sorrow, 193; = sorrow and seriousness, 195).
193 ***Bid...*make his will.** See supplementary note.
197 **mark-man** marksman (variant form), with bawdy quibble on 'fair mark...soonest hit' (198). See Partridge, under 'hit' and 'mark'; compare *LLL* 4.1.118–28.
199 **hit you miss** i.e. your aim (or guess) is wide of the mark.
200 **Dian's wit** Diana's wisdom (in eschewing love). Diana was the goddess of chastity.
201 **strong   proof** impenetrable   armour ('strong' is redundant).
202 **From...uncharmed** 'Uncharmed from' = exempt from the spell of (Kermode). Q1

'vnharm'd', an easier reading, has been adopted by most eds.
203 **stay...of** undergo the threat of capture posed by. To 'lay siege' to a lady, as to a castle or fort, was a common medieval and Renaissance metaphor (compare *AWW* 3.7.18; *Venus and Adonis* 423–4) – love as war (compare Brooke (897–900)).
205 **ope...gold** A reference to Danaë, who was seduced by Jove in the form of a golden shower. See supplementary note.
206–7, 209–11 These lines turn on the theme of the sterility of chastity ('huge waste' (209)), which kills the future ('posterity' (211)) and thus robs both men and women of immortality in their children, a theme that underlies Shakespeare's *Sonnets* 1–14 (see particularly Sonnets 1, 3, 4, 11, 14). Gibbons also compares Daniel's *Complaint of Rosamond* (239–52).

That when she dies, with beauty dies her store.

BENVOLIO Then she hath sworn that she will still live chaste? Nun?

ROMEO She hath, and in that sparing makes huge waste;

    For beauty starved with her severity   210

    Cuts beauty off from all posterity.

    She is too fair, too wise, wisely too fair,

    To merit bliss by making me despair.

    She hath forsworn to love, and in that vow

    Do I live dead, that live to tell it now.   215

BENVOLIO Be ruled by me, forget to think of her.

ROMEO O teach me how I should forget to think.

BENVOLIO By giving liberty unto thine eyes,

    Examine other beauties.

ROMEO   'Tis the way

    To call hers (exquisite) in question more: 220

    These happy masks that kiss fair ladies' brows,

    Being black, puts us in mind they hide the fair;

    He that is strucken blind cannot forget

    The precious treasure of his eyesight lost;

    Show me a mistress that is passing fair,   225

    What doth her beauty serve but as a note

    Where I may read who passed that passing fair?

---

207 beauty dies her] Q2–4, F, Q1; her dies Beauty's *Theobald*; her dies beauty *Keightley*   **208–29**] *not in* Q1
209 makes] Q4; make Q2–3, F   **212** wise, wisely too] Q2–4; wisewi:sely too F; wise; too wisely *Hanmer*
219–20 'Tis...more:] *As Pope; one line,* Q2–4, F   **223** strucken] Q5; strooken Q2–4, F *(variant form)*   **227** fair?]
Q5; faire: Q2–4; faire. F

207 when...store Dowden compares *Sonnets* 11.9–10 ('Let those whom nature hath not made for store, / Harsh, featureless, and rude, barrenly perish') and *Sonnets* 14.11–12 ('As truth and beauty shall together thrive / If from thyself to store thou wouldst convert') and explains: 'Rosaline is the possessor of beauty and also beauty's store, i.e. the reserve [or stock] of beauty (in posterity) or the propagating power of beauty. If Rosaline dies wedded, beauty indeed dies; but if she dies single beauty dies and also beauty's store.' Also compare *Sonnets* 4.13–14: 'Thy unus'd beauty must be tomb'd with thee, / Which used lives th'executor to be', and 209–11 below.

208 still always.

209 makes huge waste Compare *Sonnets* 1.11–12: 'Within thine own bud buriest thy content, / And, tender chorl, mak'st waste in niggarding'; and 142–4 above.

210 starved killed.

212–13 She...despair i.e. it is improper that her excess of beauty ('fair') and wisdom, a beauty

she hoards with too much prudence ('wisely too fair'), should earn heaven for her while driving me to despair (therefore to damnation). See supplementary note.

220 hers...more her beauty (being exquisite) into more heightened consideration ('question') by comparison. NS compares Brooke (1767–8, describing Romeo in exile).

221–2 These...fair The black masks that are happy in touching ('kiss') the brows of beautiful women by their contrast (i.e. being black) only serve to remind us of the fairness that they cover. 'These' is used generically; 'puts', a northern third per. pl. (Abbott 332). Compare *MM* 2.4.79–81: 'as these black masks / Proclaim an enshield beauty ten times louder / Than beauty could, display'd'.

223 strucken struck (Abbott 344).

225 a mistress i.e. any lady-love (other than Romeo's). 'who' (227) = Romeo's mistress.

225 passing surpassingly; 'passed' (227) = surpassed.

226 note explanatory marginal gloss.

Farewell, thou canst not teach me to forget.
BENVOLIO I'll pay that doctrine, or else die in debt.

Exeunt

[1.2] *Enter* CAPULET, COUNTY PARIS, *and the Clown* [SERVANT *to Capulet*].

CAPULET But Montague is bound as well as I,
     In penalty alike, and 'tis not hard, I think,
     For men so old as we to keep the peace.
PARIS Of honourable reckoning are you both,
     And pity 'tis, you lived at odds so long.   5
     But now, my lord, what say you to my suit?
CAPULET But saying o'er what I have said before:
     My child is yet a stranger in the world,   *innocent + ignorant*
     She hath not seen the change of fourteen years;
     Let two more summers wither in their pride,   10
     Ere we may think her ripe to be a bride.
PARIS Younger than she are happy mothers made.
CAPULET And too soon marred are those so early made.
     Earth hath swallowed all my hopes but she;
     She's the hopeful lady of my earth.   15
     But woo her, gentle Paris, get her heart,
     My will to her consent is but a part;

Act 1, Scene 2   1.2] *Capell; no scene division*, Q2–4, F, Q1   Location] *Capell*   0 SD SERVANT *to Capulet*] *NS ; Enter Countie* Paris, *old* Capulet. Q1   1–3] *not in* Q1   13 made] Q2–4, F; maried Q1, *Ulrici*   14–15] *not in* Q1   14 Earth] Q2–3, F; The earth Q4; Earth up F2   14 swallowed] Q5 (swallow'd); swallowed Q2–4, F   15 She's] Q2–3, F; She is Q4, F2   15 earth] Q2–4, F; fee *Keightley*

229 I'll...debt I'll take responsibility for teaching you that lesson ('doctrine') or pay forfeit (literally, die your debtor).

Act 1, Scene 2
  Location Verona. A street.
  0 SD COUNTY Count.
  1 bound legally obligated (to keep the peace).
  4 reckoning reputation.
  6 my suit Paris does not figure as a suitor in Brooke until after Romeus and Juliet are secretly married and Tybalt has been killed.
  9 not...years i.e. not yet fourteen years old ('change' = passage). Brooke (1860) says 'Scarce saw she yet full xvi. yeres: too yong to be a bryde'; Painter (p. 121), following Boaistuau, says 'she is

not attayned to the age of .xviii. yeares'. See supplementary note.

13 marred...made A common proverbial jingle, with play on 'married' and, perhaps, 'maid'. See Tilley M701 and Puttenham, *Arte of English Poesie* (1589; ed. Willcock and Walker, p. 207): 'The maide that soone married is, soone marred is.' Compare 2.4.95–6.

15 hopeful...earth A disputed passage; perhaps the most satisfactory gloss is: (she is) the only remaining hope of my life in this world (= 'earth'), my other children being dead, 'swallowed' by the grave (= 'Earth' in 14). See supplementary note.

17 to Either 'in proportion to' (Steevens), or 'if' (Delius).

And she agreed, within her scope of choice
Lies my consent and fair according voice.
This night I hold an old accustomed feast,   20
Whereto I have invited many a guest,
Such as I love, and you among the store,
One more, most welcome, makes my number more.
At my poor house look to behold this night
Earth-treading stars that make dark heaven light.   25
Such comfort as do lusty young men feel
When well-apparelled April on the heel
Of limping winter treads, even such delight
Among fresh fennel buds shall you this night
Inherit at my house; hear all, all see;   30
And like her most whose merit most shall be;
Which on more view of many, mine, being one,
May stand in number, though in reck'ning none.
Come go with me. [*To Servant*] Go, sirrah, trudge about
Through fair Verona, find those persons out   35
Whose names are written there [*Gives a paper.*], and to
    them say,

18–19] *not in* Q1   18 agreed] Q2; agree Q3–4, F   21 guest,] Q3–4, F, Q1; guest: Q2   23 welcome,] *Theobald (after Pope)*; welcome Q2–3, F, Q1; welcome) Q4   26 young men] Q2–4, F; youngmen Q1, *Daniel*; yeomen *conj. Johnson*   28 limping] Q2–4, F; lumping Q1, *Daniel*   29 fennel] Q2–4, F; female Q1, F2   32 Which...view] Q4; Which one more view, Q2–3, F; Such amongst view Q1, *Steevens*; On which more view *Capell*; Whilst on more view *conj. Mason*   32 mine,] *Theobald*; mine Q2–4, F, Q1   33] *Following this line*, Q1 *inserts* SD: *Enter Seruingman*.   34 SD] *Staunton (after Capell)*; *no* SD, Q2–4, F, Q1   36 SD] *Malone (after Capell)*; *no* SD, Q2–4, F, Q1

18 **And she agreed** And once she has consented. Q3 reads 'And she agree' (= if she consent) and is followed, unnecessarily, by most eds.

18–19 **within...voice** i.e. my consent and happily ('fair') assenting vote ('voice') will always be granted to whoever falls into her range ('scope') of choice – a tortured and tautologous way of saying 'I will accept whomever she chooses'; a similar vice affects 20–3 and 31–3.

20 **old accustomed feast** i.e. a feast held regularly for years past. Compare 'ancient feast' (82). In Brooke, it is the 'wonted use of banquets' at Christmas (155–8). Compare 'celebrate the feast...according to the ancient accustomed manner' in Montemayor's *Diana*, p.33.

25 **Earth-treading** i.e. mortal.

26–8 Compare *Sonnets* 98.2–3: 'When proud-pied April (dress'd in all his trim) / Hath put a spirit of youth in every thing'.

29 **fennel** Fragrant yellow-flowered plant, believed to cleanse the stomach and preserve and clear the sight (Sir John Harington, *Schoole of Salerne*

(1607; ed. F. H. Garrison, p. 105)). Most eds. prefer Q1 'female', perhaps rightly, but Durham notes that fennel was supposed to awaken passion, was thrown in the path of brides, and was especially associated with newly married couples; compare Drayton, *Poly-Olbion* (1613), Song xv, 191–8: 'Some others were again as seriously employ'd / In strewing of those herbs, at Bridalls us'd that be; / ...Strong Tansey, Fennell coole, they prodigally waste'.

30 **Inherit** Possess.

32–3 **Which...none** A passage for which no entirely satisfactory explanation has been offered. It seems to mean: Which being the case (referring to 31), on a more extensive view of the many other beauties there present, my daughter may indeed figure as one among the total ('stand in number'), though in the final calculation she may turn out to count for nothing ('one' being no number; compare *Sonnets* 136.7–8 and Tilley O52). See supplementary note.

34 **sirrah** Form of address to an inferior.

My house and welcome on their pleasure stay.

Exit [with Paris]

SERVANT Find them out whose names are written here! It is written
that the shoemaker should meddle with his yard and the tailor with
his last, the fisher with his pencil and the painter with his nets;   40
but I am sent to find those persons whose names are here writ, and
can never find what names the writing person hath here writ. I must
to the learnèd. In good time!

Enter BENVOLIO *and* ROMEO.

BENVOLIO Tut, man, one fire burns out another's burning,
One pain is lessened by another's anguish;   45
Turn giddy, and be holp by backward turning;
One desperate grief cures with another's languish:
Take thou some new infection to thy eye,
And the rank poison of the old will die.

ROMEO Your plantain leaf is excellent for that.   50

BENVOLIO For what, I pray thee?

ROMEO   For your broken shin.

BENVOLIO Why, Romeo, art thou mad?

ROMEO Not mad, but bound more than a madman is:
Shut up in prison, kept without my food,
Whipt and tormented, and – God-den, good fellow.   55

---

37 SD *with Paris*] *Rowe (subst.)*; *Exeunt*. Q1   38 written here!] Q1 (written here,); written. Here Q2–4, F   41 here writ]
Q2–3; heee writ Q4; writ F   42–3 writ. I…learnèd. In] *Pope (subst.)*; writ (I…learned) in Q2–4, F; Q1 *omits in good
time*   44 out another's] Q3–4, F, Q1; out, an others Q2   45 One] Q3–4, F, Q1; On Q2   45 by] Q2–4, F; with Q1
46 giddy…by] Q2–4, F; backward…with Q1   48 thy] Q2, Q1; the Q3–4, F   50–1.3.35] *These lines in Q2 were set
from an essentially uncorrected copy of Q1, which for these lines, therefore, becomes the copy-text; all substantive and semi-
substantive variants between Q1 and Q2 are recorded for these lines*   51 I pray thee] Q2–4, F; *not in* Q1   53 madman]
Warburton; mad man Q1–4, F   55 and –] *Rowe*; and Q1–4, F

37 on…stay wait on their will (to attend).

38–40 Typically the 'Clown' associates each
attribute with the wrong individual, complaining
that he is being asked to 'meddle' with something
(writing and reading) that is not his proper business.
See supplementary note.

39 yard measuring-rod (with play on 'yard' =
penis). Similar play on 'pencil' (40); compare
Shirley, *The Ball* 3.3.38, on English painters: 'They
ha' not active pencils.'

44–9 A string of moral 'sentences' on the
common theme that one grief or pain drives out
another grief or pain. Compare Brooke (206–8) and
see Tilley F277 (*TGV* 2.4.192; *Cor.* 4.7.54), G446
(*Lear* 3.4.8–9), P457 ('one poison expels another';
compare Brooke (219): 'loves sweete empoysonde
baite').

45 another's anguish the pain of another pain.
Compare 'another's languish' (= suffering) in 47.

46 holp helped. See Abbott 343.

46 backward turning turning in the reverse
direction.

50 plantain leaf Plantain leaves were used as
poultices for something minor like a 'broken'
(= skinned) shin (see 51). Romeo is sarcastically
referring to the stream of proverbial wisdom
Benvolio has just let loose as no better than
employing a mere poultice when a desperate remedy
is needed.

53–5 bound…tormented Romeo is speaking
of the pains and deprivations of the rejected lover,
but the terms actually describe the treatment used
to cure madness in Shakespeare's time. Compare
AYLI 3.2.400–2 and aspects of the treatment of
Malvolio in *TN* 3.4 and 4.2.

55 God-den Good evening. (Used loosely for
any time between noon and night.)

SERVANT God gi' god-den. I pray, sir, can you read?

ROMEO Ay, mine own fortune in my misery.

SERVANT Perhaps you have learned it without book; but I pray, can
    you read any thing you see?

ROMEO Ay, if I know the letters and the language.   60

SERVANT Ye say honestly, rest you merry.

ROMEO Stay, fellow, I can read.

He reads the letter.

'Signior Martino and his wife and daughters,
County Anselme and his beauteous sisters,
The lady widow of Vitruvio,   65
Signior Placentio and his lovely nieces,
Mercutio and his brother Valentine,
Mine uncle Capulet, his wife and daughters,
My fair niece Rosaline, and Livia,
Signior Valentio and his cousin Tybalt,   70
Lucio and the lively Helena.'

A fair assembly: whither should they come?

SERVANT Up.

ROMEO Whither? to supper?

SERVANT To our house.   75

ROMEO Whose house?

SERVANT My master's.

ROMEO Indeed I should have asked thee that before.

SERVANT Now I'll tell you without asking. My master is the great rich
    Capulet, and if you be not of the house of Montagues, I pray come   80
    and crush a cup of wine. Rest you merry.   *[Exit]*

chance

56 God gi' god-den] *Dyce;* Godgigoden Q1–4, F   58–9] *As prose,* Q1, *Pope¹; as verse, ending* booke / ...see Q2–4, F
58 learned] F (learn'd); learned Q1–4   63–71] *As verse, Dyce (conj. Capell); as prose,* Q1–4, F *(in italics, except for proper
names)*   63, 66, 70 Signior] *Rowe;* Seigneur Q1–4, F   63 daughters] Q1–4; *daughter* F   64 Anselme] Q1–4, F; *Anselm*
F3; Anselmo *Dyce² (conj. Capell)*   65 Vitruvio] F3; Vtruuio Q1–4, F; Utruvio Q5   68 Capulet,] F3; Capulet Q1–4, F
69 and Livia] Q1; *Liuia* Q2–4, F   71 lively] Q1–4, F; lovely *Rowe*   74–5 Whither? to supper? SERVANT To] F;
Whether to supper? *Ser:* To Q1; Whither to supper? *Ser.* To Q2; Whither to supper. *Ser?* To Q3; Whither to supper.
Ser. To Q4; Whither? *Ser.* To Supper, to *Theobald (from conj. Warburton);* Whither? / *Ser.* To *Capell*   78 thee] Q1;
you Q2–4, F   81 SD] F; *not in* Q1–4

56 **God gi' god-den** God give ye good even.
58 **without book** by heart (rote learning by ear).
61 **rest you merry** (God) give you happiness (a
form of salutation most commonly used, as again at
81, at parting).
62 SD *letter* Not, of course, strictly a letter;
Brooke (162) calls it a 'paper'.
64 **Anselme** Probably trisyllabic. Anselme is the
name of Friar John in Painter (p. 132).

65 *****Vitruvio** See supplementary note.
68 **uncle Capulet** Probably to be identified with
'Cousin Capulet' in 1.5.29; 'cousin' was used
loosely to describe any family relationship save that
between parents and children.
74–5 See collation for the various arrangements
of these lines.
78 **thee** See supplementary note.
81 **crush** drink.

BENVOLIO At this same ancient feast of Capulet's
   Sups the fair Rosaline whom thou so loves,
   With all the admirèd beauties of Verona:
   Go thither, and with unattainted eye   85
   Compare her face with some that I shall show,
   And I will make thee think thy swan a crow.
ROMEO When the devout religion of mine eye
   Maintains such falsehood, then turn tears to fires;
   And these who, often drowned, could never die,   90
   Transparent heretics, be burnt for liars.
   One fairer than my love! the all-seeing sun
   Ne'er saw her match since first the world begun.
BENVOLIO Tut, you saw her fair, none else being by,
   Herself poised with herself in either eye;   95
   But in that crystal scales let there be weighed
   Your lady's love against some other maid
   That I will show you shining at this feast,
   And she shall scant show well that now seems best.
ROMEO I'll go along no such sight to be shown,   100
   But to rejoice in splendour of mine own.

                [Exeunt]

83 loves,] *Neilson (after Collier)*; loues: Q1–4, F; lovest: F2 84 Verona:] *Rowe*; *Verona,* Q1–4, F 89 fires] *Pope*; fire Q1, Q3–4, F; fier Q2 92 love!] F2; loue, Q1–2; loue? Q3–4; loue: F 92 all-seeing] F; all seeing Q1–4, F; Tut Tut F2 96 that] Q1–4, F; those *Rowe* 97 lady's love] Q1–4, F; Lady-love *Theobald*; lady love *Capell* 97 maid] Q1, F; maide: Q2; maid, Q3–4 99 she...well] Q1–4; she shew scant shell, well, F *(some copies)*; she shall scant shell, well, F *(some copies)*; shele shew scant, well, F2 99 seems] Q1–2; shewes Q3–4, F 101 SD] *Pope*; *no* SD, Q1–4, F

83 **Rosaline** Although Rosaline is mentioned in the list of guests (69), we do not learn the name of Romeo's 'unkind' mistress until now; she is unnamed in Brooke.

83 **loves** loveth (syncopated form of second per. sing., present tense; see Franz 152).

85 **unattainted** unprejudiced.

88 **devout religion** zealous fidelity (to a principle).

89 **Maintains** Supports, upholds.

89 ***fires** Pope's emendation of Q1–4, F 'fire' may be justified by the rhyme with 'liars' (91) and by Shakespeare's tendency to use the plural to signify penitential fires (compare *Ham.* 1.5.11; *Cor.* 3.3.68), to which 91 clearly refers.

90 **these...die** i.e. these eyes that survived death though repeatedly drowned (in tears).

91 **Transparent** Manifest (with play on 'clear'; compare 'crystal scales' (eyes) in 96); 'heretics' (= renegades) and 'burnt' carry on the religious imagery initiated in 88.

93 **begun** Alternative form of past tense (began) from the old plural 'begun' (*OED*).

95 **poised** weighed, balanced.

97 **lady's love** i.e. either 'all the aspects of love you fondly associate with Rosaline', or 'the small amount of love borne you by Rosaline' (Cowden Clarke). Theobald's emendation 'Lady-love' normalises the construction with 'maid', but 'some other' may be read as elliptical for 'that of some other'.

101 **mine own** i.e. the expected sight of his own Rosaline.

[**1.3**] *Enter* CAPULET'S WIFE *and* NURSE.

LADY CAPULET Nurse, where's my daughter? call her forth to me.
NURSE Now by my maidenhead at twelve year old,
    I bade her come. What, lamb! What, ladybird!
    God forbid, where's this girl? What, Juliet!

                Enter JULIET.

JULIET How now, who calls?   5
NURSE Your mother.
JULIET Madam, I am here, what is your will?
LADY CAPULET This is the matter. Nurse, give leave a while,
    We must talk in secret. Nurse, come back again,
    I have remembered me, thou s' hear our counsel.   10
    Thou knowest my daughter's of a pretty age.
NURSE Faith, I can tell her age unto an hour.
LADY CAPULET She's not fourteen.
NURSE   I'll lay fourteen of my teeth –
    And yet to my teen be it spoken, I have but four –
    She's not fourteen. How long is it now   15
    To Lammas-tide?
LADY CAPULET   A fortnight and odd days.
NURSE Even or odd, of all days in the year,
    Come Lammas-eve at night shall she be fourteen.

Act 1, Scene 3   1.3] *Capell; no scene division,* Q1–4, F   Location] *Rowe*   1 SH LADY CAPULET] *Rowe; Wife:* Q1–4, F
(through 16, except / *W:* / *at 8,* Q1*)*   2–4] *As verse, Johnson; as prose,* Q1–4, F *(the Nurse's lines, through 79, in italics,*
except for proper names, in Q1–4*)*   2 maidenhead...old] *Pope (subst.); maiden head...old* Q1; *maidenhead,...old* Q2–4, F
8–11] *As verse, Capell; as prose,* Q1–4, F   10 thou s'] *Riverside (after Rowe); thou'se* Q1–4, F   13–49] *As verse,*
Capell (15–16 as arranged Steevens); as prose, Q1–4; *as prose,* F, *except 13–16 (Ile...tide?), arranged as irregular verse,*
ending teeth / ...spoken / ...fourteene / ...tide   12 an] Q2–4, F; *a* Q1   14 teen] Q1–4, F; teeth F2   18 shall] Q1,
Q3–4, F; *stal* Q2

Act 1, Scene 3
  Location Verona. Capulet's house. This scene,
in which Juliet learns of the proposed marriage to
Paris, is Shakespeare's invention, but the Nurse's
rambling account of Juliet's childhood was suggested
by 'a tedious long discoorse' in Brooke (651–60)
forced on Romeo by the Nurse at their later
encounter dramatised by Shakespeare in 2.4.
  2 maidenhead virginity. A vulgar oath suitable
to the Nurse; compare *Wily Beguiled* (anon.,
c. 1602; MSR, 1417, 1915–16). The reference to
'twelve year old' implies that she had lost it then.
On the bibliographical problems relating to the
Nurse's lines 2–77, see the Textual Analysis, p. 223
below.

3 What A common exclamation of impatience.
  4 God forbid i.e. either 'God forbid that any ill
may have prevented her coming', or an expression
of apology for just calling Juliet 'ladybird', which
meant not only 'sweetheart' but 'prostitute'
(slang). Compare 4.5.7.
  8 give leave leave us.
  10 thou s' thou shalt.
  11 pretty age i.e. an age at which marriage may
properly be considered.
  14 teen grief (with play on 'four', looking back
to 'fourteen' in 13).
  16 Lammas-tide 1 August. 'Lammas' =
Anglo-Saxon 'hlāfmaesse', the day of first fruits;
'tide' = time. 'Lammas-eve' (in 22) = 31 July.

Susan and she – God rest all Christian souls! –
Were of an age. Well, Susan is with God,   20
She was too good for me. But as I said,
On Lammas-eve at night shall she be fourteen,
That shall she, marry, I remember it well.
'Tis since the earthquake now aleven years,
And she was weaned – I never shall forget it –   25
Of all the days of the year, upon that day;
For I had then laid wormwood to my dug,
Sitting in the sun under the dove-house wall.
My lord and you were then at Mantua –
Nay, I do bear a brain – but as I said,   30
When it did taste the wormwood on the nipple
Of my dug, and felt it bitter, pretty fool,
To see it tetchy and fall out wi'th'dug!
'Shake!' quoth the dove-house; 'twas no need, I trow,
To bid me trudge.   35
And since that time it is aleven years,
For then she could stand high-lone; nay, by th'rood,
She could have run and waddled all about;
For even the day before, she broke her brow,
And then my husband – God be with his soul,   40
'A was a merry man – took up the child.
'Yea', quoth he, 'dost thou fall upon thy face?
Thou wilt fall backward when thou hast more wit,

23 she,] F4; *shee* Q1–4, F   24 aleven] *Riverside*; *e-/leauen* Q1 *(compare 36 below)*; *eleuen* Q2–4, F   25 weaned –…it –] *Capell; weand…it,* Q1–4, F   33 tetchy] *Malone; teachie* Q1–4, F *(variant form)*   33 wi'th'] *Riverside; with* Q1; *with the* Q2–4, F   36 aleven] *Riverside; a leauen* Q1; *a leuen* Q2–4; *a eleuen* F   36 years] Q2–4, F; *yeare* Q1   37 she could] Q2–4, F; *could* Iuliet Q1   37 high-lone] Q1 *(hyphen, Cam.); hylone* Q2; *a lone* Q3; *alone* Q4, F   37 by th'] *Rowe; byth* Q2; *bi'th* Q3–4; *bi'th'* F; *by the* Q1   38 run…about] Q2–4, F; *wadled vp and downe* Q1   39 before,] *Steevens; before* Q2–4, F, Q1   39 broke] Q2–4, F; *brake* Q1   41 'A] Q2–4, F; *hee* Q1   41–2 took…face?] Q2–4, F; *Dost thou fall forward* Iuliet? Q1   42 dost] Q1; *doest* Q2–4, F

24 **earthquake…years** See above, p. 2.
24 **aleven** eleven (variant form found in several texts (*Ham.* Q2, *MV* Q1, *LLL* Q1) most probably set from Shakespeare's autograph, as well as in the scene in *STM* believed by most to be in Shakespeare's hand). See collation.
27 **laid…dug** rubbed wormwood (a plant proverbial for its bitter taste) on my nipple. This causes the milk to taste so bitter that a baby will give up breast-feeding and be 'weaned' (25); compare 31–3. See supplementary note.
30 **bear a brain** have a good memory.
32 **fool** Used as a term of endearment; compare

Lear 5.3.306: 'my poor fool [Cordelia] is hang'd'; and 'wretch' in 45.
34 **'Shake!'** Look lively, move! (Compare the modern 'shake a leg'.) The 'dove-house', personified, expresses itself by shaking.
34 **trow** think (expressing annoyance).
35 **trudge** be off.
37 **high-lone** all by herself.
37 **rood** (Christ's) cross.
39 **broke her brow** cut or bruised her forehead (from a fall).
41 **'A** He.
43 **fall backward** With play on 'invite to sexual intercourse'.

Wilt thou not, Jule?' And by my holidam,
The pretty wretch left crying, and said 'Ay'.   45
To see now how a jest shall come about!
I warrant, and I should live a thousand years,
I never should forget it: 'Wilt thou not, Jule?' quoth he,
And, pretty fool, it stinted, and said 'Ay'.

LADY CAPULET Enough of this, I pray thee hold thy peace.   50
NURSE Yes, madam, yet I cannot choose but laugh,
To think it should leave crying, and say 'Ay':
And yet I warrant it had upon it brow
A bump as big as a young cock'rel's stone,
A perilous knock, and it cried bitterly.   55
'Yea', quoth my husband, 'fall'st upon thy face?
Thou wilt fall backward when thou comest to age,
Wilt thou not, Jule?' It stinted, and said 'Ay'.

JULIET And stint thou too, I pray thee, Nurse, say I.
NURSE Peace, I have done. God mark thee to his grace,   60
Thou wast the prettiest babe that e'er I nursed.
And I might live to see thee married once,
I have my wish.

LADY CAPULET Marry, that 'marry' is the very theme
I came to talk of. Tell me, daughter Juliet,   65
How stands your dispositions to be married?

JULIET It is an honour that I dream not of.

44 Jule] Q2–4, F; Iuliet Q1 44 holidam] Q1 (*holli-/dam*); *holydam* Q2–3; *holy dam* Q4; holy-dam F 45 wretch] Q2–4, F; *foole* Q1 46 now how] Q2–4, F; *how* Q1 47 and I…years] Q2–4, F; *you if I should liue a hundred yeare* Q1 48 Jule] Q2–4; *Iulet* F (*Juliet* F4); Iuliet Q1 48–9 quoth…said] Q2–4, F; *and by my troth she stinted and cried* Q1 50 SH LADY CAPULET] *Rowe*; *Old La.* Q2–4, F (*through 94*); Q1 *continues* / *Wife:* / *throughout the scene, though this speech is omitted* 50–8] *not in* Q1 51–8] *As verse, Capell; as prose,* Q2–4, F 60–3] *As verse, Pope; as prose,* Q2–4, F, Q1 64 Marry…very] Q2–4, F; *And that same marriage Nurce, is the* Q1, *Pope (omitting* Nurce *and retaining* very) 66 stands your dispositions] Q2–4; stands your disposition F; *stand you affected* Q1 67 honour] Q1; houre Q2–4, F

44 **holidam** Properly 'halidam' (from Anglo-Saxon hāligdōm = holiness), but here, erroneously, as often, with the sense 'holy dame' (i.e. the Virgin Mary).

46 **To…about** i.e. just look how something spoken in jest may become reality (referring to Juliet's projected married state).

49 **stinted** stopped (crying).

53 **it brow** its brow. At this period 'it' was the common form of the possessive, the only form used, for example, in the King James Bible (1611); Shakespeare's use of 'its', except for a single case in 2H6, a play not printed until 1623, occurs only

after 1600, when this 'new factitious genitive' (*OED*) first began to appear, and then only in plays printed from scribal transcripts by Ralph Crane or in collaborations (*H8* and *TNK*). See Abbott 228 and Brooke (654).

54 **young cock'rel's stone** young cock's testicle ('young' is redundant; 'cock'rel' = a young cock).

61 **prettiest babe** Compare Brooke (653–4).

66 **dispositions** inclination, feelings. A plural subject following a singular verb is common in Shakespeare (see Abbott 335 and *OED* Disposition 7).

67, 68 *honour See supplementary note.

NURSE An honour! were not I thine only nurse,
    I would say thou hadst sucked wisdom from thy teat.

LADY CAPULET Well, think of marriage now; younger than you,   70
    Here in Verona, ladies of esteem,
    Are made already mothers. By my count,
    I was your mother much upon these years
    That you are now a maid. Thus then in brief:
    The valiant Paris seeks you for his love.   75

NURSE A man, young lady! lady, such a man
    As all the world – Why, he's a man of wax.

LADY CAPULET Verona's summer hath not such a flower.

NURSE Nay, he's a flower, in faith, a very flower.

LADY CAPULET What say you, can you love the gentleman?   80
    This night you shall behold him at our feast;
    Read o'er the volume of young Paris' face,
    And find delight writ there with beauty's pen;
    Examine every married lineament,
    And see how one another lends content;   85
    And what obscured in this fair volume lies
    Find written in the margent of his eyes.
    This precious book of love, this unbound lover,
    To beautify him, only lacks a cover.
    The fish lives in the sea, and 'tis much pride   90

68–9] *As verse, Pope; as prose,* Q2–4, F, Q1   68 honour!] Q1 ; *houre,* Q2–4, F   70–5] Q2–4, F ; Well girle, the Noble Countie *Paris* seekes thee for his Wife. Q1   72 mothers. By] F ; mothers by Q2–4   72 count,] Q4 ; count. Q2–3 ; count F   76–7] *As verse, Pope; as prose,* Q2–4, F, Q1   76 lady!] *Capell;* Lady,. Q2–4, F, Q1   77 world –] F4 ; *world.* Q2–4, F ; *world,* Q1   80–96] *not in* Q1   84 married] Q2 ; seuerall Q3–4, F

68–9 were…teat Mock modesty from the Nurse. 'thy teat' = the teat (mine) that suckled you.

73 much…years at about the same age.

77 man of wax a man formed of all perfections (like an ideal wax figure). NS sees irony here ('Paris is never anything more'), a debatable slur on a character who acts sincerely and honourably.

81 This…feast Curiously, after all this preparation, Paris does not appear at the 'feast' in 1.5.

82–95 The precious and nonsensical praise of Paris (omitted in Q1) is an extended conceit describing him in terms of a book – unbound (unmarried) and bound (married), for which Shakespeare found a hint of this in Brooke (1893–6) and improved on it with unhappy results. Compare 3.2.83–4 and *John* 2.1.432–40, 484–5.

83 find delight find there promise of future happiness.

84 married harmoniously blended.

85 one…content each part bestows satisfaction

and pleasure (with play on 'substance' = the contents of the volume (82)) on each other part.

87 margent margin. The margins of early books and MSS. often contained glosses and commentary explaining the text; compare *Ham.* 5.2.155–6 and *Lucrece* 102. Thus 'his eyes' (eyes were known as the windows of the soul) serve to reveal his inner qualities.

88 book of love Paris is likened to a kind of Ovidian *Ars Amatoria*, which 'unbound' (as a lover) only fulfils itself when 'bound' (as a husband). Mason suggests that 'cover' (= binding) in 89 quibbles on law-French 'feme-couvert' (= a married woman).

90–1 The fish…hide No satisfactory explanation has been offered. Like the earlier part of the speech, these lines seem to turn on the neo-Platonic distinction between external beauty, the female principle ('fair without'), and internal beauty or virtue, the male principle ('fair within'). Perhaps they mean something like: as a fish can live only in

For fair without the fair within to hide;
That book in many's eyes doth share the glory
That in gold clasps locks in the golden story:
So shall you share all that he doth possess,
By having him, making yourself no less.   95
NURSE No less! nay, bigger women grow by men.
LADY CAPULET Speak briefly, can you like of Paris' love?
JULIET I'll look to like, if looking liking move;
But no more deep will I endart mine eye
Than your consent gives strength to make it fly.   100

Enter SERVINGMAN.

SERVINGMAN Madam, the guests are come, supper served up, you
called, my young lady asked for, the Nurse cursed in the pantry,
and every thing in extremity. I must hence to wait, I beseech you
follow straight.   [*Exit*]
LADY CAPULET We follow thee. Juliet, the County stays.   105
NURSE Go, girl, seek happy nights to happy days.

Exeunt

[1.4] *Enter* ROMEO, MERCUTIO, BENVOLIO, *with five or six other*
MASKERS, TORCH-BEARERS.

ROMEO What, shall this speech be spoke for our excuse?
Or shall we on without apology?

91 without] Q2; without, Q3–4, F   91 fair within] Q3–4, F; faire, within Q2   96 less!] *Rowe*; lesse, Q2, Q4, F; lesse Q3
96 bigger] Q2–4; bigger: F   99 endart] Q2–4, F; engage Q1, *Pope*   100 it fly] Q4, Q1; flie Q2–3, F
100 SD SERVINGMAN] F (*a Seruing man*); *Seruing.* Q2–4; *Clowne.* Q1 (*also as speech heading 101*)   104 SD] F; *no SD,*
Q2–4, Q1   105–6] *not in* Q1   105 SH LADY CAPULET] *Rowe; Mo.* Q2–4, F   Act 1, Scene 4   1.4] *Steevens; no scene
division,* Q2–4, F, Q1   Location] *Riverside (after Theobald, NS)*   0 SD] Q2–4, F; *Enter Maskers with* Romeo *and a Page.*
Q1   1 SH ROMEO] Q2–4, F, Q1; *Ben./conj. Capell*

the embracing sea, so the inwardly fair lover (Paris),
seeking the perfect condition of man ('pride'), must
achieve his outward realisation in the embracing
fairness of Juliet as his wife.
    92–3 That...story i.e. the binding (Juliet; with
play on 'clasps' = embraces) will share the honour
with the golden contents of the volume (Paris).
    96 No...men No, indeed, not smaller; women
grow larger (= swell in pregnancy) through men.
The F pointing ('No lesse, nay bigger: women grow
by men.'), usually adopted by eds., makes a sharper
contrast with 'less', but the Q2 pointing, though
admitting an awkward inversion, makes good sense.
    97 like of be pleased with.
    98 if...move (to see) if looking may conduce
to liking. Compare *John* 2.1.510–15.

99 endart shoot as a dart. Apparently a
Shakespearean coinage (see *OED*); the archery
metaphor is carried on in 100 with 'fly' (as an
arrow).
    104 straight immediately.
    105 stays waits.

Act 1, Scene 4
    Location Verona. Before Capulet's house.
    1 speech...excuse Masquers (= maskers)
often offered a prepared speech, spoken by their
'presenter' (or 'truchman'), the Cupid referred to
in 4, to explain the supposed reason (their 'excuse')
for the visit. Compare *Tim.* 1.2.116 ff. (where Cupid
is actually the 'presenter') and the masque of
Muscovites in *LLL* 5.2.158 ff.

BENVOLIO The date is out of such prolixity:
        We'll have no Cupid hoodwinked with a scarf,
        Bearing a Tartar's painted bow of lath,   5
        Scaring the ladies like a crow-keeper,
        Nor no without-book prologue, faintly spoke
        After the prompter, for our entrance;
        But let them measure us by what they will,
        We'll measure them a measure and be gone.   10
ROMEO Give me a torch, I am not for this ambling;
        Being but heavy, I will bear the light.
MERCUTIO Nay, gentle Romeo, we must have you dance.
ROMEO Not I, believe me. You have dancing shoes
        With nimble soles, I have a soul of lead   15
        So stakes me to the ground I cannot move.
MERCUTIO You are a lover, borrow Cupid's wings,
        And soar with them above a common bound.
ROMEO I am too sore enpiercèd with his shaft
        To soar with his light feathers, and so bound   20
        I cannot bound a pitch above dull woe:
        Under love's heavy burden do I sink.
MERCUTIO And to sink in it should you burden love,
        Too great oppression for a tender thing.

---

3 SH BENVOLIO] Q2–4, F, Q1; *Mer./conj. Capell*   4 hoodwinked] Q4 (hood-winckt); hudwinckt Q2, Q1; hud winckt Q3;
hood winckt F   7–8 Nor...entrance;] Q1, *Pope; not in* Q2–4, F   11 ambling;] F (ambling.); ambling, Q2–4, Q1
17–28] *not in* Q1   20 so bound] *Craig;* so bound, Q2–4; to bound: F; so bound. Q5, *Hoppe*   23 SH MERCUTIO] Q4;
Horatio. Q2–3; *Hora.* F

---

3 date...prolixity such tedious verbiage is
now out of fashion.

4 hoodwinked blindfolded. Compare 1.1.
162–3.

5 Tartar's...lath The Tartarean bow, derived
from the Greeks and Romans, was shaped like a
strongly marked upper lip (a 'Cupid's bow'), as
distinguished from the English bow shaped like the
segment of a circle. Cupid, from classical times, was
regularly pictured with a 'Tartar's bow'; 'painted
bow of lath' = counterfeit bow made of painted lath
(compare 1.1.202 and 'dagger of lath' associated
with the Vice figure in *TN* 4.2.124–30).

6 crow-keeper scarecrow (one, like a Cupid,
assigned to scare away crows with bow and arrows).

7 without-book (supposedly) memorised.
Compare Berowne's prompting of Moth in *LLL*
5.2.162, 168.

9 measure...will judge us by any standards
they may choose (with double play, in 10, on

'measure' = (1) traverse, tread, mete out; (2) a
stately dance.

11 torch As a torch-bearer, Romeo could not
join in the dancing.

12 heavy Referring to melancholy (the black
humour), with play on 'light'; compare 'soul of
lead' (15), the metal associated with the melancholy
humour.

18 common bound ordinary (1) limit, (2) leap
(in dancing), with further play on 'bound' = tied
up (like a captive) in 20.

19 enpiercèd empierced (variant form), pierced
through (only example with en- prefix in *OED*,
compare 'endart', 1.3.99).

21 pitch height (the upper limit of a falcon's
flight).

22 burden weight (of woes), with play on
'burden' = weigh down a woman in sexual
intercourse.

22 sink give way (as under a weight), with play
on 'sink' = penetrate sexually.

ROMEO Is love a tender thing? it is too rough,   25
     Too rude, too boist'rous, and it pricks like thorn.

MERCUTIO If love be rough with you, be rough with love:
     Prick love for pricking, and you beat love down.
     Give me a case to put my visage in, [*Puts on a mask.*]
     A visor for a visor! what care I   30
     What curious eye doth cote deformities?
     Here are the beetle brows shall blush for me.

BENVOLIO Come knock and enter, and no sooner in,
     But every man betake him to his legs.

ROMEO A torch for me: let wantons light of heart   35
     Tickle the senseless rushes with their heels;
     For I am proverbed with a grandsire phrase,
     I'll be a candle-holder and look on:
     The game was ne'er so fair, and I am done.

MERCUTIO Tut, dun's the mouse, the constable's own word.   40
     If thou art Dun, we'll draw thee from the mire,

---

27 love:] *Theobald (subst.)*; loue Q2–4; loue, F   29 SD] *Johnson (subst.)*; no SD, Q2–4, F, Q1   32–4] *not in* Q1 37 grandsire] F, Q1; graunsire Q2–4   39 done] F, Q1; dum Q2; dun Q3–4   41 Dun] Q1, F4; dun Q2–3, F; dnn Q4   41 mire,] *Daniel*; mire Q2–4, Q1; mire. F

---

28 Prick...down (1) Grieve love in return for wounding you and you will defeat it; (2) stimulate or goad love for the purpose of copulation and you will deflate it (*OED* Prick 2 and 10).

29 case mask.

30 A visor...visor i.e. a mask for an ugly face; compare *LLL* 5.2.387–8 and Tilley v92.

30–2 what...me (covered thus) why should I care what an inquisitive eye may note ('cote' = quote) as blemishes (in my face) since I have a mask to cover my embarrassment. 'beetle brows' = overhanging eyebrows.

34 betake...legs join in the dancing.

36 Tickle...rushes Tickle rushes which are without feeling (an impossibility, hence a waste of time suitable to 'wantons' (35)). Green rushes were still frequently strewn on floors as a form of covering (also apparently on the stage; compare Dekker, *The Guls Hornbook* (1609; ed. A. B. Grosart, II, 248): 'On the very Rushes where the Commedy is to daunce').

37 proverbed...phrase furnished (and thus supported) with a proverb by an ancient ('grandsire') saying.

38–9 I'll...done Two, not one, 'grandsire phrase(s)' have been thought to lie behind these lines: (1) 'a good candleholder proves a good gamester' (Tilley C51); (2) 'when play is at the best, it is time to leave' (Tilley P399; referred to again

at 1.5.118). But there are difficulties with the combination of these proverbs in this context and recently K. Bartenschlager (*Anglia* 100 (1982), 423–4) has proposed a single proverb ('He that worst may, must hold the candle', Tilley C40), according with Shakespeare's use of the singular 'phrase'. Romeo would thus seem to be saying, 'I'll assist you by bearing a torch and be an onlooker, but this game (of love) was never so appealing ('faire') anyway (particularly now after my experience with Rosaline)' – a nice irony in view of what follows.

40 dun's the mouse Proverbial (Tilley D644), usually with play on 'done' as here (39); exact meaning uncertain, but with implications of silence (Tilley M1224) and comparative invisibility (being dun- or mouse-coloured), hence a suitable watchword ('word') for a constable (so used in Dekker and Webster's *Westward Ho* (1607), 5.4.1–3). Mercutio is saying 'Don't be done (dun); such unsocial and drab behaviour is suitable only for a mouse.'

41 Dun...mire Proverbial (Tilley D643), meaning 'things are at a standstill' (literally, Dun (= a horse) is stuck in the mud) and continuing the play on 'done/dun'; also with reference to an old Christmas game where a log (representing Dun), supposedly stuck in the mud, was lustily extricated by the combined efforts of the players.

Or (save your reverence) love, wherein thou stickest
Up to the ears. Come, we burn daylight, ho!
ROMEO Nay, that's not so.
MERCUTIO   I mean, sir, in delay
We waste our lights in vain, like lights by day.   45
Take our good meaning, for our judgement sits
Five times in that ere once in our five wits.
ROMEO And we mean well in going to this mask,
But 'tis no wit to go.
MERCUTIO   Why, may one ask?
ROMEO I dreamt a dream tonight.
MERCUTIO   And so did I.   50
ROMEO Well, what was yours?
MERCUTIO   That dreamers often lie.
ROMEO In bed asleep, while they do dream things true.
MERCUTIO O then I see Queen Mab hath been with you:
She is the fairies' midwife, and she comes
In shape no bigger than an agate-stone   55

---

42 Or...reverence)] F *(pointing based on* F4, *Staunton)*; Or saue you reuerence Q2–4; Of this surreuerence Q1; O! save
your reverence, *conj. Johnson*; Of this (save reverence) *Collier*; Of this (sir-reverence)
Dyce[1]; Of this (save your reverence) *Craig*   44 in delay] Q2–3; in delay, Q4, Q1; I delay, F; in delay; *Capell*   45 waste...
like lights] *Johnson* (like *from* Q1 burne our lights by night, like Lampes); waste...lights lights Q2–4; wast...lights, lights,
F; waste...like lamps *Capell*; waste...light lights *Daniel (conj. Nicholson)*; waste...vain. Lights, lights *Hoppe*; waste...
light lamps *Munro (conj. Greg)*; waste our lights, in vaine light lights *Williams*   46 judgement] Q3, F, Q1; indgement
Q2; Iudgements Q4   47 five] *Malone (conj. Wilbraham)*; fine Q2–4, F; right Q1 *(reading* Three times a day, ere once
in her right wits.*)*   52 asleep,] *Capell (after Rowe)*; asleep Q2; a sleepe Q3–4, F, Q1   53] *Following this line,* Q1 *adds:*
Ben: Queene Mab whats she?, *continuing 54–91 to Benvolio; Keightley includes the* Q1 *line in his text*   54–91] *As verse,*
Pope (after the shorter verse version in Q1*); as prose,* Q2–4, F   54 fairies'] *Steevens*; Fairies Q2–4, F, Q1; Fancy's *Theobald*
(conj. Warburton)   55 an] Q2–4, Q1; *not in* F

---

42 Or...love Or, with apology, love (with play
on 'sir-reverence' = dung, *OED* sv 2, the reading
of Q1). Compare J. Cooke, *Greenes Tuquoque* (1614;
sig. H4): 'You (as the common trick is) straight
suppose, / Tis Love, (sirreverence, which makes the
word more beastly.)'.
43 burn daylight waste time (Tilley D123).
Romeo (44) takes 'daylight' literally and quibbles
that this isn't true since it is already dark.
45 *like lights See collation.
46–7 Take...wits The sense seems to be:
Accept our true meaning, for true meaning derives
from the reason ('judgement'), which is five times
as trustworthy as the interpretation which meaning
receives through the five senses ('wits'). Despite
Mercutio's plea, Romeo continues to quibble on
'mean well' (= have good intentions) and 'wit'
(= wisdom) in 48–9. See supplementary note on
'five wits'.
50 I dreamt Romeo's dream, which is not
recounted, presumably foreboded evil (see earlier
hints at 38–9, 48–9) and may be taken to underlie

his premonition of impending tragedy at 106–11.
On Shakespeare's use of dreams in *Rom.*, see
Marjorie B. Garber, *Dream in Shakespeare: From*
Metaphor to Metamorphosis, 1974, pp. 35–47.
53 Queen Mab Origin of the name Mab is
uncertain. It may ultimately be connected with the
Celtic 'Mabh' ('child' in Welsh), who was 'the
chief of the Irish fairies' (W. J. Thoms, *Three*
Notelets, 1865, pp. 106–7), but Shakespeare is the
first in England to attribute it to the fairy queen.
Shakespeare, moreover, seems to play on 'quean'
(= jade, hussy) and on 'mab' (= a slattern or loose
woman, *OED*) and suggests Mab's identity with an
incubus or succubus in 92 ('the hag' = the night-
mare). See supplementary note.
54–9 See Textual Analysis, pp. 209–10 below.
54 fairies' midwife i.e. 'the person among the
fairies whose department it was to deliver the
fancies of sleeping men of their dreams, those
"children of an idle brain" (97)' (Steevens).
55 agate-stone Refers to the tiny figures carved
in agate and set in seal rings.

On the forefinger of an alderman,
Drawn with a team of little atomi
Over men's noses as they lie asleep.
Her chariot is an empty hazel-nut,
Made by the joiner squirrel or old grub,   60
Time out a'mind the fairies' coachmakers:
Her waggon-spokes made of long spinners' legs,
The cover of the wings of grasshoppers,
Her traces of the smallest spider web,
Her collars of the moonshine's wat'ry beams,   65
Her whip of cricket's bone, the lash of film,
Her waggoner a small grey-coated gnat,
Not half so big as a round little worm
Pricked from the lazy finger of a maid.
And in this state she gallops night by night   70
Through lovers' brains, and then they dream of love,
O'er courtiers' knees, that dream on cur'sies straight,
O'er lawyers' fingers, who straight dream on fees,
O'er ladies' lips, who straight on kisses dream,
Which oft the angry Mab with blisters plagues,   75
Because their breaths with sweetmeats tainted are.

56 an alderman] Q2–4, F; a Burgomaster Q1   57 atomi] Q1; ottamie Q2; atomies Q3–4, F   58 Over] Q2–4, F; A thwart Q1, *Pope*   59–61] *These lines, not in* Q1, *are placed here following Daniel (conj. Lettsom); after 69,* Q2–4, F   61 a'] Q2–4, F; of F3; o' *Capell*   62 legs,] *Neilson*; legs: Q2–4, F; webs, Q1   64–6] Q2–4, F; The traces are the Moone-shine watrie beames, / The collers crickets bones, the lash of filmes, Q1   64 Her] Q2–4, F; The Q1, *Pope*   64 spider] Q2–4; Spiders F   65 Her] Q2–4, F; The Q1, *Pope*   65 collars] F2; collors Q2; collers Q3–4, Q1; coullers F   66 film] F2 (filme); Philome Q2–4, F; filmes Q1   69 Pricked] Q2–4, F; Pickt Q1, *Collier MS.*   69 lazy finger] Q2–4, Q1; Lazie-finger F   69 maid] Q1; man Q2–4, F; woman F2; maie (*i.e.* maiden) *conj.* Hoppe   72 O'er] Q1 (O're); On Q2–4, F   72 courtiers'] *Warburton*; Courtiers Q2–4, F, Q1; Countries F2; counties' *conj.* Tyrwhitt   73 dream] Q2–4; dreamt F; Q1 *omits 73*   74 on] Q3–4, F, Q1; one Q2   76 breaths] *Rowe*; breath Q2–4, F; breathes Q1

57 **little *atomi** creatures small as atoms (a plural); 'little' may be taken as an intensive. See supplementary note.

59–61 See supplementary note.

60 **joiner squirrel...grub** the sharp-toothed squirrel, like a 'joiner' (= furniture maker), and the mature ('old') grub (= larva of an insect, esp. the beetle, *OED*) bore holes in nuts.

62 **spinners'** spiders' or (Deighton) daddy-longlegs'.

64–6 **Her...film** See supplementary note.

66 **film** membrane, either animal or vegetable (?); gossamer (?).

67 **waggoner** driver of a chariot (*OED* sv 2); compare 3.2.2 and *TA* 5.2.48–51. 'Waggon' was used as a poetic equivalent of 'chariot' (see 59; *OED* sv 2c), which also explains the use of 'waggon-spokes' (62).

68–9 **worm...*maid** 'It was supposed... that when maids were idle, worms [ticks or mites] bred in their fingers' (Nares); compare *AWW* 1.1.141–2. See supplementary note for 'maid'.

70–88 Boswell compares Claudian, *De Sexto Consulatu Honorii Augusti*, Praefatio, 1–10, but J. C. Maxwell (*N&Q* 205 (1960), 16), following J. W. Hales, considers Chaucer's *Parliament of Fowls* (99–105) a more likely influence, since Shakespeare seems already to have used Chaucer's poem in *LLL* (see Nevill Coghill, 'Shakespeare's reading in Chaucer', in *Elizabethan and Jacobean Studies Presented to F. P. Wilson*, 1959).

70 **state** pomp, dignity.

72 **cur'sies** curtsies.

75 **blisters** N. Brooke (*Shakespeare's Early Tragedies*, 1968, p. 94) suggests a reference to venereal disease.

76 **sweetmeats** candied fruit or confectionery, perhaps with reference to 'kissing-comfits' (= per-

Sometime she gallops o'er a courtier's nose,
And then dreams he of smelling out a suit;
And sometime comes she with a tithe-pig's tail
Tickling a parson's nose as 'a lies asleep,   80
Then he dreams of another benefice.
Sometime she driveth o'er a soldier's neck,
And then dreams he of cutting foreign throats,
Of breaches, ambuscadoes, Spanish blades,
Of healths five fathom deep; and then anon   85
Drums in his ear, at which he starts and wakes,
And being thus frighted, swears a prayer or two,
And sleeps again. This is that very Mab
That plats the manes of horses in the night,
And bakes the elf-locks in foul sluttish hairs,   90
Which, once untangled, much misfortune bodes.
This is the hag, when maids lie on their backs,
That presses them and learns them first to bear,
Making them women of good carriage.
This is she –

ROMEO   Peace, peace, Mercutio, peace!   95
Thou talk'st of nothing.
MERCUTIO   True, I talk of dreams,

---

77 courtier's nose] Q2–4, F; Lawers lap Q1; lawyer's nose *Pope*; taylor's nose *conj. Theobald*; counsellor's nose *Collier²*; lawyer's lip *conj. Seymour*   79 a] Q2–4, Q1; *not in* F   80 parson's] Q3–4, F, Q1; Persons Q2   80 as 'a] Q2–4, F; that Q1, *Hudson (conj. Lettsom)*   81 he dreams] Q2–4, F; dreames he Q1, *Pope*   84 Spanish blades] Q2–4, F; countermines Q1   86 ear] Q2–4, Q1; eares F   90 bakes] Q2–4, F; plats Q1; cakes *Pope*   90 elf-locks] Q4, Q1; Elklocks Q2–3, F   91 untangled] Q2–4, F, Q1; entangled F3   92–5 This...she –] *not in* Q1   95 she –] F2; she. Q2–4, F   96 dreams,] Q1; dreames: Q2–4, F

---

fumed sweetmeats for sweetening the breath, *OED*). The context here, however, seems to suggest bad breath ('tainted') from eating too many sweets; compare Webster, *The White Devil* (1612), 2.1.166–8: 'O your breath! / Out upon sweete meates, and continued Physicke! / The plague is in them.'

77 courtier's nose See supplementary note.

78 smelling...suit discovering (by his sagacity) someone with a petition to further at court from whom he may collect a fee for his influence.

79 tithe-pig's A pig due as tithe (= a tenth part of one's income) to the church, which often ended up on the parson's table.

81 another benefice The holding of two or more church livings was still common long after Elizabethan times.

84 breaches, ambuscadoes breaking down of fortifications, ambushes.

84 Spanish blades The best swords were made from Toledo steel.

90–1 bakes...bodes Elves, who naturally hated 'sluts and sluttery' (*Wiv.* 5.5.46), were believed to cake ('bake') or mat the dirty hair of slovens, who, it was proposed, would suffer further torment at their hands if the locks were untangled. F3 'entangled' makes, perhaps, easier sense; Q2 'untangled' may be an error caught from Q1.

92 the hag Shakespeare here identifies Mab with the night-mare (Anglo-Saxon 'mare' = incubus) which induced evil, particularly sexual, dreams. Drayton makes the identification directly in his imitation of this passage ('Nimphidia', 53–6).

93 learns teaches.

93 bear (1) the weight of a man; (2) children.

94 carriage (1) deportment; (2) burden (with further play on both (1) and (2) in preceding note.

96 nothing With probably bawdy play on 'nothing' = 'O' = vagina. Compare 2.1.37 n. and 3.3.90 n.

Which are the children of an idle brain,
Begot of nothing but vain fantasy,
Which is as thin of substance as the air,
And more inconstant than the wind, who woos   100
Even now the frozen bosom of the north,
And being angered puffs away from thence,
Turning his side to the dew-dropping south.

BENVOLIO This wind you talk of blows us from ourselves:
Supper is done, and we shall come too late.   105

ROMEO I fear too early, for my mind misgives
Some consequence yet hanging in the stars
Shall bitterly begin his fearful date
With this night's revels, and expire the term
Of a despisèd life closed in my breast,   110
By some vile forfeit of untimely death.
But He that hath the steerage of my course
Direct my sail! On, lusty gentlemen.

BENVOLIO Strike, drum.

They march about the stage [and stand to one side].

98 fantasy,] F, Q1; phantasie: Q2–4, F   100 wind, who woos] Q3–4, F; wind who wooes, Q2; winde, / Which wooes
Q1   103 side] Q2–4, F; face Q1, *Pope*; tide *Collier MS.*   103 dew-dropping] Q1; dewe dropping Q2–4, F   110 breast,]
Q1; brest: Q2–4, F   111 vile...death] Q2–4, F; vntimelie forfet of vile death Q1   111 forfeit] Q3–4, F, Q1; fofreit Q2
112 steerage] Q1; stirrage Q2–4, F   113 Direct] Q2–4, F; Directs Q1, *Boswell*   113 sail] Q1; sute Q2–4, F; fate *conj. Anon.*
(in Cam.)   114 Strike,] F4; Strike Q2–4, F; Q1 *omits 114*   114 SD *and stand to one side*] Williams (subst.) ; Q2–4, F, Q1
indicate no exit; most modern eds., following Theobald, clear the stage with / Exeunt.

98 vain fantasy delusive imagination.
100 inconstant...wind Compare John 3.8
('The wind bloweth where it listeth') and Tilley
W412.
103 Turning his side Reversing his direction
(like a wooer repulsed by a cold mistress). Lines
100–3 may comment obliquely on the relations
between Romeo, Rosaline and Juliet.
103 dew-dropping south Compare Tilley
W444 ('When the wind is in the south it is in the
rain's mouth') and *AYLI* 3.5.50.
106–11 my mind...death Romeo prophesies
his premature ('untimely') death from a circumstance ('consequence') that will take its ('his')
beginning ('date') from Capulet's feast this very
night. Note the legal imagery in 'expire the term'
(= terminate the leasehold) and 'forfeit' (=

penalty). Here is the first explicit reference in the
play to the theme of 'star-crossed' love sounded in
the Prologue (6).
109 expire the term Hudson compares Daniel's
Rosamond, 1592 (239–42): 'Thou must not thinke
thy flowre can alwayes florish, / ...But that those
rayes which all these flames doe nourish, / Canceld
with Time, will have their date expyred.'
111 vile...death Q1's reading ('vntimelie forfet
of vile death') affords a more natural arrangement
of the adjectives.
112 He God. Some critics interpret 'he'
(Q2–4, F, Q1) as Cupid.
113 Direct my *sail Guide my voyage. On
'sail', see supplementary note.
114 drum i.e. one bearing the tabor or drum.

[1.5] *And* SERVINGMEN *come forth with napkins.*

FIRST SERVINGMAN Where's Potpan, that he helps not to take away?
He shift a trencher? he scrape a trencher?
SECOND SERVINGMAN When good manners shall lie all in one or two
men's hands, and they unwashed too, 'tis a foul thing.
FIRST SERVINGMAN Away with the join-stools, remove the court-   5
cupboard, look to the plate. Good thou, save me a piece of
marchpane, and as thou loves me, let the porter let in Susan
Grindstone and Nell.

[Exit Second Servingman]

Anthony and Potpan!

[Enter two more SERVINGMEN.*]*

THIRD SERVINGMAN Ay, boy, ready.   10
FIRST SERVINGMAN You are looked for and called for, asked for and
sought for, in the great chamber.
FOURTH SERVINGMAN We cannot be here and there too. Cheerly,
boys, be brisk a while, and the longer liver take all.

[They retire behind]

*Enter [*CAPULET, LADY CAPULET, JULIET, TYBALT *and his* PAGE,
NURSE, *and]* all the GUESTS *and* GENTLEWOMEN *to the Maskers.*

CAPULET Welcome, gentlemen! Ladies that have their toes   15
Unplagued with corns will walk a bout with you.
Ah, my mistresses, which of you all
Will now deny to dance? She that makes dainty,

Act 1, Scene 5   1.5] *Steevens; no scene division,* Q2–4, F, Q1   Location] *Riverside (after Pope)*   0 SD *And...napkins.*]
From the conclusion of the SD *at the end of 1.4 in* Q2–4, F; SD *not in* Q1; *following the* SD Q2–4 *insert an unnecessary* / *Enter
Romeo.* /, *not in* F   1–14] *not in* Q1   1, 5, 11 SH FIRST SERVINGMAN] *Rowe; Ser.* Q2–4, F   1–4] *As prose, Pope
(3–4 prose in* Q3–4, F*); as irregular verse,* Q2   3 SH SECOND SERVINGMAN] *Rowe;* 1. Q2–4, F   3 all] Q2–4; *not in* F
7 loves] Q2–4; *louest* F   8 Nell.] *Theobald; Nell,* Q2–4, F   8 SD] *Sisson (subst.); no* SD, Q2–4, F   9 SD] *This edn (after
Cowden Clarke); no* SD, Q2–4, F   10 SH THIRD SERVINGMAN] *Dowden (after Cowden Clarke);* 2. Q2–4, F
13 SH FOURTH SERVINGMAN] *Dowden (after Cowden Clarke);* 3. Q2–4; 1 F   13–14] *As prose, Pope; as verse,* Q2–4, F
13 Cheerly] F (*chearly*); *chearely* Q2–4   14 SD.1 *They retire behind] Malone; Exeunt.* Q2–4, F   14 SD.2–3 CAPULET
...*and] Riverside (after Capell); Enter old* Capulet *with the Ladies.* Q1   15, 33 SH CAPULET] Q1, *Capell;* 1. *Capu.* Q2–4, F
16 Unplagued] F (*Vnplagu'd*), Q1; *Vnplagued* Q2–4   16 walk a bout] *Pope (reading* have a bout *from* Q1 *haue about);*
walke about Q2–4, F   17 Ah, my] Q2–4, F; *ah ha my* Q1, *Capell;* Ah me F2; Ah me, my *Rowe*   17 mistresses]
Q3–4, F, Q1; *mistesses* Q2

Act 1, Scene 5
Location Scene continues, now as a hall in
Capulet's house.
  2 **trencher** wooden plate.
  5 **join-stools** joint-stools (variant form), stools
in which the parts were fitted by a joiner.
  5–6 **court-cupboard** sideboard.

6 **plate** silverware (flagons, salts, dishes, etc.).
7 **marchpane** marzipan.
14 **longer...all** Proverbial (Tilley L395); 'used
as encouragement to cheerfulness and a merry life'
(Kittredge). Compare the saying 'winner take all'.
16 **walk a bout** dance a round.
18 **makes dainty** seems loath or hesitant.

She I'll swear hath corns. Am I come near ye now?
Welcome, gentlemen! I have seen the day   20
That I have worn a visor and could tell
A whispering tale in a fair lady's ear,
Such as would please; 'tis gone, 'tis gone, 'tis gone.
You are welcome, gentlemen. Come, musicians, play.
                    Music plays.
A hall, a hall, give room! and foot it, girls.
                    And they dance.   25
More light, you knaves, and turn the tables up;
And quench the fire, the room is grown too hot.
Ah, sirrah, this unlooked-for sport comes well.
Nay, sit, nay, sit, good Cousin Capulet,
For you and I are past our dancing days.   30
How long is't now since last yourself and I
Were in a mask?

COUSIN CAPULET   Berlady, thirty years.

CAPULET What, man, 'tis not so much, 'tis not so much:
'Tis since the nuptial of Lucentio,
Come Pentecost as quickly as it will,   35
Some five and twenty years, and then we masked.

COUSIN CAPULET 'Tis more, 'tis more, his son is elder, sir;
His son is thirty.

CAPULET   Will you tell me that?
His son was but a ward two years ago.

20–5 I...girls.] *not in* Q1   **22** ear,] F4; eare: Q2–4, F   **24** gentlemen. Come,] *Rowe (subst.)*; gentlemen come, Q2; gentlemen, come Q3–4, F   **25** a hall] Q2–4; Hall F   **25** SD] *This edn (after Johnson)*; *part of* SD *at* 24 *in* Q2–4, F   **28** unlooked-for] *Pope*; vnlookt for Q2–4, F, Q1   **32, 37** SH COUSIN CAPULET] *Williams*; 2. *Capu.* Q2–4, F; *Cos:* Q1   **33** What,] F4; What Q2–4, F   **34** Lucentio,] F, Q1; *Lucientio:* Q2; *Lucientio,* Q3–4   **37** sir] Q2–4, F; far Q1   **38** SH CAPULET] Q1, *Capell*; 1. *Capu.* Q2–4; 3. *Cap.* F   **39** two] Q3–4, F; 2. Q2; three Q1   **39**] *Following this line* Q1 *(followed by Keightley) adds:* Good youths I faith. Oh youth's a iolly thing.

---

19 come near ye hit the target (by zeroing in on a sensitive point).

25 A hall Clear the floor (for dancing).

26 knaves fellows (used of servants, without abusive intent).

26 turn...up remove the boards and tidy the trestles out of the way.

28 Ah, sirrah Capulet is addressing himself. Compare Haughton, *Englishmen for My Money* (1598, MSR, 211). Except as self-address, with 'Ah' (see Schmidt), 'sirrah' was used only in addressing social inferiors; this makes it difficult to accept, as Kittredge (following Capell) asserts, that 'sirrah'

here (and later in 125) refers to 'Cousin Capulet' named in the next line.

28 unlooked-for sport i.e. the unexpected appearance of the maskers which has led to dancing.

29 Cousin Capulet i.e. presumably 'uncle Capulet' of the 'letter' in 1.2.68. See 1.2.68 n.

30 past...days Proverbial (Tilley D118).

32 mask masquerade or, simply, visor (see 21).

34 nuptial wedding.

37 elder older (see Franz 223, for the continued use of the umlauted form in contexts like the present).

39 ward i.e. not of age; under the control of a guardian.

ROMEO [*To a Servingman*] What lady's that which doth enrich the
    hand   40
    Of yonder knight?
SERVINGMAN I know not, sir.
ROMEO O she doth teach the torches to burn bright!
    It seems she hangs upon the cheek of night
    As a rich jewel in an Ethiop's ear –   45
    Beauty too rich for use, for earth too dear:
    So shows a snowy dove trooping with crows,
    As yonder lady o'er her fellows shows.
    The measure done, I'll watch her place of stand,
    And touching hers, make blessèd my rude hand.   50
    Did my heart love till now? forswear it, sight!
    For I ne'er saw true beauty till this night.
TYBALT This, by his voice, should be a Montague.
    Fetch me my rapier, boy.

                                          [*Exit Page*]
            What dares the slave

---

40 SD] Capell; no SD, Q2–4, F, Q1   40 lady's] Pope; Ladies Q2; Ladie is Q3–4, F, Q1   42] *not in* Q1   44 It seems she]
Q2–4, F, Q1; Her Beauty F2   44 night] Capell; night: Q2; night, Q3–4, F, Q1   45 As] Q2–4, F; Like Q1, F2   47 shows]
Q2–4, F; shines Q1, *Keightley*   50 blessèd] Q2–4, F; happie Q1, *Pope*   51 now?] Q1; now, Q2–4, F   52 ne'er] Q2–4;
neuer F, Q1 (Q1 *omits* For)   54 SD] Collier²; no SD, Q2–4, F, Q1

40–1 lady's...knight Compare Brooke (246);
in Painter it is a 'certayne Lord' (p. 101).

42 I know not, sir It seems odd that a Capulet
servant should not know Juliet's identity; the
servant's answer is omitted in Q1. Possibly the
Servingman here should be identified with one of
the Torch-bearers who accompanied the maskers
(see 1.4.0 SD).

43 torches In Brooke, but not Painter, the dance
which Romeo is watching is a 'torch-dance' (see
Brooke (246) and Painter (p. 101); Boaistuau
describes it as a 'bal de la torche'), which may have
suggested torches to Shakespeare at this point. The
form of the dance in *Rom.* is not clear, though it,
too, may have been staged as a torch-dance.
Dowden detects 'faint echoes' of *1H6* 5.3.46–71 in
the speech as a whole.

44–5 hangs...ear Compare *Sonnets* 27.11–12:
'Which like a jewel hung in ghastly night, / Makes
black night beauteous, and her old face new', and
TGV 2.6.25–6. 'Ethiop' was commonly used for
any black African.

46 Beauty...dear Beauty that is too precious
to be used in merely physical terms (with play on
'use' = increase, interest) and too valuable (with
play on 'dear' = of (too) high price) for this world.
Mahood suggests possible play on 'beauty' and
'booty'; they are still pronounced identically in the
country speech of Norfolk and Suffolk. Ironically,

this might apply equally to the forgotten Rosaline
(compare 1.1.199–207). Spencer detects foreboding
and compares 1.2.14.

47 dove...crows This comparison picks up
Benvolio's prophecy in 1.2.86–7. Note that Q1 has
'swan' for 'dove'. Compare *MND* 2.2.114.

49 place of stand Compare Brooke (249–50),
but Shakespeare does not seat the lovers as in
Brooke (253–66), where Juliet is seated between
Romeus and Mercutio, each of whom grasps one of
her hands (Romeus the left, the hand most closely
associated with the heart).

50 rude hand rough, coarse hand (compared
with Juliet's). This looks forward to 92 ff. and was
suggested by Brooke (264).

51 forswear it break your former oath (of love
to Rosaline).

53–91 Tybalt's presence at Capulet's feast and
his threatened attack on Romeo are Shakespeare's
invention. In Brooke (183–90), although Romeus
is recognised by the Capulets, 'The Capilets
disdayne the presence of theyr foe: / Yet they
suppresse theyr styrred yre, the cause I do not
knowe.'

53 by his voice A rather tenuous clue to
identity, but forced on Shakespeare by his handling
of the maskers, who, unlike those in Brooke (170),
apparently do not unmask throughout the scene.

54 What How.

Come hither, covered with an antic face,   55
To fleer and scorn at our solemnity?
Now by the stock and honour of my kin,
To strike him dead I hold it not a sin.

CAPULET Why, how now, kinsman, wherefore storm you so?

TYBALT Uncle, this is a Montague, our foe: 60
A villain that is hither come in spite,
To scorn at our solemnity this night.

CAPULET Young Romeo is it?

TYBALT   'Tis he, that villain Romeo.

CAPULET Content thee, gentle coz, let him alone,
'A bears him like a portly gentleman;   65
And to say truth, Verona brags of him
To be a virtuous and well-governed youth.
I would not for the wealth of all this town
Here in my house do him disparagement;
Therefore be patient, take no note of him;   70
It is my will, the which if thou respect,
Show a fair presence, and put off these frowns,
An ill-beseeming semblance for a feast.

TYBALT It fits when such a villain is a guest:
I'll not endure him.

CAPULET   He shall be endured.   75
What, goodman boy, I say he shall, go to!
Am I the master here, or you? go to!
You'll not endure him? God shall mend my soul,
You'll make a mutiny among my guests!
You will set cock-a-hoop! you'll be the man!   80

55 antic] Q1 (Anticke); anticque Q2; antique Q3–4, F   62 scorn] Q2–4, F; mocke Q1   63 it?] F; it. Q2–4; it not? Q1
65 'A] Q2–4, F; he Q1, *Rowe*   68 this] Q2–4, Q1; the F   73 ill-beseeming] *Pope*; illbeseeming Q2; ill beseeming Q3–4,
F, Q1   75 endured] F (endu'rd); endured Q2–4, Q1   76 to!] *Rowe* (to –); too, Q2–4, F *(Q1 reads* goe to I say, he shall,)
77 to!] *Rowe* (to –); too, Q2–4, F *(Q1 omits* go too,)   78 him?] Q1; him, Q2–4, F   79 my] Q2–4, Q1; the F

55 **antic face** grotesque mask.
56 **fleer...solemnity** jeer...festive celebra-
tion.
61 **in spite** out of malice or grudge.
65 **bears...gentleman** carries himself like a
dignified gentleman.
72 **presence** demeanour.
73 **semblance** facial appearance or expression.
76 **goodman boy** 'a double insult: a yeoman
(not a gentleman) and a youngster' (Spencer), but
here applied to a 'saucy' (82) young man.
76 **go to** An expression of protest or annoyance.
78 **God shall mend** i.e. may God amend.
Compare 'Bless me', a form of polite oath.
79 **mutiny** disturbance.

80 **set cock-a-hoop** cast off all restraint, become
reckless (*OED* 1b). From a supposed custom of
removing the spigot ('cock') from a barrel of ale and
setting it upon the barrel hoop, thus allowing the
ale to flow without intermission, as a result of which
the drinkers became 'cock-on-hoop' or at the height
of mirth and jollity (Blount, *Glossographia* (1670),
cited *OED*, which considers the explanation
suspect). Our modern meaning ('crowing with
exultation or boastfully elated', where 'cock' =
rooster) is apparently a late-seventeenth-century
development.
80 **you'll...man** i.e. you'll play the big hero,
will you?

TYBALT Why, uncle, 'tis a shame.
CAPULET   Go to, go to,
    You are a saucy boy. Is't so indeed?
    This trick may chance to scathe you, I know what.
    You must contrary me! Marry, 'tis time. –
    Well said, my hearts! – You are a princox, go,   85
    Be quiet, or – More light, more light! – For shame,
    I'll make you quiet, what! – Cheerly, my hearts!
TYBALT Patience perforce with wilful choler meeting
    Makes my flesh tremble in their different greeting:
    I will withdraw, but this intrusion shall,   90
    Now seeming sweet, convert to bitt'rest gall.   *Exit*
ROMEO [*To Juliet*] If I profane with my unworthiest hand
    This holy shrine, the gentle sin is this,
    My lips, two blushing pilgrims, ready stand
    To smooth that rough touch with a tender kiss.   95

83 scathe] F4; scath Q2–4, F, Q1 *(variant form)*   83 you,] F; you Q2–4; you one day Q1   83 what.] Q1; what, Q2–4, F
84–7] Q2–4, F; Well said my hartes. Be quiet: / More light Ye knaue, or I will make you quiet. Q1
86 or – More...light! – For shame,] *Collier (subst.);* or more light, more light for shame, Q2–3, F; or more light more
light for shame, Q4; or more light, for shame, F2; or (more light, more light, for shame) *Pope;* or – More...light. – For
shame! – *Knight; see 84–7 for* Q1   87 quiet, what! – Cheerly] *Capell (subst.,* cheerly F3*);* quiet (what) chearely Q2–4;
quiet. What, chearely F; quiet – What? cheerly *Pope*   90–1 shall, Now seeming sweet,] *Rowe;* shall / Now seeming
sweet, Q2–4, F, Q1; shall / Now-seeming sweet *Hudson (conj. Lettsom)*   91 bitt'rest] Q2; bitter Q3–4, F, Q1   91 SD]
Q2–4, F; *not in* Q1   92 SD] *Douai MS., Rowe; no* SD, Q2–4, F, Q1   92 unworthiest] Q2–4, F; vnworthie Q1, *Pope*
93 gentle] Q2–4, F, Q1; gentler *conj. Dowden*   93 sin] Q2–4, F, Q1; fine *Theobald (conj. Warburton);* pain *NS*
94 ready] Q1; did readie Q2–4, F

82 **Is't so indeed?** i.e. is this the way things are
(in your attitude toward me)?
83 **This trick...what** This behaviour may
injure your financial expectations (*OED* Scathe 1b)
and I have the power to see that it does. The threat
of financial reprisal is supported by Q1 ('This tricke
will scath you one day I know what'). See
K. Bartenschlager, *Anglia* 100 (1982), 424–5.
84 **contrary me** oppose my will; 'contrary' is
accented on the second syllable.
84 **'tis time** Addressed either (1) to Tybalt, who
perhaps indicates with some gesture his unwilling
compliance, or (2) to himself (i.e. time to turn his
attention to his guests, which he does in the first half
of 85). The light comma pointing in the early texts
makes it difficult in 84–7 to be sure exactly whom
Capulet is addressing (see collation).
85 **Well...hearts** Well done, my friends
(addressed to the dancers).
85 **princox** pert, conceited youth.
87 **Cheerly** Heartily.
88–9 **Patience...greeting** Enforced patience
encountering with obstinate anger, by the clash of
opposites, sets me trembling all over. Compare
Tilley P111, 112.
91 **seeming...gall** Tybalt's threat echoes
1.1.185.

92–105 These fourteen lines are cast as an
English (or 'Shakespearean') sonnet (compare the
Prologue), though the repetition of rhymes ('this',
'kiss') in the first and second quatrains is unusual.
This first exchange between Romeo and Juliet, with
its formal patterning and gentle expression of
human love through religious metaphor, conveys an
antiphonal ritual effect that balances the lovers'
delicate sparring with a nice blend of male ardour
and seeming maidenly reserve.
93 **holy shrine** i.e. Juliet's hand (a part for the
whole 'saint'). The Christian imagery in 92 picks
up the implication of 'blessèd' in 50 and contrasts
with Romeo's Cupid-dominated (i.e. 'profane')
attitude to Rosaline. Compare *MV* 2.7.39–40.
Echoed in Munday, *Downfall of...Huntingdon*
(1598; MSR, 2617–18).
93 **gentle...this** i.e. compared with the 'rough
touch' (95) of my hand this sin (= the kiss proposed
in 94–5) is a gentle amends. Dowden suggests
reading 'gentler', a tempting emendation. See
supplementary note.
94 **lips...pilgrims** i.e. 'pilgrims' because wor-
shipping at the 'shrine' (93); 'blushing' because
red. See supplementary note.

JULIET Good pilgrim, you do wrong your hand too much,
 Which mannerly devotion shows in this,
 For saints have hands that pilgrims' hands do touch,
 And palm to palm is holy palmers' kiss.
ROMEO Have not saints lips, and holy palmers too? 100
JULIET Ay, pilgrim, lips that they must use in prayer.
ROMEO O then, dear saint, let lips do what hands do:
 They pray, grant thou, lest faith turn to despair.
JULIET Saints do not move, though grant for prayers' sake.
ROMEO Then move not while my prayer's effect I take. 105
 Thus from my lips, by thine, my sin is purged.
    [*Kissing her.*]
JULIET Then have my lips the sin that they have took.
ROMEO Sin from my lips? O trespass sweetly urged!
 Give me my sin again.
    [*Kissing her again.*]
JULIET   You kiss by th'book.
NURSE Madam, your mother craves a word with you. 110
ROMEO What is her mother?
NURSE   Marry, bachelor,

96 much,] Q1; much Q2–4; much. F 98 hands that] Q5; hands, that Q2–4, F; hands which Q1
98 pilgrims'] *Theobald²*; Pilgrims Q2–4, F; holy Palmers Q1 *(omitting do)* 99 palmers'] *Theobald²*; Palmers Q2–4, F,
Q1 103 pray, grant thou,] *Johnson*; pray (grant thou) Q2–3, F; pray, (grant thou) Q4; pray, yeeld thou, Q1; pray; grant
thou, *Hanmer* 104 prayers'] *Warburton*; praiers Q2–4, F; Q1 *reads 104:* Saints doe not mooue though: grant nor praier
forsake. 105 prayer's] *Capell*; praiers Q2–4, F, Q1; prayers' *Warburton* 106 thine] Q2–4, F; yours Q1, *Capell*
106 SD] *Rowe*; no SD, Q2–4, F, Q1 108 lips?] F; lips, Q2–4, Q1 109 SD] *Capell*; no SD, Q2–4, F, Q1 109 by th'] F
(by'th'); bith Q2–4; by the Q1 110] *This and the remaining speeches by the Nurse in this scene are in italics and, where
distinguishable, in prose in Q1; compare 1.3*

96 **Good pilgrim** Interpreted by some to
indicate that Romeo is wearing a pilgrim's costume
(the other maskers being perhaps similarly
costumed); 'Romeo' is a term for 'pilgrim' in
Italian. Brooke (351–2) mentions Romeo as being
'in masking weede'. Costuming was common
among masking parties (compare 1.4.4–5 and *H8*
1.4), but the evidence in the play is inconclusive
since Juliet's 'Good pilgrim' arises naturally
enough out of the 'shrine/pilgrims' allusion in 93–4.
Compare the wooing of Cordella by the Gallian
King, disguised as a Palmer, in the anonymous *King
Leir* (c. 1588–94; MSR, 644–722).
97 **Which…this** Which shows a seemly reverence in this action (touching my hand). Juliet seems
to be arguing against Romeo's excuse for offering
a kiss.
98 **saints** i.e. the images of saints in shrines.
99 **palm to palm** Compare Brooke (267):
'Then she with tender hand his tender palme hath
prest'. Note play on 'palm' and 'palmer'
(= pilgrim).

102 **let…do** allow lips the same privilege (i.e.
kissing) as hands (see 99). There seems to be an echo
of this conceit in Porter's *Two Angry Women* (1598;
MSR, 2895–2903).
103 **They…despair** Lips pray, and you should
grant their prayers for fear that sound belief ('faith')
may turn to hopeless unbelief ('despair').
104 **move** take the initiative (with play on 'move
not' = stand still, in 105). Juliet says Romeo must
act for himself (i.e. kiss her).
104 **grant** i.e. they grant (through intercession
with God).
108 **urged** argued.
109 **by th'book** like an expert (as if following the
rules of gallantry); compare *AYLI* 5.4.90–1.
111 **What** Who. Compare the masking scene in
H8 1.4.63–96 (probably by Fletcher), where Henry
asks for the identity of the 'fair lady' he has just
danced with (i.e. Anne Bullen).
111 **bachelor** young gentleman.

Her mother is the lady of the house,
And a good lady, and a wise and virtuous.
I nursed her daughter that you talked withal;
I tell you, he that can lay hold of her   115
Shall have the chinks.

ROMEO   Is she a Capulet?
O dear account! my life is my foe's debt.

BENVOLIO Away, be gone, the sport is at the best.

ROMEO Ay, so I fear, the more is my unrest.

CAPULET Nay, gentlemen, prepare not to be gone,   120
We have a trifling foolish banquet towards.
[They whisper in his ear.]
Is it e'en so? Why then I thank you all.
I thank you, honest gentlemen, good night.
More torches here, come on! then let's to bed.
Ah, sirrah, by my fay, it waxes late,   125
I'll to my rest.
                        [Exeunt all but Juliet and Nurse]

JULIET Come hither, Nurse. What is yond gentleman?

NURSE The son and heir of old Tiberio.

JULIET What's he that now is going out of door?

NURSE Marry, that I think be young Petruchio.   130

JULIET What's he that follows here, that would not dance?

NURSE I know not.

JULIET Go ask his name. – If he be marrièd,
My grave is like to be my wedding bed.

116 Capulet] Q2–4, F; *Mountague* Q1   117 debt] Q2–4, F; thrall Q1   118–19] *not in* Q1   118 Away,] Q3–4, F; Away
Q2   121 SD] Q1; *no* SD, Q2–4, F; *Maskers excuse themselves with a bow.* / Capell   124–6] Q2–4, F; I promise you but
for your company, / I would haue bin a bed an houre agoe: [*compare 3.4.6–7*] / Light to my chamber hoe. Q1
124 here,...then] *NS*; here, come on, then Q2–4; here: come on, then F; here! – Come on, then, *Hudson*; here! Come
on then, *Globe*   125–6] *Addressed to* / Cousin Capulet, / Capell   126 SD] Malone; *no* SD, Q2–4, F; *Exeunt.* Q1
130 Marry...be] Q2–4, F; *That as I thinke is* Q1, Pope   131 here] Q2–4, F; there Q1, Capell   133 name.] F (name:);
name, Q2–4, Q1   134 wedding] Q2–4, Q1; wedded F

114 **withal** with.
116 **the chinks** plenty of coin (slang); perhaps with bawdy quibble.
117 **dear account** costly reckoning.
117 **my life...debt** I owe my life (in loving Juliet) as a debt to my foe. Compare Brooke (324–5).
118 **sport...best** i.e. the proper moment to leave; see 1.4.38–9 n.
119 **Ay...unrest** Romeo interprets Benvolio's comment as a foreboding of unhappiness. Compare 1.4.106–11.
121 **banquet** dessert (fruit, wine, sweets).
121 **towards** just ready.
122 **Is...so** The 'gentlemen' (= the maskers)

have made a whispered excuse (see SD from Q1) for their departure.
124 **More torches** To light the maskers out.
125 **sirrah** See 28 n. above.
127 **yond gentleman** Juliet, to conceal her special concern for Romeo from the Nurse, is careful to ask about two other young men first. Compare Brooke (347–50), who here describes Juliet as 'the yong and wyly dame'.
133–4 **If...bed** Ironic foreshadowing; 'introduction of the theme of Death as Juliet's lover' (Spencer). Compare 3.2.137, 3.5.200–1, 4.5.35–9, 5.3.102–5. See supplementary note.

NURSE His name is Romeo, and a Montague,   135
    The only son of your great enemy.
JULIET My only love sprung from my only hate!
    Too early seen unknown, and known too late!
    Prodigious birth of love it is to me,
    That I must love a loathèd enemy.   140
NURSE What's tis? what's tis?
JULIET   A rhyme I learnt even now
    Of one I danced withal.
             One calls within, 'Juliet!'
NURSE   Anon, anon!
    Come let's away, the strangers all are gone.

                                     Exeunt

        [*Enter*] CHORUS.

    Now old desire doth in his death-bed lie,
    And young affection gapes to be his heir;   145
    That fair for which love groaned for and would die,
    With tender Juliet matched is now not fair.
    Now Romeo is beloved, and loves again,
    Alike bewitchèd by the charm of looks;
    But to his foe supposed he must complain,   150
    And she steal love's sweet bait from fearful hooks.

138 seen] Q1; seene, Q2–4, F   141 tis? what's tis?] Q3; tis? whats tis Q2; tis? what tis? Q4; this? whats this F; *this?*
whats that Q1   141 learnt] Q2–4, Q1; learne F   142–3 Anon...gone.] Q2–4, F; *Come your mother staies for you, Ile*
goe a long with you. Q1   143 SD *Enter*] *Theobald; Chorus treated as end of Act 1, Theobald; as prologue to Act 2, Rowe*
144–57] *Chorus not in* Q1   147 matched] Q3–4 (matcht), F (match'd); match Q2   148 beloved] Rowe (belov'd); beloued
Q2–4, F

138 **Too...late** i.e. I fell in love with him before
I knew who he was and, now I know, there is no
going back.
  139 **Prodigious** Ominous, monstrous (half love,
half hate; compare 137).
  141 **tis** this (dialect form).
  141–2 **A rhyme...withal** Juliet is being eva-
sive; she hasn't danced with Romeo (Spencer).
  142 **Anon** Coming presently.
  144–57 Usually taken as a prologue to Act 2, but
perhaps better considered, as in classical and
neo-classical usage, as a concluding chorus to Act
1. Johnson's comment is famous: 'The use of this
chorus is not easily discovered; it conduces nothing
to the progress of the play, but relates what is
already known, or what the next scene will show;
and relates it without adding the improvement of
any moral sentiment.'
  145 **gapes** waits open-mouthed (to swallow his
inheritance), an ugly image, 'gape' being associated

in legal language with a voracious heir. The
language of the Chorus is uncharacteristically
reductive and unsympathetic (almost moralistic)
towards the lovers; see 149, 151, 157.
  146 **That fair** That fair lady (Rosaline).
  146 **for...for** Duplication of prepositions was
not uncommon in Elizabethan English; see Franz
543. Compare *AWW* 1.2.29; *AYLI* 2.7.138–9.
  148 **again** in return.
  149 **Alike...looks** Compare Brooke (487). Note
the unhappy implication of 'bewitched' and
'charm'; 'looks' = (1) appearance, or (2) looking
(at each other).
  150 **foe supposed** i.e. Juliet (because a
Capulet).
  150 **complain** lament (as a lover); compare
'groaned for' in 146.
  151 **steal...hooks** Again reductive ('steal',
'sweet bait', 'fearful hooks'; 'fearful' = threatening). Compare Brooke (388): 'As oft the poysond

Being held a foe, he may not have access
To breathe such vows as lovers use to swear,
And she as much in love, her means much less
To meet her new-belovèd any where: 155
But passion lends them power, time means, to meet,
Temp'ring extremities with extreme sweet.   [*Exit*]

[**2.1**] *Enter* ROMEO *alone.*

ROMEO Can I go forward when my heart is here?
    Turn back, dull earth, and find thy centre out.
                          [*Romeo withdraws*]

      Enter BENVOLIO *with* MERCUTIO.

BENVOLIO Romeo! my cousin Romeo! Romeo!
MERCUTIO   He is wise,
    And on my life hath stol'n him home to bed.
BENVOLIO He ran this way and leapt this orchard wall.   5
    Call, good Mercutio.
MERCUTIO   Nay, I'll conjure too.

155 new-belovèd] *Theobald*; new beloued Q2–4, F   156 means,] *Theobald*; meanes Q2–4, F   157 SD] *Theobald*; *no* SD,
Q2–4, F   Act 2, Scene 1   2.1] *Hanmer*; *no act or scene division*, Q2–4, F, Q1   Location] *This edn (after NS)*; *The Street.*
/ *Rowe*; *Wall of* Capulet's Garden. / *Capell*; *An open Place, adjoining* Capulet's Garden. / *Malone*; *Capulet's orchard*;
to the one side the outer wall with a lane beyond, to the other Capulet's *house showing an upper window* / NS   1 here?]
F, Q1; here, Q2–4   2 SD *Romeo withdraws*] *Riverside (after Hosley)*; *no* SD, Q2–4, F, Q1; *Exit.* / *Rowe*; *leaps the Wall.*
/ *Capell*; *He climbs the wall, and leaps down.* / *Malone*; *He approaches the house.* / *White*   3 Romeo! Romeo!] Q2–4,
F; *Romeo*. Q1, *Pope*   3–4 He...bed.] *As verse*, F; *one line*, Q2–4; Doest thou heare he is wise, / Vpon my life he hath
stolne him home to bed. Q1   6 SH MERCUTIO] Q4, Q1; *line continued to Benvolio*, Q2–3, F

hooke is hid, wrapt in the pleasant bayte'. Compare
Tilley B50 and Gabriel Harvey, *Pierces Supererogation* (1593), p. 58.

153 use are accustomed.

154 means much Elliptical; supply 'are' after 'means'.

157 Temp'ring extremities Allaying desperate difficulties. Compare Tilley D357 and *Lucrece* 1337.

157 extreme sweet (1) the greatest sweetness (= happiness); (2) excessive, cloying sweetness (compare 2.6.11–13); 'extreme' accented on first syllable.

Act 2, Scene 1
Location A lane running by Capulet's orchard. See note on 5 below.

1 Can...here? i.e. can my body leave this spot when my heart (Juliet) is here?

2 dull earth Figuratively, Romeo's body ('The Lord God also made the man of the dust of the ground', Gen. 2.7 (G)). Earth, the lowest and heaviest of the four elements, was associated with the melancholy humour (hence 'dull'). Compare *Sonnets* 44.

2 centre soul (= heart = Juliet). Compare *Sonnets* 146.1: 'Poor soul, the centre of my sinful earth'. As the Earth was the centre of the Ptolemaic system, so it was natural for all earthly things to seek out their own centre (= Earth).

5 leapt...wall jumped over this garden wall. Compare Brooke (829–30). On the staging of 2.1–2, see above, p. 30.

6 conjure raise him, with my magic words (see next line), like a spirit (since he is no longer visible).

Romeo! humours! madman! passion! lover!
Appear thou in the likeness of a sigh,
Speak but one rhyme, and I am satisfied;
Cry but 'Ay me!', pronounce but 'love' and 'dove',   10
Speak to my gossip Venus one fair word,
One nickname for her purblind son and heir,
Young Abraham Cupid, he that shot so trim
When King Cophetua loved the beggar-maid.
He heareth not, he stirreth not, he moveth not,   15
The ape is dead, and I must conjure him.
I conjure thee by Rosaline's bright eyes,
By her high forehead and her scarlet lip,
By her fine foot, straight leg, and quivering thigh,
And the demesnes that there adjacent lie,   20
That in thy likeness thou appear to us.

BENVOLIO And if he hear thee, thou wilt anger him.

MERCUTIO This cannot anger him; 'twould anger him
  To raise a spirit in his mistress' circle,
  Of some strange nature, letting it there stand   25
  Till she had laid it and conjured it down:
  That were some spite. My invocation
  Is fair and honest: in his mistress' name
  I conjure only but to raise up him.

7–21, 23–9] *As verse* Q2–4, F; *as prose,* Q1   7 passion! lover!] *Pope;* passion louer, Q2–3; passion, louer, Q4, F; passion, liuer, Q1   9 one] Q3–4, F, Q1; on Q2   10 Cry] Q2–4, Q1; Cry me F   10 pronounce] Q4, Q1; prouaunt, Q2–3; Prouant, F; Couply F2; couple *Rowe*   10 'dove'] Q1; day Q2–3, F; die Q4   11 gossip] Q4, Q1; goship Q2–3, F   12 heir] Q4, Q1; her Q2–3, F   13 Abraham Cupid] Q4, F; *Abraham:* Cupid Q2–3, Q1; auborn Cupid *Theobald;* Adam Cupid *Steevens (conj. Upton);* abram Cupid *conj. Dyce;* Abram Cupid *Hosley*   13 trim] Q1; true Q2–4, F   15–16] *not in* Q1   16 and] Q2–4; *not in* F   25 there] Q2–4; *not in* F; there to Q1   26 conjured] Q1 (coniurde); coniured Q2–4, F   27–8] *As Capell; two lines, ending* spight / . . .name Q2–4, F; *as prose,* Q1   28 in] Q2; and in Q3–4, F, Q1

---

7 **humours** whimsies, caprices (fancies proper to a lover).

8–9 **sigh…rhyme** Illustrated in 10 by 'ay me' and by 'love' and 'dove'; Juliet's first words in 2.2.25 are 'Ay me'.

10 ***pronounce** See supplementary notes.

11 **gossip Venus** familiar acquaintance, Venus, the goddess of love. Mercutio, according to Brooke (257–8), was a 'Lyon' among 'the bashfull maydes'.

12 **purblind** totally blind; compare 1.4.4.

13 **Abraham Cupid** i.e. rogue Cupid (from the cant term 'Abraham man', a beggar who cheated the public by pretending madness). Mercutio thus supplies the 'nickname' he calls for in 12. Upton's conj. 'Adam Cupid' (from Adam Bell, a famous bowman celebrated in ballad), was, until recently, widely accepted.

13 ***trim** neatly, accurately. Q1 'trim' (for Q2 'true') is accepted on the authority of the ballad of

King Cophetua and the Beggar-Maid (preserved in Richard Johnson's *Crowne Garland of goulden roses* (1612 edn)), referred to in 14: 'The blinded boy that shoots so trim'. Shakespeare mentions this ballad in *LLL* 1.2.109–14, 4.1.64–78; *R2* 5.3.80; *2H4* 5.3.102.

16 **ape is dead** i.e. like a performing monkey playing dead.

20 **demesnes** park lands, for use or pleasure (*OED*); probably used with a bawdy quibble.

22 **And if** If.

24 **raise…circle** Bawdy quibbling: 'raise' = (1) summon up (compare 'conjure' in 6), (2) erect (again in 29); 'spirit' = (1) ghost, (2) semen (Kermode); 'circle' = (1) magic circle, (2) vagina; carried on in 'stand' (25) and 'laid it…down' (26; compare 1.4.28).

28 **fair and honest** clear of offence and proper (with ironic play on 'honest' = chaste).

BENVOLIO Come, he hath hid himself among these trees   30
    To be consorted with the humorous night:
    Blind is his love, and best befits the dark.
MERCUTIO If love be blind, love cannot hit the mark.
    Now will he sit under a medlar tree,
    And wish his mistress were that kind of fruit   35
    As maids call medlars, when they laugh alone.
    O Romeo, that she were, O that she were
    An open-arse, thou a pop'rin pear!
    Romeo, good night, I'll to my truckle-bed,
    This field-bed is too cold for me to sleep.   40
    Come, shall we go?
BENVOLIO   Go then, for 'tis in vain
    To seek him here that means not to be found.
                              Exit [with Mercutio]

[2.2] [ROMEO *advances.*]

ROMEO He jests at scars that never felt a wound.
    But soft, what light through yonder window breaks?

---

30 these] Q2–4, F; those Q1, *Capell*   33 SH MERCUTIO] Q3–4, F, Q1; *Mar*. Q2   37 O...O] Q2–4, F; Ah...ah Q1, *Capell*
38 open-arse] *Riverside (after Hosley)*; open, or Q2–3, F; open & catera, and Q4; open Et cætera Q1; Open – or *Rowe*;
open –, and *Capell*; open-arse or *Hosley*; open-arse and *NS*   39 truckle-bed] Q2–4, F; trundle bed Q1
41–2 Go...found.] *As Pope (after* Q1*)*; *two lines, ending here / ...found* Q2–4, F; *lines continued to Mercutio,* Q1
42 SD *with Mercutio*] *Neilson (subst.)*; *Exeunt.* Q4, F; *no SD,* Q2–3, Q1   Act 2, Scene 2   2.2] *Hanmer; no scene division,*
Q2–4, F, Q1   Location] *This edn (after Riverside)*; *A Garden. / Rowe*; SCENE *changes to* Capulet's Garden. / *Theobald*
0 SD] *Neilson (subst.)*; *no SD,* Q2–4, F, Q1; *Enter* Romeo. *Rowe*

---

31 **consorted** associated.
31 **humorous** damp (with reference to 'night' as suitable for the melancholy ('humorous') lover).
33 **hit the mark** See 1.1.197 n.
36 **medlars** 'small brown-skinned apple[s], with a large cup-shaped eye' (*OED*); vulgarism for female genitalia.
37 **O...O** Probably with bawdy reference to 'O' = vagina. Compare 1.4.96 n. and 3.3.90 n.
38 ***open-arse** Slang term for 'medlar'. Compare Sir John Harington, *Schoole of Salerne* (1607; ed. Garrison, p. 102): 'They [medlars] have one name more fit to be forgotten' and Chapman, *Bussy D'Ambois* 3.2.244–7. See supplementary notes.
38 **pop'rin Pear** Pear named from Poperinghe in West Flanders; here used, because of its shape, as a vulgarism for penis (with further play on 'pop 'er in').
39 **truckle-bed** Low bed running on castors, usually pushed under a high or 'standing' bed when not in use (*OED*). Mercutio seems to be suggesting that he will go home to his own cosy little bed, in contrast to Romeo.

40 **field-bed** bed upon the ground (*OED*). The term is from Brooke (897), though there used in reference to Romeus and Juliet by the Nurse, who pictures their love-making as a kind of military conflict. See 1.1.203 n.
40 **sleep** i.e. sleep on.

Act 2, Scene 2
Location Scene continues, now in Capulet's orchard. No scene break is intended; Romeo's first line rhymes with the last line of 2.1. Gibbons (pp. 44–5) compares the ambience of this scene with the Fourth Song in Sidney's *Astrophil and Stella*. Compare an analogue to this scene in Montemayor's *Diana*, p. 128.
1 **He** i.e. Mercutio, not Benvolio.
2–3 Dowden compares Marlowe, *The Jew of Malta* 2.1.41–2: 'But stay, what starre shines yonder in the East? / The Loadstarre of my life, if *Abigall*'. The situation is similar, with Abigail 'above' and Barabas below.

It is the east, and Juliet is the sun.
Arise, fair sun, and kill the envious moon,
Who is already sick and pale with grief   5
That thou, her maid, art far more fair than she.
Be not her maid, since she is envious;
Her vestal livery is but sick and green,
And none but fools do wear it; cast it off.

[JULIET *appears aloft as at a window.*]

It is my lady, O it is my love: 10
O that she knew she were!
She speaks, yet she says nothing; what of that?
Her eye discourses, I will answer it.
I am too bold, 'tis not to me she speaks:
Two of the fairest stars in all the heaven,   15
Having some business, do entreat her eyes
To twinkle in their spheres till they return.
What if her eyes were there, they in her head?
The brightness of her cheek would shame those stars,
As daylight doth a lamp; her eyes in heaven   20
Would through the airy region stream so bright
That birds would sing and think it were not night.
See how she leans her cheek upon her hand!
O that I were a glove upon that hand,

---

5 sick] Q2–4, F, Q1; wan *conj. NS*   8 sick] Q2–4, F; pale Q1, *Singer²*   9 SD] *This edn (after Rowe); placed as in Hosley;*
after 3, Rowe; after 1, Capell; no SD, Q2–4, F, Q1   10–11] *As Johnson; one line,* Q2–4, F; *not in* Q1   16 do] Q3–4,
F, Q1; to Q2   18 head?] *Pope*; head, Q2–4, F, Q1   20 eyes] Q1; eye Q2–4, F   23 how] Q2–4, F; now Q1, *Daniel*

3 **Juliet is the sun** Compare Brooke (1726):
'For eche of them to other is, as to the world, the
sunne.' See supplementary note.

6 **her maid** i.e. a votary of Diana, goddess of the
moon and patroness of virgins.

8 **vestal livery** virgin garb (with possible play
on 'livery' = provision, allowance).

8 **sick and green** Referring to the so-called
'green-sickness', a kind of anaemia, producing a
greenish skin tone, to which girls of marriageable
age were supposed to be subject; compare 3.5.156.

9 **fools** This seems to say that anyone who
remains a virgin is a fool (a favourite libertine
argument), but perhaps all that is intended is a
reference to the fool's motley coat, which would
presumably include green.

10 **It...lady** Apparently Juliet only now becomes visible in the window.

12 **speaks...nothing** i.e. I can only see her lips
move, not hear what she says.

15 **stars** i.e. planets. Compare *Shr.* 4.5.31–2.

17 **spheres** orbits. In the Ptolemaic system each
of the seven planets was fixed in a hollow crystalline
sphere, which revolved concentrically at different
distances around the centre (the Earth).

18 **there** i.e. in the stars' spheres.

21 **airy region** the sky or upper limit of the air,
the heavens.

21 **stream** emit continuous beams of light.

23 **See...hand** Compare Brooke (518): 'In
windowe on her leaning arme, her weary hed doth
rest.'

24 **glove** The 'glove' conceit seems to be echoed
in Haughton, *Englishmen for My Money* (1598,
MSR, 78–9). See supplementary note.

That I might touch that cheek!

JULIET   Ay me!

ROMEO [*Aside*]   She speaks.   25

O speak again, bright angel, for thou art
As glorious to this night, being o'er my head,
As is a wingèd messenger of heaven
Unto the white-upturnèd wond'ring eyes
Of mortals that fall back to gaze on him,   30
When he bestrides the lazy puffing clouds,
And sails upon the bosom of the air.

JULIET O Romeo, Romeo, wherefore art thou Romeo?
Deny thy father and refuse thy name;
Or if thou wilt not, be but sworn my love,   35
And I'll no longer be a Capulet.

ROMEO [*Aside*] Shall I hear more, or shall I speak at this?

JULIET 'Tis but thy name that is my enemy;
Thou art thyself, though not a Montague.
What's Montague? It is nor hand nor foot,   40
Nor arm nor face, nor any other part
Belonging to a man. O be some other name!
What's in a name? That which we call a rose
By any other word would smell as sweet;

---

25 SD] *NS* ; *no* SD, Q2–4, F, Q1   27 this night] Q2–4, F, Q1 ; this sight *Theobald* ; my sight *conj. Hudson*   29 white-upturnèd] *Theobald²* ; white vpturned Q2–4, F, Q1   31 lazy puffing] Q2–4, F ; lasie pacing Q1, *Pope* ; lazy passing *Ulrici (conj. Collier)*   37 SD] *Rowe* ; *no* SD, Q2–4, F, Q1   39] Q2–4, F ; *not in* Q1 ; Thou'rt not thy self so, though a Montague *Hanmer* ; Thou art thyself, then not a Montague *conj. Johnson* ; Thou art thyself though, not a Montague *Malone* ; Thou art thyself, although a Montague *Ulrici (conj. Ritson)* ; Thou art thyself, though yet a Montague *conj. Ritson* ; Thou wert thyself, though not a Montague *conj. Maxwell (in NS)*   40–2 What's...name!] *Arranged Malone, incorporating* nor any other part *from* Q1 ; Whats *Mountague?* it is nor hand nor foote, / Nor arme, nor face, ô be some other name / Belonging to a man. Q2–4, F ; Whats *Mountague?* It is nor hand nor foote, / Nor arme, nor face, nor any other part. Q1, *Pope* ; O be some other name! What's Montague? / It is nor hand, nor foot, nor arm, nor face, / Nor any part belonging to a man. *NS (conj. A. Walker)*   43 What's in a name?] Q4, Q1 ; Whats in a name Q2–3 ; What? in a names F   44 word] Q2–4, F ; name Q1, *Otway, Pope*

---

28 wingèd messenger i.e. angel (means 'messenger' in Greek); compare 26.

29 white-upturnèd (eyes) showing the whites in looking up.

30 fall back i.e. tilt their heads back in 'wond'ring' (29), with a suggestion of a mere mortal's (Romeo's) loss of balance under the influence of the heavenly vision (Juliet).

31 lazy puffing clouds clouds which give the appearance of swelling or puffing up as they drift. There is, perhaps, a reference to early maps, which show small clouds with human faces and distended cheeks emitting puffs of wind. Many eds. prefer the easier, but less imaginative, Q1 'lasie pacing', which some consider a variant form of 'lazy passing'. Otway (*Caius Marius* 2.1.265) retains 'lazy puffing'.

32 bosom...air Chapman employs this phrase in *An Humorous Day's Mirth* (1597; 1.1.3).

33–42 These lines on refusing or altering one's name seem to be echoed in Drayton's 'Henry to Rosamond' (1597; 124–30), lines which are followed (133–8) by a reference to Rosamond's eyes, 'Which from a Turret like two Starres appeare'; compare above, 15–22.

39 though even if. See collation.

41 nor...part Supplied from Q1. See collation for the present arrangement of 40–2.

44 word appellation (*OED* sv II 12b). Compare 57 below and *Tit.* 3.2.33. Q1's repetition of 'name' from 43, although formerly widely adopted, is best considered as an example of the kind of repetition common in reported texts.

So Romeo would, were he not Romeo called, 45
Retain that dear perfection which he owes
Without that title. Romeo, doff thy name,
And for thy name, which is no part of thee,
Take all myself.

ROMEO   I take thee at thy word:
Call me but love, and I'll be new baptised; 50
Henceforth I never will be Romeo.

JULIET What man art thou that thus bescreened in night
So stumblest on my counsel?

ROMEO   By a name
I know not how to tell thee who I am.
My name, dear saint, is hateful to myself, 55
Because it is an enemy to thee;
Had I it written, I would tear the word.

JULIET My ears have yet not drunk a hundred words
Of thy tongue's uttering, yet I know the sound.
Art thou not Romeo, and a Montague? 60

ROMEO Neither, fair maid, if either thee dislike.

JULIET How cam'st thou hither, tell me, and wherefore?
The orchard walls are high and hard to climb,
And the place death, considering who thou art,
If any of my kinsmen find thee here. 65

ROMEO With love's light wings did I o'erperch these walls,
For stony limits cannot hold love out,

45 were] Q3–4, F, Q1; wene Q2   47 title. Romeo] Q5 (title: *Romeo*); tytle, *Romeo* Q2–4; title *Romeo*, F; title *Romeo* Q1
47 doff] Q2–4, F; part Q1; quit *Pope*   48 thy] Q2–4, F; that Q1, *Rowe*   52 bescreened] Q3–4, F; beschreend Q2; beskrind
Q1   53–4 By...am.] *As* F; one line, Q2–4; one line, omitting who I am, Q1   58 yet not] Q2–4, F; not yet Q1, *Capell*
59 thy tongue's uttering] Q3–4, F; thy tongus vttering Q2; that tongues vtterance Q1, *Malone*; that tongue's uttering *Pope*
61 maid...dislike] Q2–4, F; Saint...displease Q1, *Pope*; saint...dislike *Theobald*; maid...displease *White*   62 cam'st]
F, Q1; camest Q2–4   65 kinsmen] Q3–4, F, Q1; kismen Q2

46 owes owns, possesses.

47 doff cast aside (as an outer covering);
'doff' = do off (compare 'don').

48 for in return for.

49 take...word accept thy promise (with play
on 'word' = declaration in the form of a phrase or
sentence (*OED* sv 1 10a), i.e. 'Take all myself').

52 bescreened concealed, hidden (earliest use in
OED).

53 counsel private deliberation.

55 saint Echoes 1.5.102, as does 'mask' in 85
(Dowden).

58–9 ears...uttering Malone compares
Edward III (ed. T. Brooke, 2.1.2): 'His eare to

drink her sweet tongues utterance'. Shakespeare is
generally believed to have had a hand in this play.
'Ears drinking words' has classical precedent in
Horace, Ovid and Propertius (see W. Theobald,
Classical Element in the Plays of Shakespeare, 1909,
p. 220).

61 dislike displease.

62–5 Compare Brooke (491–4). Spencer notes:
'Juliet's questions and comments are all direct and
practical. Romeo's answers all vague and fantastic.'
For Romeo's attitude, compare Brooke (459–60).

66 o'erperch fly over. Compare Brooke (830):
'So light he wox, he lept the wall.' NS contrasts
1.4.19–22.

And what love can do, that dares love attempt:
Therefore thy kinsmen are no stop to me.

JULIET If they do see thee, they will murder thee.   70

ROMEO Alack, there lies more peril in thine eye
Than twenty of their swords. Look thou but sweet,
And I am proof against their enmity.

JULIET I would not for the world they saw thee here.

ROMEO I have night's cloak to hide me from their eyes,   75
And but thou love me, let them find me here;
My life were better ended by their hate,
Than death proroguèd, wanting of thy love.

JULIET By whose direction found'st thou out this place?

ROMEO By Love, that first did prompt me to enquire: 80
He lent me counsel, and I lent him eyes.
I am no pilot, yet wert thou as far
As that vast shore washed with the farthest sea,
I should adventure for such merchandise.

JULIET Thou knowest the mask of night is on my face,   85
Else would a maiden blush bepaint my cheek
For that which thou hast heard me speak tonight.
Fain would I dwell on form, fain, fain deny
What I have spoke, but farewell compliment.
Dost thou love me? I know thou wilt say 'Ay';   90
And I will take thy word; yet if thou swear'st,
Thou mayst prove false: at lovers' perjuries
They say Jove laughs. O gentle Romeo,
If thou dost love, pronounce it faithfully;

69 stop] Q2–4, F; let Q1, *Capell*   72 Than] Q2–4, F, Q1; Than' *(i.e.* than in*) conj. Allen (in Furness)*
72 swords.] *Rowe (subst.)*; swords, Q2–4, F, Q1   75 eyes] Q2–4, F; sight Q1, *Capell*   80 that] Q2–4, F; who Q1, *Capell*
80 prompt] Q1; promp Q2–4, F *(variant form)*   82 pilot] Q3–4, F, Q1; Pylat Q2   83 vast shore washed] Q4 (washt);
vast shore washeth Q2; vast shore washet Q3; vast-shore-washet F; vast shore, washt Q1; last shore wash'd *conj. Collier²*
83 farthest] Q2–4, F; furthest Q1, *Steevens (1793)*   84 should] Q2–4, F; would Q1, *Pope*   89 compliment] *Pope*;
complement Q2–4, F; complements Q1   90 Dost] F3; Doest Q2–4, F, Q1   90 love me? I] Q2–4; Loue? I F; loue me?
Nay I Q1; Love? O I F2   92 mayst] Q5, F4; maiest Q2–4, F, Q1   92 false:...perjuries] F, Q1; false...periuries. Q2;
false,...periuries Q3–4   93 laughs.] *Rowe (subst.)*; laughes, Q2–4; laught, F; smiles. Q1

71–2 lies...swords Conventional hyperbole,
but also ironic foreshadowing.

73 proof invulnerable (as if in armour).

75 night's cloak Compare Brooke (457): 'But
when on earth the night her mantel blacke hath
spred'.

76 but unless.

78 proroguèd, wanting of deferred, lacking.

83 vast far-stretching; but taken as a variant of
'waste' = barren, desert.

84 adventure venture, as a merchant adventurer
in pursuit of riches.

86 bepaint i.e. (would be seen to) colour.

88 Fain Gladly.

88 dwell on form observe decorum.

89 compliment the hollow game of conventional civility.

92–3 lovers'...laughs Compare Ovid, *Ars
Amatoria* I, 633: 'Iuppiter ex alto periuria ridet
amantum', and Tibullus, III.vi, 49–50; proverbial
to the Elizabethans (see Tilley J82).

Or if thou think'st I am too quickly won,   95
I'll frown and be perverse, and say thee nay,
So thou wilt woo, but else not for the world.
In truth, fair Montague, I am too fond,
And therefore thou mayst think my behaviour light:
But trust me, gentleman, I'll prove more true   100
Than those that have more coying to be strange.
I should have been more strange, I must confess,
But that thou overheard'st, ere I was ware,
My true-love passion; therefore pardon me,
And not impute this yielding to light love,   105
Which the dark night hath so discovered.

ROMEO Lady, by yonder blessèd moon I vow,
That tips with silver all these fruit-tree tops –

JULIET O swear not by the moon, th'inconstant moon,
That monthly changes in her circled orb,   110
Lest that thy love prove likewise variable.

ROMEO What shall I swear by?

JULIET   Do not swear at all;
Or if thou wilt, swear by thy gracious self,
Which is the god of my idolatry,
And I'll believe thee.

ROMEO   If my heart's dear love –   115

95 thou think'st] Q5; thou thinkest Q2–4, F; thou thinke Q1, *Pope*; you think *Theobald*   98 fond,] Q1; fond: Q2–4, F
99 mayst] Q5, F3; maiest Q2–4, F, Q1   99 behaviour] Q2–4, F; hauiour Q1, F2   99 light:] Q1; light, Q2–4, F
101 more] Q4, Q1; *not in* Q2–3, F; the *Williams*   101 coying] Q2–4, F; cunning Q1, *Pope*; coyning F2, *Williams*
104 true-love] *Kittredge*; truloue Q2; trueloue Q3; true loue Q4; true Loues F, Q1   107 blessèd] Q2–4, Q1; *not in* F
107 vow] Q2–4, F; sweare Q1, *Malone*   108 tops –] *Rowe*; tops. Q2–4, F, Q1   110 circled] Q3–4, F, Q1; circle Q2
112 What...by?] Q2–4, F; Now by Q1   113 gracious] Q2–4, F; glorious Q1, *White*   114 is] Q2–4, F; art Q1
115 heart's dear] Q2–4, F; true harts Q1, *Pope*   115 love –] F2; loue. Q2–4, F; loue Q1

95–106 See supplementary note.
97 **else** otherwise.
98 **fond** doting, over-tender.
101 **have...strange** show a greater affectation
of reserve in order to appear hard to win. 'more'
supplied from Q4, Q1 for metrical reasons. For Q2
'coying', usually emended to Q1 'cunning' (compare
Temp. 3.1.81), see Thomas Lodge, *Scillaes Metamorphosis* (1589; sig. B2ᵛ; 340–2): 'But she unkind
rewarded me with mockes, / Such are the fruites
that spring from Ladies coying, / Who smile at
teares, and are intrapt with toying'; and Nashe,
Saffron-Walden (*Works*, III, 116): 'cockering and
coying himselfe beyond imagination' (perhaps
picked up from 'coying themselves' in Harvey's
Pierces Supererogation (1593; sig. **1)).

104 **true-love** faithful-love.
105 **light** wanton, easy (with the inevitable play
on 'dark night' in 106).
106 **Which** Referring to 'yielding'.
107 **I vow** Only a hint for 107–15 in Brooke
(516): 'And therupon he sware an othe.'
109 **inconstant moon** The moon, because of its
changes, was a common type of inconstancy.
H. M. Richmond (*Shakespeare's Sexual Comedy*,
1971, p. 115) suggests possible reference here and
below (112, 116) to Matt. 5.34–6. Coincidentally,
Julia (Juliet) tells Roselo (Romeo) not to swear in
Lope de Vega's *Castelvines y Monteses* (1.4).
110 **circled orb** The sphere in which the moon
circles in the Ptolemaic astronomy.
113 **gracious self** yourself, full of all graces.

JULIET Well, do not swear. Although I joy in thee,
        I have no joy of this contract tonight,
        It is too rash, too unadvised, too sudden,
        Too like the lightning, which doth cease to be
        Ere one can say 'It lightens'. Sweet, good night: 120
        This bud of love, by summer's ripening breath,
        May prove a beauteous flower when next we meet.
        Good night, good night! as sweet repose and rest
        Come to thy heart as that within my breast.

ROMEO   O wilt thou leave me so unsatisfied?   125

JULIET What satisfaction canst thou have tonight?

ROMEO   Th'exchange of thy love's faithful vow for mine.

JULIET I gave thee mine before thou didst request it;
        And yet I would it were to give again.

ROMEO   Wouldst thou withdraw it? for what purpose, love?   130

JULIET But to be frank and give it thee again,
        And yet I wish but for the thing I have:
        My bounty is as boundless as the sea,
        My love as deep; the more I give to thee
        The more I have, for both are infinite.   135

                        [*Nurse calls within.*]

        I hear some noise within; dear love, adieu! –
        Anon, good Nurse! – Sweet Montague, be true.
        Stay but a little, I will come again.   [*Exit above*]

ROMEO   O blessèd, blessèd night! I am afeard,
        Being in night, all this is but a dream,   140
        Too flattering-sweet to be substantial.

much talk of light & dark, moon & sun, night & day (handwritten margin note)

---

116 swear....thee,] *Rowe (subst.)*; sweare,...thee: Q2–4, F; Q1 *reads 116 as* Sweare not at al, though I doo ioy in / (thee,
120 lightens'.] Q1; lightens, Q2–4, F   120–35 Sweet...infinite.] *not in* Q1   120 Sweet,] F4; sweete Q2–4, F
135 SD] *Rowe (from* F *Cals within.)*; *no* SD, Q2–4, Q1   138 SD] *Dyce (after Rowe)*; *no* SD, Q2–4, F, Q1   141 flattering-sweet]
Theobald; flattering sweete Q2–4, F; flattering true Q1   141 SD] *Rowe (from* F2 *Enter.)*; *no* SD, Q2–4, F, Q1

117 **contract** mutual agreement; accented on the second syllable.

118 **rash...unadvised** hasty...thoughtless. Compare Bel-imperia's premonition under similar clandestine circumstances in Kyd's *The Spanish Tragedy* 2.4.6–8, 14–15, and Brooke (209–10).

120 'It lightens' Compare *MND* 1.1.145–9, which in the last line ('So quick bright things come to confusion') catches the fatal premonition in the lightning image here: love may be short and deadly.

125 **wilt...unsatisfied** Compare Brooke (563–4): 'els favour found he none, / That night at lady Juliets hand, save pleasant woordes alone'.

131 **frank** (1) bounteous; (2) freely outspoken.

132 **yet...have** I only wish, however, for what I still possess (i.e. her inexhaustible love for Romeo); compare 134–5, 'the more I give to thee / The more I have'.

133–4 **bounty...deep** Gibbons compares *AYLI* 4.1.206–8. Compare also Daniel's *To Delia*, Sonnet 1: 'Unto the boundless ocean of thy beautie / Runs this poore river.'

137 **Anon** Presently, very soon.

141 **substantial** real, solid (as opposed to the stuff of dreams); quadrisyllabic.

[*Enter Juliet above.*]

JULIET Three words, dear Romeo, and good night indeed.
　　　If that thy bent of love be honourable,
　　　Thy purpose marriage, send me word tomorrow,
　　　By one that I'll procure to come to thee,   145
　　　Where and what time thou wilt perform the rite,
　　　And all my fortunes at thy foot I'll lay,
　　　And follow thee my lord throughout the world.
NURSE [*Within*] Madam!
JULIET I come, anon. – But if thou meanest not well,   150
　　　I do beseech thee –
NURSE [*Within*]　　　　　　　Madam!
JULIET　　　　　　　　　　　By and by I come –
　　　To cease thy strife, and leave me to my grief.
　　　Tomorrow will I send.
ROMEO So thrive my soul –
JULIET　　　　　　　　　A thousand times good night!

　　　　　　　　　　　　　　　　　　　　　[*Exit above*]

ROMEO A thousand times the worse, to want thy light.   155
　　　Love goes toward love as schoolboys from their books,
　　　But love from love, toward school with heavy looks.
　　　　　　　　　[*Retiring slowly.*]

　　　　　　　Enter *Juliet again* [*above*].

JULIET Hist, Romeo, hist! O for a falc'ner's voice,
　　　To lure this tassel-gentle back again:

146 rite] F3; right Q2–3, F, Q1; rights Q4　148 lord] F, Q1; L. Q2–3; Loue Q4　149–55] *not in* Q1　149, 151 SD]
Capell (from F *Within:); no* SD, Q2–4　149 Madam!] *in right margin, after* world., *148,* Q2–4; *to right of and below 148,* F
151 Madam!] *in right margin, after* I come), Q2–4; *to right of and following* thee –, F　152 strife] Q2–3, F; sute Q4
(compare Brooke, To cease your sute)　154 soul –] *Theobald;* soule. Q2–4, F　154 SD] *Dyce (from* F *Exit.); no* SD, Q2–4
157 toward] Q2–4; towards F; to Q1　157 SD.1 *Retiring slowly.*] *Malone (after Capell); no* SD, Q1　157 SD.2 above]
Capell; not in Q2–4, F; *no* SD, Q1　159 tassel-gentle] *Hanmer;* Tassel gentle Q2–4, F, Q1　159 again:] Q1; againe, Q2–4, F

143–52 Compare Brooke (533–44).
　143 **bent of love** inclination to love; compare
Brooke's 'ende and marke' (536).
　151 **By and by** Immediately.
　152 **strife** striving, endeavour. Q4 'sute'
(= suit) has been widely and unnecessarily adopted,
mainly because it seems to echo Brooke (544).
　155 **thousand...light** i.e. night, far from being
'good' (142, 154), is a thousand times blacker
('worse') lacking your radiance. Picks up and
refocuses the light imagery associated with Juliet in
lines 1–32.

156–7 **schoolboys...looks** Compare *AYLI*
2.7.145–7.
　158–9 **Hist...lure** A falconer called a hawk to
the lure (an apparatus constructed of a bunch of
feathers baited with raw flesh, to which was
attached a long cord or thong) by taking 'the lewre
at length of the string, and cast[ing] it about your
heade, crying and lewring alowde' (George
Turberville, *The Booke of Faulconrie* (1575), p.
147). See supplementary note.
　159 **tassel-gentle** tercel-gentle, a male hawk,
appropriate to a prince (Romeo).

Bondage is hoarse, and may not speak aloud,   160
Else would I tear the cave where Echo lies,
And make her airy tongue more hoarse than mine
With repetition of my Romeo's name.
ROMEO It is my soul that calls upon my name.
How silver-sweet sound lovers' tongues by night,   165
Like softest music to attending ears!
JULIET Romeo!
ROMEO   My niësse?
JULIET   What a'clock tomorrow
Shall I send to thee?
ROMEO   By the hour of nine.
JULIET I will not fail, 'tis twenty year till then.
I have forgot why I did call thee back.   *☆Time*   170
ROMEO Let me stand here till thou remember it.
JULIET I shall forget, to have thee still stand there,
Rememb'ring how I love thy company.
ROMEO And I'll still stay, to have thee still forget,
Forgetting any other home but this.   175
JULIET 'Tis almost morning, I would have thee gone:
And yet no farther than a wanton's bird,
That lets it hop a little from his hand,

---

160 hoarse] Q2–4, F, Q1 ; husht *Daniel*   162 tongue] Q2–4, F ; voice Q1, *Collier*   162–3 than mine With] Q4 (then myne / With); then / With Q2–3, F; as mine, / With Q1 ; then with / The F2; then Fame, / With *Daniel*   163 Romeo's name.] *Steevens (from Q1: Romeos* name. / *Romeo?*); *Romeo.* Q2–4, F; "Romeo!" *NS (after Hoppe)*   165 silver-sweet] F4; siluer sweete Q2–4, F, Q1   167 My niësse?] *NS* (niëss!; *question mark, Capell*); My Neece. Q2–3, F; My Deere. Q4; Madame. Q1 ; My sweete. F2   167 What] Q2–4, F; At what Q1, *Pope*   168 By] Q2–4, F; At Q1, *Capell*   169 year] Q2; yeares Q3–4, F, Q1   172 forget,] Q3–4, F; forget Q2, Q1   177 farther] Q2–4; further F, Q1   178 That] Q2–4, F; Who Q1, *Capell*   178 his] Q2–4, F; her Q1, *Pope*

---

160 **Bondage is hoarse** One in confinement, as
Juliet is under the discipline of her father's house,
must call softly (as if hoarse).
161 **cave...lies** See Ovid, *Metamorphoses* III,
359–401, known to Shakespeare in Golding's
translation (1567; III, 447–500). Punished by Juno,
Echo could repeat only the tag ends of what she
heard others say; repulsed by Narcissus, with whom
she had fallen in love, 'ever since she lyves alone
in dennes and hollow Caves' (Golding, 491).
162 **airy tongue** Metonymy ('tongue' for
'voice', the reading of Q1); compare 165. Compare
Golding (III, 495–7): 'The bloud doth vanish into
ayre from out of all her veynes, / And nought is left
but voyce and bones:... / His bones they say were
turnde to stones.'
163 **Romeo's name** See supplementary note.
165 **silver-sweet** Compare 4.5.127–35.

167 ***niësse** a young, unfledged hawk (= 'eyas';
compare *Ham.* 2.2.339, 'an aery of children, little
eyases'). Picking up 'tassel-gentle' (159), 'niësse',
Dover Wilson's brilliant emendation of Q2 'Neece',
is peculiarly apt for the young Juliet above, imaged
as a nestling in its aery (= nest). NS compares 1.2.8.
168 **nine** It is, however, twelve o'clock when the
Nurse meets Romeo in 2.4.92–3.
174 **to...still** in order to...ever.
175 **Forgetting...home** Compare Tilley L565
('The lover is not where he lives but where he
loves').
177 **wanton's** spoiled, pampered child's (most
frequently applied to boys; hence Q2 'his' is
retained for Q1 'her' in 178). Compare *John*
5.1.69–70: 'a beardless boy, / A cock'red silken
wanton'; and *Temp.* 4.1.100–1.

Like a poor prisoner in his twisted gyves,
And with a silken thread plucks it back again,   180
So loving-jealous of his liberty.

ROMEO I would I were thy bird.

JULIET   Sweet, so would I,
Yet I should kill thee with much cherishing.
Good night, good night! Parting is such sweet sorrow,
That I shall say good night till it be morrow.   [*Exit above*]   185

ROMEO Sleep dwell upon thine eyes, peace in thy breast!
Would I were sleep and peace, so sweet to rest!
Hence will I to my ghostly sire's close cell,
His help to crave, and my dear hap to tell.   *Exit*

[2.3] *Enter* FRIAR [LAWRENCE] *alone, with a basket.*

FRIAR LAWRENCE
The grey-eyed morn smiles on the frowning night,
Check'ring the eastern clouds with streaks of light;

180 silken thread] Q3–4, F; silken threed Q2; silke thred Q1, *Pope*   180 plucks it back] Q2–4, F; puls it backe Q1; plucks
it F2   181 loving-jealous] *Theobald*; louing Iealous Q2–4, F, Q1   184] *As* Q1; *two lines, ending* good night / . . . sorrow
Q2, Q4; *two lines, arranged* Good night, good night. / *Ro.* Parting . . . sorrow Q3, F   185 SD] *Dyce*; *no* SD, Q2–4, F, Q1
186 SH ROMEO] Q4, Q1; *Iu.* Q2–3, F, *Hosley*   187 Would I] Q4; *Ro.* Would I Q2–3, F; I would Q1; *Hosley assigns 187
to Juliet*   187 rest!] *Pope*; rest Q2–4; rest, F; rest. Q1   187] *Following 187* Q2–3, F *contain four lines (not in* Q4, Q1)
which are repeated, with slight variations, as the opening lines of 2.3; see notes to 2.3.1–4 below   188 ghostly sire's close]
conj. Delius (from Brooke, gostly syre*); ghostly Friers close Q2–4; ghostly Fries close F; Ghostly fathers Q1, *Capell
Act 2, Scene 3   2.3] *Hanmer*; *no scene division,* Q2–4, F, Q1   Location] *Malone*; *A Monastery. / *Rowe*; Fields near a
Convent. / *Capell*   0 SD] Q2–4, F; *Enter Frier Francis.* Q1   1 SH FRIAR LAWRENCE] *Dyce*; *Fri., Frier., Fr.* Q2–4, F,
Q1 (*throughout, except in 5.2*)   1–4] *not in* F2–4; *this second version of these lines is here considered as a revision of the
first version and hence the basic copy-text; see Textual Analysis. See above,* 2.2.187.   1 grey-eyed] Q3–4, F, Q1 (grey eyde
or gray ey'd, *all without hyphen*); grey-eyed Q2; *in first version, which appears only in* Q2–3, F, *all read* grey (*or* gray)
eyde *or* gray ey'd   2 Check'ring] Q3–4 (Checkring), F, Q1; Checking Q2; *in the first version, which appears only in* Q2–3,
F, *all read* Checkring

179 in . . . gyves (1) entwined in his fetters
(transposed adjective); (2) in his intertwined fetters.

181 loving-jealous lovingly mistrustful (with
suggestion of excessive love; compare 183).

181 his its. Regular older form of neuter
genitive. 182–3 See supplementary note.

183 kill . . . cherishing smother with too much
love. The line strikes an ominous chord.

184–7 See supplementary note.

188 ghostly *sire's spiritual father's; emended
from Brooke (559): 'He is my gostly syre' (again in
595). Q2 'ghostly Friers' is evidently wrong and
'Friers' is an easy misreading of 'Siers' (so spelled
in *Sonnets* 8.11, as NS notes). Q1 'Ghostly fathers',
apart from offering orthographic difficulties, is
likely to be a bad quarto anticipation of Q2, 2.3.45.

188 close cell Compare Brooke (1264–73):
'trusty Lawrence secret cell', where 'he was wont
in youth, his fayre frendes to bestowe' – the only
slur on Friar Lawrence in Brooke's poem.

189 dear hap good fortune.

Act 2, Scene 3
Location Verona. Friar Lawrence's cell.
1–4 See below, pp. 210–11.

1 grey-eyed having bluish-grey eyes. Compare
Ovid's *Metamorphoses* (trans. Golding), I, 69: 'the
morning grayc'; and *ibid.*, IV, 774. The meaning
'blue-eyed', sometimes assigned, does not seem to
be supported by *OED*. See 3.5.220. Probably
echoed in Haughton, *Englishmen for My Money*
(1598; MSR, 1): 'this gray-eyde Morning'.

And fleckled darkness like a drunkard reels
From forth day's path and Titan's fiery wheels:
Now ere the sun advance his burning eye,   5
The day to cheer, and night's dank dew to dry,
I must upfill this osier cage of ours
With baleful weeds and precious-juicèd flowers.
The earth that's nature's mother is her tomb;
What is her burying grave, that is her womb;   10
And from her womb children of divers kind
We sucking on her natural bosom find:
Many for many virtues excellent,
None but for some, and yet all different.
O mickle is the powerful grace that lies   15
In plants, herbs, stones, and their true qualities:
For nought so vile, that on the earth doth live,
But to the earth some special good doth give;
Nor ought so good but, strained from that fair use,
Revolts from true birth, stumbling on abuse.   20

---

3 fleckled darkness] F; fleckeld darknesse Q2–4; flecked darkenes Q1, *Steevens; first version reads* darknesse fleckted Q2, darknesse fleckeld Q3, darknesse fleckel'd F; darkness flecker'd *Pope;* flecker'd darkness *Capell;* darkness fleckèd *NS*   4 path and] *Boswell–Malone;* path, and Q2–4, F, Q1; *in the first version, which appears only in* Q2–3, F, *all read* pathway, made by   4 fiery] Q1, *Malone;* burning Q2–4, F; *not in first version,* Q2–3, F   7 l] Q2–4, F; We Q1   7 upfill] Q2–4, F, Q1; fill up *Pope*   8 precious-juicèd] *Pope;* precious iuyced Q2–4, F, Q1   9–14] *not in* Q1   13 many virtues] Q3, F; many, vertues Q2; many vertures Q4   16 plants, herbs] Q2–4, F; hearbes, plants Q1, *Capell*   18 to] Q2–4, F, Q1; to't *Hanmer*   19 ought] Q2–4, F; nought Q1; aught *Theobald²*   20 from...stumbling] Q2–4, F; to vice and stumbles Q1, *Pope;* from 's...stumbling *Hanmer*

---

3 **fleckled** dappled (with little streaks). Compare *Ado* 5.3.25–7: 'the gentle day, / Before the wheeles of Phoebus, round about / Dapples the drowsy east with spots of grey'; and *R3* 5.3.86 'flaky darkness'.

4 **From forth** Out of the way of.

4 **Titan's fiery wheels** the burning wheels of the chariot of the sun-god, the Titan Helios (driving in its daily track = 'path'). See Ovid, *Metamorphoses* II, 129–37 (Golding, II, 171–5) and 3.2.1–4 n. See suppl. note.   5 **advance** raise, lift up.

7 **osier cage** basket made of willow twigs.

7 **ours** i.e. not his, but the common property of his order, the Franciscans.

8 **baleful** full of active evil, poisonous.

8 **precious-juicèd** flowers i.e. flowers (as opposed to 'weeds') that contain rare healing essences.

9–30 For the Christian background to the doctrine of nature in these lines, see R. M. Frye, *Shakespeare and Christian Doctrine*, 1963, pp. 216–19.

9 **The earth...tomb** Steevens compares Lucretius, *De Rerum Natura* V, 259: 'Omniparens eadem rerum commune sepulcrum'; compare also *Tit.* 2.3.239–40.

12 **sucking on** receiving sustenance from. 'children' (11) = plants.

14 **None...some** Explained in 17–18 below.

15 **mickle** great. Compare Brooke (2109–11) and Gil Polo, *Enamoured Diana* (in Montemayor, p. 392): 'Herbes it brought forth / Of mickle worth.'

15 **grace** efficacious virtue in healing (Johnson).

16 **true** proper.

17–18 **For...give** Compare Tilley N327, N328; *H5* 4.1.4–5; the opening of Brooke's preface 'To the Reader'; and (for 19–20) Nashe, *Christs Teares over Jerusalem* (1593; *Works*, II, 39): 'Nothing doth profite, but perverted may hurte.'

19 **strained** unnaturally forced, perverted.

20 **true birth** i.e. its proper nature; compare 'true qualities' in 16.

20 **stumbling on abuse** falling into perversion; compare 94; the echo here seems deliberate.

Virtue itself turns vice, being misapplied,
And vice sometime by action dignified.

Enter ROMEO.

Within the infant rind of this weak flower
Poison hath residence, and medicine power:
For this, being smelt, with that part cheers each part,   25
Being tasted, stays all senses with the heart.
Two such opposèd kings encamp them still
In man as well as herbs, grace and rude will;
And where the worser is predominant,
Full soon the canker death eats up that plant.   30

ROMEO Good morrow, father.

FRIAR LAWRENCE   Benedicite!
What early tongue so sweet saluteth me?
Young son, it argues a distempered head
So soon to bid good morrow to thy bed:
Care keeps his watch in every old man's eye,   35
And where care lodges, sleep will never lie;
But where unbruisèd youth with unstuffed brain
Doth couch his limbs, there golden sleep doth reign.
Therefore thy earliness doth me assure
Thou art uproused with some distemp'rature;   40
Or if not so, then here I hit it right,
Our Romeo hath not been in bed tonight.

ROMEO That last is true, the sweeter rest was mine.

FRIAR LAWRENCE God pardon sin! wast thou with Rosaline?

---

22 sometime by action] Q2–4, F; sometimes by action Q1; sometime by action's *Theobald*; sometime's by action *Capell*
22 SD] Q2–4, F; *no* SD, Q1; *placed after 30, Pope*; ROMEO *approaches, unseen by the Friar* / NS   23 weak] Q2–4, F; small Q1, *Pope*   25 smelt, with that part] F; smelt with that part, Q2–4; smelt too, with that part Q1; smelt, with that sense *Pope*; smelt, with that act *Collier²*   26 stays] Q2; slayes Q3–4, F, Q1   27 kings] Q2–4, F; foes Q1, *Pope*; Kinds *Rowe³*; Kin *Warburton*   31 father] Q2–4, F; to my Ghostly Confessor Q1   31 Benedicite] Q3–4, Q1; Benedicitie Q2; Benedecite F   32 sweet] Q2–4, F; soone Q1, *Boswell*   33 distempered] F4 (distemper'd); distempered Q2–4, F, Q1   40 with] Q2–4, F; by Q1, *Pope*

---

22 **And vice...dignified** i.e. a quality that is in itself a fault may, under certain circumstances, result in a good action (Kittredge).
23 **infant** undeveloped, nascent.
24 **medicine power** i.e. healing hath power.
25 **that part** i.e. its scent.
26 **stays** arrests, brings to a standstill. Q3–4, F, Q1 'slayes' is sometimes wrongly preferred.
26 **with** together with.
28 **grace...will** divine virtue and unruly human volition (frequently with reference to sexual

excess). NS compares *JC* 2.1.66–9. See above, pp. 24–5.
30 **canker** canker-worm (which devours the bud secretly from within); compare 1.1.142–4.
31 **Benedicite!** Bless you!
33 **distempered** disordered (from an imbalance of the bodily humours); compare 'distemp'rature' in 40.
37 **unbruisèd...unstuffed** uninjured (by life)...unburdened (by thought).

ROMEO With Rosaline, my ghostly father? no;   45
    I have forgot that name, and that name's woe.

FRIAR LAWRENCE
    That's my good son, but where hast thou been then?

ROMEO I'll tell thee ere thou ask it me again:
    I have been feasting with mine enemy,
    Where on a sudden one hath wounded me   50
    That's by me wounded; both our remedies
    Within thy help and holy physic lies.
    I bear no hatred, blessèd man; for lo,
    My intercession likewise steads my foe.

FRIAR LAWRENCE Be plain, good son, and homely in thy drift,   55
    Riddling confession finds but riddling shrift.

ROMEO Then plainly know, my heart's dear love is set
    On the fair daughter of rich Capulet;
    As mine on hers, so hers is set on mine,
    And all combined, save what thou must combine   60
    By holy marriage. When and where and how
    We met, we wooed, and made exchange of vow,
    I'll tell thee as we pass, but this I pray,
    That thou consent to marry us today.

FRIAR LAWRENCE Holy Saint Francis, what a change is here!   65
    Is Rosaline, that thou didst love so dear,
    So soon forsaken? Young men's love then lies
    Not truly in their hearts, but in their eyes.
    Jesu Maria, what a deal of brine
    Hath washed thy sallow cheeks for Rosaline!   70
    How much salt water thrown away in waste,

---

45 father?] F; father Q2–4, Q1   50–1 me…wounded; both] F (*subst.*); me:…wounded both, Q2; me:…wounded, both Q3–4; mee…wounded, both Q1   55 and] Q2–4, Q1; rest F   61 marriage.] Q3–4 (marriage:), F, Q1; marriage, Q2   62 wooed] Q1 (woo'd), Q5; wooed Q2–4, F   62 vow,] F4; vow: Q2–4, F; vowes, Q1   66 that] Q2–4, F; whome Q1, *Pope*   67 Young] Q3, F; yonng Q2; yong Q4, Q1   71 thrown] Q2–3, F; throne Q4; cast Q1

45 **ghostly** spiritual.
51 **both our remedies** the cure for both of us.
52 **holy physic** spiritual remedy (through marriage).
54 **intercession likewise steads** petition also benefits.
54 **foe** i.e. Juliet (as a Capulet).
55 **homely** direct.
56 **Riddling** Ambiguous, enigmatic.
56 **shrift** absolution.
63 **pass** go along. Spencer notes that Romeo as usual is in a hurry. Compare 93–4 and the warning against 'rude will' (28) that 94 conveys.

65 **Saint Francis** A mild oath, proper to a member of the Franciscan order.
68 **hearts…eyes** i.e. a young man's love is based on the merely visual ('a painted banquet', *Sonnets* 47.6), a thing of the outward senses ('eyes'), not an 'inward love of heart' (*Sonnets* 46.14).
69 **Jesu Maria** (By) Jesus (and) Mary, another mild oath suitable to a priest. Shakespeare refers to the Virgin as 'Maria' nowhere else.
69 **brine** i.e. salt tears, the 'season' (72) or preservative of love.
70 **sallow** sickly yellow (from the anguish of unrequited love).

To season love, that of it doth not taste!
The sun not yet thy sighs from heaven clears,
Thy old groans yet ringing in mine ancient ears;
Lo here upon thy cheek the stain doth sit   75
Of an old tear that is not washed off yet.
If e'er thou wast thyself, and these woes thine,
Thou and these woes were all for Rosaline.
And art thou changed? Pronounce this sentence then:
Women may fall, when there's no strength in men.   80

ROMEO Thou chid'st me oft for loving Rosaline.

FRIAR LAWRENCE For doting, not for loving, pupil mine.

ROMEO And bad'st me bury love.

FRIAR LAWRENCE   Not in a grave,
To lay one in, another out to have.

ROMEO I pray thee chide me not. Her I love now   85
Doth grace for grace and love for love allow;
The other did not so.

FRIAR LAWRENCE   O she knew well
Thy love did read by rote, that could not spell.
But come, young waverer, come go with me,
In one respect I'll thy assistant be: 90
For this alliance may so happy prove
To turn your households' rancour to pure love.

ROMEO O let us hence, I stand on sudden haste.

FRIAR LAWRENCE Wisely and slow, they stumble that run fast.

Exeunt

72 it] Q2–4, F; loue Q1   73 sighs...clears,] Q1; sighes,...cleares Q2–4; sighes,...cleares, F   74 yet ringing] Q2–3, F; yet ring Q4; ring yet Q1, *Pope*   74 mine] Q2; my Q3–4, F, Q1   79 changed?] Q3–4, F; chang'd, Q2; changde, Q1   84 in, another] Q3–4, F; in an other Q2; in another Q1   85 chide...Her] Q2–4, F; chide not, she whom Q1, *Pope*   85 now] Q3–4, F, Q1; now. Q2   88 that] Q2–4, F; and Q1, *Pope*   92 households'] *Capell*; housholds Q2–4, Q1; houshould F; houshold F2   93–4] *not in* Q1

72 that...taste that (despite all the seasoning of tears) your love ('it') now appears insipid (without flavour).

73 sun...clears Compare 1.1.124 – a common conceit.

75–6 Lo...yet Compare Brooke (2557–8), though in the context of Juliet's supposed death.

77 wast thyself i.e. sincere, without pretence.

79 sentence moral maxim, aphorism.

80 may fall may be excused for falling.

86 grace favour.

88 Thy...spell i.e. the expression of your love was a schoolboy exercise of memory (rote learning) by one who couldn't read ('spell') and thus understand what he was mouthing. Compare Sidney, *Astrophil and Stella*, Second Song, 24: 'Who will read must first learne spelling.'

90 In one respect For a special reason.

91–2 For...love Compare Brooke (427–8).

92 To As to.

93 stand on insist on (as a necessity).

94 Wisely...fast Proverbial (Tilley H198; Smith 148, 'Error and repentance are the attendants on hasty decisions' (Publilius Syrus)). Compare 2.6.15.

[2.4] *Enter* BENVOLIO *and* MERCUTIO.

MERCUTIO Where the dev'l should this Romeo be?
    Came he not home tonight?
BENVOLIO Not to his father's, I spoke with his man.
MERCUTIO Why, that same pale hard-hearted wench, that Rosaline,
    Torments him so, that he will sure run mad.   5
BENVOLIO Tybalt, the kinsman to old Capulet,
    Hath sent a letter to his father's house.
MERCUTIO A challenge, on my life.
BENVOLIO Romeo will answer it.
MERCUTIO Any man that can write may answer a letter.   10
BENVOLIO Nay, he will answer the letter's master, how he dares, being
    dared.
MERCUTIO Alas, poor Romeo, he is already dead, stabbed with a white
    wench's black eye, run through the ear with a love-song, the very
    pin of his heart cleft with the blind bow-boy's butt-shaft; and is   15
    he a man to encounter Tybalt?
BENVOLIO Why, what is Tybalt?
MERCUTIO More than Prince of Cats. O, he's the courageous captain

Act 2, Scene 4 2.4] *Hanmer; no scene division,* Q2–4, F, Q1   Location] *Rowe*   0 SD *Enter*] Q3–4, F, Q1; *Bnter* Q2
1–2] *As verse, Capell,* Q1 *(var.); as prose,* Q2–4, F   1 dev'l] Q3–4 (deu'le); deule Q2; deu le F; devile F2; devil F3
4 Why] Q2–4, F; Ah Q1, *Malone;* Ay *Capell*   6–7] *As verse, Theobald,* Q1; *as prose,* Q2–4, F   6 kinsman] Q3–4, F,
Q1; kisman Q2   6 to] Q2–4, F; of Q1, *Capell*   11 master, how] Q4; maister how Q2–3, F; master if Q1 *(reading* master
if hee bee challenged *for* master...dared*)*   13 dead, stabbed] Q2–4, F; dead stab'd F; dead: stabd Q1; dead-stabd *conj.*
Daniel   14 run through] Q2–4, F; shot thorough Q1, *Capell*   17 SH BENVOLIO] F, Q1; *Ro.* Q2; *Rom.* Q3–4
17–18 Why...Cats. O] Q2–4, F; Why what is *Tybalt?* / *Mer:* More than the prince of cattes I can tell you. Oh Q1,
Capell (omitting the); Why...cats? – Oh Theobald; Why...Tybalt more...Cats? / *Mer.* O *Rann (conj. Mason)*
18 he's] Q2–4, F; he is Q1, *Capell*

Act 2, Scene 4
  Location Verona. A street.
  1 **should** can.
  2 **tonight** last night.
  9 **answer it** accept the challenge. Mercutio
pretends to misunderstand, implying that Romeo is
too love-sick to fight (NS).
  11 **how** 'as' or 'to what extent'.
  12 **dared** challenged.
  13–14 **white...eye** Compare *LLL* 3.1.196–7 on
Rosaline: 'A whitely wanton with a velvet brow, /
With two pitch-balls stuck in her face for eyes'; and
Sonnets 127, 130, 132 (describing the 'Dark Lady').
Dark hair and eyes in a woman seem alternately to
have attracted and repelled Shakespeare.
  14–15 **very pin** the centre of the centre. A 'pin'
was the black peg affixed to the centre of the clout
or prick ('the white') on an archer's target.
Compare Tilley P336.

  15 **butt-shaft** An unbarbed arrow used in
shooting at the butts (*OED*). Compare 'Cupid's
butt-shaft' in *LLL* 1.2.175–6; Shakespeare appears
to have been the first to use the term.
  18 **Prince of Cats** Tybert is the name of the cat
in *The History of Reynard the Fox* (trans. William
Caxton, from a Dutch version, in 1481). Compare
Nashe in *Saffron-Walden* (*Works*, III, 51): '*Tibault*
or *Isegrim*, Prince of Cattes'. Isegrim is the name
of the wolf in the *History*. The title 'Prince of Cats'
does not appear in the *History*, but seems to arise
naturally out of its context in Nashe. If Nashe is the
first to describe 'Tibault' as 'Prince of Cattes',
Shakespeare's use of the phrase to describe Tybalt
would seem to strengthen the case for his knowledge
of *Saffron-Walden* (see above, pp. 3–4).
  18–19 **captain of compliments** 'complete
master of all the laws of ceremony' (Johnson).
Tybalt is sarcastically described by Mercutio as one

of compliments: he fights as you sing prick-song, keeps time,
distance, and proportion; he rests his minim rests, one, two, and   20
the third in your bosom; the very butcher of a silk button, a duellist,
a duellist; a gentleman of the very first house, of the first and second
cause. Ah, the immortal 'passado', the 'punto reverso', the 'hay'!

BENVOLIO The what?

MERCUTIO The pox of such antic, lisping, affecting phantasimes, these   25
new tuners of accent! 'By Jesu, a very good blade! a very tall man!

19 compliments] *Rowe;* Complements Q2–4, F, Q1   19 he] Q2–4, F; Catso, he Q1   19 he rests...rests] Q3–4 (*reading*
minum; minim *Steevens, 1778);* he rests, his minum rests Q2; he rests his minum F; rests me his minum rest Q1, *Malone*
(minim)   22 house,] Q5; house Q2–4, F, Q1   23 reverso', the 'hay'!] *Steevens (subst.);* reuerso, the Hay. Q2–4, F,
Q1; reverso, the Hay – *Rowe;* reverso, the, hay! *Theobald;* reverso! the – hay! *Capell; reverso!* the *hai!* / *White*
25 antic] *Pope;* antique Q2–4, F; limping antique Q1   25 phantasimes] *Williams (conj. Crow);* phantacies Q2–4, F;
fantasticoes Q1, *Capell;* phantastickes *Collier MS.*   26 tuners] Q2–4, F, Q1; turners *Rowe*   26 accent] Q2–4, F; accents
Q1, *Pope*   26 'By Jesu] Q2–4, Q1; Iesu F

of the new (to England) Italianate 'duellists' (21),
who 'quarrel in print, by the book' (*AYLI* 5.4.90).
See supplementary note.

19 he fights Q1 'Catso, he fights' is tempting
because, as NS suggests, the exclamation is 'apt to
both speaker and context'. 'Catso' is from Italian
'cazzo' = penis.

19 as...prick-song very precisely, as one sings
from written or printed music ('prick-song', or
more properly 'pricked-song'). The musical analogy
with duelling is continued in 20–1.

19–20 time...proportion (1) (in duelling) the
minimum proper bodily movement and footwork,
due 'distance' from the opponent, and rhythm; (2)
(in music) tempo, properly observed intervals, and
correct relation between parts.

20–1 he...bosom (1) (in duelling) he will make
two feints, with the briefest possible pause between
each, and then on the third beat, he will strike (NS);
(2) (in music) he pauses ('rests' like a virtuoso) for
his minim notes ('rests'), which were worth 'half
the value of a semibreve and double that of a
crochet' (*OED*), one, two, three, etc.

21 butcher...button It was a trick in duelling
to show your mastery by 'pinking' your opponent's
buttons. See George Silver, *Paradoxes of Defence*
(1599), p. 69: '*Signior Rocco* [an Italian duelling
master resident in England],...thou that takst upon
thee to hit anie Englishman with a thrust upon anie
button'. Compare *Captain Thomas Stukely* (anon.,
c. 1596; MSR, 659–60): 'a wager at the ninth
button of your doublet'.

21 duellist Not, as *OED* suggests, the first use
of this word; used by Gabriel Harvey in *Pierces*
Supererogation (1593), p. 19.

22 very first house best duelling school (or
'colledge' as Signior Rocco preferred to call it),
with heraldic play on 'of the noblest birth'.

22–3 first...cause See Sir William Segar, *The*

Book of Honor and Armes (1590), pp. 22–3: 'I say
then that the causes of al quarrell wherupon it
behoveth to use the trial of Armes, may be reduced
into two:...Wherfore whensoever one man doeth
accuse another of such a crime as meriteth death,
in that case the Combat ought bee graunted. The
second cause of Combat is Honor, because among
persons of reputation, Honor is preferred before
life' (an expanded version of this appears in
Saviolo's *Practice* (1595)). Shakespeare repeats the
phrase in *LLL* 1.2.177–8; see 15 n. above.

23 immortal (1) famous, (2) fatal (Gibbons).

23 'passado'...'hay' Three technical duelling
terms: (1) a step, accompanied by a thrust, forward
or aside; (2) a back-handed (from the left side)
stroke; (3) a home-thrust (from Italian 'hai' = thou
hast it). NS links the three terms to the movements
described in 19–22. Since 'hay' here is the earliest
citation in *OED*, it is not surprising that the term
is new to Benvolio. See 'passado', *LLL* 1.2.178–9.

25 pox of plague upon (but also used for venereal disease).

25 affecting *phantasimes affected gallants
(from Italian 'fantasima', John Florio, *Queen Annas*
New World of Words (1611)). See supplementary
note.

26 new...accent those whose English is viti-
ated with new-fangled foreign words and affected
pronunciations. See preceding note and compare
Hamlet's attitude towards the 'waterfly' Osric
(5.2.105–94) and 28–30 below. See supplementary
note.

26–7 good blade...tall man...whore One
might here expect Mercutio to parody the 'new
tuners of accent', but he is apparently relieving his
feelings by letting fly with some down-to-earth
English. Some eds. explain 'blade' as meaning
'bravo' or 'gallant' (the earliest citation of this
meaning in *OED*), but perhaps the present context

a very good whore!' Why, is not this a lamentable thing, grandsire,
that we should be thus afflicted with these strange flies, these
fashion-mongers, these pardon-me's, who stand so much on the
new form, that they cannot sit at ease on the old bench? O their   30
bones, their bones!

Enter ROMEO.

BENVOLIO Here comes Romeo, here comes Romeo.
MERCUTIO Without his roe, like a dried herring: O flesh, flesh, how
art thou fishified! Now is he for the numbers that Petrarch flowed
in. Laura to his lady was a kitchen wench (marry, she had a better   35
love to berhyme her), Dido a dowdy, Cleopatra a gipsy, Helen and
Hero hildings and harlots, Thisbe a grey eye or so, but not to the

27 grandsire] F; graundsir Q2–4, Q1 *(variant form)*   29 pardon-me's] F; pardons mees Q2; pardon mees Q3;
pardona-mees Q4; pardonmees Q1; pardonnez-moy's *Theobald*; pardona-mi's *Globe*   31 bones, their bones] Q2–4, F,
Q1; *bon's,* their *bon's / Theobald*   31 SD] Q2–4, F; *not in* Q1   32 here comes Romeo] Q2–4, F; *not in* Q1, *Pope*
34 Petrarch] Q3–4, F, Q1; Petrach Q2   35 was] Q2–4, F; was but Q1, *Pope*

requires nothing more 'new-fangled' than the
common meaning 'sword'. 'tall' = strong, valiant.

27 grandsire. Mercutio pretends to address
Benvolio as one old greybeard to another, lamenting
the extravagance of soft and finical youth.

28 strange flies queer parasites (with a glance
at 'strange' = alien).

29 pardon-me's Frenchified gallants.

29–30 stand…bench are so insistent on the
latest foreign fashions in speech and dress that they
are uncomfortable with old-fashioned honest
English behaviour (with play on 'form' = a bench,
hard and uncushioned). See supplementary note.

30–1 O…bones O their aching bones (from the
hard benches), with probable play on French
'bon' = good, as in affected exclamation, and
(Gibbons) on 'bone-ache' = venereal disease ('a
malady of France', *H5* 5.1.82).

33 Without his roe (1) minus his manhood,
thin and emasculated by love ('roe' = fish eggs;
compare 'shotten herring' = a fish that has
spawned, and *1H4* 2.4.130); (2) without his dear
(playing on 'roe' = a small deer). Seymour suggests
that Romeo 'without his roe' = Me oh! or Oh me!
(a lover's sigh). Mercutio talks to Romeo as if he
were a depleted rake fresh from the bawdy house;
the Friar had already suggested something similar
in 2.3.42, 44.

34 fishified turned cold-blooded (without
sexual drive) – a dead ('dried') fish; compare
1.1.27–8.

34 for in favour of.

34–5 numbers… in the kind of verses in which
Petrarch streamed along (with suggestion of
over-facility in 'flowed'). Mercutio is referring to

the sort of 'sonnetese' practised by Romeo in the
first act – a love that is all high-flown talk and theory
without Mercutio's physicality, the only kind of love
Mercutio understands. See suppl. note.

35–8 Laura…purpose Except for Laura, to
whom Petrarch addressed his two series of sonnets,
the women named are classical figures (real or
fictional) celebrated for their beauty, none of whom
is comparable to Rosaline as Romeo, according to
Mercutio, supposedly envisions her. Mercutio
never learns of Romeo's love for Juliet.

35 to in comparison with.

35–6 better love i.e. Petrarch, who was the only
poet among those supposedly praising their various
ladies; despite this advantage, Laura appears as a
'kitchen wench' compared with Rosaline.

36 dowdy a slattern (perhaps with reference to
the fact that Dido was a widow; compare the rather
mysterious fun on 'Widow Dido' in *Temp.*
2.1.75–102). Spencer calls attention here and in
what follows to the use of alliteration as a device
satirising the sonnet mode.

36 gipsy Compare *Ant.* 1.1.9–10, where Antony
is described as the 'bellows and the fan / To cool
a gipsy's lust'. 'Gipsy' is a shortened form of
'Egyptian'; the Elizabethans believed that gipsies
came originally from Egypt. Echoed perhaps (along
with 3.5.219) in *Look about You* (anon., 1598–1600;
MSR, 2338–9).

37 hildings good-for-nothings (apparently the
earliest use as applied to a woman); compare
3.5.168.

37–8 grey eye…purpose one with the favourite
colour of eye (probably bluish-grey), but still
nothing to the point (compared with Rosaline).

purpose. Signior Romeo, 'bon jour'! there's a French salutation to your French slop. You gave us the counterfeit fairly last night.

ROMEO Good morrow to you both. What counterfeit did I give you?   40

MERCUTIO The slip, sir, the slip, can you not conceive?

ROMEO Pardon, good Mercutio, my business was great, and in such a case as mine a man may strain courtesy.

MERCUTIO That's as much as to say, such a case as yours constrains a man to bow in the hams.   45

ROMEO Meaning to cur'sy.

MERCUTIO Thou hast most kindly hit it.

ROMEO A most courteous exposition.

MERCUTIO Nay, I am the very pink of courtesy.

ROMEO Pink for flower.   50

MERCUTIO Right.

ROMEO Why then is my pump well flowered.

MERCUTIO Sure wit! Follow me this jest now, till thou hast worn out thy pump, that when the single sole of it is worn, the jest may remain, after the wearing, solely singular.   55

ROMEO O single-soled jest, solely singular for the singleness!

38 'bon jour'] F, Q1; *Bonieur* Q2, Q4; *Bon ieur* Q3   42 Pardon, good Mercutio] Q2–4; Pardon *Mercutio* F; I cry you mercy Q1   46–7] *not in* Q1   48 courteous] Q3–4, F, Q1; curtuous Q2   53 Sure wit!] *Neilson;* Sure wit Q2; Sure wit, Q3–4, F; Well said, Q1, *Capell;* Sure Wit – *Rowe;* Sheer wit! *conj. Malone;* Sir wit, *conj. Anon. (in Cam.)* 53 this jest now,] *Capell (after Rowe);* this ieast, now Q2–4, F; nowe that iest Q1   55 solely singular] *Theobald (subst.);* soly singular Q2–4, Q1; sole-/singular F   56 single-soled] F4; single solde Q2–4, F; single soald Q1   56 solely] F4; solie Q2–4, F, Q1

39 to...slop to match your loose-fitting, short breeches. Not having gone home, Romeo is still in his masking costume and dancing pumps (Crofts).

39 gave...counterfeit deceived, played a trick on us. 'counterfeit' is employed to prepare for the play in 41 on 'slip' = counterfeit coin. Compare *Tro.* 2.3.25–7; Nashe (*Unfortunate Traveller, Works,* II, 258) plays on 'counterfeit slip' and 'give the slip' in the same way.

41 conceive understand (the point of the pun).

42–7 The wit here turns on several bawdy puns: 'case' = (1) contingency, (2) male or female pudenda; 'courtesy' (with variant form 'cur'sy') = (1) good manners, (2) bow; 'bow in the hams' = make a bow, (2) show the debilitating effects of sexual indulgence or venereal disease; 'kindly hit it' = (1) graciously taken the point, (2) naturally effected sexual connection (compare 2.1.33).

49–52 pink...flowered 'pink' = (1) height, acme, (2) a kind of flower (with play on 'pink' = to

ornament by cut-out designs, hence 'flowered' or 'pinked'); compare 2.5.42. Hosley suggests a further pun on 'flowered' = floored (see 'worn out', 53).

52 pump light shoe (suitable for dancing). See 56 n. below.

53 Sure wit! 'Oh, indisputable cleverness!' or 'Oh, clever fellow!' Compare 'True wit!' in *LLL* 5.1.61.

53 Follow me Pursue for my sake ('me' = ethical dative; see Franz 294).

54 single slight, thin (perhaps suggested by 'flower' (50), which could be single or double).

55 solely singular uniquely alone. The point of this banter (clearer in Q2's variant form 'solie') seems to be that when the material sole is worn out in the pursuit of 'wit' then at least something immaterial will remain 'souly' valuable.

56 single-soled...singleness trivial, threadbare jest, remarkable ('singular') only for being one of a kind. Compare Nashe, *Saffron-Walden* (*Works,* III, 38): 'single-soald pumpes'.

MERCUTIO Come between us, good Benvolio, my wits faints.

ROMEO Swits and spurs, swits and spurs, or I'll cry a match.

MERCUTIO Nay, if our wits run the wild-goose chase, I am done; for
thou hast more of the wild goose in one of thy wits than, I am sure,   60
I have in my whole five. Was I with you there for the goose?

ROMEO Thou wast never with me for any thing when thou wast not
there for the goose.

MERCUTIO I will bite thee by the ear for that jest.

ROMEO Nay, good goose, bite not.   65

MERCUTIO Thy wit is a very bitter sweeting, it is a most sharp sauce.

ROMEO And is it not then well served in to a sweet goose?

MERCUTIO O here's a wit of cheveril, that stretches from an inch
narrow to an ell broad!

ROMEO I stretch it out for that word 'broad', which, added to the goose,   70
proves thee far and wide a broad goose.

MERCUTIO Why, is not this better now than groaning for love? Now
art thou sociable, now art thou Romeo; now art thou what thou
art, by art as well as by nature, for this drivelling love is like a great

---

57 wits faints] Q2–4, F; wits faile Q1, *Steevens;* wit faints F2; wits faint Q5   58 Swits...swits] Q2–4, F, Q1;
Switch...switch *Pope*   58 or I'll] Q2–4, F, Q1; or – I'll *Johnson;* for I *Capell*   59 our] Q2–4, F; thy Q1, *Capell*
59 am] Q2–4, F; haue Q1, *Capell*   66 bitter sweeting] Q2, Q1; bitter sweting Q3–4; Bitter-sweeting F   67 then well]
Q2; well Q3–4, F, Q1   67 in to] Q2–4, Q1; into F   67 sweet goose] Q2–4, Q1; Sweet-Goose F   71 a broad] Q2–4, Q1;
abroad F; abroad, *conj. Farmer;* abroad – *Collier*

57 **Come between us** i.e. as a second in a duel
(NS).

57 **faints** Northern plural in -s (Abbott 333).

58 **Swits and spurs** (Ride all out with) switch
and spurs, i.e. keep the game going as hard as you
can. 'Swits' is singular.

58 **cry a match** claim the victory.

59 **wild-goose chase** A kind of all-out horse-
race, popular with gentlemen, in which whoever
was in the lead chose the course, while the others had
either to win the lead or to follow wherever he
went. Suggested to Mercutio by 'Swits and spurs'
(58). See supplementary note.

60–71 This flight of the 'goose' turns on several
puns: 'goose' = (1) a bird proverbial for its
stupidity; hence (2) = a simpleton or nitwit
(60); (3) a prostitute (63). There is also perhaps
some reference to the game of goose (see *OED*).

60 **more...goose** more of the nitwit.

61 **whole five** i.e. five wits, either (1) the five
senses, or (2) the general mental faculties.

61 **Was...goose?** Did I score off you with that
word 'goose' (Kermode)?

63 **for the goose** (1) as a foolish fellow; (2) in
search of a prostitute. Compare 'Winchester goose'
(*OED*).

64 **bite...ear** A sign of fondness (*OED* Bite 16),
but Mercutio is annoyed.

65 **Nay...not** Be a 'good' goose and don't bite
(spoken ironically, with the suggestion that your
opponent is inferior (Kittredge)); proverbial (Tilley
G349). Gibbons cites Nashe, *Strange Newes* (*Works*,
I, 307): 'Good Beare, bite not'. Compare also
Porter, *Two Angry Women* (1598; MSR, 2394),
where it is connected with a fool's 'bauble' (see 75
below).

66 **bitter sweeting** Kind of apple (perhaps with
reference to the sugar-coated bitter pill; see Tilley
P325, S97).

66 **sharp sauce** (1) 'biting' riposte; (2) tart
relish.

67 **And...goose** Compare Tilley M839 ('Sweet
meat must have sour sauce').

68 **cheveril** Soft kid leather, unusually stretch-
able. 68–70 See supplementary note.

69 **ell** forty-five inches. Romeo's wit is properly
only 'an inch', i.e. very small.

71 **broad** obvious (with probable play on
'broad' = indecent; compare 'large' (78)). Staunton
suggests further play on 'brood-goose' = one that
only hatches others' eggs (here = Romeo's wit).

74 **by art** by application of acquired skill, as
opposed to 'by nature'.

natural that runs lolling up and down to hide his bauble in a hole.   75

BENVOLIO Stop there, stop there.

MERCUTIO Thou desirest me to stop in my tale against the hair.

BENVOLIO Thou wouldst else have made thy tale large.

MERCUTIO O thou art deceived; I would have made it short, for I was
come to the whole depth of my tale, and meant indeed to occupy   80
the argument no longer.

ROMEO Here's goodly gear!

Enter NURSE *and her man* [PETER].

A sail, a sail!

MERCUTIO Two, two: a shirt and a smock.

NURSE Peter!   85

PETER Anon.

NURSE My fan, Peter.

MERCUTIO Good Peter, to hide her face, for her fan's the fairer face.

NURSE God ye good morrow, gentlemen.

MERCUTIO God ye good den, fair gentlewoman.   90

NURSE Is it good den?

MERCUTIO 'Tis no less, I tell ye, for the bawdy hand of the dial is now
upon the prick of noon.

75 hide] Q2–4, Q1; hid F   75 bauble] F4; bable Q2–4, F, Q1   77 stop in] Q2–4, F; stopp Q1   78 tale large.] Q2–4,
F; tale too long? Q1   79 for] Q2–4, Q1; or F   82 SD] Q2–4, Q1; *follows 81*, F   83 A sail, a sail] Q2–4, F; *Mer:* A
saile, a saile, a saile Q1, *Capell*   84 SH MERCUTIO] Q2–4, F; *Ben:* Q1, *Capell*   85–8 Peter!...Peter,] Q2–4, F; *Peter,
pree thee giue me my fan. / Mer:* Pree thee doo good *Peter,* Q1, *Collier*   86 Anon.] Q2–4, F; Anon? *Theobald*; Anon!
Craig   88 Good] Q2–4, F; Do good *Pope (from Q1; see 85–8 above)*   88 face,] Q2–4; face? F; face: Q1   88 fairer
face.] Q2–3; fairer face, Q4; fairer face? F; fairer of the two. Q1, *Pope*   92 ye] Q2; you Q3–4, F, Q1

75 **natural** idiot, fool.

75 **lolling** sticking out his tongue (with probable
reference to 'bauble' (75)).

75 **bauble** (1) fool's short stick decorated with
a fool's head and sometimes with a bladder for
striking offenders; (2) penis.

75 **hole** With quibble on vagina.

77–82 The wit in these lines, sparked by 'bauble
in a hole' (75), turns on a series of bawdy puns:
'stop in' (77) = (1) cease, (2) stuff in; 'tale'
(77) = (1) story, (2) penis; 'against the hair'
(77) = (1) against the grain (my desire), (2) with
reference to pubic hair (punning further on
Benvolio's 'Stop there' (76), i.e. 'th'hair'); 'large'
(78) = (1) long, (2) tumescent (compare play on
'longer' in 81 and 'short' (79) = detumescent);
'come...tale' (80) = (1) reached the end of my
story, (2) achieved orgasm (with pun on 'whole'
(80) = hole); 'occupy' (80) = (1) continue in, (2)
have intercourse with (compare *2H4* 2.4.148–50);

'gear' = (1) rubbish, nonsense, (2) the organs of
generation.

82 **goodly gear** Some eds. take 'goodly gear' to
mean 'large clotheshorse' and to refer to the
approaching Nurse (following F in placing her entry
after 81), but this ignores the bawdy pun in 'gear'
(see preceding note), which links perfectly with
Mercutio's wit-play.

83–4 Q1's assignment of these lines to Mercutio
and Benvolio respectively presumably reflects stage
practice and may be correct.

84 **shirt...smock** man...woman.

90 **good den** good even (used loosely for any
time after noon). Mercutio thus corrects the Nurse's
'good morrow' = good morning.

92–3 **bawdy...noon** 'hand of the dial' (1) the
hand(s) on the clock face; (2) a woman's hand
('dial' = vagina; compare 'O', 2.1.37, 3.3.90);
'prick of noon' = (1) the point on the dial marking
twelve o'clock (compare 'noontide prick', *3H6*

NURSE Out upon you, what a man are you?

ROMEO One, gentlewoman, that God hath made, himself to mar.   95

NURSE By my troth, it is well said: 'for himself to mar', quoth'a?
Gentlemen, can any of you tell me where I may find the young
Romeo?

ROMEO I can tell you, but young Romeo will be older when you have
found him than he was when you sought him: I am the youngest   100
of that name, for fault of a worse.

NURSE You say well.

MERCUTIO Yea, is the worst well? Very well took, i'faith, wisely,
wisely.

NURSE If you be he, sir, I desire some confidence with you.   105

BENVOLIO She will indite him to some supper.

MERCUTIO A bawd, a bawd, a bawd! So ho!

ROMEO What hast thou found?

MERCUTIO No hare, sir, unless a hare, sir, in a lenten pie, that is
something stale and hoar ere it be spent.   110

---

95 One, gentlewoman] F4; One gentlewoman Q2–4, F; A Gentleman Nurse Q1   95 himself] Q2–4, F; for himselfe Q1,
Collier   96 well said:] Q1; well said, Q2–4; said, F   97 the young] Q2–4, F; yong Q1, Pope   103 well?] Q5, Q1; wel,
Q2–4, F   106 indite] Theobald; endite Q2–4, F; inuite Q1; envite F2   106 some supper] Q2–4, F; supper Q1, Capell
108 What] Q2–4, F; Why what Q1; What, NS (conj. Carr)   110 spent] Q2–4, F; eaten Q1   110 SD] Q1; not in Q2–4, F

1.4.34); (2) *penis erectus* (with further play on
'strike'). Partridge (p. 36) considers this passage
'one of the three or four most scintillating of all
Shakespeare's sexual witticisms'.

94 **what a man** what kind of a man.

95 **made...mar** Compare 1.2.12–13.

96 **troth** faith (variant of 'truth').

96 **quoth'a** literally, 'said he', but here as often
a sarcastic interjection meaning 'indeed', used
following the repetition of something just said by
another.

101 **for...worse** for lack of a worse (bearer of
that name). The usual phrase is 'for fault of a
better', but Shakespeare is setting up Mercutio's
jest in 103.

103 **is...well?** i.e. is it well to be the worst of all
those named Romeo? The Nurse's meaningless
'well' (102) gives Mercutio an opportunity to play
on Romeo's 'worse' (101).

103 **took** understood, interpreted. The Nurse, of
course, had 'understood' nothing.

105 **confidence** Usually taken as a malapropism
for 'conference', used twice elsewhere by Shakespeare (*Wiv.* 1.4.160; *Ado* 3.5.2); Kittredge,
however, questions the blunder (so too in *Wiv.*)
and defines as 'private conversation'. Probably
accented on second syllable.

106 **indite** Benvolio means 'invite' (the reading
of Q1), but is presumably represented as mimicking
the Nurse's supposed malapropism. Compare *2H4*
2.1.28.

107 **bawd** (1) procurer, go-between; (2) hare (in
North-Midland dialect). See 109.

107 **So ho!** Hunter's cry on sighting his quarry.
Compare Peele, *Edward I* (1593; MSR, 1009): 'Saw
haw, maister, I have found, I have found'; see
following note.

108 **What...found** i.e. What game animal have
you started? Compare the implications of Cupid as
a 'hare-finder' in *Ado* 1.1.184.

109–10 **hare...lenten pie...hoar** The Nurse
is no hare, or if she is, she is as mouldy ('hoar') and
stale ('stale' as a noun = whore) as an old hare
(= 'whore') in a lenten pie. Technically, a lenten
pie should contain no meat, the implication being
that no fresh meat was properly available in Lent
(compare 113, 'Is very good meat in Lent', where
'meat' = whore, with the meaning that even an old
mouldy whore ('hare') is better than none in a time
of prohibition). Dowden cites William Rowley (?),
A Match at Midnight (ed. S. B. Young, 5.2.143), in
which a 'Hare Pye' is the figurative equivalent for
a bawd.

110 **spent** used up.

[*He walks by them and sings.*]

An old hare hoar,

And an old hare hoar,

Is very good meat in Lent;

But a hare that is hoar

Is too much for a score,   115

When it hoars ere it be spent.

Romeo, will you come to your father's? We'll to dinner thither.

ROMEO I will follow you.

MERCUTIO Farewell, ancient lady, farewell, lady, [*Singing.*] 'lady,

lady'.   120

Exeunt [*Mercutio and Benvolio*]

NURSE I pray you, sir, what saucy merchant was this that was so full
of his ropery?

ROMEO A gentleman, Nurse, that loves to hear himself talk, and will
speak more in a minute than he will stand to in a month.

NURSE And 'a speak any thing against me, I'll take him down, and 'a   125
were lustier than he is, and twenty such Jacks; and if I cannot, I'll
find those that shall. Scurvy knave, I am none of his flirt-gills, I
am none of his skains-mates. [*She turns to Peter, her man.*] And thou
must stand by too and suffer every knave to use me at his pleasure!

PETER I saw no man use you at his pleasure; if I had, my weapon should   130
quickly have been out. I warrant you, I dare draw as soon as another
man, if I see occasion in a good quarrel, and the law on my side.

111–16] *As Capell; two lines, ending* lent / ...spent Q2–4, F; *four lines, ending* hore / ...Lent / ...score / ...spent
QI   119 SD *Singing*] *This edn (after Hosley, from conj. Farmer, following* farewell *119); no* SD, Q2–4, F, QI
120 SD *Exeunt...Benvolio*] F (*Exit. Mercutio, Benuolio.*); *Exeunt.* Q2–4; *Exeunt Benuolio, Mercutio.* QI   121 I pray] Q2–4,
F; Marry farewell. Pray QI; Marry, farewell! – I pray *Malone*   122 ropery] Q2–4, F; roperipe QI   125 And 'a speak]
Q2–4, F; If hee stand to QI   127 flirt-gills] F, QI; flurt gills Q2–3; Gil-flurts Q4   128 skains-mates] F4; skaines mates
Q2–4, F, QI   128 SD] QI; *not in* Q2–4, F   130–2 my...side.] Q2–4, F; I would soone haue drawen: you know my toole
is as soone out as anothers if I see time and place. QI

115 **too...score** not worth marking up on the
reckoning ('score').

116 **hoars** (1) turns mouldy; (2) whores.

117 **dinner** In Elizabethan times dinner was
eaten about midday.

119–20 **'lady, lady'** Mercutio ironically applies
a refrain-tag to the Nurse from a ballad, 'The
Constancy of Susanna' (*Roxburghe Ballads*, I, 190):
'There dwelt a man in Babylon, / of reputation
great by fame; / He tooke to wife a faire woman,
/ Susanna she was call'd by name; / A woman faire
and vertuous: / Lady, Lady, / Why should wee not
of her learne thus / to live godly?' Compare *TN*
2.3.78–9.

121 **merchant** fellow.

122 **ropery** knavery. Compare QI 'roperipe' =
ready for the hangman.

125 **take him down** humble him (with the usual
bawdy pun looking back to 'stand to' in 124).

126 **Jacks** ill-mannered fellows, knaves.

127 **flirt-gills** loose women (from 'Gill', a girl's
name). Earliest citation in *OED*.

128 **skains-mates** Unexplained, but perhaps =
cut-throat companions (from 'skene' = a long
dagger, originally associated with the Irish kerns).
As Kittredge shows, female desperadoes ('roaring
girls') were armed with knives.

129 **use...pleasure** treat me as he pleased
(picked up by Peter in 130 with a bawdy twist on
'use' and 'pleasure' and the inevitable play on
'weapon' in 130). Compare 1.1.28–9.

NURSE Now afore God, I am so vexed that every part about me quivers.
Scurvy knave! Pray you, sir, a word: and as I told you, my young
lady bid me enquire you out; what she bid me say, I will keep to   135
myself. But first let me tell ye, if ye should lead her in a fool's
paradise, as they say, it were a very gross kind of behaviour, as they
say; for the gentlewoman is young; and therefore, if you should deal
double with her, truly it were an ill thing to be offered to any
gentlewoman, and very weak dealing.   140

ROMEO Nurse, commend me to thy lady and mistress. I protest unto
thee –

NURSE Good heart, and i'faith I will tell her as much. Lord, Lord, she
will be a joyful woman.

ROMEO What wilt thou tell her, Nurse? thou dost not mark me.   145

NURSE I will tell her, sir, that you do protest, which, as I take it, is a
gentleman-like offer.

ROMEO Bid her devise
    Some means to come to shrift this afternoon,
    And there she shall at Friar Lawrence' cell   150
    Be shrived and married. Here is for thy pains.

NURSE No truly, sir, not a penny.

ROMEO Go to, I say you shall.

NURSE This afternoon, sir? Well, she shall be there.

ROMEO And stay, good Nurse, behind the abbey wall: 155
    Within this hour my man shall be with thee,
    And bring thee cords made like a tackled stair,

133 quivers.] Q1 (quiuers:); quiuers, Q2–4, F 135 bid…bid] Q2–4, F; bad…bad Q1, *Capell* 136 in] Q2–4, F; into
Q1, *Theobald* 140 weak] Q2–4, F, Q1; wicked *Collier MS.*; wicke [= wicked] *conj. Fleay* 141 SH ROMEO] Q2–4, Q1;
Nur. F 141–2 I…thee –] F2 *(reading* I, protest onto*)*; I protest vnto thee. Q2–4, F; tell her I protest. Q1, *Daniel*
145 dost] F3; dooest Q2; doest Q3–4, F *(*Nurse…me. *not in* Q1) 145 me.] Q5; me? Q2–4, F 148–51 Bid…married.]
Q2–4, F; Bid her get leaue to morrow morning / To come to shrift to Frier *Laurence* cell: Q1 *(transferring the rest of
151–4 after 159)* 148–9] As *Delius*; one line, Q2–3, F; as verse, Q4; as prose, ending shrift / …afternoon *Capell*
151 shrived] F (shriu'd); shrieued Q2–4 154 This…there.] Q2–4, F; Weil, to morrow morning she shall not faile. Q1
154 sir?] F; sir, Q2–4 155 stay] Q2–4; stay thou F, Q1 155 Nurse,] F4; Nurse Q2–4, F, Q1; Nurse; *White*
155 wall:] *Pope*; wall, Q2–4, F, Q1; wall *White* 157 thee] Q2–4, F; the Q1, F2

136–7 lead…paradise i.e. seduce her.
140 weak dealing (?) behaviour lacking in
moral fibre. Perhaps the Nurse means to say
'wicked' (Singer, after Collier). Cowden Clarke
defends 'weak': 'the Nurse intends to use a most
forcible expression, and blunders upon a much
feebler one'.
141 commend me convey my best wishes.
141 protest solemnly undertake or vow (the
sense which the Nurse jumps at in her comment
about a 'gentleman-like offer' (147), though
Romeo may only be using it as an asseveration
meaning 'declare' (*OED* sv *v* 1c)).

145 mark me pay attention to what I am saying.
149 shrift confession.
151 shrived given absolution after confession.
Compare Brooke (633–4): 'On Saterday quod he,
if Juliet come to shrift, / She shalbe shrived and
maried' (Romeus talking to the Nurse).
151 Here…pains In Brooke (667) Romeus
gives the Nurse '.vi. crownes of gold' and she makes
not even a token resistance as in Shakespeare (152).
'pains' = trouble.
157 tackled stair rope ladder; in Brooke (813),
'corden ladder'.

Which to the high top-gallant of my joy
Must be my convoy in the secret night.
Farewell, be trusty, and I'll quit thy pains.   160
Farewell, commend me to thy mistress.

NURSE Now God in heaven bless thee! Hark you, sir.

ROMEO What say'st thou, my dear Nurse?

NURSE Is your man secret? Did you ne'er hear say,
      'Two may keep counsel, putting one away'?   165

ROMEO 'Warrant thee, my man's as true as steel.

NURSE Well, sir, my mistress is the sweetest lady – Lord, Lord! when
      'twas a little prating thing – O, there is a nobleman in town, one
      Paris, that would fain lay knife aboard; but she, good soul, had as
      lieve see a toad, a very toad, as see him. I anger her sometimes, 170
      and tell her that Paris is the properer man, but I'll warrant you,
      when I say so, she looks as pale as any clout in the versal world.
      Doth not rosemary and Romeo begin both with a letter?

ROMEO Ay, Nurse, what of that? Both with an R.

NURSE Ah, mocker, that's the dog-name. R is for the – no, I know it   175

160 quit] Q2; quite Q3–4, F, Q1   161–79 Farewell…times.] *not in* Q1   164–5] *As verse, Rowe; as prose,* Q2–4, F
164 hear] F; here Q2–4   166 'Warrant] *Riverside;* Warrant Q2–4, F; I warrant F2   166 man's] Q2–4; man F
167–81] *As prose,* Q2–4, F; *as verse, Capell*   167 lady –] *Capell;* Lady, Q2–4, F   168 thing –] *Rowe;* thing. Q2–4, F
168 nobleman] Q4; Noble man Q2–3, F   170 see a] Q2–4; a see F   175 Ah,] *Rowe;* A Q2–4, F   175 dog-name.]
Hoppe; dog, name Q2; dogsname. Q3, F; Dogges name. Q4; dogs letter; *Daniel (conj. Farmer)*   175 R is…no,] *Delius
(conj. Ritson);* R. is for the no, Q2–4, F; R. is for Thee? No; *Theobald (conj. Warburton);* R. is not for thee, *Hanmer;*
R is for the nonce; *Steevens (1773, conj. Johnson);* R for thee? no; *Capell;* R is for the dog. No; *Steevens (1778, conj.
Tyrwhitt)*

158 high top-gallant A 'top' (= a railed
platform) at the head of the topmast (*OED*), hence
the highest point. The nautical imagery, suggested
by 'tackled' (157), is continued in 'convoy'
(159) = conveyance, guide.

160 quit reward.

161 mistress Trisyllabic, as not infrequently at
this time.

164 secret to be trusted with a secret. Compare
'keep counsel' in 165.

165 'Two…away' Proverbial (Tilley T257);
compare *Tit.* 4.2.144: 'Two may keep counsel when
the third's away.' But the meaning here is
ambiguous; 'one' may mean either 'a third party'
or one of the 'two' first mentioned.

166 'Warrant I warrant.

166 as…steel Proverbial (Tilley s840).

167–8 Lord…thing Compare Brooke (653–4):
'A prety babe… / Lord how it could full pretely
have prated with it tong.'

169 lay knife aboard assert his claim (with
probable bawdy pun on 'lay aboard' = attack, and
'knife' = phallic symbol). Crofts explains the

phrase as arising from the custom of placing a knife
on the table ('aboard' = on the board) at an
ordinary to reserve a place. See suppl. note.

170 lieve lief, willingly.

170 sometimes Here, and in 3.5.237–9, it has
been suggested by Cowden Clarke that Shakespeare
is consciously employing so-called 'double-time' to
convey the impression of a longer passage of time
than is warranted by the play's actual time-scheme.
Simple inadvertence on Shakespeare's part seems
more likely.

171 properer handsomer.

172 clout washed-out rag.

172 versal universal (vulgarism), whole.

173 rosemary 'There's rosemary, that's for
remembrance' (*Ham.* 4.5.175). a herb associated
with weddings, but also with funerals (see 4.5.95
SD).

173 both with a with the same.

175 dog-name See Persius, *Satires* I, 109:
'Sonat hic de nare canina littera'; Ben Jonson,
English Grammar (VIII, 491): '*R* is the *Dogs* letter,
and hurreth in the sound'; and Nashe, *Summers*

begins with some other letter – and she hath the prettiest sententious
of it, of you and rosemary, that it would do you good to hear it.

ROMEO Commend me to thy lady.

NURSE Ay, a thousand times.

[Exit Romeo]

　　　　　　　Peter!

PETER Anon.   180

NURSE *[Handing him her fan.]* Before and apace.

Exit [after Peter]

[2.5] *Enter* JULIET.

JULIET The clock struck nine when I did send the Nurse;
　　　In half an hour she promised to return.
　　　Perchance she cannot meet him: that's not so.
　　　O, she is lame! Love's heralds should be thoughts,
　　　Which ten times faster glides than the sun's beams,   5
　　　Driving back shadows over low'ring hills;
　　　Therefore do nimble-pinioned doves draw Love,
　　　And therefore hath the wind-swift Cupid wings.
　　　Now is the sun upon the highmost hill

---

179 times. Peter!] Q3 (*Peter?*), F; times *Peter.* Q2; times *Peter?* Q4   **179** SD] Q1 (*Exit*); no SD, Q2–4, F   **181** SD *Handing…fan.*] *Riverside (based on* Q1 *version of 181; see below)*   **181** Before, and apace.] Q2–4, F; *Peter,* take my fanne, and goe before. Q1, *Steevens*; Take my fan, and go before. *Pope*; Before; / And walk apace. *Capell*; Peter, take my fan, and go before, and apace. *Globe*   **181** SD *after Peter*] *Riverside; Ex. omnes.* Q1   Act 2, Scene 5   2.5] *Hanmer;* no scene division, Q2–4, F, Q1   Location] *Globe (after Capell)*; Capulet's House. / *Rowe*   **1** struck] *Rowe*³; strooke Q2–4, F; stroke Q1 *(variant forms)*   **2** promised] Q1 (promist); promised Q2–4, F   **4** Love's] F (Loues), Q1; loues Q2–4   **4** heralds] Q2–3, Q1; Herauld Q4, F   **5–17**] Q2–4, F; And runne more swift, than hastie powder fierd, / Doth hurrie from the fearfull Cannons mouth. Q1 *(see 5.1.64–5)*   **7** nimble-pinioned] *Pope;* nimble piniond Q2–4, F   **7** Love] F; loue Q2–4   **8** wind-swift] Q3, F; wind swift Q2, Q4

Last Will and Testament (*Works*, III, 254): 'They [dogs] arre and barke at night against the Moone.'

175–6 for the – no…letter P. Williams suggests the Nurse is about to say 'arse'. Obviously she can't read or spell, and because of its rude associations she decides that 'Romeo' and 'rosemary' must begin with some other letter.

176 sententious Probably a malapropism for 'sentences' = witty or moral sayings.

177 you NS suggests a play on 'yew', commonly associated with graveyards and funerals.

181 apace quickly. See collation for other readings of 181.

Act 2, Scene 5
Location Verona. Capulet's orchard.

4 lame slow, infirm (from age).

5 glides Northern third per. pl. in -s (Abbott 333).

7 nimble-pinioned doves swift-winged doves (which were reputed to draw Venus's chariot). Compare *Venus and Adonis* 1190–1; *MND* 1.1.171; *Temp.* 4.1.92–4. Doves were sacred to Venus and an emblem of affection and chastity.

9 highmost hill i.e. the meridian. NS compares Golding's *Ovid* (II, 84–6): (Phoebus to Phaëton) 'Now first the morning way / Lyes steepe upright, so that the steedes… / have much a doe to climbe against the Hyll'; and *Sonnets* 7.5–10: 'And having climb'd the steep-up heavenly hill,… / …from highmost pitch, with weary car, / Like feeble age he reeleth from the day.'

Of this day's journey, and from nine till twelve   10
Is three long hours, yet she is not come.
Had she affections and warm youthful blood,
She would be as swift in motion as a ball;
My words would bandy her to my sweet love,
And his to me.   15
But old folks, many feign as they were dead,
Unwieldy, slow, heavy, and pale as lead.

Enter NURSE [*with* PETER].

O God, she comes! O honey Nurse, what news?
Hast thou met with him? Send thy man away.
NURSE Peter, stay at the gate.   20

[*Exit Peter*]

JULIET Now, good sweet Nurse – O Lord, why look'st thou sad?
Though news be sad, yet tell them merrily;
If good, thou shamest the music of sweet news
By playing it to me with so sour a face.
NURSE I am a-weary, give me leave a while.   25
Fie, how my bones ache! What a jaunce have I!
JULIET I would thou hadst my bones, and I thy news.
Nay, come, I pray thee speak, good, good Nurse, speak.
NURSE Jesu, what haste! can you not stay a while?
Do you not see that I am out of breath?   30

---

11 Is three] Q3–4; Is there Q2; I three F; Ay three *Rowe*   15–19] *Continued to Juliet*, Q4, F; *assigned to* / *M.* / Q2–3 (*with period after* loue *in 14*)   15–16] *As Rowe*; *one line*, Q2–4, F   16 folks, many feign] Q2–4, F; folks, marry, feign *Johnson*; folks, marry, seem *Keightley*; folks, marry, fare *White*; folks tarry, faith *conj. Bullock*; folks move, i'faith *Hudson* (*conj. Dyce*); folks many seem *conj. Kinnear*   17 SD *with* PETER] *Theobald*   19–24] *not in* Q1   20 SD] *Theobald*; *no* SD, Q2–4, F, Q1   21 Nurse –] *Rowe*; Nurse, Q2–4; Nurse: F   21 look'st] Q4; lookest Q2–3, F; lookes F2   23 shamest] Q2–3; sham'st Q4, F   25–53] Q2–4, F; Oh I am wearie, let mee rest a while. Lord how my bones ake. Oh wheres my man? Giue me some aqua vitæ. / *Iul*: I would thou hadst my bones, and I thy newes. / *Nur*: Fie, what a iaunt haue I had: and my backe a tother side. Lord, Lord, what a case am I in. / *Iul*: But tell me sweet Nurse, what sayes *Romeo*? / *Nur*: Romeo, nay, alas you cannot chuse a man. Hees no bodie, he is not the Flower of curtesie, he is not a proper man: and for a hand, and a foote, and a baudie, wel go thy way wench, thou hast it ifaith. Lord, Lord, how my head beates? / *Iul*: What of all this? tell me what sayes he to our mariage? Q1   25 a-weary] *Capell* (aweary); a wearie Q2–4, F; wearie Q1   25 give me leave] Q2–4, F; let mee rest Q1, *Pope*   26 jaunce] Q2–3; iaunt Q4, F, Q1   26 I!] *Hoppe*; I? Q2; I had? Q3–4, F; I had: Q1   28 come,] Q4; come Q2–3, F   29–34] *Pope substitutes* Give me some *Aqua vitæ*./*from* Q1 *for 29–34* (*part of an anticipation from 3.2.88*)

---

14 **bandy** strike (as a ball) to and fro.

16 **old...dead** some old people like to take advantage of their age by pretending to be immobile ('dead').

17 **pale as lead** Shakespeare may be referring to white lead (= ceruse), then often used in facial make-up to give a fashionable pallor (Paul Chipchase, privately). Lead was also associated with the melancholy humour, the colour of which was 'pale'.

22 **them** 'news' was treated as either plural or singular; compare 'it' in 24.

26 **jaunce** Literally, 'a prance', i.e. a tiring jolting journey; compare 'jauncing' in 51. Echoed in Porter, *Two Angry Women* (1598; MSR, 2222–3). See supplementary note.

29 **stay a while** wait a moment.

JULIET How art thou out of breath, when thou hast breath
      To say to me that thou art out of breath?
      The excuse that thou dost make in this delay
      Is longer than the tale thou dost excuse.
      Is thy news good or bad? Answer to that.   35
      Say either, and I'll stay the circumstance:
      Let me be satisfied, is't good or bad?

NURSE Well, you have made a simple choice, you know not how to
      choose a man: Romeo? no, not he; though his face be better than
      any man's, yet his leg excels all men's, and for a hand and a foot   40
      and a body, though they be not to be talked on, yet they are past
      compare. He is not the flower of courtesy, but I'll warrant him, as
      gentle as a lamb. Go thy ways, wench, serve God. What, have you
      dined at home?

JULIET No, no! But all this did I know before.   45
      What says he of our marriage, what of that?

NURSE Lord, how my head aches! what a head have I!
      It beats as it would fall in twenty pieces.
      My back a't'other side – ah, my back, my back!
      Beshrew your heart for sending me about   50
      To catch my death with jauncing up and down!

JULIET I'faith, I am sorry that thou art not well.
      Sweet, sweet, sweet Nurse, tell me, what says my love?

NURSE Your love says, like an honest gentleman,
      And a courteous, and a kind, and a handsome,   55
      And I warrant a virtuous – Where is your mother?

JULIET Where is my mother? why, she is within,

33–4 dost...dost] Q3–4, F; doest...doest Q2   38–44] *As prose, Q2–4, F; as verse, Capell*   39 he;] *Theobald;* he Q2–3, F; he, Q4   40 leg excels] Q2–4; legs excels F   41 a body] Q2–3, F; body Q4; a baudie Q1; a bawdy F2; a Baw-dy *Rowe;* a bo-dy *Pope*   43 as a] Q2–4; a F   45 this] Q2–4; this this F   49 ah] Q5; a Q2–4; o F   51 jauncing] Q2–3 (iaunsing); iaunting Q4, F   52 not well] Q2–4; so well F; so ill F2   54–6] *As verse, Q2–4, F; as prose, Q1, Globe (conj. S. Walker)*   55 And] Q3–4, F; An Q2   57–8] *As Rowe; two lines, ending* be / ...repliest Q2–4; *three lines, ending* Mother / ...be / ...repli'st F; *as prose,* Q1

33 in in regard to.

36 **stay the circumstance** wait for the details; compare 5.3.181.

38 **simple** foolish, silly (like a simpleton).

39–40 **though...yet** The construction is intentionally a non sequitur; compare the same construction in 41. The Nurse is babbling nonsense just to tease Juliet. Brooke (686) offers a hint for the Nurse's teasing.

41 **body** Some eds. suggest a pun on 'bawdy'; Q1 reads 'baudie'; F2 'bawdy'.

41 **be...on** are not worth talking about.

42 See supplementary note.

42 **flower** height. Compare 2.4.49–50.

43 **Go...God** We've had enough of this, girl, behave yourself.

45–6 **No...that** Compare Brooke (683–4).

48 **beats** throbs.

49 **a't'other** on the other.

50 **Beshrew** Literally 'curse', but commonly used as a mild oath; compare 3.5.221.

51 **jauncing...down** prancing, trudging back and forth.

54 **honest** honourable, trustworthy; compare 77.

Where should she be? How oddly thou repliest:
'Your love says, like an honest gentleman,
"Where is your mother?"'

NURSE   O God's lady dear,   60
Are you so hot? Marry come up, I trow;
Is this the poultice for my aching bones?
Henceforward do your messages yourself.

JULIET Here's such a coil! Come, what says Romeo?

NURSE Have you got leave to go to shrift today?   65

JULIET I have.

NURSE Then hie you hence to Friar Lawrence' cell,
There stays a husband to make you a wife.
Now comes the wanton blood up in your cheeks,
They'll be in scarlet straight at any news.   70
Hie you to church, I must another way,
To fetch a ladder, by the which your love
Must climb a bird's nest soon when it is dark.
I am the drudge, and toil in your delight;
But you shall bear the burden soon at night.   75
Go, I'll to dinner, hie you to the cell.

JULIET Hie to high fortune! Honest Nurse, farewell.

                                                           Exeunt

[2.6] *Enter* FRIAR [LAWRENCE] *and* ROMEO.

FRIAR LAWRENCE So smile the heavens upon this holy act,
That after-hours with sorrow chide us not.

63] Q2–4, F; next arrant youl haue done, euen doot your selfe. Q1   67 hie] Q1 (hye); high Q2–4, F   68] Q2–4, F;
And frame a scuse that you must goe to shrift: / There stayes a Bridegroome to make you a Bride. Q1
70–1 They'll…church,] *not in* Q1   70 They'll…any] Q2–4, F, They'll be in scarlet straightway at my *Hanmer*; They'll
be in scarlet straight at my next *conj. S. Walker*; They will be straight in scarlet at my *Keightley*   73 climb] Q2, Q4,
Q1; climde Q3, F   76–7] Q2–4, F; Doth this newes please you now? / *Iul:* How doth her latter words reuiue my hart.
/ Thankes gentle Nurse, dispatch thy busines, / And Ile not faile to meete my *Romeo.* Q1   Act 2, Scene 6   2.6] *Hanmer*;
no scene division, Q2–4, F, Q1   Location] *Capell (after Rowe)*   0 SD] Q2–4, F; *Enter Romeo, Frier.* Q1   2 after-hours]
Pope; after houres Q2–4, F   1–37] *The following version of 2.6 in* Q1 *differs almost completely from that in* Q2–4, F: *Rom:*

---

60 **God's lady** i.e. the Virgin Mary.
   61 **hot** over-eager (with undertone of 'lustful';
compare 'wanton' in 69). Echoed in Porter, *Two
Angry Women* (1598; MSR, 2255–6).
   61 **Marry come up** A form of reprimand,
meaning 'Behave yourself.'
   64 **coil** disturbance, fuss.
   69 **wanton** undisciplined, rebellious.
   70 **in…news** 'Any sudden news always makes

your cheeks scarlet in a second' (Kittredge, after
Dowden).
   75 **bear the burden** carry (1) the responsibility,
(2) the weight of your lover (Spencer).

Act 2, Scene 6
   Location Verona. Friar Lawrence's cell.
   1 **So…heavens** May the heavens so smile.
   2 **That** So that.

ROMEO Amen, amen! but come what sorrow can,
        It cannot countervail the exchange of joy
        That one short minute gives me in her sight.   5
        Do thou but close our hands with holy words,
        Then love-devouring Death do what he dare,
        It is enough I may but call her mine.
FRIAR LAWRENCE These violent delights have violent ends,
        And in their triumph die like fire and powder,   10
        Which as they kiss consume. The sweetest honey
        Is loathsome in his own deliciousness,
        And in the taste confounds the appetite.   *antithesis*
        Therefore love moderately, long love doth so;
        Too swift arrives as tardy as too slow.   15

                    Enter JULIET.

Now Father *Laurence*, in thy holy grant / Consists the good of me and *Iuliet*. / *Fr:* Without more words I will doo all I may, / To make you happie if in me it lye. / *Rom:* This morning here she pointed we should meet, / And consumate those neuer parting bands, / Witnes of our harts loue by ioyning hands, / And come she will. / *Fr:* I gesse she will indeed, / Youths loue is quicke, swifter than swiftest speed. / *Enter* Iuliet *somewhat fast, and embraceth Romeo.* / See where she comes. / So light of foote nere hurts the troden flower: / Of loue and ioy, see see the soueraigne power. / *Iul: Romeo.* / *Rom:* My *Iuliet* welcome. As doo waking eyes / (Cloasd in Nights mysts) attend the frolicke Day, / So *Romeo* hath expected *Iuliet*, / And thou art come. / *Iul:* I am (if I be Day) / Come to my Sunne: shine foorth, and make me faire. / *Rom:* All beauteous fairnes dwelleth in thine eyes. / *Iul: Romeo* from thine all brightnes doth arise. / *Fr:* Come wantons, come, the stealing houres do passe / Defer imbracements till some fitrer time, / Part for a while, you shall not be alone, / Till holy Church haue ioynd ye both in one. / *Rom:* Lead holy Father, all delay seemes long. / *Iul:* Make hast, make hast, this lingring doth vs wrong. / *Fr:* O, soft and faire makes sweetest worke they say. / Hast is a common hinder in crosse way. *Exeunt omnes.*   7 Death] F4; death Q2–4, F   8 enough I] Q2–4; inough. I F   10 triumph] Q2–4; triumph: F   10 powder,] F4; powder: Q2; powder; Q3–4, F   15 SD] Q2–4, F; *Enter* Iuliet *somewhat fast, and embraceth Romeo.* Q1

3–4 come...joy whatever sorrow may be able to do, it cannot outweigh ('countervail') the joy that I receive (in advance) in exchange for any future woe (Kittredge). Such a reading is better than to take 'exchange' in the sense of 'reciprocal giving and receiving'. With 3–8, compare Brooke (859–62, spoken by Juliet).
  6 close join (in marriage).
  9 violent...ends See Tilley B262 ('Such beginning such end') and N321 ('Nothing violent can be permanent'). Compare *Lucrece* 894; *Ham.* 2.1.99–103.
  10 triumph moment of rapturous joy (the sexual connection underlined by 'kiss' and 'consume' (= (1) be destroyed; (2) achieve consummation) in 11).

11–13 honey...appetite Proverbial; compare Tilley H560 and *MND* 2.2.137–8.
  12 his its.
  13 taste confounds the tasting ruins or destroys.
  14 moderately...so Proverbial; compare Tilley L559 ('Love me little love me long') and *MV* 3.2.111–12.
  15 Too...slow Compare 2.3.94.
  15 SD The Q1 SD (*Enter* Iuliet *somewhat fast, and embraceth Romeo.*), adopted only by Spencer and Gibbons, suggests a wanton quality to Juliet's entrance that is more suitable to Q1's almost wholly different version of this scene (see collation) than to Shakespeare's.

Here comes the lady. O, so light a foot
Will ne'er wear out the everlasting flint;
A lover may bestride the gossamers
That idles in the wanton summer air,
And yet not fall, so light is vanity.   20

JULIET Good even to my ghostly confessor.

FRIAR LAWRENCE Romeo shall thank thee, daughter, for us both.

[Romeo kisses Juliet.]

JULIET As much to him, else is his thanks too much.

[Juliet returns his kiss.]

ROMEO Ah, Juliet, if the measure of thy joy
Be heaped like mine, and that thy skill be more   25
To blazon it, then sweeten with thy breath
This neighbour air, and let rich music's tongue
Unfold the imagined happiness that both
Receive in either by this dear encounter.

JULIET Conceit, more rich in matter than in words,   30
Brags of his substance, not of ornament;
They are but beggars that can count their worth,
But my true love is grown to such excess
I cannot sum up sum of half my wealth.

---

17 ne'er] F4; nere Q2–4, F, Q1   18–19 gossamers…idles] Q2–4, F; Gossamour…idles F4; gossamours…idle *Malone*
22 SD] *This edn; no SD,* Q2–4, F, Q1   23 is] Q2–3; in Q4, F   23 SD] *This edn (after conj. Allen in Furness); no SD,* Q2–4,
F, Q1   24 SH ROMEO] Q2–4; *Fri.* F   27 music's] Q4 (Musickes), F; musicke Q2–3   33 such] Q2–4; such such F
34 sum up…my] Q2–3; summe vp some of halfe my Q4, F; sum up one half of my *Pope;* sum up sums of half my
Johnson; sum up half my sum of *Capell;* sum the sum of half my *Rann*

16–17 light…flint The general sense here is
clear enough: Juliet moves so lightly that she barely
touches the ground and hence will never wear out
the flint cobble-stones over which she has 'walked'
to come to Romeo – an example of hyperbole
perhaps a little surprising coming from the Friar.
See supplementary notes.
19 idles Northern third per. pl. in -s (Abbott
333).
19 wanton sportive, playful.
20 vanity the insubstantiality of earthly happiness('vanity'literally = emptiness, hence'light').
The Friar's last comment recovers his momentarily
lapsed didactic tone.
21 confessor Accented on the first syllable.
23 As…much i.e. I must repay him in kind (a
kiss) or I shall have been overpaid.
24 measure quantity, amount (that properly
contained in a measuring cup).
25 heaped i.e. his joy overflows the 'measure'.

25 and that and if.
26 blazon celebrate, portray.
27 rich music's tongue i.e. the harmony of
Juliet's words.
28 imagined inner, but unexpressed.
29 in either in each other.
30 Conceit Understanding (the 'imagined'
idea).
30 matter substance (the true 'inner' content as
opposed to the 'outer' expression = 'words').
31 Brags…ornament Takes just pride in its
truth not in dressing itself in mere words (i.e. strong,
true feeling does not need words).
32 worth wealth. Compare Martial, VI.xxxiv, 8,
and *Ant.* 1.1.15: 'There's beggary in the love that
can be reckon'd.'
34 sum up sum total up the full amount.
Compare Sidney, *Astrophil and Stella*, Sonnet
85.10: 'See Beautie's totall summe summ'd in her
face.'

FRIAR LAWRENCE
> Come, come with me, and we will make short work,   35
> For by your leaves, you shall not stay alone
> Till Holy Church incorporate two in one.
>
>   [*Exeunt*]

[3.1] *Enter* MERCUTIO [*and his* PAGE], BENVOLIO, *and* MEN.

BENVOLIO I pray thee, good Mercutio, let's retire:
> The day is hot, the Capels are abroad,
> And if we meet we shall not scape a brawl,
> For now, these hot days, is the mad blood stirring.

MERCUTIO Thou art like one of these fellows that, when he enters the   5
confines of a tavern, claps me his sword upon the table, and says
'God send me no need of thee!'; and by the operation of the second
cup draws him on the drawer, when indeed there is no need.

BENVOLIO Am I like such a fellow?

MERCUTIO Come, come, thou art as hot a Jack in thy mood as any in   10
Italy, and as soon moved to be moody, and as soon moody to be
moved.

BENVOLIO And what to?

MERCUTIO Nay, and there were two such, we should have none shortly,
for one would kill the other. Thou? why, thou wilt quarrel with   15
a man that hath a hair more or a hair less in his beard than thou
hast; thou wilt quarrel with a man for cracking nuts, having no other

---

37 SD] F2; *no SD*, Q2–4, F; *Exeunt omnes.* Q1   Act 3, Scene 1   3.1] *Rowe; no act or scene division*, Q2–4, F, Q1   Location]
Capell (after Rowe)   0 SD *and his* PAGE] *This edn (after Capell)*; *Enter Benvolio, Mercutio.* Q1   2 Capels are] Q1;
Capels Q2–3; *Capulets* Q4, F   3–4] *As verse, Rowe; as prose,* Q2–4, F; *not in* Q1; *as prose (including 1–2), Hosley*
5 these] Q2–4, F; *those* Q1, F4   8 him] Q2–4, F; *it* Q1, *Pope*   13 to] *Pope; too* Q2–4, F, Q1   15–17 *for...hast;] not
in* Q1   15 Thou?] *Hoppe; thou,* Q2–4, F; *Thou! Rowe*

Act 3, Scene 1
Location Verona. A public place.
1–4 The day...stirring In 1.3.16 we are told
that events are taking place about the middle of July,
the dog-days so-called, in which physical violence,
particularly in Italy, was noted as especially rife.
2 Capels Capulets (the form occurs occasionally
in Brooke).
5–26 Mercutio's characterisation of Benvolio as
a quarrelsome gallant who will pick a fight under
the most whimsical pretexts, or for none, is borne
out by nothing we learn of Benvolio in the play; if
anything, he is the opposite. Thus, in his pique at
Benvolio's suggestion that they should withdraw
because 'the Capels are abroad', Mercutio's

criticism tells us more about himself than about
Benvolio. See supplementary note.
6 claps me places (noisily); 'me' = ethical
dative (compare 'him' in 8; see Franz 294). This
is the action of a braggart and in itself a covert
invitation to quarrel.
7 operation effect, influence.
8 drawer tapster.
10 mood anger, quarrelsome humour.
11–12 as soon moved...moved as quickly
provoked to be angry and as quickly angry for being
provoked.
14 two Mercutio plays on Benvolio's 'to' in 13.
17 cracking nuts Prepares for the pun on
'hazel' (18).

reason but because thou hast hazel eyes. What eye but such an eye
would spy out such a quarrel? Thy head is as full of quarrels as
an egg is full of meat, and yet thy head hath been beaten as addle   20
as an egg for quarrelling. Thou hast quarrelled with a man for
coughing in the street, because he hath wakened thy dog that hath
lain asleep in the sun. Didst thou not fall out with a tailor for
wearing his new doublet before Easter? with another for tying his
new shoes with old riband? and yet thou wilt tutor me from   25
quarrelling?

BENVOLIO And I were so apt to quarrel as thou art, any man should
    buy the fee-simple of my life for an hour and a quarter.

MERCUTIO The fee-simple? O simple!

Enter TYBALT, PETRUCHIO, *and others.*

BENVOLIO By my head, here comes the Capulets.   30

MERCUTIO By my heel, I care not.

TYBALT Follow me close, for I will speak to them.
    Gentlemen, good den, a word with one of you.

MERCUTIO And but one word with one of us? couple it with something,
    make it a word and a blow.   35

TYBALT You shall find me apt enough to that, sir, and you will give
    me occasion.

MERCUTIO Could you not take some occasion without giving?

TYBALT Mercutio, thou consortest with Romeo.

MERCUTIO Consort? what, dost thou make us minstrels? And thou   40

19–21 Thy...quarrelling.] *not in* Q1   25 from] Q2–4, F; of Q1; for Q5, *Pope*   27–9 And...simple!] *not in* Q1
29 fee-simple?] F; fee-simple, Q2–4   29 SD] Q2–4, F; *Enter Tybalt.* Q1 *(after 30)*; *Enter* Tybalt, *and others.* / *Hanmer*
30 comes the Capulets] Q2–4, F; comes a *Capolet* Q1; come the *Capuletes* F2   34 us?] Q3–4, F, Q1; vs, Q2   39 consortest]
Q2–4; consort'st F; consorts Q1   39 Romeo.] Q2–4, F; *Romeo?* Q1; *Romeo –* / *Rowe*   40 Consort?] F; Consort, Q2–4;
Consort Zwounes consort? Q1   40 dost] Q3–4, F; doest Q2

---

20 **meat** edible substance (yolk and white).

20–1 **addle...for** as muddled and worthless as
a bad egg as a result of; compare 'addle-pated'.

24 **his new doublet** i.e. the new jacket he has
just created. NS suggests that the tailor was
advertising his new line in advance of Easter when
'lenten' wear was abandoned.

24–5 **his new shoes** i.e. the new shoes supplied
by him (NS).

25 **riband** ribbon (variant form). Ribbons were
used as shoelaces.

25 **tutor me from** warn me against (as a tutor
might warn his pupil).

27 **apt** prone.

27–8 **any...quarter** i.e. it would be a bargain
for me to sell all rights to my life ('fee-
simple' = absolute possession) to anyone who
would buy them for as little as an hour and a

quarter, since I would expect to be dead before the
time was up.

29 **simple** weak-minded, stupid (with perhaps
some play on 'simple' = absolute).

29 SD PETRUCHIO Presumably the 'young
Petruchio' mentioned by the Nurse in 1.5.130; he
has no lines.

31 **By my heel** Derogatory, as the extreme
opposite of the head.

35 **word...blow** Proverbial (Tilley w763: 'He
is but a word and a blow', and w824).

37 **occasion** excuse.

38 **Could...giving?** Mercutio is presumably
annoyed by Tybalt's insistence on punctilio.
'without giving' = without its having been offered.

40 **Consort?** Mercutio intentionally misinter-
prets Tybalt's 'consortest' (= keepest company
with) to mean 'performest musically with' as a

make minstrels of us, look to hear nothing but discords. Here's my
fiddlestick, here's that shall make you dance. 'Zounds, consort!

BENVOLIO We talk here in the public haunt of men:
Either withdraw unto some private place,
Or reason coldly of your grievances,   45
Or else depart; here all eyes gaze on us.

MERCUTIO Men's eyes were made to look, and let them gaze;
I will not budge for no man's pleasure, I.

Enter ROMEO.

TYBALT Well, peace be with you, sir, here comes my man.

MERCUTIO But I'll be hanged, sir, if he wear your livery.   50
Marry, go before to field, he'll be your follower;
Your worship in that sense may call him man.

TYBALT Romeo, the love I bear thee can afford
No better term than this: thou art a villain.

ROMEO Tybalt, the reason that I have to love thee   55
Doth much excuse the appertaining rage
To such a greeting. Villain am I none;
Therefore farewell, I see thou knowest me not.

TYBALT Boy, this shall not excuse the injuries
That thou hast done me, therefore turn and draw.   60

ROMEO I do protest I never injuried thee,
But love thee better than thou canst devise,
Till thou shalt know the reason of my love;

---

42 'Zounds] Q2–4 (zounds); Come F; *see 40 above for* Q1   43–8] *not in* Q1   45 Or] Q2–4, F; And *Capell*
45–6 grievances,…depart;] F4 *(comma also in* Q5*)*; greeuances: depart, Q2–4, F   53 love] Q2–4, F; hate Q1, *Pope*
58 knowest] Q2–3; know'st Q4, F, Q1   61 injuried] Q2; iniured Q3–4, Q1; iniur'd F   62 love] Q2–4, Q1; lou'd F
62 thou] Q3–4, F, Q1; thon Q2   62 devise,] Q1, Q5; deuise: Q2–3, F; deuise. Q4

member of a 'consort' or troupe of professional
musicians or 'minstrels' (= fiddlers, etc.) – an
insult to a gentleman. Compare 'give you the
minstrel' in 4.5.110–11.

42 fiddlestick i.e. rapier (to which he points).

42 'Zounds A corruption of 'By God's (=
Christ's) wounds'.

45 reason coldly of discuss dispassionately.

46 depart go your separate ways.

50 wear your livery Mercutio again quibbles
with Tybalt, taking 'my man' (49) to mean 'my
servant', one who would properly wear Tybalt's
'livery' (= uniform or heraldic badge). Compare
similar play in 51 on 'follower' (= (1) one who
accepts a challenge; (2) an attendant servant).

51 go…field lead the way to the place of
combat (i.e. set an example).

53 love Surprisingly ironic coming from the
forthright Tybalt. Some eds. prefer Q1 'hate'.

54 villain A very serious insult demanding
reprisal, carrying not only the sense of 'depraved
scoundrel' but undertones of 'low-born fellow'
(= villein); compare 86.

55–8, 61–5 Compare Brooke (999–1002,
1011–15); Painter (p. 112), however, seems much
closer in tone and feeling to Shakespeare. See
supplementary note.

56 appertaining appropriate (to a member of
the Capulet family).

59 Boy A term of contempt; compare Brooke
(1016) and *Cor.* 5.6.100–16.

61 injuried injured (variant form from 'to
injury').

And so, good Capulet, which name I tender
As dearly as mine own, be satisfied.   65

MERCUTIO O calm, dishonourable, vile submission!
'Alla stoccata' carries it away. [*Draws.*]
Tybalt, you rat-catcher, will you walk?

TYBALT What wouldst thou have with me?

MERCUTIO Good King of Cats, nothing but one of your nine lives that   70
I mean to make bold withal, and as you shall use me hereafter,
dry-beat the rest of the eight. Will you pluck your sword out of
his pilcher by the ears? Make haste, lest mine be about your ears
ere it be out.

TYBALT I am for you. [*Drawing.*]   75

ROMEO Gentle Mercutio, put thy rapier up.

MERCUTIO Come, sir, your 'passado'.

> [*They fight.*]

ROMEO Draw, Benvolio, beat down their weapons.
Gentlemen, for shame forbear this outrage!
Tybalt, Mercutio, the Prince expressly hath   80
Forbid this bandying in Verona streets.

> [*Romeo steps between them.*]

64–5] *not in* Q1   65 mine] Q2; my Q3–4, F   67 'Alla stoccata'] *Knight; Alla stucatho* Q2–4, F; *Allastockado* Q1; *Ah!
la Stoccata / Theobald; Ha! la stocatto / Hanmer; A la stoccato / Capell; Allo steccato / Hoppe; Alla stoccatho / Hosley;
Alla stoccato / Riverside*   67 SD] *Capell; no* SD, Q2–4, F, Q1   69 wouldst] Q2; *woulds* Q3–4, F; *wouldest* Q1
70–82 Good…hurt.] Q2–4, F; *Nothing King of Cates, but borrow one of your nine liues, therefore come drawe your
rapier out of your scabard, least mine be about your eares ere you be a ware. / Rom: Stay Tibalt, hould Mercutio: Benuolio
beate downe their weapons.* Q1   71 me hereafter,] *Pope; mee hereafter* Q2–4, F; me, hereafter *Rowe*   72 dry-beat]
Rowe; drie beate Q2–4, F   73 pilcher] Q2–4, F; *scabard* Q1; *pilche Warburton; pitcher Singer²; pilch, sir, conj. Staunton*
75 SD] *Rowe; no* SD, Q2–4, F, Q1   77 SD] *Rowe (subst.); no* SD, Q2–4, F, Q1   81 Forbid this] Q2; Forbid Q3–4; Forbidden F
81 SD] *Riverside (from Douai MS.); no* SD, Q2–4, F, Q1; *striving to part them. / Capell (after 79)*

64 **tender** value, hold in regard.
67 **'Alla stoccata'** Literally 'at the thrust', an
Italian fencing term of the kind Mercutio despises;
here used as a nickname for Tybalt (Cowden Clarke)
and implying, with 'carries it away' (= wins the
day), that his verbal onslaught has apparently
unarmed Romeo (Kermode).
68 **rat-catcher** i.e. 'King of Cats' (70). Compare
2.4.18, and Nashe, *Saffron-Walden (Works*, III, 67).
71 **withal** with.
71–2 **as…dry-beat** depending on your future
behaviour to me, thrash or cudgel ('dry-beat'
properly means 'to beat without drawing blood' but
was vaguely used to mean 'beat hard' (*OED*)).
Mercutio suggests that another time he will not
accord Tybalt the honour of armed combat proper
to a gentleman, but will thrash him with his bare
hands as one would a servant.

73 **pilcher** Contemptuous term for 'scabbard'
(the reading of Q1), from 'pilch' = a leather jacket,
though 'pilcher' is otherwise unrecorded in this
sense. Scabbards were commonly made of leather
reinforced with metal. Perhaps Mercutio is sneer-
ing at a mere leather scabbard as compared with
more costly ones (such as his?) wholly of metal.
NS proposes that 'pluck…ears' (72–3) 'suggests
a reluctant sword' – an insult to Tybalt as its
wearer.
75 **I…you** i.e. I accept the challenge.
77 **Come…'passado'** 'Come, sir, show your
thrust that you are so fond of talking about'
(Kittredge). Compare 2.4.23.
81 **bandying** contention, strife (literally, 'exchange of strokes').

Hold, Tybalt! Good Mercutio!
[Tybalt under Romeo's arm thrusts Mercutio in.]
                              Away Tybalt [with his followers]
MERCUTIO   I am hurt.
A plague a'both houses! I am sped.
Is he gone and hath nothing?
BENVOLIO   What, art thou hurt?
MERCUTIO Ay, ay, a scratch, a scratch, marry, 'tis enough.   85
    Where is my page? Go, villain, fetch a surgeon.
                                        [Exit Page]

ROMEO Courage, man, the hurt cannot be much.
MERCUTIO No, 'tis not so deep as a well, nor so wide as a church-door,
    but 'tis enough, 'twill serve. Ask for me tomorrow, and you shall
    find me a grave man. I am peppered, I warrant, for this world. A   90
    plague a'both your houses! 'Zounds, a dog, a rat, a mouse, a cat,
    to scratch a man to death! a braggart, a rogue, a villain, that fights
    by the book of arithmetic. Why the dev'l came you between us?
    I was hurt under your arm.
ROMEO I thought all for the best.   95
MERCUTIO Help me into some house, Benvolio,
    Or I shall faint. A plague a'both your houses!   repetition
    They have made worms' meat of me. I have it,
    And soundly too. Your houses!
                                        Exit [with Benvolio]

82 SD.1 *Tybalt...in.] from* Q1 (*Tibalt vnder Romeos arme thrusts Mercutio, in and flyes.*); *not in* Q2–4, F   82 SD.2 *Away Tybalt*] *centred as* SD *in* Q2–4; *Exit Tybalt.* F; *Williams (conj. Greg) assigns as dialogue to Petruchio; Spencer assigns to / A Follower.*   82 SD.2 *with his followers*] *Globe (after Malone)*   83, 91, 97 plague] Q2–4, F; poxe Q1   83 a'both] Q2–4 (a both); a both the F; on your Q1; of both the F2; on both *the Johnson*; o' both your *Dyce*   85 Ay, ay] *Rowe*; I, I Q2–4, F   86] *Following this line* Q1 *adds: Boy:* I goe my Lord.   86 SD] *Capell; no* SD, Q2–4, F, Q1   91 a'both] Q2–4 (a both), F; of your Q1; of both F2; on both *Johnson*; o' both *Capell*   91–9 'Zounds...houses!] Q2–4, F; I shall be fairely mounted vpon foure mens shoulders: For your house of the *Mountegues* and the *Capolets*: and then some peasantly rogue, some Sexton, some base slaue shall write my Epitapth, that *Tybalt* came and broke the Princes Lawes, and *Mercutio* was slaine for the first and second cause. Wher's the Surgeon? / *Boy:* Hee's come sir. / *Mer:* Now heele keepe a mumbling in my guts on the other side, come *Benuolio*, lend me thy hand: a poxe of your houses. Q1   91 'Zounds] Q5; sounds Q2–4; What F   98–9 I...houses!] *As Dyce; one line*, Q2–4, F   99 soundly too.] F3 (soundly too,); soundly, to Q2; soundly to Q3–4, F; soundly too F2; soundly too. Plague o' your houses! *Theobald*   99 SD] *Rowe (subst.); Exit.* Q2–4, F; *Exeunt* Q1

82 SD.1 *thrusts Mercutio in* i.e. runs Mercutio through. Compare Brooke (1005–6) for Romeo's interference.
82 SD.2 *Away Tybalt* See collation.
83 **sped** dispatched, done for. Compare 'I have it' in 98.
85 **a scratch** With rueful reference to Tybalt as 'King of Cats' (NS); compare 92.
86 **villain** fellow (without social slur here).

90 **grave** i.e. dead (and buried); compare the play on 'grave' in *R2* 2.1.82–3.
90 **peppered...world** dead, I swear, so far as this life is concerned.
92–3 **fights...arithmetic** fences precisely, by the numbers (i.e. a textbook fencer); compare 2.4.19–21.
98–9 See supplementary note.

ROMEO This gentleman, the Prince's near ally,   100
My very friend, hath got this mortal hurt
In my behalf; my reputation stained
With Tybalt's slander – Tybalt, that an hour
Hath been my cousin. O sweet Juliet,
Thy beauty hath made me effeminate,   105
And in my temper softened valour's steel!

Enter Benvolio.

BENVOLIO O Romeo, Romeo, brave Mercutio is dead.
That gallant spirit hath aspired the clouds,
Which too untimely here did scorn the earth.
ROMEO This day's black fate on moe days doth depend,   110
. This but begins the woe others must end.

[Enter Tybalt.]

BENVOLIO Here comes the furious Tybalt back again.
ROMEO Again, in triumph, and Mercutio slain?
Away to heaven, respective lenity,
And fire-eyed fury be my conduct now!   115
Now, Tybalt, take the 'villain' back again
That late thou gavest me, for Mercutio's soul
Is but a little way above our heads,
Staying for thine to keep him company:
Either thou or I, or both, must go with him.   120
TYBALT Thou wretched boy, that didst consort him here,
Shalt with him hence.

101 got this] Q2; gott his Q3; got his Q4, F; tane this Q1, *Ridley*   102 reputation] Q2–4, F, Q1; reputation's *Hudson*
(conj. S. Walker)   104 cousin] Q2–4, F; kinsman Q1, *Capell*   107 Mercutio is] Q2–4, Q1; *Mercutio's* is F; *Mercutio's*
F2   108 gallant] Q3–4, F, Q1; gallanr Q2   110 moe] Q2–4, F; more Q1, Q5, F4   111 begins…others] Q5; begins, the
wo others Q2–4, F; begins what other dayes Q1; begins the Woe, others F4   111 SD] F, Q1; *not in* Q2–4   113 Again,]
Capell (Again?); He gan Q2; He gon Q3–4, F; A liue Q1; He gone Q5, F3; Alive? *Pope*; He gay *Hoppe*; He yare *Williams*;
'A live *conj. this edn*   113 slain?] F, Q1; slaine Q2–4   115 fire-eyed] *Pope* (fire-ey'd; *from* Q1 fier eyed); fier end Q2;
fier and Q3–4, F   117 gavest] Q2–4; gau'st F, Q1   120 Either] Q2–4, F; Or Q1, *Pope*   121–2] *not in* Q1

100 **ally** relative.

101 **very** true.

103 **slander** i.e. the insults heaped on Romeo
which he had failed to answer, as the terms of
honour dictated, by duelling.

106 **in…steel** weakened the (manly) steel-like
courage of my natural disposition ('temper', with
play on the technical 'tempering of steel').

108 **aspired** mounted up to (intransitive use
common in Elizabethan English).

109 **untimely** prematurely.

110 **day's…depend** the malignant consequence

('black fate') of today's events is contingent ('doth
depend' = hangs) on the future ('moe [= more]
days'). Compare 1.4.107–9.

111 **others** i.e. other days to come.

113 *****Again** See supplementary note.

114 **respective lenity** considerate mildness
(mercy being an attribute of heaven; 'fire-eyed
fury' (115) a 'conduct' (= guide) from hell).
Spencer suggests that Romeo's language is now that
of the typical hero of revenge tragedy; compare 162.

119 **Staying** Waiting.

121 **consort** associate with. Compare 40.

ROMEO   This shall determine that.
                    They fight; Tybalt falls.
BENVOLIO Romeo, away, be gone!
          The citizens are up, and Tybalt slain.
          Stand not amazed, the Prince will doom thee death   125
          If thou art taken. Hence be gone, away!
ROMEO O, I am fortune's fool. *fortune/fate v. God*
BENVOLIO   Why dost thou stay?

                                              Exit Romeo

          Enter Citizens [as OFFICERS *of the Watch].*

OFFICER Which way ran he that killed Mercutio?
         Tybalt, that murderer, which way ran he?
BENVOLIO There lies that Tybalt.
OFFICER   Up, sir, go with me;   130
         I charge thee in the Prince's name obey.

          Enter PRINCE, *old* MONTAGUE, CAPULET, *their* WIVES,
                        and all.

PRINCE Where are the vile beginners of this fray?
BENVOLIO O noble Prince, I can discover all
          The unlucky manage of this fatal brawl;
          There lies the man, slain by young Romeo,   135
          That slew thy kinsman, brave Mercutio.
LADY CAPULET Tybalt, my cousin! O my brother's child!
          O Prince! O husband! O, the blood is spilled
          Of my dear kinsman. Prince, as thou art true,
          For blood of ours, shed blood of Montague.   140
          O cousin, cousin!

123 away,] Q4, Q1 ; away Q2–3, F   125 amazed] F (amaz'd); amazed Q2–4   126 be gone,] Q4, F; be gone Q2 ; begone
Q3, Q1   127 Why…stay?] *not in* Q1   127 SD.1] Q2–4, F; *Exeunt* Q1   127 SD.2 *as* OFFICERS *of the Watch*] *This edn
(after* Q1 *speech headings; see below)*   128 SH OFFICER] *This edn (after* Q1 *speech heading / Watch.)*; *Citti.* Q2; *Citi.*
Q3–4, F; 1. *O. / Capell;* 1. *Cit. / Malone; Citizens. / Hosley*   129 murderer] Q3–4, F (murtherer); mutherer Q2; villaine
Q1   130 SH OFFICER] *This edn (after* Q1 *speech heading / Watch:)*; *Citi.* Q2–4, F; 1. *O. / Capell;* 1. *Cit. / Malone;
Citizen. / Hosley*   131 name] Q2–4; names F; Q1 *omits 131*   131 SD] Q2–4, F; *Enter Prince, Capolets wife.* Q1
133 all] F, Q1 ; all: Q2–4   134 brawl] Q1 ; brall Q2–4, F   136, 139 kinsman] Q3–4, F, Q1; kisman Q2   137 SH LADY
CAPULET] *Rowe; Capu. Wi.* Q2–4; *Cap. Wi.* F; *M:* Q1   138 O Prince…O,] *Capell (later withdrawn), Dyce;* O Prince,
O Cozen, husband, O Q2–4, F; Vnhappie sight! Ah Q1, *Malone;* Unhappy sight! alas *Pope;* Prince – cousin –
husband – O – *Johnson;* Unhappy sight! ah me, *conj. Malone*   141 O cousin, cousin!] *not in* Q1, *Pope*

124 **up** aroused.   133 **discover** reveal.
125 **amazed** filled with consternation.   134 **manage** conduct.
127 **fool** dupe, sport. Compare 'time's fool', 138 **O Prince! O husband!** See supplementary
1H4 5.4.81.   note.
130 **Up** Benvolio is still apparently kneeling by
Tybalt's body.

PRINCE Benvolio, who began this bloody fray?

BENVOLIO Tybalt, here slain, whom Romeo's hand did slay.
    Romeo, that spoke him fair, bid him bethink
    How nice the quarrel was, and urged withal   145
    Your high displeasure; all this, utterèd
    With gentle breath, calm look, knees humbly bowed,
    Could not take truce with the unruly spleen
    Of Tybalt deaf to peace, but that he tilts
    With piercing steel at bold Mercutio's breast,   150
    Who, all as hot, turns deadly point to point,
    And with a martial scorn, with one hand beats
    Cold death aside, and with the other sends
    It back to Tybalt, whose dexterity
    Retorts it. Romeo he cries aloud,   155
    'Hold, friends! friends, part!' and swifter than his tongue,
    His agile arm beats down their fatal points,
    And 'twixt them rushes; underneath whose arm
    An envious thrust from Tybalt hit the life
    Of stout Mercutio, and then Tybalt fled;   160
    But by and by comes back to Romeo,
    Who had but newly entertained revenge,
    And to't they go like lightning, for, ere I
    Could draw to part them, was stout Tybalt slain;
    And as he fell, did Romeo turn and fly.   165
    This is the truth, or let Benvolio die.

LADY CAPULET He is a kinsman to the Montague,
    Affection makes him false, he speaks not true:

---

142 bloody] Q2–4; *not in* F, Q1   145–61 and...Romeo,] Q2–4, F; But *Tibalt* still persisting in his wrong, / The stout
Mercutio drewe to calme the storme, / Which *Romeo* seeing cal'd stay Gentlemen, / And on me cry'd, who drew to part
their strife, / And with his agill arme yong *Romeo*, / As fast as tung cryde peace, sought peace to make. / While they
were enterchanging thrusts and blows, / Vnder young *Romeos* laboring arme to part, / The furious *Tybalt* cast an enuious
thrust, / That rid the life of stout *Mercutio*. / With that he fled, but presently return'd, / And with his rapier braued
Romeo: Q1   146 displeasure;] F *(subst.)*; displeasure Q2–4   146 this, utterèd] *Capell (subst., after Pope)*; this vttered,
Q2, F; this vttered. Q3–4   147 bowed] F (bow'd); bowed Q2–4   148 take] Q2–4, F; make *conj. Capell*   149 Tybalt]
Q2–4; *Tybalts* F   155 it] Q2–4, F; it home *Collier MS*.   157 agile] Q4, Q1; aged Q2–3, F; able F2   162 entertained]
Q2–4 (entertaind), Q1; entertained Q3, F   163 to't] Q4 (too't), F; toote Q2–3   167 SH LADY CAPULET] *Rowe; Ca.
Wi.* Q2–4, F *(subst.); Mo:* Q1   167–8] Q2–4, F; He is a *Mountagew* and speakes partiall, Q1   167 kinsman] Q3–4,
F; kisman Q2

---

144 **bethink** consider.

145 **nice** insignificant, trifling.

148 **take truce** make peace.

148 **unruly spleen** ungoverned fiery temper.
The spleen was considered the seat of the morose
passions and anger.

152–3 **with one...other** i.e. Mercutio parries
the blow with his dagger and thrusts at Tybalt with
his sword.

155 **Retorts it** Returns the thrust ('cold death').

157 **arm** i.e. sword (metonymy).

159 **envious** malicious.

160 **stout** strong, brave.

162 **entertained** allowed the thought of.

168 **Affection** Partial inclination or love.

168 **he...true** Though Benvolio's account is
relatively accurate, he is guilty of some 'affection':
(1) he is careful to stress Mercutio's kinship with

Some twenty of them fought in this black strife,
And all those twenty could but kill one life.   170
I beg for justice, which thou, Prince, must give:
Romeo slew Tybalt, Romeo must not live.
PRINCE Romeo slew him, he slew Mercutio;
Who now the price of his dear blood doth owe?
MONTAGUE Not Romeo, Prince, he was Mercutio's friend;   175
His fault concludes but what the law should end,
The life of Tybalt.
PRINCE   And for that offence
Immediately we do exile him hence.
I have an interest in your hearts' proceeding:
My blood for your rude brawls doth lie a-bleeding;   180
But I'll amerce you with so strong a fine
That you shall all repent the loss of mine.
I will be deaf to pleading and excuses,
Nor tears nor prayers shall purchase out abuses:
Therefore use none. Let Romeo hence in haste,   185
Else, when he is found, that hour is his last.
Bear hence this body, and attend our will:
Mercy but murders, pardoning those that kill.

                                             Exeunt

173–7 Romeo...Tybalt.] *not in* Q1   174 owe?] *Theobald²*; owe. Q2–4, F   175 SH MONTAGUE] Q4; *Capu.* Q2; *Cap.* Q3, F; *La. Cap.* / *Rowe*; *La. Mont.* / *Theobald*   179 hearts'] *Johnson*; hearts Q2–4, F; hates Q1; heats' *Hanmer*; hates' *Capell*; hate's *Knight*   183 I] Q4, Q1; It Q2–3, F   184–5 abuses:...none.] *Theobald (subst.)*; abuses. / ...none, Q2–4, F; abuses. Q1   184 out] Q2–4; our F; for Q1   185–8] Q2–4, F; Pittie shall dwell and gouerne with vs still: / Mercie to all but murdrers, pardoning none that kill. Q1   188 but] Q2–4; not F   188 SD] F; *Exit.* Q2–4; *Exeunt omnes.* Q1

the Prince (136); (2) he implies that Tybalt was the aggressor against Mercutio and that only he was 'deaf to peace' (149), when, in fact, Mercutio was the aggressor (68–74).

169 Some twenty Lady Capulet has received the usual sort of exaggerated account of the fight from a Capulet source and is suggesting 'foul play' on Romeo's and Benvolio's parts.

174 Who...owe? Who then should pay the cost for Mercutio's dear (= (1) loved, honourable, (2) costly, precious) blood?

175 SH *MONTAGUE See collation.

176 concludes but only finishes.

177 for that offence i.e. for taking the law into his own hands. The Prince turns Montague's defence back on him.

179 interest...proceeding personal concern in the reaction dictated by your feelings. The heart

was considered the seat of the emotions generally. Q1 'hates' (i.e. hate's or hates'), adopted by most earlier eds. (since Capell), is an easier reading. In Secretary hand 'heart' and 'hate' could be misread either way. NS quotes *1H6* 3.1.26 ('From envious malice of thy swelling heart') in support of Q2 'hearts'.

180 My blood i.e. Mercutio, the Prince's kinsman.

180 lie a-bleeding Proverbial phrase (Tilley A159).

181 amerce punish, penalise.

182 loss of mine either (1) the loss of my blood, or (2) my loss.

184 purchase out buy out, make amends for.

188 Mercy...kill Mercy only leads to further murders by pardoning murderers.

[3.2] *Enter* JULIET *alone.*

JULIET Gallop apace, you fiery-footed steeds,
        Towards Phoebus' lodging; such a waggoner
        As Phaëton would whip you to the west,
        And bring in cloudy night immediately.
        Spread thy close curtain, love-performing Night,   5
        That runaways' eyes may wink, and Romeo
        Leap to these arms, untalked of and unseen:
        Lovers can see to do their amorous rites
        By their own beauties, or if love be blind,
        It best agrees with night. Come, civil Night,   10
        Thou sober-suited matron all in black,
        And learn me how to lose a winning match,
        Played for a pair of stainless maidenhoods.
        Hood my unmanned blood, bating in my cheeks,
        With thy black mantle, till strange love grow bold,   15
        Think true love acted simple modesty.

Act 3, Scene 2   3.2] *Rowe; no scene division,* Q2–4, F, Q1   Location] *Rowe; Capulet's Garden. / Capell*   0 SD *alone]
not in* Q1   1 SH JULIET] F, Q1 ; *not in* Q2–4   1 fiery-footed] *Rowe;* fierie footed Q2–4, F, Q1   2 lodging] Q2–4, F ;
mansion Q1, *Pope*   3 Phaëton] Q3–4, F, Q1 ; *Phaetan* Q2   5–33] *not in* Q1   6 runaways'] *Delius;* runnawayes Q2–4;
run-awayes F ; jealous *Otway;* th' Run-away's *Theobald (conj. Warburton)* ; run-away's *Rann;* run-away *Blackstone (in
Johnson–Steevens, 1785)* ; Rumour's *Hudson (conj. Heath, withdrawn)* ; unawares *Knight (conj. Jackson)* ; runagates' *conj.
Becket;* Luna's *conj. Mitford;* rumourers' *Singer²;* Cynthia's *conj. S. Walker;* enemies' *Collier MS.;* rude day's *Dyce;*
envious *or* curious *conj. Cowden Clarke;* cunningest *conj. Dover Wilson (in NS)*   7 unseen:] Q5 ; vnseene, Q2–4, F *(conj.
Dowden, with period after* armes*)*   8 rites] F4 ; rights Q2–4, F   9 By] Q4 ; And by Q2–3, F   11 sober-suited] F4 ; sober
suted Q2–4, F   13 maidenhoods] Q2–3, F ; maiden-heads Q4 ; Maidenheads F2   15 mantle,] Q2–4, F ; mantle: Q5,
Theobald   15 grow] Q2–4, F ; grown *Rowe*

Act 3, Scene 2 See suppl. note.
  Location Verona. Capulet's house.
  1–4 Gallop...immediately This speech as a
whole was first associated with the epithalamium (or
wedding hymn) by H. N. Halpin ·in 1845. See
supplementary note.
  2 lodging i.e. the west, below the horizon.
Compare Brooke (1527): 'The golden sonne, was
gonne to lodge him in the west.'
  5 close curtain curtain ensuring privacy, like
the curtains of a fourposter bed. See 4.5.58 SD.
  5 love-performing Night i.e. night, the time
for love. Gibbons compares Daniel, *Rosamond*
(432–4): 'night... / Who with her sable mantle
friendly covers / The sweet-stolne sports, of joyfull
meeting Lovers'.
  6 That...wink So that the eyes of (1) the horses
of the sun – or (2) vagrant night wanderers – may
(1) close in sleep (compare Brooke (1709)) – or (2)
pretend to see nothing. See supplementary note.

  8–9 Lovers...beauties Malone compares Marlowe, *Hero and Leander*, I, 191: 'darke night is
Cupids day'; NS adds II, 240–2: 'Rich jewels in the
darke are soonest spide. / Unto her was he led, or
rather drawne, / By those white limmes, which
sparckled through the lawne' and II, 318–22.
Marlowe also uses 'amorous rites' in II, 64.
  9 By See supplementary note.
  10 civil grave, sober.
  12 learn teach.
  14 Hood...unmanned...bating Cover, blind-
fold...untamed (i.e. not trained by a man, with play
on 'husbandless' (NS))...fluttering (to break
loose); all terms from falconry.
  15 strange...bold reserved, shy love become
courageous.
  16 Think Elliptical: supply 'And' before
'Think'. Many eds. prefer Rowe's 'grown' for
'grow' (15), but unnecessarily.
  16 modesty chastity.

Come, Night, come, Romeo, come, thou day in night,
For thou wilt lie upon the wings of night,
Whiter than new snow upon a raven's back.
Come, gentle Night, come, loving, black-browed Night, 20
Give me my Romeo, and when I shall die
Take him and cut him out in little stars,
And he will make the face of heaven so fine
That all the world will be in love with night,
And pay no worship to the garish sun. 25
O, I have bought the mansion of a love,
But not possessed it, and though I am sold,
Not yet enjoyed. So tedious is this day
As is the night before some festival
To an impatient child that hath new robes 30
And may not wear them. O, here comes my Nurse,

Enter NURSE, *with* [*the ladder of*] *cords* [*in her lap*].

And she brings news, and every tongue that speaks
But Romeo's name speaks heavenly eloquence.
Now, Nurse, what news? What hast thou there? the cords
That Romeo bid thee fetch?

NURSE   Ay, ay, the cords. 35

[*Throws them down.*]
JULIET Ay me, what news? Why dost thou wring thy hands?

19 new snow upon] Q2–3, F; snow vpon Q4; new Snow on F2   20 black-browed] Q4 (black-browd); black browd Q2; blackbrowd Q3, F   21 I] Q2–3, F; hee Q4, *Otway*   28 enjoyed.] *Rowe (subst.)*; enioyd, Q2–4, F   31 SD *the ladder of...in her lap*] *from* Q1 (*Enter Nurse wringing her hands, with the ladder of cordes in her lap.*); *not in* Q2–4, F   33 Romeo's name] Q2–4; *Romeos*, name F   34 there?] F; there, Q2–4, Q1   34–5 the cords...fetch?] *As Hanmer; one line*, Q2–4, F; the cordes? Q1   35 SD] *Capell (subst.)*; *no* SD, Q2–4, F, Q1

19 new snow upon See supplementary note.

20 Come, gentle Night Compare Lyly, *Woman in the Moon* 4.1.254: 'Come night, come gentle night, for thee I stay.' See above, 1–4.

21–5 Give...sun i.e. let me have Romeo to myself as long as I am alive, and when I die then I will share him with the whole world as a source of light that will put the sun to shame. Q4 'he' for 'I' in 21, adopted by many eds., too suddenly changes the focus to Romeo's death, something, as Delius points out, Juliet 'cannot, in her present happiness, conceive'. Accepting 'he', Dover Wilson (NS) paraphrases: 'if, gentle night, you will give him to me now, you may have him when he is dead to make stars of'.

25 garish showy, glaring.

26–7 bought...sold A sudden shift in metaphor: (1) Juliet has bought a lordly new dwelling place (= Romeo's love) of which she has not yet taken physical possession; (2) Juliet has sold herself (for love), but the new tenant (= Romeo) has not entered into possession. 'mansion of a love' = the body as the vehicle of love's physical activities' (Partridge). Compare *TGV* 5.4.7–10.

31 SD *in her lap* Q1's detail suggests that the Nurse is carrying the ladder of cords bundled up in her cloak or apron for concealment. Q1's '*wringing her hands*' seems to be an anticipation of Q2, line 36 (omitted Q1), since she could not very well wring her hands until she had set down the ladder of cords.

NURSE Ah weraday, he's dead, he's dead, he's dead!
    We are undone, lady, we are undone.
    Alack the day, he's gone, he's killed, he's dead!
JULIET Can heaven be so envious?
NURSE   Romeo can,   40
    Though heaven cannot. O Romeo, Romeo!
    Who ever would have thought it? Romeo!
JULIET What devil art thou that dost torment me thus?
    This torture should be roared in dismal hell.
    Hath Romeo slain himself? Say thou but 'ay',   45
    And that bare vowel 'I' shall poison more
    Than the death-darting eye of cockatrice.
    I am not I, if there be such an 'ay',
    Or those eyes shut, that makes thee answer 'ay'.
    If he be slain, say 'ay', or if not, 'no':   50
    Brief sounds determine my weal or woe.
NURSE I saw the wound, I saw it with mine eyes
    (God save the mark!), here on his manly breast:
    A piteous corse, a bloody piteous corse,
    Pale, pale as ashes, all bedaubed in blood,   55
    All in gore blood; I sounded at the sight.
JULIET O break, my heart, poor bankrout, break at once!

37 Ah] *Pope*; A Q2–4, F   37 weraday] Q2; weladay Q3–4; welady F; Alack the day Q1   37 he's dead, he's dead, he's dead] Q2–4, Q1; hee's dead, hee's dead F   42 it? Romeo!] *Capell*; it *Romeo*? Q2; it *Romeo*. Q3–4, F   44 roared] F (roar'd), Q1; rored Q2–4   45–51] *not in* Q1   45 'ay'] *Rowe*; I Q2–4, F   47 death-darting] Q3–4, F; death arting Q2   48 'ay',] *Rowe (comma,* Q5*)*; I. Q2–4, F   49 eyes shut, that makes thee] *Capell*; eyes shot, that makes thee Q2–4, F; eyes shot, that makes the F2; Eyes short that makes the *Rowe*; eyes shut, that make thee *Steevens (conj. Johnson)*; eyes' shot that makes thee *Hoppe*   49, 50 'ay'] *Rowe*; I Q2–4, F   51 Brief sounds] Q5; Briefe, sounds, Q2–4, F   51 my] Q2–4; of my F; or *Collier²*; me my *conj. J. C. Maxwell*   53 mark!), here] *Theobald*; marke, here Q2–4, F; sample, Q1   53 breast:] Q1; brest, Q2–4, F   56 sounded] Q2–4, F; swounded Q1, *Collier*; swouned Q5; swooned F4   57–60] Q2–4, F; Ah *Romeo, Romeo*, what disaster hap / Hath seuerd thee from thy true *Iuliet*? / Ah why should Heauen so much conspire with Woe, / Or Fate enuie our happie Marriage, / So soone to sunder vs by timelesse Death? Q1   57 bankrout] Q2–4, F; bankrupt Q5, F4

37 **weraday** alas (variant of 'well-a-day').
40 **envious** malicious.
44 **torture** i.e. the Nurse's manner of telling her news.
45 **'ay'** Here, and through 50, Shakespeare plays tiresomely on 'ay' (= yes, spelled 'I' in Elizabethan orthography) and 'I', as well as on the homonym 'eye'.
47 **death-darting...cockatrice** A fabled creature with the body of a serpent and the head of a cock (often = 'basilisk'), which could kill with a glance. Compare *TN* 3.4.195–6; see Sir Thomas Browne, *Pseudodoxia Epidemica* (1646), III, viii.

49 **those eyes** i.e. Romeo's eyes. See collation for 'shut'.
53 **God...mark!** Exclamation, used as apology when something horrible (as here), disgusting, indecent or profane has been mentioned (*OED* 'mark' 18). 'save' = avert; 'mark' = ?sign or omen.
54 **corse** corpse.
56 **gore blood** thickened (i.e. partially congealed) blood.
56 **sounded** swooned (variant form).
57 **bankrout** bankrupt (variant form), with following play on 'break' (= become insolvent or valueless).

To prison, eyes, ne'er look on liberty!
Vile earth, to earth resign, end motion here,
And thou and Romeo press one heavy bier!   60

NURSE O Tybalt, Tybalt, the best friend I had!
O courteous Tybalt, honest gentleman,
That ever I should live to see thee dead!

JULIET What storm is this that blows so contrary?
Is Romeo slaughtered? and is Tybalt dead?   65
My dearest cousin, and my dearer lord?
Then, dreadful trumpet, sound the general doom,
For who is living, if those two are gone?

NURSE Tybalt is gone and Romeo banishèd,
Romeo that killed him, he is banishèd.   70

JULIET O God, did Romeo's hand shed Tybalt's blood?

NURSE It did, it did, alas the day, it did!

JULIET O serpent heart, hid with a flow'ring face!
Did ever dragon keep so fair a cave?
Beautiful tyrant, fiend angelical!   *oxymorons*   75
Dove-feathered raven, wolvish-ravening lamb!
Despisèd substance of divinest show!
Just opposite to what thou justly seem'st, *antithesis*
A damnèd saint, an honourable villain!   *chiasmus*
O nature, what hadst thou to do in hell   80
When thou didst bower the spirit of a fiend

---

59 to] Q3–4, F; too Q2   60 one] Q4, F; on Q2–3   66 dearest] Q2–4, F; deare loude Q1, *Pope* (dear-lov'd)   66 dearer]
Q2–4, F; dearest Q1   67 dreadful trumpet] Q2–4, F; let the trumpet Q1, *Pope*   69 gone] Q2–4, F; dead Q1, *Pope*
72 SH NURSE] Q1, Q5, F4; *line continued to Juliet*, Q2–4, F   73 SH JULIET] Q1, F2; *Nur*. Q2–4 *(assigning 74–84 to / Iu.)*, F
74–82] Q2–4, F; O painted sepulcher, including filth. Q1   75 Beautiful] Q2–4, F; bountiful *or* pityful *conj. Daniel*;
merciful *conj. Staunton (in Daniel)*   76 Dove-feathered] *Theobald (hyphen, F)*; Rauenous douefeatherd Q2–3; Rauenous
dove, feathred Q4; Rauenous Doue-feather'd F   76 wolvish-ravening] Q3, F; woluishrauening Q2; woluish rauening Q4
77–8 show!...seem'st,] *Theobald*; showe:...seemst, Q2–4, F; show,...seemst –*Hoppe*; show,...seem'st, *Sisson*
79 damnèd] Q4; dimme Q2–3; dimne F   81 bower] Q2–3, F; power Q4; poure Q5

---

59 **Vile earth** i.e. her body.
59 **resign** surrender.
59 **motion** physical movement, i.e. the property
of life. Compare *MM* 3.1.119–20.
62 **honest** honourable.
64 **so contrary** i.e. from Romeo's death to
Tybalt's.
67 **trumpet** i.e. 'the last trump' (1 Cor. 15.52),
which would announce the Last Judgement
('general doom').
73–85 Juliet rings the changes on the theme of
appearance and reality, the outward 'show'
compared with the inner 'substance' (77). Compare
Romeo's string of oxymorons in 1.1.167–72.

73 **serpent...face** Compare Tilley S585
('Snake in the grass'); Brooke (386): 'And so the
snake that lurkes in grasse, thy tender heart hath
stong?' (Juliet wrestling with herself over the wiles
of men and possibly of Romeo); and *Mac.* 1.5.65–6.
Kittredge compares the Virgilian 'latet anguis in
herba' (*Eclogues* III, 93).
74 **keep** inhabit (as the guardian).
76 **Dove-feathered raven** See supplementary
note.
78 **Just...justly** Exact...exactly.
79 *****damnèd** See supplementary note.
81 **bower** lodge (as in an arbour).

In mortal paradise of such sweet flesh?
Was ever book containing such vile matter
So fairly bound? O that deceit should dwell
In such a gorgeous palace!

NURSE   There's no trust,   85
No faith, no honesty in men, all perjured,
All forsworn, all naught, all dissemblers.
Ah, where's my man? Give me some aqua-vitae;
These griefs, these woes, these sorrows make me old.
Shame come to Romeo!

JULIET   Blistered be thy tongue   90
For such a wish! he was not born to shame:
Upon his brow shame is ashamed to sit;
For 'tis a throne where honour may be crowned
Sole monarch of the universal earth.
O what a beast was I to chide at him!   95

NURSE Will you speak well of him that killed your cousin?
JULIET Shall I speak ill of him that is my husband?
Ah, poor my lord, what tongue shall smooth thy name,
When I, thy three-hours wife, have mangled it?
But wherefore, villain, didst thou kill my cousin?   100
That villain cousin would have killed my husband.
Back, foolish tears, back to your native spring,
Your tributary drops belong to woe,
Which you mistaking offer up to joy.
My husband lives that Tybalt would have slain,   105
And Tybalt's dead that would have slain my husband:

85–7 There's...dissemblers.] *As Capell (after Pope); two lines, ending* men / ...dissemblers Q2–4, F; There is no truth,
no faith, no honestie in men: / All false, all faithles, periurde, all forsworne. Q1; Theres no trust, / No faith, no honestie
in men; all naught, / All periurde, all dissemblers, all forsworn. *Daniel (conj. Fleay); two lines, Hosley (omitting* all
naught *as part of a first version);* Theres no trust, / No faith, no honestie in men, all naught, / All perjurde, all forsworne,
all dissemblers, *Williams*   88] Q2–4, F; *follows* ache! *in* 2.5.26, Q1   93–9] *not in* Q1   95 at him] Q2–4; him F; him
so F2   99 three-hours] *Theobald;* three houres Q2–4, F   102–6] *not in* Q1   106 Tybalt's] Q2–4; *Tibalt*
106 slain] Q2–4, F; kil'd F2

83–4 **book...bound** Compare 1.3.82–93.
85–7 See collation.
87 **All...dissemblers** Read 'forsworn' as trisyllabic, with heavy stress on each 'all'.
87 **naught** wicked, vicious.
88 **aqua-vitae** strong drink (e.g. brandy);
literally, 'water of life'. See supplementary note.
90 **Blistered...tongue** Compare Tilley R84
('Report hath a blister on her tongue'); slander
proverbially was believed to blister the tongue
(Kittredge).

98 **poor my lord** i.e. my poor lord (transposed
adjective; Franz 328). Compare 3.5.198.
98–9 **smooth...it** assuage, make whole (by
speaking well of) the mutilation ('mangled' =
hacked to bits) your honour ('name') has suffered
(from my words). Compare Brooke (1144–54).
103 **tributary drops** tears paid as tribute.
104 **mistaking** i.e. her tears wrongly take what
is a glad occasion (Romeo's survival) for a sad one.
105 **that...slain** that Tybalt wished to slay.

All this is comfort, wherefore weep I then?
Some word there was, worser than Tybalt's death,
That murdered me; I would forget it fain,
But O, it presses to my memory,   110
Like damnèd guilty deeds to sinners' minds:
'Tybalt is dead, and Romeo banishèd.'
That 'banishèd', that one word 'banishèd',
Hath slain ten thousand Tybalts. Tybalt's death
Was woe enough if it had ended there;   115
Or if sour woe delights in fellowship,
And needly will be ranked with other griefs,
Why followed not, when she said 'Tybalt's dead',
'Thy father' or 'thy mother', nay, or both,
Which modern lamentation might have moved?   120
But with a rear-ward following Tybalt's death,
'Romeo is banishèd': to speak that word,
Is father, mother, Tybalt, Romeo, Juliet,
All slain, all dead. 'Romeo is banishèd!'
There is no end, no limit, measure, bound,   125
In that word's death, no words can that woe sound.
Where is my father and my mother, Nurse?
NURSE Weeping and wailing over Tybalt's corse.
        Will you go to them? I will bring you thither.
JULIET Wash they his wounds with tears? mine shall be spent,   130
        When theirs are dry, for Romeo's banishment.
        Take up those cords. Poor ropes, you are beguiled,
        Both you and I, for Romeo is exiled.

107–26 wherefore...sound.] Q2–4, F; But there yet remaines / Worse than his death, which faine I would forget: / But
ah, it presseth to my memorie, / *Romeo* is banished. Ah that word Banished / Is worse than death. *Romeo* is banished,
/ Is Father, Mother, *Tybalt*, *Iuliet*, / All killd, all slaine, all dead, all banished. Q1   108 word there was] Q2, F2; words
there was Q3–4, F; words there were Q5   109 murdered] *Johnson* (murder'd); murd'red Q2–3; murdered Q4, F;
118 followed] *Pope* (follow'd); followed Q2–4, F   120 moved] F (mou'd); moued Q2–4   121 with] Q2–4; which F
121 rear-ward] F (rere-ward); rereward Q2–4; rear-word *Hudson* (conj. *Collier*)   122 banishèd': to] Q2; banished to
Q3–4, F   130 tears?] Q2; teares: Q3–4, F   132–9] *not in* Q1   133 I,] Q5; I Q2–4, F

116 **woe...fellowship** Proverbial (Tilley
C571); compare *Lucrece* 790.
117 **needly...griefs** of necessity must be
associated with other griefs in order of importance
(*OED* Rank v 3). Juliet is saying, here and in what
follows, that if 'sour woe' demands company, why
couldn't Tybalt's death have been 'ranked' with
something comparable, news of her parents' death
(a lesser woe), rather than with the fact of Romeo's
banishment (a greater woe).
120 **modern...moved** might have given rise to
the ordinary ('modern') expression of grief (proper
to the death of parents).
121 **rear-ward** rearguard (suggesting a surprise
attack from behind), perhaps with play on
'rear-word'. Dowden compares *Sonnets* 90.5–6.
126 **that word's death** the death–dealing power
of that word ('banishèd'). 'word's' is an objective
genitive; compare 3.3.20.
126 **sound** (1) give adequate expression to; (2)
plumb the depth of.

He made you for a highway to my bed,
But I, a maid, die maiden-widowèd.   135
Come, cords, come, Nurse, I'll to my wedding bed,
And death, not Romeo, take my maidenhead!

NURSE Hie to your chamber. I'll find Romeo
To comfort you, I wot well where he is.
Hark ye, your Romeo will be here at night.   140
I'll to him, he is hid at Lawrence' cell.

JULIET O find him! Give this ring to my true knight,
And bid him come to take his last farewell.

Exeunt

[3.3] *Enter* FRIAR [LAWRENCE].

FRIAR LAWRENCE
Romeo, come forth, come forth, thou fearful man:
Affliction is enamoured of thy parts,
And thou art wedded to calamity.

[*Enter*] ROMEO.

ROMEO Father, what news? What is the Prince's doom?
What sorrow craves acquaintance at my hand,   5
That I yet know not?

FRIAR LAWRENCE   Too familiar
Is my dear son with such sour company!
I bring thee tidings of the Prince's doom.

ROMEO What less than doomsday is the Prince's doom?

FRIAR LAWRENCE A gentler judgement vanished from his lips: 10

135 maiden-widowèd] *Rowe*; maiden widowed Q2–4, F   136 cords] Q2; cord Q3–4, F   143 SD] Q1; *Exit.* Q2–4, F   Act
3, Scene 3   3.3] *Rowe*; *no scene division*, Q2–4, F, Q1   Location] *Capell (after Rowe)*; The Monastery. / *Rowe*
0 SD] *Capell (after Q1 Enter Frier.)*; *Enter Frier and* Romeo. Q2–4, F *(see 3 below)*   3 SD] Q1; *see above for* Q2–4, F
10 vanished] Q2–4 (vanish), F, Q1; even'd *Warburton*; issued *conj. Heath*; vented *conj. Bailey*; – 'banish'd' – *conj.
Dowden*; vantaged *conj. Dover Wilson (in NS)*

139 wot know.

Act 3, Scene 3
Location Verona. Friar Lawrence's cell.
1 **fearful** full of fear, timorous. Spencer
proposes, in view of 2–3, that it also carries some
suggestion of Romeo as 'terrible' (= 'fearful') and
threatening, a fated figure.
2 **parts** qualities, endowments.
3 **wedded** married (but with a strong sense of
'bound forever'). Lines 2–3 are powerfully ironic,

since both 'Affliction' and 'calamity' may be felt as
identified with Juliet.
4 **doom** judgement, sentence.
5 **sorrow...hand** what new sorrow is now
seeking to introduce itself to me (literally, to shake
hands with me).
9 **doomsday** the final judgement (i.e. death).
10 **vanished** (1) ? breathed out like so much air
(compare 'airy word', 1.1.80 and 'airy tongue',
2.2.162); (2) ? issued without possibility of recall
(Kermode, after Spencer). The reading may be

Not body's death, but body's banishment.

ROMEO Ha, banishment? be merciful, say 'death':

For exile hath more terror in his look,

Much more than death. Do not say 'banishment'!

FRIAR LAWRENCE Here from Verona art thou banishèd.   15

Be patient, for the world is broad and wide.

ROMEO There is no world without Verona walls,

But purgatory, torture, hell itself:

Hence 'banishèd' is banished from the world,

And world's exile is death; then 'banishèd'   20

Is death mistermed. Calling death 'banishèd',

Thou cut'st my head off with a golden axe,

And smilest upon the stroke that murders me.

FRIAR LAWRENCE O deadly sin! O rude unthankfulness!

Thy fault our law calls death, but the kind Prince,   25

Taking thy part, hath rushed aside the law,

And turned that black word 'death' to 'banishment'.

This is dear mercy, and thou seest it not.

ROMEO 'Tis torture, and not mercy. Heaven is here

Where Juliet lives, and every cat and dog   30

And little mouse, every unworthy thing,

Live here in heaven, and may look on her,

But Romeo may not. More validity,

More honourable state, more courtship lives

In carrion flies than Romeo; they may seize   35

On the white wonder of dear Juliet's hand,

And steal immortal blessing from her lips,

---

14 Much...death] Q2–4, F; Than death it selfe Q1, *Pope*   15 Here] Q2–4, F; Hence Q1, *Hanmer*   19 banished] Q3–4, F, Q1; blanisht Q2   20 world's exile] Q2–4, F; world exilde Q1, *Pope* (world-exil'd)   21 death mistermed. Calling] Q5 (*subst.*), *Theobald*; death, mistermd, calling Q2–3, F; death mistearm'd, calling Q4; Q1 *omits* then...mistermd *in 20–1*   21 banishèd] Q2–4, F; banishment Q1, *Pope*   26 rushed] Q2–4, F; rushd Q1; push'd *conj. Capell*; brush'd *Collier MS.;* thrust *conj. NS*   28 dear] Q2–4, F; meere Q1, *Pope*

corrupt; see collation for suggested emendations. R. W. Bond (ed.), *TGV*, 1906, 3.1.216) suggests some possible connection with Launce's misuse of 'vanished' for 'banished'.

15 Here See supplementary note.

16 Be patient Compose yourself. Compare Brooke (1223): 'With patience arme thy selfe.'

17 without outside the bounds of.

20 world's exile exile from the world (Verona). Accent on 'exile' in Elizabethan English could vary; here 'exíle', but 'éxile' in 13 above. Compare Romeo's speeches, through 60, with Valentine's lament (probably also in-

fluenced by Brooke) on his banishment in *TGV* 3.1.170–87.

21 mistermed called by the wrong name (i.e. a name which pretends to mercy, a euphemism); compare 'golden axe' (22) and 'smilest' (23).

26 rushed aside forced out of place (*OED* Rush *v* 2b), i.e. against the strict letter (of the law).

28 dear precious.

30–2 cat...her Compare Tilley C141 ('A cat may look on a king').

33 validity true worth.

34 state...courtship estate...courtly position (with play on 'court' = to woo).

Who even in pure and vestal modesty
Still blush, as thinking their own kisses sin;
But Romeo may not, he is banishèd.   40
Flies may do this, but I from this must fly;
They are free men, but I am banishèd:
And sayest thou yet that exile is not death?
Hadst thou no poison mixed, no sharp-ground knife,
No sudden mean of death, though ne'er so mean,   45
But 'banishèd' to kill me? 'Banishèd'?
O Friar, the damnèd use that word in hell;
Howling attends it. How hast thou the heart,
Being a divine, a ghostly confessor,
A sin-absolver, and my friend professed,   50
To mangle me with that word 'banishèd'?

FRIAR LAWRENCE Thou fond mad man, hear me a little speak.

ROMEO O thou wilt speak again of banishment.

FRIAR LAWRENCE I'll give thee armour to keep off that word:
Adversity's sweet milk, philosophy,   55
To comfort thee though thou art banishèd.

ROMEO Yet 'banishèd'? Hang up philosophy!
Unless philosophy can make a Juliet,
Displant a town, reverse a prince's doom,
It helps not, it prevails not; talk no more.   60

In left margin: Why 3rd person

38–9] *not in* Q1   **40–3**] *Arranged as in Globe (after conj. Steevens);* This may flyes do, when I from this must flie, / And sayest thou yet, that exile is not death? / But *Romeo* may not, he is banished. / Flies may do this, but I from this must flie: / They are freemen, but I am banished. Q2–4; This may Flies doe, when I from this must flie, / And saist thou yet, that exile is not death? / But *Romeo* may not, hee is banished. F; But *Romeo* may not, he is banished. / Flies may doo this, but I from this must flye. Q1; Flies...but...fly; / They...banished. *Capell;* Flies...when...fly; / They...banished. / And...death? / But Romeo...banished. *Steevens (1773);* But Romeo...banished: / Flies... when...fly; / They... banished. / And...death? *Malone (conj. Steevens);* But Romeo...banished. / This may... when...fly; / And...death? *Hudson;* But Romeo...banished. / This may...when...fly: / They...banished. / And...death? *White;* But Romeo...banished: / This may...but...fly: / And...death? *Cam.* Flies...but...fly; / They...banished. / And...death? *Craig;* But Romeo...banished. / Flies...but...fly; / They ...banished. *Sisson;* This may...when...fly; / And...death? *NS*   **42** free men] Q5; freemen Q2–4   **44** sharp-ground] F4; sharpe ground Q2–4, F, Q1   **48** Howling attends] Q2–4, Q1; Howlings attends F; Howlings attend F2   **50** sin-absolver] F; sin obsoluer Q2–4; sinne absoluer Q1   **51** 'banishèd'] Q2–4, F; Banishment Q1, *Pope*   **52** Thou] Q4, Q1; Then Q2–3, F; *not in* F2   **52** hear...speak] Q2–4; heare me speake F; heare me but speake a word Q1, *Malone*   **54** keep off that] Q2–4, F; beare off this Q1; bear off that *Pope*

---

38 vestal maidenly, virgin.

39 kisses i.e. the coming together of the lips, a conceited way of saying that Juliet's lips are red ('blush').

40–3 See supplementary note.

45 mean...mean method, instrument...low, base.

49 ghostly spiritual. 'confessor' accented on first syllable.

52 fond foolish (with play on 'doting').

55 Adversity's sweet milk A palliative against adversity. Compare Brooke (1393–4).

57 Hang up philosophy! Let philosophy go hang itself! – (like disused armour on the wall; compare 54). Echoed in Haughton, *Englishmen for My Money* (1598; MSR, 67).

59 Displant Uproot (i.e. move Verona from one place to another).

FRIAR LAWRENCE O then I see that mad men have no ears.
ROMEO How should they when that wise men have no eyes?
FRIAR LAWRENCE Let me dispute with thee of thy estate.
ROMEO Thou canst not speak of that thou dost not feel.

Wert thou as young as I, Juliet thy love,   65
An hour but married, Tybalt murderèd,
Doting like me, and like me banishèd,
Then mightst thou speak, then mightst thou tear thy hair,
And fall upon the ground as I do now,
Taking the measure of an unmade grave.   70

Enter Nurse [within] and knock.

FRIAR LAWRENCE Arise, one knocks. Good Romeo, hide thyself.
ROMEO Not I, unless the breath of heart-sick groans
Mist-like infold me from the search of eyes.
Knock.

FRIAR LAWRENCE
Hark how they knock! – Who's there? – Romeo, arise,
Thou wilt be taken. – Stay a while! – Stand up;   75
Loud knock.
Run to my study. – By and by! – God's will,
What simpleness is this? – I come, I come!
Knock.
Who knocks so hard? whence come you? what's your will?
NURSE [*Within*] Let me come in, and you shall know my errand:
I come from Lady Juliet.

61 mad men] Q3–4, F; mad man Q2; madmen Q1   62 that] Q2, Q1; *not in* Q3–4, F   62 wise men] Q2–4, Q1; wisemen
F   62 eyes?] F; eyes. Q2–4, Q1   63 dispute] Q2–4, Q1; dispaire F   64 that] Q2–4, F; what Q1, *Pope*   65 as…thy]
Q2–4, Q1; as *Iuliet* my F   68] *As* Q1; *two lines, ending* speake / …hayre Q2–4, F   68 mightst…mightst] Q1, Q5;
mightest…mightst Q2; mightest…mightest Q3–4, F   70 SD] Q2; *Enter Nurse, and knockes.* Q3, F; *Nurse knocks.* Q4,
Q1   70 SD *within*] *Rowe*   71–80] Q2–4, F; *Romeo* arise, stand vp thou wilt be taken, / I heare one knocke, arise and
get thee gone. / *Nu:* Hoe Fryer. / *Fr:* Gods will what wilfulnes is this? / *Shee knockes againe.* / *Nur:* Hoe Fryer open
the doore, / *Fr:* By and by I come. Who is there? / *Nur:* One from Lady Iuliet. / *Fr:* Then come neare. Q1
73 SD] Q4, F; *They knocke.* Q2–3   74 Who's] Q4, F; whose Q2–3; Who is Q1   75 taken. – …while! –] *Rowe (subst.)*;
taken,…while, Q2–3, F; taken (stay a while) Q4; taken, Q1   75 SD] *Anon. conj. (in Cam.)*; *Slud knock.* Q2–3; *Knocke
againe.* Q4; *Knocke.* F; *Shee knockes againe.* Q1   76 study. – …by! –] *Rowe (subst.)*; studie by and by, Q2–3; studie
(by and by) Q4; study: by and by, F; By and by Q1   77 simpleness] Q2–4, F; wilfulnes Q1, *Pope*   79 SD] *Rowe*; *no
SD*, Q2–4, F, Q1   79 errand] Q4, F; errant Q2–3 *(variant form)*

61–2 **no ears…no eyes** no ears to listen (to
good counsel)…no eyes to see (be moved by
feeling; compare 64). Compare Brooke (1317):
'That no advise can perce, his close forstopped
eares'.
63 **dispute…estate** discuss your present
situation.
64 **Thou…feel** With Romeo's attitude towards

his mentor, compare Sidney's in Sonnet 21 of
Astrophil and Stella.
67 **Doting** Deranged (by love), love-sick.
68 **tear thy hair** Compare Brooke (1291–4).
75 **Stay a while!** Wait a moment (to the Nurse)!
76 **By and by!** In a moment!
77 **simpleness** foolish behaviour.

FRIAR LAWRENCE   Welcome then. [*Unlocks the door.*]   80

Enter NURSE.

NURSE O holy Friar, O tell me, holy Friar,
    Where's my lady's lord? where's Romeo?
FRIAR LAWRENCE
    There on the ground, with his own tears made drunk.
NURSE O he is even in my mistress' case,
    Just in her case. O woeful sympathy!   85
    Piteous predicament! even so lies she,
    Blubb'ring and weeping, weeping and blubb'ring.
    Stand up, stand up, stand, and you be a man;
    For Juliet's sake, for her sake, rise and stand;
    Why should you fall into so deep an O?   90
ROMEO Nurse! [*He rises.*]
NURSE Ah, sir, ah, sir, death's the end of all.
ROMEO Spakest thou of Juliet? how is it with her?
    Doth not she think me an old murderer,
    Now I have stained the childhood of our joy   95
    With blood removed but little from her own?
    Where is she? and how doth she? and what says
    My concealed lady to our cancelled love?
NURSE O she says nothing, sir, but weeps and weeps,
    And now falls on her bed, and then starts up,   100
    And Tybalt calls, and then on Romeo cries,
    And then down falls again.
ROMEO   As if that name,
    Shot from the deadly level of a gun,
    Did murder her, as that name's cursèd hand
    Murdered her kinsman. O tell me, Friar, tell me,   105

80 SD.1 *Unlocks the door.*] *Riverside; no* SD, Q2–4, F, Q1 *; opens. / Capell*   80 SD.2 *Enter* NURSE.] *As Rowe; after 78,* Q2–4,
F; *not in* Q1   82 Where's] Q2–4, F; Where is Q1, *Rowe*   83] *As* Q1, *Pope; two lines, ending* ground / . . . drunke Q2–4, F
85–6 O . . . predicament!] *Assigned to Friar Lawrence, Steevens (conj. Farmer)*   88 man;] Q1 (man.); man, Q2–4, F
91 SD] Q1 *; no* SD, Q2–4, F   92 sir, death's] Q2–4, F; Wel death's Q1, *Malone*   93 Spakest] Q2–4, Q1; Speak'st F
94 not she] Q2–4, F; she not Q1, *Capell*   96 removed] Q1 (remou'd); remoued, Q2–4, Q1;   98 cancelled] Q2–4, Q1;
conceal'd F   99 and weeps] Q2–4, F; and pules Q1   101 calls . . . cries] Q2–4, F; cryes . . . calles Q1, *Pope*
102–3 As . . . gun,] *As Rowe; one line,* Q2–4, F, Q1   103 deadly] Q2–4, Q1; dead F

85 **woeful sympathy** mutual sharing of grief.
90 **deep an O** profound groan (with bawdy pun
suggested by 'stand' (89)). Compare 1.4.96 n.;
2.1.37 n.
94 **old** accustomed. Compare 1.2.20.

98 **concealed lady** secret wife. 'concealed'
accented on first syllable.
98 **cancelled** rendered void, nullified (legal
term).
101 **cries** exclaims against.
103 **level** aim.

In what vile part of this anatomy
Doth my name lodge? Tell me, that I may sack
The hateful mansion.

[*He offers to stab himself, and Nurse snatches the dagger away.*]   *suicidal*

FRIAR LAWRENCE   Hold thy desperate hand!   *unstable*
Art thou a man? thy form cries out thou art;
Thy tears are womanish, thy wild acts denote   *"she makes me* 10
The unreasonable fury of a beast.   *effeminate"*
Unseemly woman in a seeming man,
And ill-beseeming beast in seeming both,   *"Be a man!"*
Thou hast amazed me. By my holy order,
I thought thy disposition better tempered.   *"Boys don't cry"* 115
Hast thou slain Tybalt? wilt thou slay thyself,
And slay thy lady that in thy life lives,
By doing damnèd hate upon thyself?
Why rail'st thou on thy birth? the heaven and earth?
Since birth, and heaven, and earth, all three do meet   120
In thee at once, which thou at once wouldst lose.
Fie, fie, thou sham'st thy shape, thy love, thy wit,
Which like a usurer abound'st in all,
And usest none in that true use indeed
Which should bedeck thy shape, thy love, thy wit: 125
Thy noble shape is but a form of wax,

108 SD] Q1 (*following this* SD Q1 *adds* / *Nur:* Ah?); *no* SD, Q2–4, F; *Drawing his Sword.* / *Theobald*; *drawing out a Dagger.* / *Capell (after 105)*   110 denote] Q4, F, Q1; deuote Q2–3; doe note F2   113 And] Q2–4, F; Or Q1, *Steevens* 117 that...lives] F4; that in thy life lies Q2–4, F; too, that liues in thee Q1, *Pope*   118–34] *not in* Q1   119 rail'st] F; raylest Q2–4   121 lose] Q5; loose Q2–4, F   122 sham'st] F; shamest Q2–4   123 all,] *Rowe*; all: Q2–4, F

109–54 Compare Brooke (1353–1480).
111 unreasonable irrational. Man's God-given reason, his rational soul, distinguished him from the beasts, the next step below him in the great chain of being; *Ham.* 1.2.150: 'a beast that wants discourse of reason'.
112–13 Romeo, in outward appearance ('seeming') a man, is behaving in a manner improper ('Unseemly') even to a woman and in this mixture ('seeming both') is a kind of *lusus naturae*, unnatural ('ill-beseeming') even among beasts.
114 amazed astonished.
115 tempered balanced (literally, mixed, compounded) in terms of the four humours.
119–21 Compare Brooke (1325–48). As Malone points out, Shakespeare seems closer to Brooke here than to what Romeo has earlier said in the scene.

120 birth...earth i.e. nativity and parentage, spiritual part (soul), and physical body.
121 lose i.e. by suicide (105–8) Romeo would damn his soul.
122 shape...wit form as a man (made in the image of God), sworn faith to Juliet (see 128), and reason or intellect.
123–5 Which...wit i.e. a usurer 'misused' his money by making it breed interest ('use') against nature (*MV* 1.3.134); Romeo is misusing his natural wealth (shape, love, wit), like a usurer, making it breed unnaturally instead of putting it to natural productive and beneficial use ('true use'). 'Which' = who.
126 form of wax wax image (not a real man). Contrast the Nurse's 'man of wax' in 1.3.77.

Digressing from the valour of a man;
Thy dear love sworn but hollow perjury,
Killing that love which thou hast vowed to cherish;
Thy wit, that ornament to shape and love,   130
Misshapen in the conduct of them both,
Like powder in a skilless soldier's flask,
Is set afire by thine own ignorance,
And thou dismembered with thine own defence.
What, rouse thee, man! thy Juliet is alive,   135
For whose dear sake thou wast but lately dead:
There art thou happy. Tybalt would kill thee,
But thou slewest Tybalt: there art thou happy.
The law that threatened death becomes thy friend,
And turns it to exile: there art thou happy.   140
A pack of blessings light upon thy back,
Happiness courts thee in her best array,
But like a mishavèd and sullen wench,
Thou pouts upon thy fortune and thy love:
Take heed, take heed, for such die miserable.   145
Go get thee to thy love as was decreed,
Ascend her chamber, hence and comfort her;
But look thou stay not till the Watch be set,
For then thou canst not pass to Mantua,
Where thou shalt live till we can find a time   150

130 ornament] F4; ornament, Q2–4, F   131 both,] *Rowe*; both: Q2–4, F   133 afire] *Collier*; a fier Q2–4, F   136 dead:]
Q1; dead. Q2–4, F   137 happy. Tybalt] F, Q1; happie, *Tybalt* Q2–4   138 slewest...happy] *Knight (subst.)*; slewest
Tibalt,...happie Q2–4; slew'st *Tybalt*,...happie F; sluest *Tybalt*,...happy too Q1, F2 *(reading* slew'st*)*; slew'st Tybalt;
there thou'rt happy too *Pope*; slew'st Tybalt; there too art thou happy *Capell*   139–40] *not in* Q1   139 becomes]
Q2–4; became F   140 turns] Q2, Q4; turne Q3; turn'd F   141 of blessings] Q2, Q4, Q1; of blessing Q3; or blessing F
141 light] Q2–3, F; lights Q4, Q1, *Steevens*   143 mishavèd and] Q2–3; misbehau'd and Q4; mishaped and F; misbehaude
and Q1; mis-shaped and a F2; mis shapen and a F4; mis-hav'd and a *Rowe*   144 pouts upon] Q4 (powts vpon); puts
vp Q2–3; puttest vp F; frownst vpon Q1; pout'st vpon Q5   150–4] *not in* Q1

127 **Digressing** (If it) deviates, falls away from.
So 'Killing' (129) = (if it) kills.
131 **Misshapen** Wrongly directed (with play on
'shape').
131 **conduct** guidance.
132 **flask** powder horn.
133–4 **Is...defence** i.e. your reason ('wit'),
which should be your defence (like a soldier's
powder), turned to passion ('set afire') through
your misuse of it ('ignorance'), has become the
means to destroy you ('thou dismembered'). Compare 2.6.9–11 and 5.1.63–5 for the powder/fire
image.
136 **wast...dead** i.e. just now tried to kill
thyself.

137 **happy** fortunate, blessed.
137 **would** wished. See Abbott 329.
141 **light** Third per. pl., by attraction of
'blessings'.
143 **mishavèd** misbehaved. Crow defends 'mishavèd' on the analogy of Shakespeare's use of
'haviour'; see also *OED* under 'mishave'. Echoed
in Haughton, *Englishmen for My Money* (1598;
MSR, 1001).
146 **decreed** determined.
148 **Watch be set** With the posting of the guard,
the city gates would be closed. Brooke (1729–31)
reports that the gates of Verona were 'set open' in
the early morning and the Watch 'discharged'.

To blaze your marriage, reconcile your friends,
Beg pardon of the Prince, and call thee back
With twenty hundred thousand times more joy
Than thou went'st forth in lamentation.
Go before, Nurse, commend me to thy lady,   155
And bid her hasten all the house to bed,
Which heavy sorrow makes them apt unto.
Romeo is coming.
NURSE O Lord, I could have stayed here all the night
To hear good counsel. O, what learning is!   160
My lord, I'll tell my lady you will come.
ROMEO Do so, and bid my sweet prepare to chide.
  [Nurse offers to go in, and turns again.]
NURSE Here, sir, a ring she bid me give you, sir.
Hie you, make haste, for it grows very late.
ROMEO How well my comfort is revived by this.   165
                                        [Exit Nurse]

FRIAR LAWRENCE
Go hence, good night, and here stands all your state:
Either be gone before the Watch be set,
Or by the break of day disguised from hence.
Sojourn in Mantua; I'll find out your man,
And he shall signify from time to time   170
Every good hap to you that chances here.
Give me thy hand, 'tis late. Farewell, good night.
ROMEO But that a joy past joy calls out on me,
It were a grief, so brief to part with thee:
Farewell.   175
                                        Exeunt

---

152 the] Q2, Q4; thy Q3, F   159 all the night] Q2–4; all night F; all this night Q1   162 SD] Q1; *no SD,* Q2–4, F
163] Q2–3, F; Here...bids...sir Q4; Heere is a ring Sir, that she bad me giue you Q1 *(omitting 164),* Dyce²; Here,
sir,'s a Ring...sir *conj.* Daniel   165 SD] Q1; *after* good night, 166, Capell; *after* 164, Malone; *no SD,* Q2–4, F
166–8] *not in* Q1   168 disguised] Q3–4, F; disguise Q2   168 hence.] *Johnson;* hence, Q2–4, F   175 SD] Q2–4, F; *no*
SD, Q1

---

151 blaze make known, proclaim.
151 friends relatives (of both families).
160 O...is Compare *Shr.* 1.2.159: 'O this
learning, what a thing it is!'
162 chide i.e. reprimand him for Tybalt's death.
166 here...state i.e. on this condition rests
your (future) fortune.

167–8 Friar Lawrence suddenly gives Romeo a
second option; compare 148.
169 find...man i.e. keep in touch with your
personal servant (Balthasar).
174 brief hastily.

[3.4] *Enter old* CAPULET, *his* WIFE, *and* PARIS.

CAPULET Things have fall'n out, sir, so unluckily
   That we have had no time to move our daughter.
   Look you, she loved her kinsman Tybalt dearly,
   And so did I. Well, we were born to die.
   'Tis very late, she'll not come down tonight.   5
   I promise you, but for your company,
   I would have been abed an hour ago.
PARIS These times of woe afford no times to woo.
   Madam, good night, commend me to your daughter.
LADY CAPULET I will, and know her mind early tomorrow;   10
   Tonight she's mewed up to her heaviness.
   [*Paris offers to go in, and Capulet calls him again.*]
CAPULET Sir Paris, I will make a desperate tender
   Of my child's love: I think she will be ruled
   In all respects by me; nay more, I doubt it not.
   Wife, go you to her ere you go to bed,   15
   Acquaint her here of my son Paris' love,
   And bid her – mark you me? – on Wednesday next –
   But soft, what day is this?
PARIS   Monday, my lord.
CAPULET Monday, ha, ha! Well, Wednesday is too soon,
   A'Thursday let it be – a'Thursday, tell her,   20

Act 3, Scene 4 3.4] *Rowe; no scene division,* Q2–4, F, Q1 Location] *Rowe* 0 SD] Q2–4, F; *Enter olde Capolet and his Wife, with County Paris.* Q1 2 daughter.] Q1; daughter, Q2–4; Daughter: F 5–7] Q2–4, F; Wife wher's your daughter, is she in her chamber? / I thinke she meanes not to come downe to night. Q1 *(6–7 inserted earlier at 1.5.124–6)* 7 abed] *Rowe*³; a bed Q2–4, F, Q1 8 times to] Q2–4, F; time to Q1, *Rowe* 10–11]*not in* Q1 11 she's mewed] *Theobald (mew'd; after Rowe);* shees mewed Q2; she is mewed Q3–4, F; she is mew'd *Rowe* 11 SD] Q1; *no SD,* Q2–4, F 13 be] Q3–4, F, Q1; me Q2 14–17 nay…next –] *not in* Q1 16 here of] Q4; here, of Q2, F; hereof, Q3; ear of *NS* 17 next –] *Rowe*; next. Q2; next, Q3–4, F 20–2] Q2–4, F; On Thursday let it be: you shall be maried. Q1, *Pope* 20 A'…a'] *Riverside*; A…a Q2–4, F; *see above for* Q1; On…o' *Theobald*; O'…o' *Capell*

Act 3, Scene 4
 Location Verona. Capulet's house.
 2 move propose the matter to.
 6 but for were it not for.
 8 no times Duthie (NS) defends 'times' (most eds. read 'time' with Q1) on the parallelism of 'times of woe' with 'times to woo', with word-play on 'woe/woo'.
 11 mewed…heaviness shut up (literally, caged like a moulting hawk) with her sorrow.
 12 desperate tender bold offer (implying some risk). The suggestion for marriage at this point originates with Lady Capulet in Brooke (1842–53).

 15 Wife…bed As Spencer points out, this order creates a moment of tension, since we know that Romeo is now with Juliet.
 16 son i.e. son-in-law (a courtly anticipation).
 17 mark you me? are you paying close attention to me?
 18 soft wait a moment.
 19 ha, ha! i.e. the humming sound one makes while considering something; not laughter.
 20 Thursday Capulet later (4.2.23 ff.) returns to his original Wednesday in his haste to take advantage of what seems to be Juliet's sudden acquiescence in the marriage with Paris.

She shall be married to this noble earl.
Will you be ready? do you like this haste?
Well, keep no great ado – a friend or two,
For hark you, Tybalt being slain so late,
It may be thought we held him carelessly,   25
Being our kinsman, if we revel much:
Therefore we'll have some half a dozen friends,
And there an end. But what say you to Thursday?
PARIS My lord, I would that Thursday were tomorrow.
CAPULET Well, get you gone, a'Thursday be it then. –   30
Go you to Juliet ere you go to bed,
Prepare her, wife, against this wedding day.
Farewell, my lord. Light to my chamber, ho!
Afore me, it is so very late that we
May call it early by and by. Good night.   35

Exeunt

[3.5] *Enter* ROMEO *and* JULIET *aloft* [*as at the window*].

JULIET Wilt thou be gone? It is not yet near day:
It was the nightingale, and not the lark,
That pierced the fearful hollow of thine ear;

23 Well, keep] Q2; Weele keep Q3–4, F; Wee'le make Q1   30 a'] *Riverside;* a Q2–4, F; Q1 *omits 30;* on *Pope;* o' *Capell* 34–5] *As Theobald (reading* 'Fore); *two lines, ending* and by / ...Goodnight Q2–4, F; *two lines (omitting* Goodnight), *ending* late / ...and by Q1   34 it...very] Q2–4, F; it is so very very Q1, *Dyce*¹; 'tis so very late *Dyce*²
Act 3, Scene 5 3.5] *Rowe; no scene division,* Q2–4, F; *Q1 marks a break by two rows of printer's ornaments, one at foot of sig.* G2ᵛ, *the other above opening* SD *on sig.* G3ʳ   Location] *Globe; The Garden. / Rowe;* Juliet's Chamber looking to the Garden. / *Theobald;* Anti-room of Juliet's Chamber. / *Capell*   0 SD as at the window] *This edn (from* Q1 at the window)

23 **Well, keep** Most eds. read 'We'll keep' (following Q3–4, F, Q1), but Duthie in NS (after Mommsen) feels that lines 20–8 ('...there an end.') are addressed to Lady Capulet and that Q2 'Well,' reflects the look of dismay on her face at the prospect of such sudden preparations. See Brooke (2255–76) on the feast.
32 **against** in anticipation of.
34 **Afore me** A mild oath ('I swear, taking my self to witness', Kittredge). Possibly, however, it should be taken as a direction to one of the servants to carry the 'Light' (33) ahead of him to his chamber.
35 **by and by** immediately (as usual in

Elizabethan usage). Compare *TN* 2.3.1–2: 'Not to be a-bed after midnight is to be up betimes.'

Act 3, Scene 5
Location Verona. Capulet's orchard. See, however, note on 67 SD below.
1–36 These lines may be considered as a dramatic variation on the 'aubade' or dawn-song, spoken or sung by a lover at the unwelcome intrusion of day. Compare Donne's 'Breake of Day' and Ovid's *Amores* I.xiii.
1–7 Wilt...nightingale The genesis of these lines is complicated; see supplementary note.
3 **fearful** timorous (because afraid to hear).

> Nightly she sings on yond pomegranate tree.
> Believe me, love, it was the nightingale.   5

ROMEO It was the lark, the herald of the morn,
> No nightingale. Look, love, what envious streaks
> Do lace the severing clouds in yonder east:
> Night's candles are burnt out, and jocund day
> Stands tiptoe on the misty mountain tops.   10
> I must be gone and live, or stay and die.

JULIET Yond light is not daylight, I know it, I:
> It is some meteor that the sun exhaled
> To be to thee this night a torch-bearer,
> And light thee on thy way to Mantua.   15
> Therefore stay yet, thou need'st not to be gone.

ROMEO Let me be tane, let me be put to death,
> I am content, so thou wilt have it so.
> I'll say yon grey is not the morning's eye,
> 'Tis but the pale reflex of Cynthia's brow;   20
> Nor that is not the lark whose notes do beat
> The vaulty heaven so high above our heads.
> I have more care to stay than will to go:
> Come, death, and welcome! Juliet wills it so.
> How is't, my soul? Let's talk, it is not day.   25

---

4 yond] Q2–4, F; yon Q1, *Warburton*   9 jocund] Q3–4, F, Q1; iocand Q2   10 mountain] Q2, Q1; Mountaines Q3–4, F   13 exhaled] *Hosley*; exhale Q2; exhales Q3–4, F, Q1   16] Q2–4, F; Then stay a while, thou shalt not goe soone. Q1, *Pope (reading so soon)*   17–18] Q2–4, F; Let me stay here, let me be tane, and dye: / If thou wilt haue it so, I am content. Q1; Let me then stay, let...content. *Pope*   19 the] Q3–4, F, Q1; the the Q2   20 brow] Q2–4, F, Q1; bow *Collier, Singer MSS.*   21–3] Q2–4, F *(the last omitting the in 21)*; Ile say it is the Nightingale that beates / The vaultie heauen so high aboue our heads, / And not the Larke the Messenger of Morne. Q1, *Pope (reading heav'ns from F3 Heavens)*   21 the] Q2–4, Q1; *not in* F   23 care...will] Q2–4, F; will...care *conj. Johnson*   25 How...soul?] Q2; How ist my soule, Q3–4, F; What sayes my Loue? Q1, *Pope*   25 talk,...not] Q4, F; talke it is not Q2–3; talke, tis not yet Q1

---

4 she...tree The pomegranate tree was traditionally associated with the nightingale, though it was the male that did most of the singing. Dowden suggests that the common reference (as here and in the quotations from Eliot and Lyly in supplementary note to 1–7 above) to 'she' arose from the Ovidian tale of Tereus and Philomela, who was turned into a nightingale (*Metamorphoses* VI, 433 ff.)

7 **envious** malicious (as jealous of the night).

8 **severing** Streaks of light are parting (1) the clouds, (2) the lovers.

9 **Night's candles** The stars. Compare *Mac.* 2.1.4–5. Echoed in Haughton, *Englishmen for My Money* (1598; MSR, 1324).

9 **jocund** sprightly, cheerful (ironic in view of the situation; see 36).

13 **meteor...°exhaled** Meteors were believed

to be formed by vapours drawn up from the earth by the sun and then ignited. Compare *LLL* 4.3.67–8. Hosley's 'exhaled' ('exhale', Q2) for the more usually adopted 'exhales' (Q3–4, F, Q1) is necessary, since Juliet's argument is that the sun is not now 'exhaling'. Final 'e/d' confusion in reading Secretary hand is common; see 3.3.168 and 31 below for similar examples.

20 **reflex...brow** reflection of the moon's (i.e. Cynthia's) face.

21–2 **beat...heaven** Compare *Cym.* 2.3.20–1: 'Hark, hark, the lark at heaven's gate sings, / And Phoebus gins arise.' 'vaulty' = arched like a vault; see supplementary note to 1–7 above.

23 **care...will** desire, concern...inclination (the two words mean essentially the same).

JULIET It is, it is, hie hence, be gone, away!
    It is the lark that sings so out of tune,
    Straining harsh discords and unpleasing sharps.
    Some say the lark makes sweet division:
    This doth not so, for she divideth us. 30
    Some say the lark and loathèd toad changed eyes;
    O now I would they had changed voices too,
    Since arm from arm that voice doth us affray,
    Hunting thee hence with hunt's-up to the day.
    O now be gone, more light and light it grows. 35
ROMEO More light and light, more dark and dark our woes!

Enter NURSE [*hastily*].

NURSE Madam!
JULIET Nurse?
NURSE Your lady mother is coming to your chamber.
    The day is broke, be wary, look about. [*Exit*] 40
JULIET Then, window, let day in, and let life out.
ROMEO Farewell, farewell! one kiss, and I'll descend.
[He goeth down.]
JULIET Art thou gone so, love, lord, ay husband, friend?
    I must hear from thee every day in the hour,
    For in a minute there are many days. 45

26 hence, be gone, away] F4; hence be gone away Q2–4, F; be gone, flye hence away Q1   30 she] Q2–4, F; this Q1
31 changed] *Rowe*³ (chang'd); change Q2–4, F, Q1   35 light it] Q2–4, Q1; itli ght F; it light F2   36] *Pope substitutes*
Farewell my Loue, one kisse and Ile descend., Q1 *version of 42*   36 and light,] Q2–4, F, Q1; and light? – *Theobald*
36 SD] Q1 *(following 59)*; *Enter Madame and Nurse.* Q2–4, F; *Enter Nurse. | Rowe*   37–8] *not in* Q1   38 Nurse?]
Theobald; Nurse. Q2–4, F   40 SD] *Theobald*; *no* SD, Q2–4, F, Q1; *she goes*; *Juliet bolts the door* /NS   42 SD] Q1; *no*
SD, Q2–4, F; Romeo *comes down by the Ladder into the Garden. | Rowe*; *he lowers the ladder and descends | NS*
43 love...friend?] Q2–4 (friend,), F; my Lord, my Loue, my Frend? Q1, *Boswell*; Love, Lord, ah Husband, Friend,
F2; my love! my lord! my friend! *Malone*; love-lord, ay, husband-friend! *Dowden*; love, lord? Ay, husband, friend. *Hoppe*;
love? Lord, my husband, friend, *Hosley*   45] *Following 45, Daniel inserts from* Q1: Minutes are dayes, so will I number
them:

28 **sharps** shrill notes above the regular and true pitch (*OED*). The lark's beautiful song has become ugly to Juliet because of its implications.

29 **division** The execution of a rapid melodic passage, originally conceived as the dividing of each of a succession of long notes into several short ones (*OED*), with play on 'divide' (= separate) in 30.

31 **lark...*changed eyes** Warburton cites a not well authenticated belief that the lark exchanged ('changed') its originally beautiful eyes for the toad's ugly eyes. Rowe's 'chang'd' for 'change' (Q2) seems called for by the parallelism with 32 and by the fact that the exchange is something which happened in the past, not something that continues to happen.

32 **would...too** 'If the toad and lark exchanged voices, the lark's croak would be no signal for day' (Heath).

33 **affray** startle (making us separate).

34 **hunt's-up** A morning song serenading the bride the day after the wedding (so called from a song melody sung or played to arouse hunters to early sport). But Romeo and Juliet have ironically become the hunted not the hunters.

36 Compare Brooke (1725): 'Then hath these lovers day an ende, their night begonne.'

43 **friend** lover. For 'ay', see supplementary note.

44–5 **day...days** i.e. because each minute seems like many days. Compare Brooke (747, 821–3).

O, by this count I shall be much in years
Ere I again behold my Romeo!

ROMEO [*From below*] Farewell!
I will omit no opportunity
That may convey my greetings, love, to thee.   50

JULIET O think'st thou we shall ever meet again?

ROMEO I doubt it not, and all these woes shall serve
For sweet discourses in our times to come.

JULIET O God, I have an ill-divining soul!
Methinks I see thee now, thou art so low,   55
As one dead in the bottom of a tomb.
Either my eyesight fails, or thou look'st pale.

ROMEO And trust me, love, in my eye so do you:
Dry sorrow drinks our blood. Adieu, adieu!   *Exit*

JULIET O Fortune, Fortune, all men call thee fickle;   60
If thou art fickle, what dost thou with him
That is renowned for faith? Be fickle, Fortune:
For then I hope thou wilt not keep him long,
But send him back.

Enter Mother [LADY CAPULET *below*].

LADY CAPULET   Ho, daughter, are you up?

JULIET Who is't that calls? It is my lady mother.   65
Is she not down so late, or up so early?
What unaccustomed cause procures her hither?
[*She goeth down from the window and enters below.*]

48 SD] *Neilson; no SD*, Q2–4, F, Q1   51 think'st] Q2, Q1; thinkest Q3–4, F   52 I...not] Q2–4, F; No doubt, no doubt Q1; Ay, doubt it not *conj. Daniel*   53 our times] Q2; our time Q3–4, F; the time Q1   54 SH JULIET] Q4, F, Q1; *Ro.* Q2–3 *(but catchword / Iu.)*   54 ill-divining] *Pope*; ill diuining Q2–4, F, Q1   55 thee now,] Q2–4, F; thee, now *Pope*   55 so low] Q2–4, F; below Q1, *Pope*   57 look'st] F, Q1; lookest Q2–4   60–4 O Fortune...back.] *not in* Q1   62 renowned] F (renown'd); renowmd Q2–4 *(variant form)*   64 SD] *This edn*; Enter Mother. Q2–4, F; *Enter Iuliets Mother, Nurse.* Q1 *(preceded by a line of printer's ornaments, used elsewhere to indicate a break between scenes)*; Q2–4, F SD *placed after* 67, *Capell* (Lady Capulet's Ho...up? *in* 64 *being spoken within*)   64 SH LADY CAPULET] *Rowe; La.* Q2–4 *(through* 87*)*; Lad. / *or* / La. F *(through* 87*)*; Moth: Q1 *(throughout scene, except* / Mo: / *at* 175*)*   64–7 Ho...hither?] Q2–4, F; Where are you Daughter? / *Nur:* What Ladie, Lambe, what *Iuliet?* / *Iul:* How now, who calls? / *Nur:* It is your Mother. Q1   65 It is] Q2–4; Is it F   67 procures] Q2–4, F; provokes *Hanmer*   67 SD *She...window*] Q1 *(follows* 39–40, *which are placed after* 59 *in* Q1 *preceding this* SD*)*; *no* SD, Q2–4, F   67 SD *and enters below*] *This edn*

46 **count** method of computation.
46 **much in years** aged.
54 **ill-divining** intuitively anticipating evil. Compare *Ham.* 1.5.40 ('prophetic soul'); *R3* 3.2.18.
55 **low** i.e. Romeo standing below looking up at Juliet.   54–6 See suppl. note.
59 **Dry...blood** Compare Tilley s656 ('Sorrow is dry [= thirsty]'). It was believed that each sigh took a drop of blood from the heart ('blood-sucking sighs', *3H6* 4.4.22) and hence shortened life.

61 **what dost thou** why are you concerned with?
62 **for faith** for steadfastness (as opposed to fortune's fickleness).
66 **Is...early?** Has she not yet been abed at such a late hour or (has she) got up again at such an early hour?
67 SD **She...below.** On the staging here, see above, p. 31.
70–1 Compare Brooke (1211–12, 1797).

LADY CAPULET Why how now, Juliet?

JULIET   Madam, I am not well.

LADY CAPULET Evermore weeping for your cousin's death?
          What, wilt thou wash him from his grave with tears?   70
          And if thou couldst, thou couldst not make him live;
          Therefore have done. Some grief shows much of love,
          But much of grief shows still some want of wit.

JULIET Yet let me weep for such a feeling loss.

LADY CAPULET So shall you feel the loss, but not the friend   75
          Which you weep for.

JULIET   Feeling so the loss,
          I cannot choose but ever weep the friend.

LADY CAPULET Well, girl, thou weep'st not so much for his death
          As that the villain lives which slaughtered him.

JULIET What villain, madam?

LADY CAPULET   That same villain Romeo.   80

JULIET [*Aside*] Villain and he be many miles asunder. –
          God pardon him, I do with all my heart:
          And yet no man like he doth grieve my heart.

LADY CAPULET That is because the traitor murderer lives.

JULIET Ay, madam, from the reach of these my hands.   85
          Would none but I might venge my cousin's death!

LADY CAPULET We will have vengeance for it, fear thou not:
          Then weep no more. I'll send to one in Mantua,
          Where that same banished runagate doth live,
          Shall give him such an unaccustomed dram   90
          That he shall soon keep Tybalt company;
          And then I hope thou wilt be satisfied.

71–3] *not in* Q1   74–9] Q2–4, F; I cannot chuse, hauing so great a losse. / *Moth:* I cannot blame thee. / But it greeues
thee more that Villaine liues. Q1   76 weep] Q2–4, F; do weep *Theobald*   81 SD] *Hanmer;* no SD, Q2–4, F, Q1
81 be] Q2–4, F; are Q1, *Pope*   82–8 God…more.] *not in* Q1   82 pardon] Q3–4; padon Q2   82 him] Q4; *not in*
Q2–3, F   83 like he doth] Q5; like he, doth Q2–4, F; like, he doth *Williams*   84 murderer] Q2; *not in* Q3–4, F
88–104 I'll…girl.] Q2–4, F; Content thee Girle, if I could finde a man / I soone would send to *Mantua* where he is,
/ That should bestow on him so sure a draught, / As he should soone beare *Tybalt* companie. / *Iul:* Finde you the meanes,
and Ile finde such a man: / For whilest he liues, my heart shall nere be light / Till I behold him, dead is my poore
heart. / Thus for a Kinsman vext? / *Moth:* Well let that passe. I come to bring thee ioyfull newes? Q1, *Pope (with some
variation)*   90] Q2–4, F; That shall bestow on him so sure a draught *Steevens (from Q1)*

72–3 Therefore…wit Compare *Ham.*
1.2.87–106.
74 feeling sensible (touching the feelings),
affecting.
75 feel…friend i.e. your grief is more for the
loss to yourself than for the person lost.
83 yet…heart no other man grieves (= (1)
pains with longing; (2) angers) my heart so much
as he does. 'like he' = Elizabethan colloquial usage
(see Abbott 204, 206). Juliet's lines, through 102,

are intended to deceive her mother and hence
intentionally ambiguous.
85 from the reach out of the (1) touch, (2) grasp
(with implication of harming).
89 runagate fugitive, renegade.
90 unaccustomed dram unusual draught (of
poisoned liquor). Lady Montague's Mantuan
poisoner anticipates ironically Romeo's Mantuan
apothecary of 5.1.
91 company i.e. in death.

JULIET Indeed I never shall be satisfied
         With Romeo, till I behold him – dead –
         Is my poor heart, so for a kinsman vexed.   95
         Madam, if you could find out but a man
         To bear a poison, I would temper it,
         That Romeo should upon receipt thereof
         Soon sleep in quiet. O how my heart abhors
         To hear him named and cannot come to him,   100
         To wreak the love I bore my cousin
         Upon his body that hath slaughtered him!
LADY CAPULET Find thou the means, and I'll find such a man.
         But now I'll tell thee joyful tidings, girl.
JULIET And joy comes well in such a needy time.   105
         What are they, beseech your ladyship?
LADY CAPULET Well, well, thou hast a careful father, child,
         One who, to put thee from thy heaviness,
         Hath sorted out a sudden day of joy,
         That thou expects not, nor I looked not for.   110
JULIET Madam, in happy time, what day is that?
LADY CAPULET Marry, my child, early next Thursday morn,
         The gallant, young, and noble gentleman,
         The County Paris, at Saint Peter's Church,
         Shall happily make thee there a joyful bride.   115
JULIET Now by Saint Peter's Church and Peter too,
         He shall not make me there a joyful bride.
         I wonder at this haste, that I must wed
         Ere he that should be husband comes to woo.
         I pray you tell my lord and father, madam,   120

---

94 him – dead –] *Pope;* him. Dead *Q2–4,* F; him, dead Q1; him – Dead *Rowe*   97 it,] *Cam.*; it: Q2–4; it; F
101 cousin] Q2–4, F; Cozin, *Tybalt* F2; slaughter'd Cousin *Theobald;* murdered cousin *conj. Malone*   103 SH LADY
CAPULET] *Rowe; Mo. / or / M.* Q2–4, F *(through 125); see 64 for* Q1   105 needy] Q2–4, F; needfull Q1, *Pope*
106 beseech] Q2–3, F; I beseech Q4, F2; Q1 *omits 106*   110 expects] Q2–4, F; Q1 *omits 110;* expect'st *Rowe*   111 that]
Q2–4, Q1; this F   115 there] Q2–4, Q1; *not in* F   118–20 I...father,] *not in* Q1

94 –dead– Pope's pointing allows 'dead' to be
taken with what precedes (for Lady Capulet's
benefit), while Juliet continues her ambiguous
expression of love-longing for Romeo.
97 temper mix, compound, with play on (1)
prepare a particularly virulent poison to produce
death ('sleep'); (2) ameliorate the poison so that it
becomes a sleeping draught bringing the balm of
rest.
101 wreak the love (1) avenge the love (for
Tybalt); (2) bestow the love (on Romeo).

105 needy time time that stands in need of
(joy).
106 beseech See supplementary note.
107 careful solicitous (for your good).
109 sorted out selected, appointed.
109 sudden speedy, coming quickly.
110 expects Common as second pers. sing. in
verbs ending in 't' (Abbott 340; Franz 152).
Compare 'counterfeits' in 131.

> I will not marry yet, and when I do, I swear
> It shall be Romeo, whom you know I hate,
> Rather than Paris. These are news indeed!

LADY CAPULET Here comes your father, tell him so yourself;
And see how he will take it at your hands.   125

Enter CAPULET *and Nurse.*

CAPULET When the sun sets, the earth doth drizzle dew,
But for the sunset of my brother's son
It rains downright.
How now, a conduit, girl? What, still in tears?
Evermore show'ring? In one little body   130
Thou counterfeits a bark, a sea, a wind:
For still thy eyes, which I may call the sea,
Do ebb and flow with tears; the bark thy body is,
Sailing in this salt flood; the winds, thy sighs,
Who, raging with thy tears and they with them,   135
Without a sudden calm, will overset
Thy tempest-tossèd body. How now, wife,
Have you delivered to her our decree?

LADY CAPULET Ay, sir, but she will none, she gives you thanks.
I would the fool were married to her grave.   140

121 I swear] Q2–4, F; *not in* Q1, *Pope*   125 SD] Q2–4, F; *Enter olde Capolet.* Q1   126–8] *not in* Q1, *Pope*   126 earth]
Q2–3, F; Ayre Q4, *Theobald*   128–9 It...tears?] *As* Q4, F; *one line,* Q2–3; Why how now, Q1   129 girl?] *Rowe*; girle,
Q2–4, F   129 tears?] F; tears Q2–3; teares. Q4   130 show'ring?...body] Q1; showring...body? Q2–3, F; showring:
...body? Q4   131 counterfeits a] F; countefaits. A Q2; counterfaits. A Q3; counterfeits, a Q4; counterfeit'st a Q5, *Pope*;
resemblest a Q1   132–7 For...body.] Q2–4, F; For this thy bodie which I tearme a barke, / Still floating in thy euerfalling
teares, / And tost with sighes arising from thy hart: / Will without succour ship wracke presently. Q1   133–4 is,...flood;]
Pope (subst.); is:...floud, Q2–4; is...floud, F   135 Who] Q2–4, F; Which *Pope*   135 thy] Q2–4; the F   138 delivered]
Rowe (deliver'd); delivered Q2–4, F   139 SH LADY CAPULET] *Rowe*; La. Q2–4 *(through 157)*; *Lady. / or / La.* F *(through
175)*; Moth: Q1   139 gives you thanks] Q3–4, F; giue you thankes Q2; thankes ye Q1

126 earth...dew earth sheds fine spray-like
drops (*OED* Drizzle *v* 2). Shakespeare imagines the
'earth' weeping at the death of the sun (= sunset).
Q4 'Ayre' for 'earth' (adopted by some eds.) loses
the sun/earth planetary comparison. Malone
compares *Lucrece* 1226: 'But as the earth doth weep,
the sun being set'. S. K. Heniger (*Handbook of
Renaissance Meteorology*, 1960, p. 67) notes that,
though without support from serious meteoro-
logians, some poets describe the earth as sweating
dew.

128 It rains downright i.e. there is an absolute
flood (of tears from Juliet).

129 conduit fountain. Conduits were often
made in the form of human figures (Malone).

136 Without...calm Unless you quickly cease
weeping and sighing and 'calm down'.

139 will...thanks refuses the 'decree', thank
you very much (i.e. Juliet answers sarcastically).
Lines 139–95 are freely imitated in *Wily Beguiled*
(anon., *c*. 1602; MSR, 1170–80).

140 I...grave Tilley (G426) gives as proverbial,
doubtfully perhaps. Shakespeare's line seems to be
echoed in Porter, *Two Angry Women* (1598; MSR,
1628), where it is associated (1619) with 'minion'
addressed to a girl who wishes to marry against her
mother's desire (see 151 below), and in Haughton's
Englishmen for My Money (1598; MSR, 2494).

CAPULET Soft, take me with you, take me with you, wife.
How, will she none? doth she not give us thanks?
Is she not proud? doth she not count her blest,
Unworthy as she is, that we have wrought
So worthy a gentleman to be her bride?   145

JULIET Not proud you have, but thankful that you have:
Proud can I never be of what I hate,
But thankful even for hate that is meant love.

CAPULET How how, how how, chopt-logic? What is this?
'Proud', and 'I thank you', and 'I thank you not',   150
And yet 'not proud', mistress minion you?
Thank me no thankings, nor proud me no prouds,
But fettle your fine joints 'gainst Thursday next,
To go with Paris to Saint Peter's Church,
Or I will drag thee on a hurdle thither.   155
Out, you green-sickness carrion! out, you baggage!
You tallow-face!

LADY CAPULET   Fie, fie, what, are you mad?

JULIET Good father, I beseech you on my knees,
Hear me with patience but to speak a word.

               [*She kneels down.*]

CAPULET Hang thee, young baggage, disobedient wretch!   160
I tell thee what: get thee to church a'Thursday,
Or never after look me in the face.

142 How,] F; How Q2–4; What Q1 *(omitting 141)*   143–5 doth…bride?] *not in* Q1   145 bride] Q2; Bridegroome Q3–4, F   147 hate] Q2–4, Q1; haue F   149 How how, how how,] *Neilson*; how, how, howhow, Q2; How now, how now, Q3–4; How now? / How now? F   149 chopt-logic?] *Durham*; chopt lodgick, Q2–4; Chopt Logicke? F; chop logicke. Q1   150–1] Q2–4; F *omits 151*; Q1 *omits* mistresse minion you?; *Proud, and yet not proud, and, I thank you not; / And yet I thank you.* Mistress minion, you, *Hudson (1880; conj. Lettsom)*   151 proud',] *Hoppe*; proud Q2–3; proud: Q4; proud. Q1; proud! – *Theobald*   151 mistress] Q2–4; Why, Mistress *Theobald*; Misteress *Keightley*   151 you?] Q2–4; You, *Theobald*   153 fettle] Q2–4, F, Q1; settle F2   154 Church,] Q1; Church: Q2–4, F   156 Out, you] You Q2–3 *(catchword)*   156 green-sickness] F4; greene sicknesse Q2–4, F, Q1   157 You] Q2–4, F; out you Q1, F4   157 tallow-face] F4; tallow face Q2–4, F, Q1   157 Fie…mad?] *not in* Q1   159 SD] Q1; *no* SD, Q2–4, F   160 CAPULET] Q1 *(throughout rest of scene)*; Fa. Q2–4, F *(throughout rest of scene)*

141 take…you let me understand you.

143 proud sensible of, pleased with, the honour (being done her).

144 wrought persuaded.

145 bride i.e. bridegroom (but archaic in Shakespeare's time).

146 Not…have i.e. not pleased that such an arrangement has been made, but grateful for the thought that prompted it.

149 chopt-logic (1) sophistical argument; (2) one who argues sophistically (*OED*; spelling variant of Q1 'chop-logic').

151 mistress minion madam spoiled darling.

153 fettle make ready, prepare (a stable term carried on in 'fine joints').

155 hurdle Flat frame on which traitors were drawn through the streets to execution (*OED*). In his present role as tyrant-father Capulet views Juliet as a traitor; compare 'disobedient wretch' (160).

156 green-sickness carrion someone as pale as a corpse (see 2.2.8 n.). Juliet's pallor is stressed again in 'tallow-face' (157).

156 baggage hussy, good-for-nothing.

157 Fie…mad? Addressed to either Capulet or Juliet.

Speak not, reply not, do not answer me!
My fingers itch. Wife, we scarce thought us blest
That God had lent us but this only child,   165
But now I see this one is one too much,
And that we have a curse in having her.
Out on her, hilding!

NURSE   God in heaven bless her!
You are to blame, my lord, to rate her so.

CAPULET And why, my Lady Wisdom? Hold your tongue,   170
Good Prudence, smatter with your gossips, go.

NURSE I speak no treason.

CAPULET   O God-i-goden!

NURSE May not one speak?   *sassy! talking back!*

CAPULET   Peace, you mumbling fool!
Utter your gravity o'er a gossip's bowl,
For here we need it not.

LADY CAPULET   You are too hot.   175

CAPULET God's bread, it makes me mad! Day, night, work, play,
Alone, in company, still my care hath been
To have her matched; and having now provided
A gentleman of noble parentage,
Of fair demesnes, youthful and nobly ligned,   180

---

164 itch. Wife,] Q5 (itch: Wife,),; itch, wife, Q2–4; itch, wife: F; ytch. / Why wife, Q1   165 lent] Q2–4, F; sent Q1,
Pope   167 curse] Q2–4, F; crosse Q1, *conj. Grant White*   170 Wisdom?] F3; wisdome, Q2–4; wisedome? F, Q1
171 Prudence, smatter] Q3–4, F; Prudence smatter, Q2; prudence smatter Q1   171 gossips,] Q3–4, Q1; gossips Q2; gossip, F
172 SH CAPULET] Q1; *Fa.* Q4; Q2–3, F read Father *in roman, as if it were part of the Nurse's speech*   172 God-i-goden] F
(subst.); Godigeden Q2–4; goddegodden Q1; God gi' goode'en F4   173 SH NURSE] Q4; *not in* Q2–3, F, Q1
173 May…fool!] *not in* Q1   173 speak] Q2–4, F; speak t'ye *Daniel (conj. Fleay)*   173 Peace, you mumbling] Q2–4,
F; Peace, peace, you mumbling *Theobald*; Peace, you old mumbling *conj. Seymour*   174 gossip's] *Rowe*; Goships Q2;
Gossips Q3–4, F, Q1   174 bowl] Q2–4, F; bowles F   175 SH LADY CAPULET] *Rowe; Wi.* Q2–4; *La.* F; *Mo:* Q1
176 God's…play] *As Hoppe; two lines, ending mad / …play* Q2–4,   F *(see following note)*
176–7 Day…company] *Hoppe;* Day, night, houre, tide [ride F], time, worke, play, / Alone [Alone, Q4] in companie
Q2–4, F; Day, night, early, late, at home, abroad, / Alone, in company, waking or sleeping Q1, *Pope (reading late, early)*;
Day, night, hour, tide, time, work, and play, / Alone, in company *Rowe*; day, night, hour, tide, work, play, / Alone,
in company *Johnson (omitting Gods bread at beginning of 176)*   177 Alone,] Q4, Q1; Alone Q2–3, F   179 noble] Q2–4,
F; Princely Q1, *Capell*   180 ligned] *Gibbons (conj. Jenkins, from* lien'd *conj. Crow)*; liand Q2; allied Q3–4, F; trainde
Q1, *Capell;* 'lianc'd *conj. Capell;* limb'd *Hosley*

---

169 **rate** berate.

171 **smatter** prate, chatter.

171 **gossips** tattling women.

172 **God-i-goden** Exclamation of annoyance
(literally, 'God give ye good even'). 'Good night'
is still used in a similar way.

174 **gravity** wise advice (ironic).

176 **God's bread** An oath by the body
(= 'bread') of God.

176–7 **Day…company** See supplementary
note.

179–82 T. W. Baldwin (*MLN* 65 (1950),
111–12) connects these lines with the typical 'laus'

(= praise) formula proposed in Apthonius's *Pro-
gymnasmata* (1555 edn).

180 **demesnes** estates (by inheritance).

180 **nobly *ligned** descended, by line, from
noble forebears. The form 'ligned' for Q2 'liand',
adopted by Gibbons from a conjecture of Harold
Jenkins's based on John Crow's conjecture 'lien'd'
(one who had noble 'liens de famille'), although,
like 'lien'd', a nonce-form, receives some support
from *OED* under 'line' (*sb²* 24b 'By line: by lineal
descent'). See collation for other readings. See
Brooke (1961–8).

Stuffed, as they say, with honourable parts,
Proportioned as one's thought would wish a man,
And then to have a wretched puling fool,
A whining mammet, in her fortune's tender,
To answer 'I'll not wed, I cannot love;   185
I am too young, I pray you pardon me.'
But and you will not wed, I'll pardon you:
Graze where you will, you shall not house with me.
Look to't, think on't, I do not use to jest.
Thursday is near, lay hand on heart, advise: 190
And you be mine, I'll give you to my friend;
And you be not, hang, beg, starve, die in the streets,
For by my soul, I'll ne'er acknowledge thee,
Nor what is mine shall never do thee good.
Trust to't, bethink you, I'll not be forsworn.   *Exit*   195

JULIET Is there no pity sitting in the clouds
That sees into the bottom of my grief?
O sweet my mother, cast me not away!
Delay this marriage for a month, a week,
Or if you do not, make the bridal bed   200
In that dim monument where Tybalt lies.

LADY CAPULET Talk not to me, for I'll not speak a word.
Do as thou wilt, for I have done with thee.   *Exit*

JULIET O God! – O Nurse, how shall this be prevented?
My husband is on earth, my faith in heaven;   205

---

182 thought would] Q2–4, F; heart coulde Q1, *Capell*   184 fortune's] *Theobald*; fortunes Q2–4, F, Q1   190 advise:]
F4 *(subst.)*; aduise, Q2–4, F, Q1   199 month, a week] Q2–4, F; day or two Q1   202 SH LADY CAPULET] *Rowe; Mo.*
Q2–4, F; *Moth*: Q1   204–12 O God...Nurse.] Q2–4, F; Ah Nurse what comfort? what counsell canst thou giue me. Q1
204 God!] F; God, Q2; God. Q3(?)–4

---

181 **Stuffed** Crammed full.

181 **parts** qualities.

183 **puling fool** crying, whining child (the image carried on in 'mammet' (= doll, puppet) in 184). Compare Brooke (1969): 'dainty foole, and stubberne gyrle'.

184 **in...tender** at the moment when fortune offers you a gift ('tender'). Compare Brooke (1970): 'Thou dost refuse thy offred weale'. Possibly, however, following Q2–4, F, we should read 'in her fortunes tender', i.e. in her future happiness uncertain, unless she marries Paris, since I intend to disinherit her; see 188–94.

187 **I'll pardon you** Ironic repetition of 'pardon' (= give permission to go anywhere, except remain here as my daughter); compare 'Graze' (188) = turned loose like an animal.

189 **do...jest** am not in the habit of jesting (i.e. when I say something I mean it). Compare Brooke (1984): 'And thinke not that I speake in sport'.

190 **lay...advise** consider deeply, take counsel (within yourself); compare 'bethink you' (195).

198 **sweet my mother** my sweet mother (see Franz 328).

200–1 **bridal...lies** Ironic foreshadowing; compare 54–6 above.

205–8 **My...earth** i.e. only by Romeo's death may Juliet's faith (her sacred vow to Romeo as her husband) be given again to any other man.

How shall that faith return again to earth,
Unless that husband send it me from heaven
By leaving earth? Comfort me, counsel me.
Alack, alack, that heaven should practise stratagems
Upon so soft a subject as myself!   210
What say'st thou? hast thou not a word of joy?
Some comfort, Nurse.
NURSE   Faith, here it is:
Romeo is banished, and all the world to nothing
That he dares ne'er come back to challenge you;
Or if he do, it needs must be by stealth.   215
Then since the case so stands as now it doth,
I think it best you married with the County.
O, he's a lovely gentleman!
Romeo's a dishclout to him. An eagle, madam,
Hath not so green, so quick, so fair an eye   220
As Paris hath. Beshrew my very heart,
I think you are happy in this second match,
For it excels your first, or if it did not,
Your first is dead, or 'twere as good he were
As living here and you no use of him.   225
JULIET Speak'st thou from thy heart?
NURSE And from my soul too, else beshrew them both.
JULIET Amen.
NURSE What?

212–13 Faith...nothing,] *As* F; *one line*, Q2–4; *two lines, ending* Romeo / ...nothing *Capell (reading here* 'tis *and retaining* banishèd *in 213)*; Now trust me Madame, I know not what to say: / Your *Romeo* he is banisht, and all the world to nothing Q1   213 banished] Q1 (banisht); banished Q2–4, F   215–16] *not in* Q1   218 he's] Q2–4, F; he is Q1; 'faith, he is *Hanmer*   218 lovely gentleman] Q2–4, F; gallant Gentleman Q1; lovely gentleman! Romeo! *Capell;* lovely gentleman *in sooth! Keightley*   219 Romeo's] Q5; *Romios* Q2; *Romeos* Q3–4, F; Romeo is but Q1   219–21 An...hath.] *not in* Q1   220 green] Q2–4, F; keen *Hanmer*   221 hath.] *Rowe (subst.);* hath, Q2–4, F   221 Beshrew] Q5; beshrow Q2–4, F *(variant form)*   222 you are] Q2–4, F; you Q1, *Pope*   225 here] Q2–4, F; hence *Hanmer;* there *conj. Anon. (Cam.)*   226 Speak'st thou] Q2; Speakest thou Q3–4, F; Speakst thou this Q1, *Kittredge*   227 And from] Q2–4, F; I and from Q1, *Malone (*Ay, and from, *omitting* too*)*; And *conj. Capell;* From *Steevens (1793)*   227 too, else] Q2; too, or else Q3–4, F; or els Q1, *Hanmer*   228 Amen.] Q2–4, F, Q1; Amen! *Capell*   229 What?] Q2–4, F; What say you Madame? Q1; To what? *Hanmer;* What say you? *conj. Dyce²;* What to? *Keightley*

210 **soft** (1) gentle, tenderhearted; (2) weak, impressionable. Juliet suggests that it is beneath heaven's dignity to devise plots ('practise stratagems') against such a 'subject'.
212–35 Compare Brooke (2295–2312).
213 **all...nothing** all odds against none.
214 **challenge you** claim you as his.
219 **dishclout** to dishrag by comparison with.
220 **green** Green eyes were considered especially admirable and rare.
220 **quick** lively, keen. Eagles were known for

the extraordinary keenness of their sight. Compare Tilley E6 and Apuleius (*The Golden Asse*, trans. W. Adlington (1566), ch. 8): 'his graye and quicke eies like unto the Egle'.
225 **living** i.e. you living.
225 **use** As usual the Nurse's mind moves only on the physical level.
228 **Amen** So be it. Juliet takes the Nurse's 'beshrew' (= curse) in 227 literally and the Nurse's confusion is shown by her question ('What?').

JULIET Well, thou hast comforted me marvellous much.   230
    Go in, and tell my lady I am gone,
    Having displeased my father, to Lawrence' cell,
    To make confession and to be absolved.
NURSE Marry, I will, and this is wisely done.   [*Exit*]
JULIET [*She looks after Nurse.*]
    Ancient damnation! O most wicked fiend!   235
    Is it more sin to wish me thus forsworn,
    Or to dispraise my lord with that same tongue
    Which she hath praised him with above compare
    So many thousand times? Go, counsellor,
    Thou and my bosom henceforth shall be twain.   240
    I'll to the Friar to know his remedy;
    If all else fail, myself have power to die.   *Exit*

[4.1] *Enter* FRIAR [LAWRENCE] *and* COUNTY PARIS.

FRIAR LAWRENCE On Thursday, sir? the time is very short.
PARIS My father Capulet will have it so,
    And I am nothing slow to slack his haste.
FRIAR LAWRENCE You say you do not know the lady's mind?
    Uneven is the course, I like it not.   5
PARIS Immoderately she weeps for Tybalt's death,
    And therefore have I little talked of love,
    For Venus smiles not in a house of tears.
    Now, sir, her father counts it dangerous
    That she do give her sorrow so much sway;   10
    And in his wisdom hastes our marriage

---

233 absolved] Q3–4, F, Q1; obsolu'd Q2   234 SD] Q4; *no* SD, Q2–3, F, Q1   235 SD] Q1; *no* SD, Q2–4, F   235 wicked] Q2–4, F; cursed Q1, *Dyce*²; wither'd *conj. S. Walker*   236 Is it] Q2–4, Q1; It is F   242 SD] Q2–4, Q1; *Exeunt.* F   Act 4, Scene 1   4.1] *Rowe; no act or scene division,* Q2–4, F; Q1 *indicates a break by a row of printer's ornaments above opening* SD   Location] *Capell (after Rowe)*   0 SD COUNTY] Q2–4, F; *not in* Q1   3 slow to slack] Q2–4, F; slacke to slow Q1; slow to back *conj. Johnson*   7 talked] Q1 (talkt); talke Q2–4, F, *Houghton*   10 do] Q2; doth Q3–4, F, Q1; should F3

235 **Ancient damnation!** Cursed old woman!
240 **bosom** inmost secret thoughts. Compare Brooke (2290): 'The secret counsell of her hart the nurce childe seekes to hide.'
240 **twain** separated, estranged. Compare Tilley T648.

Act 4, Scene 1
  Location Friar Lawrence's cell.

3 **nothing slow** in no way reluctant.
5 **Uneven...course** The manner of proceeding is inequitable (i.e. one-sided).
8 **Venus smiles not** i.e. Venus does not cast a favourable aspect on the affairs of love (an astrological reference carried on, Mahood suggests, in 'house of tears' = an inauspicious section of the heavens).
11 **marriage** Trisyllabic.

To stop the inundation of her tears,
Which too much minded by herself alone
May be put from her by society.
Now do you know the reason of this haste.   15
FRIAR LAWRENCE [*Aside*]
    I would I knew not why it should be slowed. –
    Look, sir, here comes the lady toward my cell.

Enter JULIET.

PARIS Happily met, my lady and my wife!
JULIET That may be, sir, when I may be a wife.
PARIS That 'may be' must be, love, on Thursday next.   20
JULIET What must be shall be.
FRIAR LAWRENCE   That's a certain text.
PARIS Come you to make confession to this father?
JULIET To answer that, I should confess to you.
PARIS Do not deny to him that you love me.
JULIET I will confess to you that I love him.   25
PARIS So will ye, I am sure, that you love me.
JULIET If I do so, it will be of more price,
    Being spoke behind your back, than to your face.
PARIS Poor soul, thy face is much abused with tears.
JULIET The tears have got small victory by that,   30
    For it was bad enough before their spite.
PARIS Thou wrong'st it more than tears with that report.
JULIET That is no slander, sir, which is a truth,
    And what I spake, I spake it to my face.
PARIS Thy face is mine, and thou hast slandered it.   35
JULIET It may be so, for it is not mine own.

---

12 tears,] F; teares. Q2–4, Q1   16 SD] *Theobald;* no SD, Q2–4, F, Q1   16 slowed] F (slow'd), Q1; slowed Q2–4
17 toward] Q2; towards Q3–4, F; to Q1   17 SD] Q2–4, F; *Enter Paris.* Q1 *(after 16)*   18 Happily met] Q2–4, F; Welcome
my loue Q1, *Pope*   18 wife] Q2–4, F, Q1; life *conj. Johnson*   20 'may be'] *Hosley;* may be Q2–4, F, Q1   23 I should]
Q2–4, F; were to Q1, *Pope*   26 ye] Q2–4, F; you Q1, *Capell (Q1 reading* So I am sure you will that*)*   26 sure,] F;
sure Q2–4, F, Q1   33 slander…truth] Q2–4, F; wrong sir, that is a truth Q1, *Malone;* slaunder sir, which is truth F2;
slander, Sir, which is but truth *Rowe;* wrong, sir, that is but a truth *Capell;* wrong, sir, that is a truth *Malone;* slander,
sir, that is a truth *Steevens (1793)*   34 my] Q2–4, Q1; thy F

---

13 **too…alone** too mind-consuming when she
is without company.

14 **society** companionship.

19–36 Juliet's cool verbal sparring with Paris
marks the beginning of a new self-reliance under the
pressure of her sudden isolation. This chance
meeting with Paris is not in Brooke.

21 **What…be** Proverbial (Tilley M1331). Com-

pare Marlowe, *Dr Faustus* 1.1.74–5: '*Che sera, sera*:
/ What will be, shall be.'

26 **will ye** i.e. ye will (confess to him).

27 **more price** greater worth.

31 **bad enough** 'conventional self-depreciation
in dealing with a compliment' (Kittredge).

34 **to my face** (1) openly; (2) about my face.
Looks back to 28.

Are you at leisure, holy father, now,
Or shall I come to you at evening mass?
FRIAR LAWRENCE My leisure serves me, pensive daughter, now.
My lord, we must entreat the time alone.   40
PARIS God shield I should disturb devotion!
Juliet, on Thursday early will I rouse ye;
Till then adieu, and keep this holy kiss.   *Exit*
JULIET O shut the door, and when thou hast done so,
Come weep with me, past hope, past cure, past help!   45
FRIAR LAWRENCE O Juliet, I already know thy grief,
It strains me past the compass of my wits.
I hear thou must, and nothing may prorogue it,
On Thursday next be married to this County.
JULIET Tell me not, Friar, that thou hearest of this,   50
Unless thou tell me how I may prevent it.
If in thy wisdom thou canst give no help,
Do thou but call my resolution wise,
And with this knife I'll help it presently.
God joined my heart and Romeo's, thou our hands,   55
And ere this hand, by thee to Romeo's sealed,
Shall be the label to another deed,
Or my true heart with treacherous revolt
Turn to another, this shall slay them both:

40 we] Q2–4, Q1; you F; I F2   41 God shield] Q1; Godshield, Q2–4; Godsheild: F   42–3] Q2–4, F; *Iuliet* farwell, and keep this holy kisse. Q1, *Pope*   42 ye] Q2–4, F; you *Theobald*   43 SD] Q2–4; *Exit Paris.* F, Q1   44 O] Q2–4, F; Goe Q1, *Pope*   45 cure] Q1, *Rowe*; care Q2–4, F, *Houghton*   46 O] Q2–4, F; Ah Q1, *Capell*   47] *not in* Q1, *Pope*   47 strains] Q2–4; streames F   52–60] *not in* Q1   54 with this] Q2–4; with' his F; with' this F2   55 heart and Romeo's,] F4; heart, and *Romeos* Q2; heart, and *Romeos*, Q3–4, F   56 Romeo's] Q5; *Romeos* Q2–4; *Romeo* F   56 sealed,] Q5; seald: Q2–4, F

38 **evening mass** Shakespeare has been accused of ignorance or carelessness because mass was not normally celebrated in the evening, but as *OED* points out (Mass *sb*[1] 2c) 'evening mass' is a direct rendering of Latin *missa vespertina*, where *missa* has the general sense of 'religious service'. In any case, we know that a mass was said about six o'clock in the evening at the Charter-House, London, in the lodgings of the Portuguese ambassador in 1576 (*Queen Elizabeth and Her Times*, ed. Thomas Wright, 1838, II, 37–41).

39 **pensive** sad, mournful. Paris would understand 'pensive' only in reference to Tybalt's death.

40 **entreat...alone** pray you now to leave us privately together.

41 **shield** forbid.

45 ***cure** A few eds. (Hoppe most recently) retain Q2 'care' on the grounds that 'past cure' merely anticipates 'past help', but most prefer Q1

'cure' and interpret 'past cure, past help' as meaning 'beyond any final solution, beyond even remedial action'. Compare Tilley C921, *LLL* 5.2.28, *R2* 2.3.171. See the same 'care/cure' misreading in 4.5.65, where 'cure' is necessary to the sense.

47 **strains...wits** forces me beyond the limits of my power to think clearly.

48 **prorogue** postpone, delay.

54 **knife** Elizabethan ladies sometimes wore small household knives at their girdles.

54 **it** i.e. the intolerable situation, not her 'resolution' (53).

54 **presently** immediately. Compare 'present counsel' (= immediate advice) in 61.

56 **sealed** contracted. The legal imagery is carried on (57) in 'label' (= seal), a slip of parchment inserted in a 'deed' (= contract), which bore the signature and seal of the person 'setting his hand' to the document.

Therefore, out of thy long-experienced time,   60
Give me some present counsel, or, behold,
'Twixt my extremes and me this bloody knife
Shall play the umpire, arbitrating that
Which the commission of thy years and art
Could to no issue of true honour bring.   65
Be not so long to speak, I long to die,
If what thou speak'st speak not of remedy.
FRIAR LAWRENCE Hold, daughter, I do spy a kind of hope,
Which craves as desperate an execution
As that is desperate which we would prevent.   70
If, rather than to marry County Paris,
Thou hast the strength of will to slay thyself,
Then is it likely thou wilt undertake
A thing like death to chide away this shame,
That cop'st with Death himself to scape from it;   75
And if thou dar'st, I'll give thee remedy.
JULIET O bid me leap, rather than marry Paris,
From off the battlements of any tower,
Or walk in thievish ways, or bid me lurk
Where serpents are; chain me with roaring bears,   80
Or hide me nightly in a charnel-house,
O'ercovered quite with dead men's rattling bones,
With reeky shanks and yellow chapless skulls;

---

60 long-experienced] *Pope;* long experienst Q2–3; long experien'st Q4; long expetien'st F   63 umpire] Q4; umpeer Q2–3, F, Q1 *(variant form)*   66 Be…I long] Q2–4, F; Speake not, be briefe: for I desire Q1, *Pope;* Speak now, be brief; for I desire *Hanmer*   72 of] Q2–4, F; or Q1, *Pope*   72 slay] Q4, Q1; stay Q2–3, F   75 cop'st] F4; coapst Q2–3, Q1; coop'st Q4; coap'st F; copest *Globe*   75 Death himself] Q3–4, F *(all reading* death*);* death, himselfe Q2; death it selfe Q1   75 from] Q2–4, Q1; fro F   76 And if] Q2–4, F, Q1; An if *conj. Delius*   76 dar'st] F; darest Q2–4; doost Q1   78 off] Q5, Q1; of Q2–4, F   78 any] Q2–4, F; yonder Q1, *Pope*   79–80] Q2–4, F; Or chaine me to some steepie mountaines top, / Where roaring Beares and sauage Lions are: Q1, *Pope (reading* roam *for* are*)* ; Or chain me to some steepy mountain's top, / Where savage bears and roaring lions roam; *conj. Johnson*   81 hide] Q2–4, F; shut Q1, *Pope*   83 reeky] Q2–4, Q1; reckie F   83 yellow] Q4, F; yealow Q2–3; yeolow Q1   83 chapless] Q4; chapels Q2; chappels Q3, F; chaples Q1

60 **long-experienced time** i.e. the wisdom of age; compare 'years and art' (64).
62 **extremes** desperate straits.
62 **bloody** Used anticipatively, or = cruel (NS). Compare Brooke (496, 1915).
64 **commission** authority, warrant.
64 **art** skill derived from experience and knowledge.
66 **long** slow ('long' here chosen for the following quibble on 'long to die').
75 **cop'st** (art willing) to deal or encounter.
75 **it** i.e. shame (74).
77–8 Compare Brooke (1602–4).
79 **thievish ways** lanes haunted by thieves.

81 **charnel-house** A small building attached to a church containing the bones of those whose graves have been dug up to make way for new burials. Compare *Ham.* 5.1 and the warning on Shakespeare's gravestone against such desecration.
83 **reeky** emitting vapour, steamy, full of rank moisture (*OED* sv *a* 1a); the more modern sense of 'reek' (*OED* 3) as 'a strong and disagreeable fume or smell', used adjectivally, seems more applicable here.
83 *chapless lacking the lower jaw. Q2 'chapels' may have been influenced by a misunderstanding of the Q1 form 'chaples' (= chapless).

Or bid me go into a new-made grave,
And hide me with a dead man in his shroud – 85
Things that to hear them told have made me tremble –
And I will do it without fear or doubt,
To live an unstained wife to my sweet love.

FRIAR LAWRENCE Hold then, go home, be merry, give consent
To marry Paris. Wednesday is tomorrow; 90
Tomorrow night look that thou lie alone,
Let not the Nurse lie with thee in thy chamber.
Take thou this vial, being then in bed,
And this distilling liquor drink thou off,
When presently through all thy veins shall run 95
A cold and drowsy humour; for no pulse
Shall keep his native progress, but surcease;
No warmth, no breath shall testify thou livest;
The roses in thy lips and cheeks shall fade
To wanny ashes, thy eyes' windows fall, 100
Like Death when he shuts up the day of life;
Each part, deprived of supple government,
Shall stiff and stark and cold appear like death,
And in this borrowed likeness of shrunk death
Thou shalt continue two and forty hours, 105

84–5] Q2–4, F; Or lay me in tombe with one new dead: QI   84 new-made] *Rowe*; new made Q2–4, F   85 hide] Q2–4, F; lay QI, *NS*   85 his shroud –] Q4 (his shroud,); his, Q2–3; his graue F, *Sisson*; his tomb, *conj. Malone (suggested by QI, above)*, Williams   86 told] Q2–4, F; namde QI, *Pope*   88 unstained] Q2–4 (vnstaind), QI; vnstained F   89–93] Q2–4, F; Hold *Iuliet*, hie thee home, get thee to bed, / Let not thy Nurse lye with thee in thy Chamber: / And when thou art alone, take thou this Violl, QI, *Pope*   92 the] Q2; thy Q3–4, F, QI   94 distilling] Q2–4, F; distilled QI, *Pope*   96 cold...humour] Q2–4, F; dull and heauie slumber QI   96–7 for...surcease;] Q2–4, F; which shall seaze / Each vitall spirit: for no Pulse shall keepe / His naturall progresse, but surcease to beate: QI, *Pope*   98 breath] Q3–4, F, QI; breast Q2   99–103] *not in* QI   99 fade] Q3–4, F; fade: Q2   100 To wanny] *Hoppe (conj. Kellner)*; Too many Q2–3; Too paly Q4; To many F; To mealy F2   100 thy] Q2; the Q3–4, F   100 fall,] F (fall); fall: Q2–4   101 shuts] Q2–4; shut F   104 borrowed] Q5 (borrow'd); borrowed Q2–4, F, QI

85 *shroud grave-clothes. Word omitted in Q2–3; supplied from Q4. Compare 4.3.42–3; 5.3.97. See collation. The horror of the idea reflects Juliet's morbid sensibility at this terrifying moment.

94 distilling 'distilled' (see Abbott 372) or 'infusing (the body)' (*OED* sv *v* 3). Compare 95: 'through all thy veins shall run'. Most eds. accept the easier QI 'distilled', but it is difficult to see how '-ed' could be misread as '-ing'.

96 A cold...humour A fluid ('humour') inducing cold and drowsiness. Compare *Ham.* 1.5.61–70.

97 his...surcease its natural movement, but cease.

98 *breath Q2's 'breast' (= voice in singing, breath (*OED*)) makes perhaps possible sense, but,

since the context favours 'breath' (Q3–4, F, QI), eds. have never accepted it.

100 *wanny pale. Q2 'many' is obviously wrong. Compare *2H6* 3.2.141 'paly lips'. See collation. This description seems to contradict Romeo's statement in 5.3.94–6.

100 eyes' windows fall eyelids close ('windows' = shutters), a confusing metaphor since the eyes were commonly considered as the 'windows' of the soul, but compare *R3* 5.3.116.

102 supple government control of muscular movement.

103 stark rigid; essentially = 'stiff'.

105 two and forty hours No specific time in Brooke; Painter (p. 127) says Juliet will 'abide in such extasie the space of .40. houres at the least', a

And then awake as from a pleasant sleep.
Now when the bridegroom in the morning comes
To rouse thee from thy bed, there art thou dead.
Then as the manner of our country is,
In thy best robes, uncovered on the bier,   110
Thou shall be borne to that same ancient vault
Where all the kindred of the Capulets lie.
In the mean time, against thou shalt awake,
Shall Romeo by my letters know our drift,
And hither shall he come, and he and I   115
Will watch thy waking, and that very night
Shall Romeo bear thee hence to Mantua.
And this shall free thee from this present shame,
If no inconstant toy, nor womanish fear,
Abate thy valour in the acting it.   120

JULIET Give me, give me! O tell not me of fear.

FRIAR LAWRENCE Hold, get you gone, be strong and prosperous
In this resolve; I'll send a friar with speed
To Mantua, with my letters to thy lord.

JULIET Love give me strength, and strength shall help afford.   125
Farewell, dear father.

Exeunt

106–26] Q2–4, F; And when thou art laid in thy Kindreds Vault, / Ile send in hast to *Mantua* to thy Lord, / And he shall come and take thee from thy graue. / *Iul*: Frier I goe, be sure thou send for my deare *Romeo*. Q1   110 In] Q3–4, F; Is Q2   110 uncovered] Q3–4 (vncouerd), F; vncoured Q2   110] *Following 110, Q2–4, F read*: Be borne to buriall in thy kindreds graue: 111 shall] Q2; shalt Q3–4, F   115–16 and...waking] Q2–4 *(subst.)*; *not in* F   115 and] Q3–4; an Q2   116 waking] Q3–4; walking Q2   121 Give...not me] Q2–3, F; Giue me, giue me, O tell me not Q4; Give me, oh give me, tell not me *Pope*[1]; Give me, oh give me, tell me not *Pope*[2]   121 fear.] Q3–4; feare Q2; care. F   122 prosperous] Q2–4; prosperous: F   123 resolve;] *Theobald*; resolue, Q2–4, F   126 SD] Q4, Q1; *Exit*. Q2–3, F

detail that may have suggested Shakespeare's forty-two hours, a figure that raises a problem in the time-scheme. Otway (*Caius Marius* 4.521) changes the time to 'Two Summer-days'. See above, p. 10, n.5, and Furness, p. 428.

107–8 bridegroom...bed It was customary for the bridegroom to serenade the bride early in the morning on the wedding-day.

110 See supplementary note.

110 uncovered...bier Compare Brooke (2523–5) and *Ham.* 4.5.165: 'They bore him barefac'd on the bier.'

111 Thou shall For this syncopated form of 'shalt', see Franz 152.

112 Capulets Metrically awkward; perhaps Shakespeare wrote 'Capels' as in 3.1.2, etc.

113 against in anticipation of the time when.

114 drift purpose.

116 watch be on hand for.

119 inconstant...fear From Brooke: 'inconstant toy' (2190), 'womannish dread' (2145). 'toy' = whim, caprice.

122 Hold Enough.

[4.2] *Enter Father* CAPULET, *Mother* [LADY CAPULET], NURSE, *and*
SERVINGMEN, *two or three.*

CAPULET So many guests invite as here are writ.

[Exit Servingman]

    Sirrah, go hire me twenty cunning cooks.

SERVINGMAN You shall have none ill, sir, for I'll try if they can lick
    their fingers.

CAPULET How canst thou try them so?   5

SERVINGMAN Marry, sir, 'tis an ill cook that cannot lick his own
    fingers; therefore he that cannot lick his fingers goes not with me.

CAPULET Go, be gone.

[Exit Servingman]

    We shall be much unfurnished for this time.

    What, is my daughter gone to Friar Lawrence?   10

NURSE Ay forsooth.

CAPULET Well, he may chance to do some good on her.

    A peevish self-willed harlotry it is.

Enter JULIET.

NURSE See where she comes from shrift with merry look.

CAPULET How now, my headstrong, where have you been gadding?   15

JULIET Where I have learnt me to repent the sin

    Of disobedient opposition

    To you and your behests, and am enjoined

Act 4, Scene 2   4.2] *Rowe; no scene division, Q2–4, F; Q1 indicates a break by a row of printer's ornaments above opening*
SD   Location] *Rowe*   0 SD] Q2–4, F; *Enter olde Capolet, his Wife, Nurse, and Seruingman.* Q1   1–11] Q2–4, F; *Where
are you sirra?* / *Ser:* Heere forsooth. / *Capo:* Goe, prouide me twentie cunning Cookes. / *Ser:* I warrant you Sir, let
me alone for that, Ile knowe them by licking their fingers. / *Capo:* How canst thou know them so? / *Ser:* Ah Sir, tis
an ill Cooke cannot licke his owne fingers. / *Capo:* Well get you gone. / *Exit Seruingman.* / But wheres this Head-strong?
/ *Moth:* Shees gone (my Lord) to Frier *Laurence* Cell / To be confest. Q1   1 SD] *Capell (subst.); no SD, Q2–4, F, Q1;
Exit First Servant.* / *Dyce*   3, 6 SH SERVINGMAN] *Williams; Ser. Q2–4, F, Q1; 1. S.* / *Capell; 2. Serv.* / *Malone*
8–9 Go…time.] *As Pope; one line, Q2–4, F*   8 SD] *no SD, Q2–4, F; Exit Servant.* / *Capell*   13 self-willed harlotry]
*Q4; selfewieldhar lottry Q2 (some copies); selfeweild harlotry Q2 (other copies, perhaps a corrected state); self willde harlotry
Q3; selfe-wild harlotry F; selfe wild harlotrie Q1*   14 comes…look] Q2–4, F; *commeth from Confession Q1; comes from
her confession Pope; line given to* / *Moth:* Q1

Act 4, Scene 2

  Location Verona. Capulet's house.

  2 cunning skilled. Capulet's 'twenty cunning
cooks' seems to reflect Brooke's 'costly feast'
(2258); he (or Shakespeare) seems to have forgotten
his earlier frugal intentions in 3.4.23–8.

  3 none ill no bad ones.

  3 try test them by observing.

  3–4 can…fingers Proverbial (Tilley c636: 'He
is an ill cook that cannot lick his own fingers'),
i.e. he is one who endorses his cooking by tasting
it.

  9 this time i.e. the wedding festivities (then
planned for Thursday).

  13 harlotry silly girl, hussy. Compare *1H4*
3.1.196: 'a peevish self-will'd harlotry'. The word
generally had a stronger sense of sexual
impropriety.

  15 How…gadding Echoed in Porter, *Two
Angry Women* (1598; MSR, 692).

By holy Lawrence to fall prostrate here
To beg your pardon.
>   [*She kneels down.*]
>   Pardon, I beseech you!   20
Henceforward I am ever ruled by you.
CAPULET Send for the County, go tell him of this.
I'll have this knot knit up tomorrow morning.
JULIET I met the youthful lord at Lawrence' cell,
And gave him what becomèd love I might,   25
Not stepping o'er the bounds of modesty.
CAPULET Why, I am glad on't, this is well, stand up.
This is as't should be. Let me see the County;
Ay, marry, go, I say, and fetch him hither.
Now afore God, this reverend holy Friar,   30
All our whole city is much bound to him.
JULIET Nurse, will you go with me into my closet,
To help me sort such needful ornaments
As you think fit to furnish me tomorrow?
LADY CAPULET No, not till Thursday, there is time enough.   35
CAPULET Go, Nurse, go with her, we'll to church tomorrow.
>   *Exeunt* [*Juliet and Nurse*]
LADY CAPULET We shall be short in our provision,
'Tis now near night.
CAPULET   Tush, I will stir about,
And all things shall be well, I warrant thee, wife:

20–1] Q2–4, F; And craue remission of so foule a fact. / She kneeles downe. / Moth: Why thats well said. Q1
20 SD] Q1; no SD, Q2–4, F   24–29] not in Q1   25 becomèd] Q4, F; becomd Q2–3; becoming Rowe   28 as't] Q4, F;
ast Q2–3   30 reverend holy] Q2–4, F; holy reuerent Q1; holy reverend Q5, Capell   31 to him] Q2–4, F; vnto Q1, conj.
Steevens   35, 37 SH LADY CAPULET] Rowe; Mo. Q2–4, F; Moth: Q1   35–6] Q2–4, F; I pree thee doo, good Nurse
goe in with her, / Helpe her to sort Tyres, Rebatoes, Chaines, / And I will come vnto you presently, / Nur: Come
sweet hart, shall we goe: / Iul: I pree thee let vs. / Exeunt Nurse and Iuliet. / Moth: Me thinks on Thursday would
be time enough. / Capo: I say I will haue this dispatcht to morrow, / Goe one and certefie the Count thereof. / Moth:
I pray my Lord, let it be Thursday. / Capo: I say to morrow while shees in the mood. Q1   35 there is] Q2–4; there's F
36, 38 SH CAPULET] Q1 (Capo:); Fa. Q2–4, F   36 SD] F, Q1 (Nurse and Iuliet); Exeunt. Q2–4   38–46 Tush…
reclaimed.] Q2–4, F; Let me alone for that, goe get you in, / Now before God my heart is passing light, / To see her
thus conformed to our will. Q1

23 tomorrow morning In his gratification at Juliet's apparent capitulation, Capulet changes the marriage day to Wednesday, a sudden change that will have fatal consequences. See supplementary note.

25 becomèd befitting, becoming. The form, found only in Shakespeare, seems to represent the reverse process found in 'distilling' in 4.1.94.

29 Capulet's order is ignored because, as he notes in 42–5, no servant is available at this point to carry it out. Shakespeare seems to have forgotten that he was more generous with attending servants in the 0 SD (*Seruingmen, two or three*).

31 bound beholden.

32 closet private sitting-room.

33 sort choose.

38 now near night Shakespeare is turning the dramatic clock ahead to achieve a greater sense of urgency. Strict clock-time would place this scene not later than early afternoon, since Juliet visited the

Go thou to Juliet, help to deck up her;   40
I'll not to bed tonight; let me alone,
I'll play the huswife for this once. What ho!
They are all forth. Well, I will walk myself
To County Paris, to prepare up him
Against tomorrow. My heart is wondrous light,   45
Since this same wayward girl is so reclaimed.

Exeunt

[4.3] *Enter* JULIET *and* NURSE.

JULIET Ay, those attires are best, but, gentle Nurse,
  I pray thee leave me to myself tonight:
  For I have need of many orisons
  To move the heavens to smile upon my state,
  Which, well thou knowest, is cross and full of sin.   5

Enter Mother [LADY CAPULET].

LADY CAPULET What, are you busy, ho? need you my help?
JULIET No, madam, we have culled such necessaries
  As are behoveful for our state tomorrow.
  So please you, let me now be left alone,
  And let the Nurse this night sit up with you,   10
  For I am sure you have your hands full all,
  In this so sudden business.

41 tonight;] *Johnson (subst.)*; to night, Q2–4, F 41 alone,] *Capell*; alone: Q2–4, F; Let me alone for that, Q1 44 up him] Q2–4; him vp F 45 heart is] Q2–4, F, Q1; heart's *Pope* 46 SD] Q4, Q1; *Exit.* Q2–3; *Exeunt Father and Mother.* F Act 4, Scene 3 4.3] *Rowe*; *no scene division*, Q2–4, F; Q1 *indicates a break by a row of printer's ornaments above opening* SD Location] *Riverside*; *Juliet's Chamber. / Rowe* 1–13 SD JULIET Ay,...*Nurse*] Q2–4, F; *Nur:* Come, come, what need you anie thing else? / *Iul:* Nothing good Nurse, but leaue me to my selfe: / For I doo meane to lye alone to night. / *Nur:* Well theres a cleane smocke vnder your pillow, and so good night. *Exit. / Enter Mother. / Moth:* What are you busie, doo you need my helpe? / *Iul:* No Madame, I desire to lye alone, / For I haue manie things to thinke vpon. / *Moth:* Well then good night, be stirring *Iuliet*, / The Countie will be earlie here to morrow. *Exit.* Q1 5 knowest] Q2–4; know'st F 6, 12 SH LADY CAPULET] *Rowe*; *Mo.* Q2–4, F; *Moth:* Q1 6 ho? need you] Q2–4, F; doo you need Q1, *Pope* 8 behoveful] F4; behoofefull Q2–4; behoouefull F

Friar in the morning (see end of 3.5 and 4.1) and has apparently just returned from seeing him when she enters at 14 above. See supplementary note.
 41 let me alone leave me to myself.
 42 huswife housewife (pronounced 'húsif').
 45 heart...light Tilley (L277: 'A lightening (light'ning) before death') associates the implication of this line with 5.1.2–5 and 5.3.88–90.

Act 4, Scene 3
 Location Verona. Capulet's house.
 1–5 Compare Brooke (2320–31).
 4 state condition.
 5 cross contrary to my desire, unfavourable.
 7 culled picked out.
 8 behoveful needful, fitting.
 8 state social degree.
 12 business Trisyllabic.

LADY CAPULET   Good night.
　　Get thee to bed and rest, for thou hast need.
　　　　　　　　　　　Exeunt [Lady Capulet and Nurse]
JULIET Farewell! God knows when we shall meet again.
　　I have a faint cold fear thrills through my veins   15
　　That almost freezes up the heat of life:
　　I'll call them back again to comfort me.
　　Nurse! – What should she do here?
　　My dismal scene I needs must act alone.
　　Come, vial.   20
　　What if this mixture do not work at all?
　　Shall I be married then tomorrow morning?
　　No, no, this shall forbid it; lie thou there.
　　　　　　　　　　[Laying down her dagger.]
　　What if it be a poison which the Friar
　　Subtly hath ministered to have me dead,   25
　　Lest in this marriage he should be dishonoured,
　　Because he married me before to Romeo?
　　I fear it is, and yet methinks it should not,
　　For he hath still been tried a holy man.
　　How if, when I am laid into the tomb,   30
　　I wake before the time that Romeo
　　Come to redeem me? There's a fearful point!
　　Shall I not then be stifled in the vault,
　　To whose foul mouth no healthsome air breathes in,
　　And there die strangled ere my Romeo comes?   35
　　Or if I live, is it not very like
　　The horrible conceit of death and night,

13 SD] *Capell; Exeunt.* Q2–4, F; *Exit.* Q1   15–20] Q2–4, F; Ah, I doo take a fearfull thing in hand. Q1   16 life] Q2–4; fire F   18 Nurse! –] *Hanmer (after Rowe);* Nurse, Q2–4, F   20–1 Come…all] *As Hanmer; one line,* Q2–4, F   20 vial] Q3–4, F; Violl Q2; phial *Johnson*   22] Q2–4, F; Must I of force be married to the Countie? Q1, *Malone;* Shall I of force be marry'd to the Count? *Pope*   23 No…lie] Q2–4, F; This shall forbid it. Knife, lye Q1, *conj. Lettsom*   23 SD] *Johnson; no SD,* Q2–4, F, Q1 ; *Lyes down a penknife. / Douai MS.; Pointing to a dagger. / Rowe*   29 man.] Q2–4, F; Man: / I will not entertaine so bad a thought. Q1, *Steevens*   30–58] Q2–4, F; What if I should be stifled in the Toomb? / Awake an houre before the appointed time: / Ah then I feare I shall be lunaticke, / And playing with my dead forefathers bones, / Dash out my franticke braines. Me thinkes I see / My Cosin *Tybalt* weltring in his bloud, / Seeking for *Romeo*: stay *Tybalt* stay. / *Romeo* I come, this doe I drinke to thee. Q1   33 stifled] F, Q1 ; stiffled Q2–4

15–58 Compare Brooke (2353–2402).
15 faint cold causing faintness and coldness.
15 thrills pierces, shivers. Compare Brooke (2387–91).
19 dismal (1) fatal; (2) full of dread; (3) miserable.
24–7 This passing suspicion of the Friar's motives is not in Brooke or Painter. By coincidence, Julia (Juliet) expresses a similar suspicion in Lope de Vega's *Castelvines y Monteses* (3.1).
25 Subtly Cunningly, craftily.
29 tried tested, proved.
37 conceit of conception induced by the thought of.

Together with the terror of the place –
As in a vault, an ancient receptacle,
Where for this many hundred years the bones   40
Of all my buried ancestors are packed,
Where bloody Tybalt, yet but green in earth,
Lies fest'ring in his shroud, where, as they say,
At some hours in the night spirits resort –
Alack, alack, is it not like that I,   45
So early waking – what with loathsome smells,
And shrieks like mandrakes' torn out of the earth,
That living mortals hearing them run mad –
O, if I wake, shall I not be distraught,
Environèd with all these hideous fears,   50
And madly play with my forefathers' joints,
And pluck the mangled Tybalt from his shroud,
And in this rage, with some great kinsman's bone,
As with a club, dash out my desp'rate brains?
O look! methinks I see my cousin's ghost   55
Seeking out Romeo that did spit his body
Upon a rapier's point. Stay, Tybalt, stay!
Romeo, Romeo, Romeo! Here's drink – I drink to thee.
[She falls upon her bed, within the curtains.]

40 this] Q2; these Q3–4, F   47 mandrakes'] *Capell*; mandrakes Q2–4, F   49 O, if I wake] *Hanmer*; O if I walke Q2–3, F; Or if I wake Q4; Or if I walke F2   57 a] Q2–4; my F; his F2   58] Q2–4, F; *Romeo* I come, this doe I drinke to thee. Q1, *Pope; Romeo*, here's drink! *Romeo*, I drink to thee. *Johnson;* Romeo, Romeo, Romeo, I drink to thee. *Knight* 58 SD] Q1; *no SD*, Q2–4, F; *Exit. / Rowe; She throws herself on the bed. / Pope; throws away the Vial, and casts herself upon the Bed. Scene closes. / Capell*

39 **As** As being.
39 **receptacle** Accented on the first syllable.
42 **green in earth** freshly buried.
47 **mandrakes'** The mandrake plant (mandragola), apart from its medical qualities, was popularly believed to be generated from the droppings of dead bodies at the gallows' foot, to resemble a man because of its bifurcated foot, and to shriek as it was pulled out of the earth. To hear the mandrake's shriek was supposed to cause either death or madness. Browne (*Pseudodoxia Epidemica*, II, 6)

considers all this as 'ridiculous and false below confute'.
50 **Environèd** Surrounded.
53 **rage** madness, frenzy.
53 **great** 'earlier by one or more generations, as in great-grandfather' (Kermode).
58 The dramatically extra-metrical quality of this line (a kind of extended cry) is often unnecessarily regularised by eds.
58 SD For the staging at this point, see above, p. 33.

[4.4] *Enter lady of the house* [LADY CAPULET] *and* NURSE [*with herbs*].

LADY CAPULET Hold, take these keys and fetch more spices, Nurse.
NURSE They call for dates and quinces in the pastry.

Enter old CAPULET.

CAPULET Come, stir, stir, stir! the second cock hath crowed,
         The curfew bell hath rung, 'tis three a'clock.
         Look to the baked meats, good Angelica,   5
         Spare not for cost.
NURSE   Go, you cot-quean, go,
         Get you to bed. Faith, you'll be sick tomorrow
         For this night's watching.
CAPULET No, not a whit. What, I have watched ere now
         All night for lesser cause, and ne'er been sick.   10
LADY CAPULET Ay, you have been a mouse-hunt in your time,
         But I will watch you from such watching now.
                            Exeunt Lady [*Capulet*] *and Nurse*

Act 4, Scene 4 4.4] *Rowe; no scene division,* Q2–4, F*;* Q1 *indicates a break by a row of printer's ornaments above opening*
SD Location] *Riverside; A Hall. / Rowe;* SCENE *changes to Capulet's Hall. / Theobald*   0 SD *with herbs*] *from* Q1 SD*:*
Enter Nurse with hearbs, Mother.; not in Q2–4, F   1, 11 SH LADY CAPULET] *Rowe; La.* Q2–4, F *(Lady. / in* F *at 1);*
Moth: Q1   1] Q2–4, F*;* Thats well said Nurse, set all in redines, / The Countie will be heere immediatly. Q1 *(omitting
the Nurse's speech in 2)*   2 SD *old* CAPULET] Q2–4, F*; Oldeman* Q1   3 crowed] F *(Crow'd); crowed* Q2–4   4 rung]
F, Q1*; roong* Q2*; roung* Q3–4   4 three] Q2–4, F*; foure* Q1   6 SH NURSE] Q2–4, F, Q1*; La. Cap. / Singer (conj. Jackson)*
6 Go] Q2–4, F, Q1*; Go, go Theobald*   10 lesser] Q2*; lesse* Q3–4, F*; a lesse* F2   12 SD *Exeunt*] *Hanmer; Exit* Q2–4, F*;
no* SD, Q1

Act 4, Scene 4
Location Scene continues.

2 pastry Room where pie paste was prepared;
compare 'pantry', 'buttery'.

3 second cock The conventional times of
cockcrowing were (1) midnight, (2) three a.m., (3)
an hour before day (Kittredge).

4 curfew bell Strictly, curfew (French 'couvre
feu') was rung at eight in the evening, but the term
was loosely used for other ringings. Perhaps all
Shakespeare means is that the same bell (the curfew
bell) was used for the 'matin bell'. In any case,
'three a'clock' is extremely early; Q1 correctly reads
'four a clocke'.

5 baked meats pasties, meat pies.

5 Angelica Either the name of Lady Capulet or
the Nurse, probably the Nurse's since she answers.
If it is the Nurse, Spencer suggests an ironic/comic

contrast with Angelica the pagan princess 'of
exquisite beauty and heartless coquetry' in Ariosto's
Orlando Furioso.

6 cot-quean Used of a man who usurped the
place of housewife. Jackson objects that the Nurse's
speech is too familiar and rude as addressed to her
master and should be assigned to Lady Capulet.
This misses the Nurse's privileged position as an
'ancient' retainer – comparable to that of an
'allowed fool'. Capulet's bustling on the eve of a
wedding is imitated by Pisaro in Haughton's
Englishmen for My Money (1598; MSR, 2241–6).

8 watching loss of sleep (with play in 9 and 12
on 'watched' (= stayed awake) and 'watch'
(= keep an eye on, prevent)).

11 mouse-hunt Literally, a weasel, but here
= woman-chaser. 'Mouse' was an amorous term of
endearment for a woman.

CAPULET A jealous hood, a jealous hood!

Enter three or four [SERVINGMEN] *with spits and logs and baskets.*

                                           Now, fellow,
    What is there?
FIRST SERVINGMAN Things for the cook, sir, but I know not what.   15
CAPULET Make haste, make haste.

                              [*Exit First Servingman*]
                Sirrah, fetch drier logs.
    Call Peter, he will show thee where they are.
SECOND SERVINGMAN I have a head, sir, that will find out logs,
    And never trouble Peter for the matter.
CAPULET Mass, and well said, a merry whoreson, ha!   20
    Thou shalt be loggerhead.

            [*Exeunt Second Servingman and any others*]
              Good faith, 'tis day.
    The County will be here with music straight,
    For so he said he would.

              (*Play music* [*within*].)
               I hear him near.
    Nurse! Wife! What ho! What, Nurse, I say!

Enter Nurse.

    Go waken Juliet, go and trim her up,   25
    I'll go and chat with Paris. Hie, make haste,

13–14 A jealous...there?] *As Capell (after Q1); one line, Q2–4; two lines, ending* hood / ...there? F; A Ielous hood, a Ielous hood: How now sirra? / What haue you there? Q1   13 SD] *Placed as in Cam. (after Capell); after 14,* Q2–4, F; *Enter Seruingman with Logs & Coales.* Q1 (*before 13*)   13 SD SERVINGMEN] *Cam. (after Capell); not in Q2–4, F;* Seruingman Q1   14 What is] Q2–4; what F; What haue you Q1; whats F2   15 SH FIRST SERVINGMAN] *Capell (subst.); Fel.* Q2–4, F; *Ser:* Q1   15] Q2–4, F; Forsooth Logs. Q1   16 haste. Sirrah,] Q5 (*subst.*); haste sirra, Q2–4; hast, sirrah, F   16 SD] *Capell (subst.); no SD,* Q2–4, F, Q1   17] Q2–4, F; Will will tell thee where thou shalt fetch them. Q1   18 SH SECOND SERVINGMAN] *Capell (subst.); Fel.* Q2–4, F; *Ser:* Q1 (*only one Servingman in* Q1)   21 Thou] Q3–4, F, Q1; Twou Q2   21 SD] *This edn (after Capell, following 19); no SD,* Q2–4, F; *Exit.* Q1 (*after 18;* Q1 *omits 19*)   21 faith] Q4; father Q2–3, F   23 SD within] *Cam. (after Capell, following 22); SD after 21,* Q2–4, F; *no SD,* Q1   23–8] Q2–4, F; Gods me hees come, Nurse call vp my daughter. Q1

---

13 **jealous hood** Meaning uncertain, probably = jealous woman; 'one who wears jealousy all the time as if it were a hood' (Kittredge), citing Greene's *Mamillia*, Pt II (1593; II, 292), in which an old jealous husband is described as wearing 'a jelous cap'. See supplementary note.
20 **Mass** i.e by the mass.

21 **loggerhead** (1) the head of the logging contingent; (2) blockhead (the Second Servingman has implied (18) that his head has a natural affinity to a block of wood).
21 ***faith** See supplementary note.
22 **straight** immediately.

Make haste, the bridegroom he is come already,
Make haste, I say.   [*Exit*]

[4.5]

NURSE Mistress, what mistress! Juliet! Fast, I warrant her, she.
Why, lamb! why, lady! fie, you slug-a-bed!
Why, love, I say! madam! sweet heart! why, bride!
What, not a word? You take your pennyworths now;
Sleep for a week, for the next night I warrant   5
The County Paris hath set up his rest
That you shall rest but little. God forgive me!
Marry and amen! How sound is she asleep!
I needs must wake her. Madam, madam, madam!
Ay, let the County take you in your bed,   10
He'll fright you up, i'faith. Will it not be?
        [*Draws back the curtains.*]
What, dressed, and in your clothes, and down again?
I must needs wake you. Lady, lady, lady!
Alas, alas! Help, help! my lady's dead!
O weraday that ever I was born!   15
Some aqua-vitae, ho! My lord! My lady!

        [*Enter Mother,* LADY CAPULET.]

LADY CAPULET What noise is here?
NURSE   O lamentable day!

27–8] *As* F; *one line*, Q2–4   28 SD] *Rowe; no* SD, Q2–4, F, Q1   Act 4, Scene 5 4.5] *Pope; no scene division,* Q2–4,
F, Q1   Location] *Riverside (after Rowe);* SCENE *draws and discovers* Juliet *on a Bed.* / *Rowe;* SCENE *changes to Juliet's
Chamber,* Juliet *on a bed.* / *Theobald; Anti-room of* Juliet's *Chamber. Door of the Chamber open, and* Juliet *upon her Bed.*
/ *Capell*   1–16] Q2–4, F; Goe, get you gone. What lambe, What Lady birde? *fast I warrant. What* Iuliet? well, let
the County take you in your bed: yee sleepe for a weeke now, but the next night, the Countie *Paris* hath set vp his rest
that you shal rest but little. What lambe I say, fast still: what Lady, Loue, what bride, what Iuliet? Gods me how sound
she sleeps? Nay then I see I must wake you indeed. Whats heere, laide on your bed, drest in your cloathes and down,
ah me, alack the day, some Aqua vitæ hoe. Q1   1 mistress! Juliet!] *Rowe;* mistris, Iuliet, Q2–4; Mistris? Iuliet? F; mistris
Iuliet! *Daniel*   7 little. God] Q5 (little: God); little, God Q2–4, F   9 needs must] Q2; must needs Q3–4, F; must Q1
11 SD] *Capell; no* SD, Q2–4, F, Q1   15 weraday] *Kittredge;* wereaday Q2; weladay Q3; weladay Q4, F; alack the day
Q1   16 SD] F, Q1; *no* SD, Q2–4   17 SH LADY CAPULET] *Rowe;* Mo. Q2–4, F *(throughout scene, except* / M. / *at* 24
in Q2–3, F*)* / *Nur:* Alack the day, shees dead, shees dead,
shees dead. / *Moth:* Accurst, vnhappy, miserable time. / *Enter Oldeman.* / *Cap:* Come, come, make hast, wheres my
daughter? / *Moth:* Ah shees dead, shees dead. / *Cap:* Stay, let me see, all pale and wan. / Accursed time, vnfortunate
olde man. Q1

Act 4, Scene 5
Location Scene continues.
1 Fast Fast asleep. Compare the Nurse's
discovery of Juliet in Brooke (2403–23).
4 pennyworths i.e. what little you can get.
6 set…rest resolved to play the limit (a term
from the card game of primero), but with obvious

bawdy double meaning. Nashe (*Terrors of the Night*
(1594), *Works*, I, 384–5) makes the same play on 'set
up' and 'rest'.
7–8 God…amen A half-hearted apology for
the sexual innuendo, an offence she immediately
repeats in 'take you' (10) and 'fright [= freight] you
up' (11). Compare 1.3.3–4.

LADY CAPULET What is the matter?
NURSE   Look, look! O heavy day!
LADY CAPULET O me, O me, my child, my only life!
          Revive, look up, or I will die with thee.   20
          Help, help! Call help.

Enter Father [CAPULET].

CAPULET For shame, bring Juliet forth, her lord is come.
NURSE She's dead, deceased, she's dead, alack the day!
LADY CAPULET Alack the day, she's dead, she's dead, she's dead!
CAPULET Hah, let me see her. Out alas, she's cold,   25
          Her blood is settled, and her joints are stiff:
          Life and these lips have long been separated;
          Death lies on her like an untimely frost
          Upon the sweetest flower of all the field.
NURSE O lamentable day!
LADY CAPULET   O woeful time!   30
CAPULET Death that hath tane her hence to make me wail
          Ties up my tongue and will not let me speak.

Enter FRIAR [LAWRENCE] *and the* COUNTY [PARIS *with the*
                    MUSICIANS].

FRIAR LAWRENCE Come, is the bride ready to go to church?
CAPULET Ready to go, but never to return. –
          O son, the night before thy wedding day   35
          Hath Death lain with thy wife. There she lies,
          Flower as she was, deflowerèd by him.
          Death is my son-in-law, Death is my heir,

---

21 SD] Q2–4, F; *Enter Oldeman.* Q1   22 SH CAPULET] Q1; *Fa.* Q2–4, F (*throughout rest of scene, except* / *Fat.* / *at 59*)
23 dead, deceased] *Rowe*; dead: deceast Q2–4, F   29 field.] Q2–4, F; field. / Accursed time! unfortunate old man! *Pope*
(*from* Q1)   32 SD *Enter...*COUNTY] Q2–4, F; *Enter Fryer and Paris.* Q1   32 SD *with the* MUSICIANS] Q4; *not in* Q2–3,
F, Q1   33 SH FRIAR LAWRENCE] Q2–4, F; *Par:* Q1   36 wife] Q2–4, F; bride Q1, *Steevens (1778)*   36 There] Q2–4,
F; see, where Q1; see thdre F2   37 deflowered] *Steevens (1793, after Johnson)*; deflowred Q2–4, F; Deflowerd Q1;
deflowred now F2   38–40] Q2–4, F; Death is my Sonne in Law, to him I giue all that I haue. Q1

25 **Out** An exclamation of lament. Compare
Brooke 'out alas' (2424).
28–9 Dowden (from W. J. Craig) compares
Marlowe, *Jew of Malta* 1.2.378–80: 'A faire young
maid scarce fourteene yeares of age, / The sweetest
flower in *Citherea's* field, / Cropt from the pleasures
of the fruitfull earth'.
30 **O lamentable day!** Compare Brooke
(2459–60): 'If ever there hath been a lamentable day, / A day ruthfull, unfortunate, and
fatall,...'
31–2 Compare Brooke (2451–4).
37 **deflowerèd** Quadrisyllabic.
38 **Death...son-in-law** The theme of death as
Juliet's paramour, earlier broached in 1.5.134,
3.2.137, and 3.5.200–1, is picked up again in
5.3.102–5. See note on 5.3.92–115, where the
influence of Daniel's *Rosamond* is suggested.

My daughter he hath wedded. I will die,
And leave him all; life, living, all is Death's.   40
PARIS Have I thought long to see this morning's face,
And doth it give me such a sight as this?
LADY CAPULET Accursed, unhappy, wretched, hateful day!
Most miserable hour that e'er time saw
In lasting labour of his pilgrimage!   45
But one, poor one, one poor and loving child,
But one thing to rejoice and solace in,
And cruel Death hath catched it from my sight!
NURSE O woe! O woeful, woeful, woeful day!
Most lamentable day, most woeful day   50
That ever, ever, I did yet behold!
O day, O day, O day, O hateful day!
Never was seen so black a day as this.
O woeful day, O woeful day!
PARIS Beguiled, divorcèd, wrongèd, spited, slain!   55
Most detestable Death, by thee beguiled,
By cruel, cruel thee quite overthrown!
O love! O life! not life, but love in death!
CAPULET Despised, distressèd, hated, martyred, killed!

---

40 all; life, living,] *Collier (after Capell)* ; all life liuing, Q2–3, F; all, life, liuing, Q4; all; life leauing, *Capell*   41 long]
Q3–4, F, Q1; loue Q2   42–95] Q2–4, F; And doth it now present such prodegies? / Accurst, vnhappy, miserable man,
/ Forlorne, forsaken, destitute I am: / Borne to the world to be a slaue in it. / Distrest, remediles, and vnfortunate.
/ O heauens, O nature, wherefore did you make me, / To liue so vile, so wretched as I shall. / *Cap:* O heere she lies
that was our hope, our ioy, / And being dead, dead sorrow nips vs all. / *All at once cry out and wring their hands.* /
All cry: And all our ioy, and all our hope is dead, / Dead, lost, vndone, absented, wholy fled. / *Cap:* Cruel, vniust,
impartiall destinies, / Why to this day haue you preseru'd my life? / To see my hope, my stay, my ioy, my life, / Depriude
of sence, of life, of all by death, / Cruell, vniust, impartiall destinies. / *Cap:* O sad fac'd sorrow map of misery, / Why
this sad time haue I desird to see. / This day, this vniust, this impartiall day / Wherein I hop'd to see my comfort full,
/ To be depriude by suddaine destinie. / *Moth:* O woe, alacke, distrest, why should I liue? / To see this day, this miserable
day. / Alacke the time that euer I was borne, / To be partaker of this destinie. / Alacke the day, alacke and welladay.
/ *Fr:* O peace for shame, if not for charity. / Your daughter liues in peace and happines, / And it is vaine to wish it
otherwise. / Come sticke your Rosemary in this dead coarse, / And as the custome of our Country is, / In all her best
and sumptuous ornaments, / Conuay her where her Ancestors lie tomb'd, / *Cap:* Let it be so, come wofull sorrow mates,
/ Let vs together taste this bitter fate. Q1 *(Capulet's third speech must belong to Paris)*   51 behold] Q3–4, F; bedold
Q2; bedole *conj. this edn*   54] Q2–4, F; O wofull day! O wofull, wofull day! *Daniel (conj. Fleay and Allen)*   57 cruel
thee] F2; cruell, thee Q2; cruell thee, Q3–4, F   58] Q2–4, F; O life! not life, O loue! but loue in death! *conj. Dowden*

---

41 thought *long been impatient. Compare
Brooke (2274): 'And now his longing hart thinkes
long for theyr appoynted howre.' Q2 'loue' has been
defended (Spencer) as a possible vocative, but the
close parallel between Brooke and Q1 makes a good
case for 'long'.
43–64 These lines of exclamatory and repetitive
lament, turning on the themes of time, day, life and
love, strike a modern audience as unbearably

artificial and appear almost as a parody of grief. See,
supplementary note.
48 catched snatched.
56 detestable Accented on the first syllable.
58 O love...death 'Not "my life", as I have
so often called you, but still in death my loved one'
(Deighton). H. Levin (*SQ* 11 (1960), 6) compares
Kyd, *Spanish Tragedy* 3.2.2: 'Oh life, no life, but
lively fourme of death'.

Uncomfortable time, why cam'st thou now   60
To murder, murder our solemnity?
O child, O child! my soul, and not my child!
Dead art thou. Alack, my child is dead,
And with my child my joys are burièd.
FRIAR LAWRENCE Peace ho, for shame! Confusion's cure lives not   65
In these confusions. Heaven and yourself
Had part in this fair maid, now heaven hath all,
And all the better is it for the maid:
Your part in her you could not keep from death,
But heaven keeps his part in eternal life.   70
The most you sought was her promotion,
For 'twas your heaven she should be advanced,
And weep ye now, seeing she is advanced
Above the clouds, as high as heaven itself?
O, in this love, you love your child so ill   75
That you run mad, seeing that she is well.
She's not well married that lives married long,
But she's best married that dies married young.
Dry up your tears, and stick your rosemary
On this fair corse, and as the custom is,   80
And in her best array, bear her to church;
For though fond nature bids us all lament,
Yet nature's tears are reason's merriment.
CAPULET All things that we ordainèd festival,

---

63 Dead art thou.] *Theobald (subst., reading* Dead art Thou! dead;*);* Dead art thou, Q2–4, F*;* Dead, dead, art thou! *conj.*
Malone   65–83] Q2–4, F*;* Pope *substitutes* Q1*'s version of this speech (see 42–95, above), omitting only* if not for charity,
*and inserting 66–7 (*heauen…all,*) from* Q2–4, F *following the Friar's third line in* Q1   65 Confusion's cure] *Theobald;*
confusions care Q2*;* confusions, care Q3–4*;* confusions: Care F*;* Confusions? Care *Rowe*   65 lives] Q2–4, F*;* lies *conj.*
Lettsom   66 confusions.] Q5 *(subst.)*; confusions Q2*;* confusions, Q3–4, F   81 And in] Q2–4, F*;* In all Q1, *Capell;* All
in *Rowe*   82 fond] F2*;* some Q2–4, F*;* soon *conj. Dowden*   82 us all] Q2–4*;* all vs F

---

60 **Uncomfortable** Causing discomfort.

61 **solemnity** festive (marriage) rites.

65 **Confusion's *cure** The remedy for this state
of frenzied disorder, or (Kittredge) calamity. Note
play on 'confusions' (= unrestrained outcries) in
66. Theobald's 'cure' for Q2–4, F 'care' has never
been challenged. Compare 4.1.45.

71 **promotion** material advancement.

72 **advanced** promoted (raised socially through
an advantageous marriage).

75 **in this love** in your concern for her merely
earthly welfare (as compared with the love of
heaven).

76 **is well** Proverbially spoken of the dead;
compare Tilley H347 ('He is well since he is in

heaven'), 5.1.17, and *Ant.* 2.5.32–3: 'we use / To
say the dead are well'.

77 **not…long** i.e. a long marriage is not
necessarily a good marriage. Does the Friar slip in
associating Juliet (78) with one 'that dies married
young'?

79 **rosemary** See 2.4.173 n. and 95 SD below.

82–3 'For though human nature, which is weak
("fond") in judgment, prompts us all to lament,
yet reason bids us rejoice – for "death is to me
advantage" [Phil. 1.21, Bishops']' (Kittredge). On
'*fond', see supplementary note.

84 **ordainèd festival** intended to be festive.
Compare Brooke (2507–14). Echoed by Munday,
Death of…Huntingdon (1598; MSR, 831–2).

Turn from their office to black funeral: 85
Our instruments to melancholy bells,
Our wedding cheer to a sad burial feast;
Our solemn hymns to sullen dirges change;
Our bridal flowers serve for a buried corse;
And all things change them to the contrary.   90
FRIAR LAWRENCE Sir, go you in, and, madam, go with him,
And go, Sir Paris. Every one prepare
To follow this fair corse unto her grave.
The heavens do low'r upon you for some ill;
Move them no more by crossing their high will.   95
        [*They all, but the Nurse and the Musicians, go forth,
        casting rosemary on her, and shutting the curtains*]
FIRST MUSICIAN Faith, we may put up our pipes and be gone.
NURSE Honest good fellows, ah put up, put up,
For well you know this is a pitiful case.   [*Exit*]
FIRST MUSICIAN Ay, by my troth, the case may be amended.

        Enter PETER.

PETER Musicians, O musicians, 'Heart's ease', 'Heart's ease'! O,   100

---

87 burial] Q2–4, F; funerall Q5   95 SD] Q1 *(and the Musicians / inserted by NS from Q4 SD: Exeunt manent Musici.);
Fxeunt manet. Q2; Exeunt: manet. Q3; Exeunt F; following this SD Q1 adds: Enter Musitions.*   96 SH FIRST MUSICIAN]
Capell; Musi. Q2–4; *Mu.* F; 96 *not in* Q1   98 SD] Q1; *no SD,* Q2–4, F   99 SH FIRST MUSICIAN] *Capell; Fid.* Q2–4;
Mu. F; *I.* Q1   99 by my] Q3–4, F, Q1; my my Q2   99 amended.] F; amended. / *Exit omnes.* Q2; amended. / *Exeunt
omnes.* Q3–4; mended. Q1   99 SD PETER] Q4, F; *Will Kemp* Q2–3; *Seruingman* Q1; *another* Servant *Capell*   100 SH
PETER] Q2–4, F; *Ser:* Q1, *Capell*   100–4] Q2–4, F; Alack alack what shal I doe, come Fidlers play me some mery dumpe.
Q1   100–1] *As prose, Pope; two lines, ending* ease / ...ease Q2–4; *three lines, ending* Musitions / ...ease / ...ease F
100 'Heart's...ease'!] *Pope;* harts ease, harts ease, Q2–4; Hearts ease, hearts ease, F

---

85 **office** function.
87 **cheer** fare, viands.
88 **sullen** mournful, heavy.
89 **corse** corpse.
94 **ill** sin (committed by you).
95 **Move** Provoke.
96 **put...pipes** Proverbial (Tilley P345), figurative for 'pack up' or 'give up (one's hope or intention)'. There is no necessary implication that any of the musicians is a piper. Both the Q2–4 speech headings (see collation) and the generically descriptive names assigned to them by Peter (see 124, 126, 129) indicate they are string-players, one of whom, as Gibbons suggests, may have doubled as a singer. See supplementary note.
98 **pitiful case** state of affairs arousing pity.
99 **the case...amended** (1) the state of affairs might be improved; (2) the box, or bag, in which I keep my instrument might benefit from repair. Dowden compares *WT* 4.4.814–15.
99 Following this line Q2 inserts *Exit [Exeunt*

Q3–4] *omnes.*, obviously wrongly as the text now stands. Dover Wilson (in NS) suggests (1) that Shakespeare originally intended the scene to end here (99 is a suitable exit line), but then added some 'fat' for Will Kemp as Peter; or (2) that, because of the Nashe connections noted above (96), Nashe himself was responsible for adding lines 100–38. In view of the fairly numerous Nashe echoes throughout the play, the second proposal seems highly unlikely.
99 SD *Enter* PETER. Q2–3 read *Enter Will Kemp.*, the name of the well known comedian of Shakespeare's company, who played Peter. He also played Dogberry in *Ado*, where his name occurs in the speech headings of 4.2, and probably Falstaff.
100 'Heart's ease' An earlier song, of which only the tune survives (see F. W. Sternfeld, *Music in Shakespearean Tragedy*, rev. edn, 1967, p. 102). *Wily Beguiled* (anon., *c.* 1602) associates 'hearts ease' with having money: 'O this red chink, and silver coine' (MSR, 4–6).

and you will have me live, play 'Heart's ease'.

FIRST MUSICIAN Why 'Heart's ease'?

PETER O musicians, because my heart itself plays 'My heart is full'.
O play me some merry dump to comfort me.

MUSICIANS Not a dump we, 'tis no time to play now. 105

PETER You will not then?

FIRST MUSICIAN No.

PETER I will then give it you soundly.

FIRST MUSICIAN What will you give us?

PETER No money, on my faith, but the gleek; I will give you the 110
minstrel.

FIRST MUSICIAN Then will I give you the serving-creature.

PETER Then will I lay the serving-creature's dagger on your pate. I will
carry no crotchets, I'll re you, I'll fa you. Do you note me?

FIRST MUSICIAN And you re us and fa us, you note us. 115

SECOND MUSICIAN Pray you put up your dagger, and put out your
wit.

PETER Then have at you with my wit! I will dry-beat you with an iron

---

102 SH FIRST MUSICIAN] *Capell; Fidler.* Q2–4; *Mu.* F 103–4] *As prose, Pope; two lines, ending* full / ...me Q2–4;
two lines, ending Musitions / ...full F *(omitting* O play...me.) 103 'My...full'] *Distinguished as a quotation, Pope*
103 full] Q2–3, F; full of woe Q4, *Pope* 105 SH MUSICIANS] *Hoppe; Minstrels.* Q2–4; *Mu.* F; *1.* QI; *1. M. / Capell*
107, 109, 112, 115, 136 SH FIRST MUSICIAN] *Capell; Minst. / Minstrel. / or / Min.* Q2–4; *Mu.* F; *1.* QI *(omitting 112,*
136) 110–15] Q2–4, F; The fidler, Ile re you, Ile fa you, Ile sol you. QI 110–11] *As prose, Theobald (after Pope);*
two lines, ending gleeke / ...Minstrell Q2–4, F 113–14] *As prose,* Q4, F; *three lines, ending* pate / ...fa / ...me Q2;
three lines (first two prose), ending your / ...fa / ...me Q3 116–17] *not in* QI 116 SH SECOND MUSICIAN] F3;
2. M. Q2–4, F 118 SH PETER] Q4; Q2–3, F *continue* Then...wit. *to Second Musician* 118–19 I...dagger.] *As prose,*
QI, *Theobald; one line,* Q2–4; *two lines, ending* wit / ...Dagger F 118–19 an iron wit] Q2–4, F; my wodden wit QI

---

103 'My heart is full' As Steevens noted,
probably a reference to a song (only later printed)
called 'Ballad of Two Lovers', of which the last line
of the first stanza was 'Hey, ho! my heart is full of
woe.' Q4 reads 'My heart is full of woe' and is
followed, perhaps correctly, by many eds.

104 merry dump An oxymoron, 'dump' meaning a mournful song. The sudden comic incongruity
focuses the tone of the remainder of the scene.
Compare 'doleful dumps' in 121; in Painter (p.
132), on the discovery of Juliet's supposed death,
those attending were struck 'into sutch sorrowfull
dumpes' that they could neither speak nor weep.

108 soundly thoroughly (with play on 'berate
with words [i.e. 'sounds']' and on their profession
as musicians).

110 gleek scoffing rebuke (from 'to give the
gleek' = to scoff or jeer at).

110–11 give...minstrel i.e. describe you as a
worthless fellow. A 1572 Act of Parliament included
minstrels along with bear-keepers, fencers, etc., as
rogues, vagabonds, and sturdy beggars (Dowden).

A play on 'gleek' and 'gleeman' (= minstrel) has
been suggested, though the latter word was archaic
by Shakespeare's time.

112 serving-creature A riposte in 'kind'
('creature' for 'man' being intentionally
derogatory).

114 carry no crotchets (1) put up with no
whims or airs; (2) take no part in singing quarter-
notes or such frivolities.

114 re...fa Notes of the scale used figuratively
as verbs meaning 'to give you a beating' (with possible play on 'ray' (= befoul) and 'fay' (= cleanse),
Ulrici).

114 note mark, pay heed to (with play on 're'
and 'fa' above and, in 115, on 'note' = (1) reprimand; (2) score (i.e. make us look like a musical
score with nicks and bruises)).

116 put up...put out sheathe...(1) lay out,
display; (2) extinguish (Peter answers in terms of
(2)).

118 dry-beat See 3.1.71–2 n.

wit, and put up my iron dagger. Answer me like men:

'When griping griefs the heart doth wound,   120
And doleful dumps the mind oppress,
Then music with her silver sound –'

Why 'silver sound'? why 'music with her silver sound'? What say
you, Simon Catling?

FIRST MUSICIAN Marry, sir, because silver hath a sweet sound.   125

PETER Prates! What say you, Hugh Rebeck?

SECOND MUSICIAN I say 'silver sound' because musicians sound for
silver.

PETER Prates too! What say you, James Soundpost?

THIRD MUSICIAN Faith, I know not what to say.   130

PETER O, I cry you mercy, you are the singer; I will say for you: It
is 'music with her silver sound' because musicians have no gold
for sounding.

'Then music with her silver sound
With speedy help doth lend redress.'   *Exit*   135

FIRST MUSICIAN What a pestilent knave is this same!

SECOND MUSICIAN Hang him, Jack! Come, we'll in here, tarry for the
mourners, and stay dinner.

Exeunt

119] Q1 *breaks Peter's speech at this point with* / *1* Lets heare.   120–2] *As verse*, Q1 ; *one line (omitting 121)*, Q2–4 ; *as prose*, F *(omitting 121)*   120 griefs] Q2–4, F ; griefe Q1 *(as in Edwardes)*, Hanmer   121] Q1, Capell ; *not in* Q2–4, F   123–4] *As prose*, Q4, F ; *one line*, Q2–3 ; *as prose in* Q1 *version*   124 Simon Catling] Q2–4, F ; Simon found Pot Q1   125 SH FIRST MUSICIAN] *Johnson* ; Minst. Q2 ; Min. Q3–4 ; Mu. F ; *1*. Q1   125 Marry] Q5 ; Mary Q2–4, F   126 Prates!] *Ulrici* ; Prates, Q2 ; Pratest, Q3 ; Pratee, Q4 ; Pretie, Q1   126 Hugh Rebeck] *Rowe* ; Hugh Rebick Q2–4, F ; Mathew minikine Q1   127 SH SECOND MUSICIAN] F3 ; *2*. M. Q2–4, F ; *2*. Q1   129 Prates too!] *Ulrici* ; Prates to, Q2 ; Pratest to, Q3, F ; Pratee to, Q4 ; Prettie too: Q1 ; Pratest too, F3   129 James Soundpost] Q2–4, F *(subst.)* ; Samuel Sound-board / *Pope*   130 SH THIRD MUSICIAN] F ; *3* M. Q2–4 ; *3*. Q1   131–3] *As prose, Pope* ; *three lines, ending* singer / ...sound / ...sounding Q2–4, F ; *as prose in* Q1 *version*   134–5] *As verse, Johnson* ; *one line*, Q2–4 ; *as prose*, F ; *not in* Q1 ; *The Musick...Sound / Doth lend Redress. / Theobald*   135 SD] Q2–4, F, Q1 ; *Exit, singing. / Theobald*   136–8] Q2–4, F ; Farewell and be hangd: come lets goe. Q1   137 SH SECOND MUSICIAN] F4 ; M. *2*. Q2–4, F ; *1*. Q1   137 him, Jack!] *Theobald (subst.)* ; him Iack, Q2–4, F   138 SD] Q4, Q1 ; Exit. Q2–3, F

120–2 The opening three lines, with slight
variations, of a song by Richard Edwardes, 'In
commendation of Musick', printed in *The Paradyse
of Daynty Devises* (1576; ed. Rollins, p. 63); the
fourth line is quoted below at 135. Line 121,
omitted in Q2–4, F, is supplied from Q1.

124 Catling 'A small lute [or fiddle] string
made out of catgut' (Steevens).

126 Prates (He) talks but says nothing. See
collation for other readings. See suppl. note.

126 Rebeck An early, three-stringed form of
fiddle.

127 sound i.e. play or sing.

129 Soundpost 'A small peg of wood fixed
beneath the bridge of a [fiddle], serving as a support
for the belly and as a connecting part between this
and the back' (*OED*).

131 cry...singer beg your pardon for asking a
'singer' to speak ('say').

132–3 have...sounding (1) receive no gold for
playing or singing; (2) have no gold for jingling in
their pockets. See supplementary note on 4.5.96.

138 stay dinner wait till dinner is served.

[**5.1**] *Enter* ROMEO.

ROMEO If I may trust the flattering truth of sleep,
     My dreams presage some joyful news at hand.
     My bosom's lord sits lightly in his throne,
     And all this day an unaccustomed spirit
     Lifts me above the ground with cheerful thoughts.   5
     I dreamt my lady came and found me dead
     (Strange dream that gives a dead man leave to think!),
     And breathed such life with kisses in my lips
     That I revived and was an emperor.
     Ah me, how sweet is love itself possessed,   10
     When but love's shadows are so rich in joy!

       Enter Romeo's man [BALTHASAR, *booted*].

     News from Verona! How now, Balthasar?
     Dost thou not bring me letters from the Friar?
     How doth my lady? Is my father well?
     How doth my Juliet? That I ask again,   15
     For nothing can be ill if she be well.
BALTHASAR Then she is well and nothing can be ill:
     Her body sleeps in Capels' monument,
     And her immortal part with angels lives.

Act 5, Scene 1   5.1] *Rowe; no act or scene division*, Q2–4, F; Q1 *indicates a break by a row of printer's ornaments above opening* SD   Location] *Rowe, Capell*   1 flattering truth of] Q2–4, F; flattering Eye of Q1, *Malone*; flattery of *Pope (after Otway)*; flattering ruth of *Warburton; etc. (see Cam.²)*   2 at hand.] F (at hand:); at hand, Q2–4; to come, Q1   3 lord] Q4, Q1; L. Q2–3, F   3 throne,] Q1; throne: Q2–4, F   4–5] Q2–4, F; And I am comforted with pleasing dreames. Q1   4 this day an] Q2–4; thisan day an F; this winged F2   7 (Strange...think!),] F, Q1 *(reading* dreames *and* giue*)*; Strange...thinke, Q2–4 (Q4 *reading* dreames)   7 dead man] Q3–4, F, Q1; deadman Q2   10–11] *not in* Q1   11 SD BALTHASAR, *booted*] *from* Q1 SD: *Enter Balthasar his man booted.; Enter* Romeos man. Q2–3, F; *Enter* Romeos man Balthazer. Q4   12 Balthasar] Q1; *Balthazer* Q2–4, F; *Balthazar* F2   15 doth my Juliet] *Pope*; doth my Lady *Iuliet* Q2–4, F; fares my *Iuliet* Q1, *Steevens*   17 SH BALTHASAR] Q1; *Man.* Q2–4, F *(throughout scene)*   18 Capel's] *Rolfe*; Capels Q2–4, F, Q1; *Capulet's* F4; Capels' *Malone*   19 lives] Q2–4; liue F; dwell Q1 *(reading parts)*

Act 5, Scene 1
  Location Mantua. A street.
  1–9 J. W. Hales (*Quarterly Review* 134 (1873), 252–3) compares Chaucer's *Troilus and Criseyde*, V, 1163–9, where Troilus has a similar false presentiment of good fortune. No suggestion of this in Brooke or Painter.
  1 If...sleep 'If I may trust that as true which sleep has revealed to me of a flattering nature' (Delius). Some eds. unnecessarily prefer Q1 'Eye' for 'truth'. Romeo has earlier (2.2.139–41) spoken of the illusive nature of dreams (compare Tilley D587, 588), but, ironically, morning dreams were proverbially believed to be truthful (Tilley D591).

  3 bosom's lord...throne Love (or Cupid)... heart. Compare *Oth.* 3.3.448: 'Yield up, O love, thy crown and hearted throne.'
  4 unaccustomed spirit unwonted liveliness (high spirits).
  5 Lifts...ground i.e. he is figuratively walking on air.
  8 breathed...lips Malone compares Marlowe, *Hero and Leander*, II, 3: 'He kist her, and breath'd life into her lips.'
  11 love's shadows i.e. dreams.
  14 lady Juliet, not his mother (see 15).
  15 How...Juliet? See supplementary note.

I saw her laid low in her kindred's vault,   20
And presently took post to tell it you.
O pardon me for bringing these ill news,
Since you did leave it for my office, sir.
ROMEO Is it e'en so? then I defy you, stars! *night*
Thou knowest my lodging, get me ink and paper,   25
And hire post-horses; I will hence tonight.
BALTHASAR I do beseech you, sir, have patience:
Your looks are pale and wild, and do import
Some misadventure.
ROMEO   Tush, thou art deceived.
Leave me, and do the thing I bid thee do.   30
Hast thou no letters to me from the Friar?
BALTHASAR No, my good lord.
ROMEO   No matter, get thee gone,
And hire those horses; I'll be with thee straight.

                                        Exit [Balthasar]

Well, Juliet, I will lie with thee tonight.
Let's see for means. O mischief, thou art swift   35
To enter in the thoughts of desperate men!
I do remember an apothecary,
And hereabouts 'a dwells, which late I noted
In tattered weeds, with overwhelming brows,
Culling of simples; meagre were his looks,   40

20–3] Q2–4, F; Pardon me Sir, that am the Messenger of such bad tidings. Q1   **24** e'en] *Collier;* in Q2; euen Q3–4, F, Q1   **24** defy you] *Pope;* denie you Q2–4, F; defie my Q1   **27**] Q2–4, F; Pardon me Sir, I will not leaue you thus, Q1, *Steevens (1793);* Pardon me, sir, I dare not leaue you thus. *Pope (dare from the concluding line of Balthasar's speech in Q1:* I dare not, nor I will not leaue you yet.*)*   **30–3**] Q2–4, F; Doo as I bid thee, get me incke and paper, / And hyre those horse: stay not I say. Q1   **32** my good] Q2–4, F; good my *Rowe*   **32** No matter] Q2–4; Mo matter F   **33** SD] Q1 *(placed as in Rowe);* Exit. *(after* lord., *32),* Q2–4, F   **35–6** O...men!] *not in* Q1   **36** thoughts] Q2–4, F; thought *Rowe*   **37–46**] Q2–4, F; As I doo remember / Here dwells a Pothecarie whom oft I noted / As I past by, whose needie shop is stufft / With beggerly accounts of emptie boxes: / And in the same an *Aligarta* hangs, Q1   **38** hereabouts] F3; here abouts Q2–4, F; here about Q1   **38** 'a dwells] Q2–4; dwells F; he dwells Q1, F2   **38** which] Q2–4, F; whom Q1, *Pope*

---

21 presently took post at once set out with post-horses (see 26).

23 for my office as my duty.

24 *e'en Q2 'in' seems to be a Shakespearean spelling for 'e'en'; compare *Ant.* 4.15.73.

24 *defy Q2 'denie' makes good sense (= disown, repudiate (Dowden)), but Q1 'defie' (which receives some support from Brooke (1347), though in an earlier context) is almost universally accepted by eds. since Pope, on the grounds that Romeo is not repudiating judicial astrology but challenging the universe (Dover Wilson) and his own particular fate. Compare 5.3.111.

26 post-horses Horses kept at an inn for hire by travellers or post riders (*OED*). See Brooke (2612).

27 patience Trisyllabic.

34 lie with i.e. (1) in death; (2) as a lover.

35 see for means consider how to accomplish it.

37 apothecary Compare Brooke (2567–88).

39 weeds garments.

39 overwhelming overhanging.

40 Culling of simples Gathering medicinal herbs. There is a powerfully ironic reflection here of Friar Lawrence, another 'culler of simples', whose life-giving potion will turn out to be as fatal as the Apothecary's deadly poison.

40–1 meagre...bones Malone compares Sackville's description of 'Miserie' in his Induction to

Sharp misery had worn him to the bones;
And in his needy shop a tortoise hung,
An alligator stuffed, and other skins
Of ill-shaped fishes, and about his shelves
A beggarly account of empty boxes,   45
Green earthen pots, bladders, and musty seeds,
Remnants of packthread, and old cakes of roses
Were thinly scattered, to make up a show.
Noting this penury, to myself I said,
'And if a man did need a poison now,   50
Whose sale is present death in Mantua,
Here lives a caitiff wretch would sell it him.'
O this same thought did but forerun my need,
And this same needy man must sell it me.
As I remember, this should be the house.   55
Being holiday, the beggar's shop is shut.
What ho, apothecary!

[*Enter* APOTHECARY.]

APOTHECARY   Who calls so loud?

ROMEO Come hither, man. I see that thou art poor.
Hold, there is forty ducats; let me have

---

42 tortoise] Q2–4; Tortoyrs F   44 ill-shaped] *Rowe*; ill shapte Q2–4, F   48 scattered] *Warburton* (scatter'd); scattered
Q2–4, F   50 And] Q1; An Q2–4, F   56 holiday] Q1; holy day Q2–4, F; holy-day *Rowe*   57 SD] F, Q1; *no* SD, Q2–4
58 SH ROMEO] Q3–4, F, Q1; *Kom.* Q2   59 forty ducats] Q2–4, F; twentie duckates Q1

A Mirror for Magistrates (1563; 253–4; ed. L. B.
Campbell): 'His face was leane, and sumdeale
pyned away, / And eke his handes consumed to the
bone.'
42–8 Shakespeare embellishes Brooke's account
of the Apothecary's shop. Malone compares Nashe,
Saffron-Walden (1596; *Works*, III, 67): 'the next rat
he seazed on hee made an Anatomie of,...and after
hangd her over his head in his studie, in stead of
an Apothecaries Crocodile, or dride *Alligatur*'. See
Hogarth's *Marriage-a-la-Mode*, Plate III (for the
alligator, fish, boxes and pots) and his plate of
Sidrophel's house in Butler's *Hudibras* (for the
alligator and tortoise).
45 **beggarly account** poor store or number.
Compare Brooke (2569): 'his boxes were but fewe'.
47 **Remnants of packthread** Bits of stout
twine for tying up bundles.
47 **cakes of roses** Rose leaves dried and pressed
into small cakes. Since they were 'old' they had lost
their fragrance.

50–2 Romeo's recollection of the Apothecary
(37–8) and his earlier thought of his possible utility
suggest that suicide had not been far from his mind
during his banishment – a brilliant touch not in
Brooke or Painter.
50 **And if** If.
51 **Whose...death** The sale of which carries
the punishment of immediate death (to the seller).
52 **caitiff** miserable, pitiable.
56 **Being holiday** This is Shakespeare's detail;
why this Wednesday should have been designated
as a holiday is unexplained.
59 **forty ducats** The ducat was a small gold
coin then worth about ten shillings; forty ducats was
then a substantial sum. Brooke (2577) has 'fiftie
crownes of gold'; Painter's version of Boaistuau (p.
134), 'Fifty Ducates'; Q1, 'twentie duckates'.
Gibbons suggests Shakespeare's 'forty' was
influenced by recollection of the Courtesan's line
in *Err.* 4.3.96: 'For forty ducats is too much to
lose.'

A dram of poison, such soon-speeding gear   60
As will disperse itself through all the veins,
That the life-weary taker may fall dead,
And that the trunk may be discharged of breath
As violently as hasty powder fired
Doth hurry from the fatal cannon's womb.   65
APOTHECARY Such mortal drugs I have, but Mantua's law
Is death to any he that utters them.
ROMEO Art thou so bare and full of wretchedness,
And fearest to die? Famine is in thy cheeks,
Need and oppression starveth in thy eyes,   70
Contempt and beggary hangs upon thy back;
The world is not thy friend, nor the world's law,
The world affords no law to make thee rich;
Then be not poor, but break it and take this.
APOTHECARY My poverty, but not my will, consents.   75
ROMEO I pay thy poverty and not thy will.
APOTHECARY Put this in any liquid thing you will
And drink it off, and if you had the strength
Of twenty men, it would dispatch you straight.
ROMEO There is thy gold, worse poison to men's souls,   80
Doing more murder in this loathsome world,
Than these poor compounds that thou mayst not sell.

60 such soon-speeding] F4; such soone speeding Q2–4, F; some such speeding Q1; such soone spreading Q5
61–5] Q2–4, F; As will dispatch the wearie takers life, / As suddenly as powder being fierd / From forth a Cannons
mouth. Q1   62 life-weary taker] Q5; life-wearie-taker Q2–4, F; wearie takers life Q1   66, 75, 77 SH APOTHECARY] F,
Q1; *Poti.* Q2; *Poti. / or / Po.* Q3–4   69–74] Q2–4, F; And doost thou feare to violate the Law? / The Law is not
thy frend, nor the Lawes frend, / And therefore make no conscience of the law: / Vpon thy backe hangs ragged Miserie,
/ And starued Famine dwelleth in thy cheekes. Q1   69 fearest] Q2–4; fear'st F; doost thou feare Q1   69 die?] F; die,
Q2–4   70 starveth in] Q2–4, F; stareth in *Rowe*³ *(from Otway's* Caius Marius*)*; stare within *Pope*; starteth in *conj. Anon.
(in Cam.)*   71] Q2–4, F; Vpon thy backe hangs ragged Miserie, Q1, *Steevens*   71 hangs upon] Q2–4, F; *see* 69–74
for Q1; hang on F2; hang upon Q5   76 pay] Q4, Q1; pray Q2–3, F   80 There is thy] Q2–4; There's thy F; Hold, take
this Q1   81–4] Q2–4, F; Than this which thou hast giuen me. Goe hye thee hence, / Goe buy the clothes, and get
thee into flesh. Q1   82 mayst] Q4; maiest Q2–3, F

60 dram draught or drink (literally, half a fluid
ounce). In Brooke (2583, 2640) the poison seems to
be a solid.
60 soon-speeding gear quick-working stuff.
Compare Brooke (2585): 'speeding gere'.
61 disperse...veins Seems to echo Daniel's
Rosamond (603); see supplementary note on
5.3.92–115.
63 trunk body (with secondary reference to
'trunk' = a cylindrical case to contain or discharge
explosives (*OED* sv III 11); compare the image of
the cannon in 64–5).
67 any he any man.

67 utters sells.
70 Need and oppression Oppressive poverty
(hendiadys; see Franz 673(c) and compare 'Contempt and beggary' (= contemptible beggarliness)
in 71).
70 starveth 'are hungry' (Dowden).
71 hangs i.e. as in tatters.
74 it i.e. the law.
76 *pay Q2 'pray' may be taken to mean
'intercede with or address', but, as Dyce points out,
'pay' (Q4, Q1) properly looks back to 'take this' in
74.

I sell thee poison, thou hast sold me none.
Farewell, buy food, and get thyself in flesh.

[*Exit Apothecary*]

Come, cordial and not poison, go with me   85
To Juliet's grave, for there must I use thee.   *Exit*

[**5.2**]   *Enter* FRIAR JOHN.

FRIAR JOHN   Holy Franciscan Friar, brother, ho!

Enter [FRIAR] LAWRENCE.

FRIAR LAWRENCE   This same should be the voice of Friar John.
Welcome from Mantua. What says Romeo?
Or if his mind be writ, give me his letter.
FRIAR JOHN   Going to find a barefoot brother out,   5
One of our order, to associate me,
Here in this city visiting the sick,
And finding him, the searchers of the town,
Suspecting that we both were in a house
Where the infectious pestilence did reign,   10
Sealed up the doors, and would not let us forth,
So that my speed to Mantua there was stayed.
FRIAR LAWRENCE   Who bare my letter then to Romeo?
FRIAR JOHN   I could not send it – here it is again –
Nor get a messenger to bring it thee,   15

83 none.] F4; none, Q2–4, F   84 SD] NS; no SD, Q2–4, F, Q1   86 SD] NS; Exeunt. Q2–4, F, Q1   Act 5, Scene 2
5.2] Rowe; no scene division, Q2–4, F; Q1 indicates a break by a row of printer's ornaments above opening SD   Location]
Capell (after Rowe)   0 SD] Q1 (omitting any entry for Friar Lawrence); Enter Frier Iohn to Frier Lawrence. Q2–4, F
1 SH FRIAR JOHN] Capell; Ioh. / or / Iohn. Q2–4, F, Q1 (throughout scene)   1 SD] Theobald (subst., from opening
SD, Q2–4, F); no SD, Q1   2 SH FRIAR LAWRENCE] Capell; Law. Q2–4, F (throughout scene); Laur: Q1 (throughout scene)
8–12] Q2–4, F; Whereas the infectious pestilence remaind: / And being by the Searchers of the Towne / Found and
examinde, we were both shut vp. Q1   14–16] Q2–4, F; I haue them still, and here they are. Q1

85 cordial Medicine which invigorates the
heart. The implication seems to be that the poison
will defend the integrity of love's 'throne' (i.e. the
heart; see 3 above).

Act 5, Scene 2
   Location Verona. Friar Lawrence's cell.
   5–8 These lines are syntactically confusing;
supply 'I' before 'Going' (5) and 'finding' (8).
   5 find...out search for. 'barefoot brother' = a
Franciscan. Compare Brooke (2485–97).
   6 associate me act as my companion. The

Franciscan order required brothers to travel in pairs
as a check on each other's behaviour. Compare
Brooke (2490).
   8 searchers of the town Health officers, whose
duty it was to view dead bodies and report on the
cause of death (*OED* 2e).
   9 house It is not clear whether 'house' = a
monastery (as in Brooke and Painter) or = a private
dwelling.
   12 my speed successful performance (of my
journey).

So fearful were they of infection.

FRIAR LAWRENCE Unhappy fortune! By my brotherhood,
The letter was not nice but full of charge,
Of dear import, and the neglecting it
May do much danger. Friar John, go hence,   20
Get me an iron crow and bring it straight
Unto my cell.

FRIAR JOHN Brother, I'll go and bring it thee.   *Exit*

FRIAR LAWRENCE Now must I to the monument alone,
Within this three hours will fair Juliet wake.   25
She will beshrew me much that Romeo
Hath had no notice of these accidents;
But I will write again to Mantua,
And keep her at my cell till Romeo come,
Poor living corse, closed in a dead man's tomb!   *Exit*   30

[5.3] *Enter* PARIS *and his* PAGE [*with flowers and sweet water and a torch*].

PARIS Give me thy torch, boy. Hence, and stand aloof.
Yet put it out, for I would not be seen.
Under yond yew trees lay thee all along,
Holding thy ear close to the hollow ground,
So shall no foot upon the churchyard tread,   5
Being loose, unfirm with digging up of graves,

---

17 fortune! By] F (Fortune: by); fortune, by Q2–4   19–23] Q2–4, F; Goe get thee hence, and get me presently / A
[*catchword* As] spade and mattocke. / *Iohn:* Well I will presently go fetch thee them. Q1   25–30] Q2–4, F; Least that
the Ladie should before I come / Be wakde from sleepe. I will hye / To free her from that Tombe of miserie. Q1   Act
5, Scene 3   5.3] *Rowe; no scene division,* Q2–4, F; Q1 *indicates a break by a row of printer's ornaments above opening* SD
Location] *Rowe (subst.)*   0 SD.1 PARIS] Q2–4, F; *Countie Paris* Q1   0 SD.1 *with...water*] Q1; *not in* Q2–4, F
0 SD.2 *and a torch*] *Capell (after Rowe)*   1–11] Q2–4, F; Put out the torch, and lye thee all along / Vnder this Ew-tree,
keeping thine eare close to the hollow ground. / And if thou heare one tread within this Churchyard, / Staight giue
me notice. / *Boy:* I will my Lord. Q1   1 aloof] Q2–4; aloft F   3 yew trees] *Pope (from* Q1 Ew-tree); young Trees
Q2–4, F   4 Holding thy] Q2–4, F; keeping thine Q1; Laying thy F3; Holding thine *Capell*   6 unfirm] Q2–4, F; unfirm,
F4

18 **nice** unimportant, trivial.
18 **charge** weighty matter.
19 **dear import** important consequence (with possible play on 'dear' = grievous, costly).
19 **neglecting** it failure to deliver its contents.
21 **crow** crowbar.
26 **beshrew** reprove, blame.
27 **accidents** happenings.

Act 5, Scene 3
   Location Verona. A churchyard; in it a tomb belonging to the Capulets.
   0 SD *sweet* perfumed.
   1 **stand aloof** withdraw to a distance. Paris's visit to the tomb and consequent death are not in Brooke or Painter.
   3 *yew trees See supplementary note.
   3 **lay...along** lie stretched out.

But thou shalt hear it. Whistle then to me
As signal that thou hear'st something approach.
Give me those flowers. Do as I bid thee, go.

PAGE [*Aside*] I am almost afraid to stand alone   10
Here in the churchyard, yet I will adventure.   [*Retires*]

[*Paris strews the tomb with flowers.*]

PARIS Sweet flower, with flowers thy bridal bed I strew –
O woe, thy canopy is dust and stones! –
Which with sweet water nightly I will dew,
Or wanting that, with tears distilled by moans.   15
The obsequies that I for thee will keep
Nightly shall be to strew thy grave and weep.

Whistle Boy.

The boy gives warning, something doth approach.
What cursèd foot wanders this way tonight,
To cross my obsequies and true love's rite?   20
What, with a torch? Muffle me, night, a while.   [*Retires*]

Enter ROMEO *and* [BALTHASAR *with a torch, a mattock, and a crow
of iron*].

ROMEO Give me that mattock and the wrenching iron.
Hold, take this letter; early in the morning
See thou deliver it to my lord and father.
Give me the light. Upon thy life I charge thee,   25
What e'er thou hear'st or seest, stand all aloof,
And do not interrupt me in my course.

8 hear'st] *Rowe*³; hearest Q2–4, F   8 something] Q4; some thing Q2–3, F   10 SH PAGE] Q2–4, F; *Boy:* Q1   10 SD]
Capell; no SD, Q2–4, F, Q1   11 SD.1 *Retires*] *Capell; no* SD, Q2–4, F, Q1; *Exit.* F2   11 SD.2 *Paris…flowers.*] Q1; *no* SD,
Q2–4, F   12–17] Q2–4, F; Sweete Flower, with flowers I strew thy Bridale bed: / Sweete Tombe that in thy circuite
dost containe, / The perfect modell of eternitie: / Faire *Iuliet* that with Angells dost remaine, / Accept this latest fauour
at my hands, / That liuing honourd thee, and being dead / With funerall praises doo adorne thy Tombe. Q1, *Steevens;*
Pope retains 12 and substitutes the last four lines of Q1, *reading* hand *for* hands *and* obsequies *for* praises   12–13 strew – …
stones! –] *Staunton;* strew…stones, Q2; strew,…stones, Q3–4; strew:…stones, F   13 canopy] F; Canapie Q2–4
15 moans.] Q3–4, F *(subst.);* mones, Q2   16 keep] *Capell;* keepe: Q2; keepe, Q3–4, F   17 be to] *Collier;* be, to
Q2–4, F; be – to *Capell*   17 SD] Q2–4, F; *Boy whistles and calls.* My Lord. Q1   18 warning,] Q2–4, F, Q1; warning;
Steevens; warning *Collier*   19 way] Q2–4; wayes F; was Q1   20 rite] *Pope*²; right Q2–4, F; rites Q1, *Pope*   21 SD.1
Retires] *Capell; no* SD Q2–4, F, Q1; Steps aside. *Douai MS.*   21 SD.2 BALTHASAR…iron] Q1 *(after 17)*; *and* Peter Q2–3,
F; *and* Balthazar *his man* Q4   25–7] Q2–4, F; So get thee gone and trouble me no more. Q1   25 light. Upon] Q3–4,
F *(subst.);* light vpon Q2   26 hear'st] F; hearest Q2–4

10 **stand** stay.
13 **thy canopy** i.e. of thy bed.
15 **wanting** lacking.
15 **distilled by** extracted out of.
20 **cross** thwart, interfere with.
21 SD.2 BALTHASAR *Collier* (followed by
Greg) suggests that the confusion between Q2

'Peter' and 'Balthasar' (Q4, Q1) arose from
doubling, Kemp playing both roles (though see
above, p. 28, n. 4), but as Hosley points out
'Peter' is the name of Romeo's man in Brooke
(2697), an equally likely source of confusion.
21 SD.2 *mattock* a kind of pick-axe.
27 **course** intended proceeding.

Why I descend into this bed of death
Is partly to behold my lady's face,
But chiefly to take thence from her dead finger   30
A precious ring, a ring that I must use
In dear employment; therefore hence, be gone.
But if thou, jealous, dost return to pry
In what I farther shall intend to do,
By heaven, I will tear thee joint by joint,   35
And strew this hungry churchyard with thy limbs.
The time and my intents are savage-wild,
More fierce and more inexorable far
Than empty tigers or the roaring sea.

BALTHASAR I will be gone, sir, and not trouble ye.   40

ROMEO So shalt thou show me friendship. Take thou that,
                    [*Gives a purse.*]
Live and be prosperous, and farewell, good fellow.

BALTHASAR [*Aside*] For all this same, I'll hide me hereabout,
His looks I fear, and his intents I doubt.   [*Retires*]

ROMEO Thou detestable maw, thou womb of death,   45
Gorged with the dearest morsel of the earth,
Thus I enforce thy rotten jaws to open,
And in despite I'll cram thee with more food.
                    [*Romeo begins to open the tomb.*]

PARIS This is that banished haughty Montague,
That murdered my love's cousin, with which grief   50
It is supposèd the fair creature died,
And here is come to do some villainous shame
To the dead bodies. I will apprehend him.
                    [*Steps forth.*]

---

34 farther] Q2–4; further F, Q1   37 savage-wild] *Steevens (1778)*; sauage wilde Q2–4, F; sauage, wilde Q1, *Pope*
38–9] *not in* Q1   40, 43 SH BALTHASAR] Q4, Q1; *Pet.* Q2–3, F   40 ye] Q2; you Q3–4, F, Q1   41 show me friendship]
Q3–4, F; shew me friendshid Q2; win my fauour Q1, *Pope*   41 SD] *This edn (after Capell, Collier)*; *no* SD, Q2–4, F, Q1
43 SD] *Capell*; *no* SD, Q2–4, F, Q1   43–4] Q2–4, F; Yet for all this will I not part from hence. Q1   44 SD] *Hanmer*;
no SD, Q2–4, F, Q1; *Exit.* F2   46 earth,] *Theobald*; earth: Q2–4, F; earth. Q1   47 open] Q2–4, F; ope Q1   48 SD] *NS
(from* Q1 SD *Romeo opens the tombe.* / *after* 44*)*; *placed as in Cam.*; *no* SD, Q2–4, F; *Breaking open the Monument.* /
Rowe (after 47*)*; *Tomb opens.* / *Capell (after* 47*, with an earlier* SD*, after* 45*,* / *fixing his Mattock in the Tomb.)*
49 SH PARIS] F, Q1; *Pa.* Q2–4   50–3 with…bodies.] *not in* Q1   53 SD] *Douai MS.*; *no* SD, Q2–4, F, Q1; *draws, and
rushes forward.* / *Capell (after* 54*)*; *advances.* / *Malone*; *Comes forward.* / *Cam.*

30–1 chiefly…ring Romeo invents this (not in   45 womb belly.
Brooke or Painter) to mislead Balthasar as to his real   48 in despite 'to spite thee – by making thee
intention.   eat when thou art already gorged with food'
  32 dear employment important business.   (Kittredge).
  33 jealous suspicious.   52 do…shame dismember the bodies (in
  44 fear…doubt distrust…fear.   revenge). Suggested perhaps by Brooke (2795–8).
  45 detestable Accented on first syllable.   53 apprehend arrest.

Stop thy unhallowed toil, vile Montague!
Can vengeance be pursued further than death?   55
Condemnèd villain, I do apprehend thee.
Obey and go with me, for thou must die.

ROMEO I must indeed, and therefore came I hither.
    Good gentle youth, tempt not a desp'rate man,
    Fly hence and leave me. Think upon these gone,   60
    Let them affright thee. I beseech thee, youth,
    Put not another sin upon my head,
    By urging me to fury: O be gone!
    By heaven, I love thee better than myself,
    For I come hither armed against myself.   65
    Stay not, be gone; live, and hereafter say,
    A madman's mercy bid thee run away.

PARIS I do defy thy conjuration,
    And apprehend thee for a felon here.

ROMEO Wilt thou provoke me? then have at thee, boy!   70
                    [*They fight.*]

PAGE O Lord, they fight! I will go call the Watch.   [*Exit*]

PARIS O, I am slain! [*Falls.*] If thou be merciful,
    Open the tomb, lay me with Juliet. [*Dies.*]

ROMEO In faith, I will. Let me peruse this face.
    · Mercutio's kinsman, noble County Paris!   75
    What said my man, when my betossèd soul
    Did not attend him as we rode? I think
    He told me Paris should have married Juliet.
    Said he not so? or did I dream it so?
    Or am I mad, hearing him talk of Juliet,   80
    To think it was so? O give me thy hand,

54 unhallowed] *Pope* (unhallow'd); vnhallowed Q2–4, F, Q1   55 pursued] Q4 (pursu'd); pursued Q2–3, F, Q1
60–1] *not in* Q1   60 these] Q2–4; those F   62 Put] Q2–4, F; Heape Q1, *Malone*; Pull *Rowe*; Pluck *Capell*
66–7] *not in* Q1, *Pope*   66 be gone] Q3–4, F; begone Q2   67 madman's] *Theobald*; mad mans Q2–4, F   67 bid] Q2–4,
F; bad Q5, *Theobald*¹; bade *Theobald*²   68 conjuration] *Capell (after* Q1 coniurations); commiration Q2; commisseration
Q3, F; commiseration Q4; commination *Williams (conj. Mommsen)*   69 apprehend] Q2–4, F; doe attach Q1, *Malone*
70 SD] Q1; *no* SD, Q2–4, F; They fight, Paris falls. / *Rowe*   71 SH PAGE] Q4; *line unassigned, centred and in italics as
a* SD, Q2–3; *Pet.* F; Boy: Q1   71 SD] *Capell; no* SD, Q2–4, F, Q1   72 SD] *Capell (after Rowe); no* SD, Q2–4, F, Q1
73 SD] *Theobald; no* SD, Q2–4, F, Q1   75 Mercutio's] Q2, Q4, Q1; *Mercutius* Q3, F   80–6] Q2–4, F; But I will satisfie
thy last request, / For thou hast prizd thy loue aboue thy life. Q1

55 Suggested perhaps by Brooke (2663–6),
though in a different context.
68 *conjuration admonition, solemn entreaty.
Q2 'commiration' is an easy minim misreading of
'coniuration' (Q1 'coniurations'). Q3, F 'commisseration' is not a bad compositorial guess (= offered

pity), but metrically awkward. Mommsen's 'commination' (= threatenings, especially of divine
vengeance, *OED*), an equally easy minim misreading, does not fit the placatory tone of Romeo's
speech.
78 should have was to have.

One writ with me in sour misfortune's book!
I'll bury thee in a triumphant grave.
A grave? O no, a lantern, slaughtered youth;
For here lies Juliet, and her beauty makes   85
This vault a feasting presence full of light.
Death, lie thou there, by a dead man interred.
            [*Laying Paris in the tomb.*]
How oft when men are at the point of death
Have they been merry, which their keepers call
A light'ning before death! O how may I   90
Call this a light'ning? O my love, my wife,
Death, that hath sucked the honey of thy breath,
Hath had no power yet upon thy beauty:
Thou art not conquered, beauty's ensign yet
Is crimson in thy lips and in thy cheeks,   95
And Death's pale flag is not advancèd there.
Tybalt, liest thou there in thy bloody sheet?
O, what more favour can I do to thee
Than with that hand that cut thy youth in twain
To sunder his that was thine enemy?   100
Forgive me, cousin. Ah, dear Juliet,
Why art thou yet so fair? Shall I believe
That unsubstantial Death is amorous,
And that the lean abhorrèd monster keeps

---

82 book!] *Capell;* booke, Q2, F2; booke. Q3–4, F   84 no,] Q3–4, F; no. Q2   84 lantern] *Malone;* Lanthorne Q2–4, F
(variant form)   87 Death] Q2–4, F, Q1; Dead *Dyce² (conj. Lettsom)*   87 SD] *Theobald (subst.);* no SD, Q2–4, F, Q1;
enters the Tomb, carrying in the Body. / Capell   90 how] Q2–4, F, Q1; now *conj. Johnson*   91–117 O my...pilot,] Q2–4,
F; Ah dear *Iuliet,* / How well thy beauty doth become this graue? / O I beleeue that vnsubstanciall death, / Is amorous,
and doth court my loue. / Therefore will I, O heere, O euer heere, / Set vp my euerlasting rest / With wormes, that
are thy chamber mayds. / Come desperate Pilot Q1   94 art] Q2–4; are F   97 liest] Q2–4; ly'st F   100 thine] Q2–4;
thy F   102 Shall I believe] *Theobald;* I will beleeue, / Shall I beleeue Q2–4, F; O I beleeue Q1; I will believe *Pope*

---

83 **triumphant** magnificent, glorious (with
overtones of 'victorious', forerunning the theme of
death swallowed up in victory).

84 **lantern** 'a spacious round or octagonal turret
full of windows, by means of which cathedrals, and
sometimes halls, are illuminated' (Steevens).

86 **feasting presence** festival presence-chamber
(used by the sovereign (Juliet) for receiving
important visitors (Paris, Romeo)).

87 **Death...man** i.e. Paris...Romeo.

89 **keepers** (1) sick-nurses; (2) jailors.

90 **light'ning before death** 'that exhilara-
tion or revival of spirits...supposed to occur...
before death' (*OED* Lightening *vbl sb²* b).
Proverbial (Tilley L277); compare 5.1.1–5 and

Munday, *Death of...Huntingdon* (1598; MSR,
1315–16).

90–1 **how...light'ning** how, under these tragic
circumstances, may I consider my imaginations of
the dead Juliet as a 'light' (85–6) as reflecting the
proverbially 'merry' mood of one about to die?

92–115 Apart from Romeo's apology to Tybalt,
these lines owe almost nothing to Brooke (2631–86).
The effective dramatic irony in Romeo's comments
on Juliet's lifelike appearance in 'death' and the
extended metaphor of Death as 'paramour' seem to
have been suggested, as noted by Malone and
Steevens, by Daniel's *Rosamond*. See supplementary
note.

102 **Shall I believe** See supplementary note.

Thee here in dark to be his paramour? 105
For fear of that, I still will stay with thee,
And never from this palace of dim night
Depart again. Here, here will I remain
With worms that are thy chambermaids; O here
Will I set up my everlasting rest, 110
And shake the yoke of inauspicious stars
From this world-wearied flesh. Eyes, look your last!
Arms, take your last embrace! and, lips, O you
The doors of breath, seal with a righteous kiss
A dateless bargain to engrossing Death! 115
Come, bitter conduct, come, unsavoury guide!
Thou desperate pilot, now at once run on
The dashing rocks thy seasick weary bark!
Here's to my love! [*Drinks.*] O true apothecary!
Thy drugs are quick. Thus with a kiss I die. [*Dies.*] 120

Enter FRIAR [LAWRENCE] *with lantern, crow, and spade.*

FRIAR LAWRENCE Saint Francis be my speed! how oft tonight
Have my old feet stumbled at graves! Who's there?
BALTHASAR Here's one, a friend, and one that knows you well.

107 palace] Q3–4, F; pallat Q2; pallet *Hosley*   107 night] Q3–4, F; night. Q2   108 Depart again. Here] Q4, *Theobald*; Depart againe, come lye thou in my arme, / Heer's to thy health, where ere thou tumblest in. / O true Appothecarie! / Thy drugs are quicke. Thus with a kisse I die. / Depart againe, here Q2–3, F (F *reading* armes); Depart again: come lye thou in my arms, / Here's to thy health. – Here *Pope*   112 world-wearied] Q3–4, F; world wearied Q2   118 thy] Q2–4, F; my *Pope*   118 bark] Q2–4, F; barge Q1   119 SD] *Douai MS., Theobald*; no SD, Q2–4, F, Q1   120 SD.1 Dies.] *Douai MS., Theobald*; no SD, Q2–4, F; Falls. Q1   120 SD.2 Enter...spade.] Q2 (*Entrer*), Q3–4, F; *Enter Fryer with a Lanthorne.* Q1 (*a break indicated by a row of printer's ornaments above this* SD); *Enter, at the other end of the Yard, Friar Lawrence...spade. / Capell*   121 Francis] Q3–4, F; Frances Q2

107 *palace See supplementary note.
108 Depart again. Here See supplementary note.
110 set...rest make a final desperate commitment of myself. Compare 4.5.6.
111–18 Walter Whiter (*A Specimen of a Commentary on Shakspeare*, 1794, pp. 123–4) notes how images here drawn from the stars, the law and the sea 'succeed each other in the same order, though with a different application' as in Romeo's speech of fatal premonition in 1.4.106–13.
114 doors of breath Compare *2H4* 4.5.31: 'gates of breath'.
115 A dateless...Death an everlasting ('dateless' = without date of termination) contract ('bargain') with all-devouring ('engrossing' = monopolising) death. The legal image of 'seal' in 114 is carried on by 'bargain' and 'engrossing'. Compare *TGV* 2.2.7

116 conduct i.e. the poison.
118 seasick weary bark small ship worn out by the buffeting of the sea. Compare Brooke's first sonnet 'To the Reader' ('The lode starres are, the wery pilates marke, / In stormes to gyde to haven the tossed barke') and 'wracke thy sea beaten barke' (808); also 1365–70, 1519–26, and *R3* 4.4.233–5. Muir (p. 45) compares Sonnet 85 in Sidney's *Astrophil and Stella*. See supplementary note.
120 quick fast-acting (with play on 'quick' = life-giving). Compare 166.
121 speed aid. Compare *Troublesome Reigne of King John* (Bullough, IV, line 1289): 'S. Fraunces be your speed.'
122 stumbled at graves Considered a bad omen ('graves' simply heightens the threat). See 2.3.94; *3H6* 4.7.10–12; *R3* 3.4.84.

FRIAR LAWRENCE Bliss be upon you! Tell me, good my friend,
    What torch is yond that vainly lends his light   125
    To grubs and eyeless skulls? As I discern,
    It burneth in the Capels' monument.
BALTHASAR It doth so, holy sir, and there's my master,
    One that you love.
FRIAR LAWRENCE   Who is it?
BALTHASAR   Romeo.
FRIAR LAWRENCE How long hath he been there?
BALTHASAR   Full half an hour.   130
FRIAR LAWRENCE Go with me to the vault.
BALTHASAR   I dare not, sir.
    My master knows not but I am gone hence,
    And fearfully did menace me with death
    If I did stay to look on his intents.
FRIAR LAWRENCE Stay then, I'll go alone. Fear comes upon me.   135
    O, much I fear some ill unthrifty thing.
BALTHASAR As I did sleep under this yew tree here,
    I dreamt my master and another fought,
    And that my master slew him.   *[Retires]*
FRIAR LAWRENCE   Romeo!
    [Friar stoops and looks on the blood and weapons.]
    Alack, alack, what blood is this which stains   140
    The stony entrance of this sepulchre?
    What mean these masterless and gory swords
    To lie discoloured by this place of peace?
    [Enters the tomb.]
    Romeo! O, pale! Who else? What, Paris too?
    And steeped in blood? Ah, what an unkind hour   145

---

123 SH BALTHASAR] Q4; *Man.* Q2–3, F, Q1 *(throughout, except 272)*   124] Q2–4, F; Who is it that consorts so late the dead, Q1, *Steevens (inserted after 122)*   127 the Capels'] *Malone;* the Capels Q2–4, F; *Capels* Q1; the *Capulet's* F4; the *Capulets'/Theobald*   128–9 It...love.] *As Johnson; one line,* Q2–4; *two lines, ending* sir / ...loue F; It doth so holy Sir, and there is one / That loues you dearely. Q1   135–6] Q2–4, F; Then must I goe: my minde presageth ill. Q1   135 Stay then, I'll] Q5, *Theobald;* Stay then ile Q2; Stay, then ile Q3–4, F   135 Fear comes] Q2–4; feares comes F; feares come F2   136 unthrifty] Q2; vnluckie Q3–4, F   137–9] *not in* Q1   137 yew] *Pope;* yong Q2; young Q3–4, F   139 SD.1 *Retires*] *This edn (after Collier MS.) / Exit.*); *no SD* Q2–4, F, Q1   139 Romeo!] Q2–4 *(subst.)*, F; Romeo? – *[leaves him, and goes forward.* / *Capell;* Romeo? – *[advances.* / *Malone*   139 SD.2 *Friar...weapons.*] Q1; *no SD,* Q2–4, F   143 SD] *Douai MS., Capell (subst.)*; *no SD,* Q2–4, F, Q1

---

124 good my friend my good friend. Compare 3.5.198 n.

136 unthrifty unfortunate (i.e. lacking in 'thrift' = success). Q3–4, F 'vnluckie' is merely a more commonplace synonym.

143 To lie i.e. lying (a gerundive use of the infinitive, common after 'mean' (142); see Abbott 356).

143 discoloured unnaturally stained (with blood).

145 unkind unnatural, injurious (with suggestion of bad astrological influence). Accented on first syllable.

Is guilty of this lamentable chance!
  [*Juliet rises.*]
The lady stirs.

JULIET O comfortable Friar, where is my lord?
I do remember well where I should be;
And there I am. Where is my Romeo?   150
  [*Noise within.*]

FRIAR LAWRENCE I hear some noise, lady. Come from that nest
Of death, contagion, and unnatural sleep.
A greater power than we can contradict
Hath thwarted our intents. Come, come away.
Thy husband in thy bosom there lies dead;   155
And Paris too. Come, I'll dispose of thee
Among a sisterhood of holy nuns.
Stay not to question, for the Watch is coming.
Come go, good Juliet, I dare no longer stay.   *Exit*

JULIET Go get thee hence, for I will not away.   160
What's here? a cup closed in my true love's hand?
Poison I see hath been his timeless end.
O churl, drunk all, and left no friendly drop
To help me after? I will kiss thy lips,
Haply some poison yet doth hang on them,   165
To make me die with a restorative.
Thy lips are warm.

CAPTAIN OF THE WATCH [*Within*] Lead, boy, which way?

---

146 SD] Q1; *no* SD, Q2–4, F; *Juliet awaking. / Pope (after 147)*; Juliet *wakes, and looks about her. / Capell (after 147)*
148 where is] Q2–4; where's F; Q1 *omits* where…Lord? **150**] Q2–4, F; And what we talkt of: but yet I cannot see / Him for whose sake I vndertooke this hazard. Q1 **150** SD] Capell; *no* SD, Q2–4, F, Q1 **151–9**] Q2–4, F; Lady come foorth, I heare some noise at hand, / We shall be taken, *Paris* he is slaine, / And *Romeo* dead: and if we heere be tane / We shall be thought to be as accessarie. / I will prouide for you in some close Nunery. / *Iul*: Ah leaue me, leaue me, I will not from hence. / *Fr*: I heare some noise, I dare not stay, come, come. Q1 **151** noise, lady.] *Hoppe*; noyse Lady, Q2–4, F; noise, Q1; noise! Lady *Pope* **159** SD] Q2–4, F; *not in* Q1; *after 160, Dyce* **163** O] Q2–4, F; Ah Q1, *Staunton* **163** drunk…left] Q2; drinke all, and left Q3–4; drinke all? and left F; drinke all, and leaue Q1, *Pope* **164–7** I…warm.] *not in* Q1 **168** SH CAPTAIN OF THE WATCH] *This edn*; *Watch.* Q2–4, F, Q1; 1. W. / *Capell*; *Chief Watch / Hoppe* **168** SD] *Capell*; *no* SD, Q2–4, F; *the duplication of* Q1 SD / Enter watch. / *preceding 168 and again following 170, may perhaps be interpreted to indicate that 168 was spoken within; a row of printer's ornaments follows 170 in* Q1 **168** way?] Q3–4, F; way. Q2

---

148 comfortable affording comfort.

152 unnatural sleep i.e. the sleep of death.

155 in thy bosom If Romeo has fallen across Juliet's body, as this implies and Brooke (2681–2) states, one must attribute Juliet's question in 150 ('Where is my Romeo?') to her confusion on suddenly awaking from her drugged sleep.

159 The Friar's fear and his attempt to escape (also in Brooke (2762–4)) are not properly in character. See above, pp. 23–4.

161 cup i.e. presumably, the vial containing the poison. Spencer suggests stage business with a cup or beaker when Romeo drinks.

162 timeless untimely (but with suggestion of 'beyond time', 'eternal'; compare 'dateless' (115).

163–6 Juliet's wish to share the poison and her hope of dying through a poisoned kiss are not in Brooke or Painter. Compare Horatio's desire to follow Hamlet (5.2.340–2) by drinking the dregs of the poisoned cup.

163 churl niggard (literally, unmannerly rustic).

166 a restorative i.e. the kiss Juliet claims from Romeo.

JULIET Yea, noise? Then I'll be brief. O happy dagger,
        [Taking Romeo's dagger.]
    This is thy sheath;
           [Stabs herself.]
           there rust, and let me die.   170
[Falls on Romeo's body and dies.]

    Enter [Paris's] Boy and WATCH.

PAGE This is the place, there where the torch doth burn.
CAPTAIN OF THE WATCH
    The ground is bloody, search about the churchyard.
    Go, some of you, whoe'er you find attach.
            [Exeunt some of the Watch]
    [The Captain enters the tomb and returns.]
    Pitiful sight! here lies the County slain,
    And Juliet bleeding, warm, and newly dead,   175
    Who here hath lain this two days burièd.
    Go tell the Prince, run to the Capulets,
    Raise up the Montagues; some others search.
            [Exeunt others of the Watch]
    We see the ground whereon these woes do lie,
    But the true ground of all these piteous woes   180

169 SD] *Douai MS., Capell; no* SD, Q2–4, F, QI *; Finding a dagger. / Pope*   170] Q2–4, F; *thou shalt end my feare, /
Rest in my bosome, thus I come to thee.* QI *(Hazlitt first reads* QI *Rest for* rust*)*   170 This is] Q2, Q4; 'Ti's is Q3;
'Tis in F   170 SD.1 *Stabs herself.*] *Douai MS., Capell; no* SD, Q2–4; *Kils herselfe.* F *(after* die.*); She stabs herselfe and
falles.* QI   170 SD.2 *Falls…dies.*] *Malone; no* SD, Q2–4; *see preceding note for* F *and* QI; *dyes Douai MS., Grant White;
throws herself upon her Lover, and expires. / Capell*   170 SD.3 *Enter…*WATCH.] *Kittredge (after Capell) ; Enter Boy
and Watch.* Q2–4, F *(after 167) ; Enter watch.* QI *(after 170; see 168* SD)   171 SH PAGE] *Capell; Watch boy.* Q2–3; *Boy.*
Q4, F; QI *omits Page's entry and 171*   171 place,] Q3–4, F; place Q2   172 SH CAPTAIN OF THE WATCH] *This edn
(from* QI *Cap:); Watch.* Q2–4, F; 1. W. / *Capell; Chief Watch / Hoppe*   172–81] Q2–4, F; *Come looke about, what
weapons haue we heere? / See frends where Iuliet two daies buried, / New bleeding wounded, search and see who's
neare, / Attach and bring them to vs presently.* QI   173 SD.1 *Exeunt…Watch*] *Hanmer; no* SD, Q2–4, F, QI;
Exeunt…Watch, the rest enter the Tomb. / Capell   173 SD.2 *The…returns.*] *This edn (after Capell); no* SD, Q2–4, F,
QI   175 dead,] F4; dead: Q2–4; dead F   176 this] Q2; these Q3–4, F   178] *S. Walker suggests a line lost after 178,
rhyming with woes in 180*   178 SD] *Capell (subst.); no* SD, Q2–4, F, QI

169 **happy** (1) fortunate in being ready to hand;
(2) successful, fortunate in itself (with quibble on
'die') (Mahood).
    170 **sheath** Compare Nashe, *Unfortunate
Traveller* (*Works*, II, 295): 'Point, pierce, edge,
enwiden, I patiently afforde thee a sheath:…So
(throughlie stabd) fell she downe, and knockt her
head against her husbands bodie [whom she
believed to be dead].'
    170 **rust** Many eds. prefer QI 'Rest', a blander
and easier reading. Dover Wilson declares 'rust'
'hideously unpoetical', but 'rust' carries with it a

vivid sense of the physical decay attendant on death
(Gibbons) and recalls the 'discoloured' swords of
143. See supplementary note.
    176 **this two days** Two days accords closely
enough with the forty-two-hour period promised by
the Friar in 4.1.105, but there are difficulties with
the forty-two hours (see above, p. 10, n. 5). 'this' =
these ('two days' being taken as a collective
singular).
    179 **ground…woes** scene…woeful creatures.
    180 **ground…woes** reason…woeful happen-
ings.

We cannot without circumstance descry.

Enter [one of the Watch with] Romeo's man [Balthasar].

SECOND WATCHMAN
Here's Romeo's man, we found him in the churchyard.
CAPTAIN OF THE WATCH
Hold him in safety till the Prince come hither.

Enter Friar [Lawrence] and another Watchman.

THIRD WATCHMAN Here is a friar that trembles, sighs, and weeps.
We took this mattock and this spade from him,   185
As he was coming from this churchyard's side.
CAPTAIN OF THE WATCH A great suspicion. Stay the friar too.

Enter the PRINCE [with others].

PRINCE What misadventure is so early up,
That calls our person from our morning rest?

Enter Capels [CAPULET, LADY CAPULET].

CAPULET What should it be that is so shrieked abroad?   190
LADY CAPULET O, the people in the street cry 'Romeo',
Some 'Juliet', and some 'Paris', and all run
With open outcry toward our monument.
PRINCE What fear is this which startles in your ears?
CAPTAIN OF THE WATCH
Sovereign, here lies the County Paris slain,   195
And Romeo dead, and Juliet, dead before,
Warm and new killed.
PRINCE Search, seek, and know how this foul murder comes.

181 SD] *This edn (after* Q1, *Rowe)* ; *Enter Romeos man.* Q2–4, F; *Enter one with Romets Man.* Q1 *(after 187)* ; *Enter Romeo's Man and a Watchman.* / *Hoppe*   182 SH SECOND WATCHMAN] *Rowe; Watch.* Q2–4, F; *1.* Q1   183, 187 SH CAPTAIN OF THE WATCH] *This edn (after* Q1 *Cap:, Capt:)* ; *Chief. watch.* Q2–4, *Hoppe; Con.* F; 1 *Watch.* / *Rowe*   183 come] Q2–4, F; comes F2   183 SD] Q2–4, F; *Enter one with the Fryer.* Q1 *(following* Q1 *version of 172–81)*   184 SH THIRD WATCHMAN] Q2–4, F; *1.* Q1   186 churchyard's] Q2; Church-yard Q3, F; Churchyard Q4   187 too] F; too too Q2; too, too Q3–4   187 SD *with others*] Q1; *not in* Q2–4, F; *and Attendants* / *Rowe*   189 morning] Q2–3; mornings Q4, F   189 SD] Q2–4, F; *Enter olde Capolet and his Wife.* Q1 *(after 198)* ; *Enter* Capulet, *his Lady, and Others.* / *Capell*   190 is so shrieked] *Daniel (subst.)* ; is so shrike Q2; they so shrike Q3–4, F; they so shriek F4   191, 206 SH LADY CAPULET] *Rowe; Wife.* Q2–4, F; *Moth:* Q1 *(191 only)*   191 O, the people] Q2–4, F; The people Q1, *Pope*   192–3 and some…monument.] Q2–4, F; as if they alone / Had beene the cause of such a mutinie. Q1   193] *Following this line, Capell adds* SD: Prince, *and the rest, enter the Monument.*   194 your] Q2–4, F; Q1 *omits 194*; our Capell *(conj. Heath, Johnson)*   195 SH CAPTAIN OF THE WATCH] *This edn (after* Q1 *Capt:)* ; *Watch.* Q2–4; *Wat.* F; *1. W.* / *Capell; Chief Watch* / *Hoppe*

181 **circumstance** detailed information.
183 **in safety** under guard.
186 **this churchyard's side** this side of the churchyard (Hoppe).
190 ***shrieked** See supplementary note.

191 **O, the people** See supplementary note.
194 **startles** springs up, rises with startling sound (Kittredge).
194 **your** The Heath–Johnson conj. 'our' is an easier reading, but 'your' makes adequate sense.

CAPTAIN OF THE WATCH
    Here is a friar, and slaughtered Romeo's man,
    With instruments upon them, fit to open   200
    These dead men's tombs.
        [*Capulet and Lady Capulet enter the tomb.*]
CAPULET O heavens! O wife, look how our daughter bleeds!
    This dagger hath mistane, for lo his house
    Is empty on the back of Montague,
    And it mis-sheathèd in my daughter's bosom!   205
LADY CAPULET O me, this sight of death is as a bell
    That warns my old age to a sepulchre.
        [*They return from the tomb.*]

        Enter MONTAGUE.

PRINCE Come, Montague, for thou art early up
    To see thy son and heir now early down.
MONTAGUE Alas, my liege, my wife is dead tonight;   210
    Grief of my son's exile hath stopped her breath.
    What further woe conspires against mine age?
PRINCE Look and thou shalt see.
        [*Montague enters the tomb and returns.*]
MONTAGUE O thou untaught! what manners is in this,
    To press before thy father to a grave?   215
PRINCE Seal up the mouth of outrage for a while,
    Till we can clear these ambiguities,

199 SH CAPTAIN OF THE WATCH] *This edn; Wat.* Q2–3, F; *Watch.* Q4; *1.* Q1; *1. W.* / *Capell; Chief Watch* / *Hoppe* 199 slaughtered] Q3 (slaughter'd), F; *Slaughter* Q2; slaughtred Q4 201 SD] *This edn (suggested by* Q2–3 SD, *following 201,* / *Enter Capulet and his wife.* / *; since it appears to duplicate their earlier entry at 189, it was omitted in* Q4, F *and by subsequent eds.*); *no* SD, Q4, F, Q1 202 heavens] Q2; heauen Q3–4, F 205 it] Q2; is Q3–4, F; it is Q1 205 mis-sheathèd] F4; missheathd Q2; misheath'd Q3–4; misheathed F; sheathed Q1 206–7] *not in* Q1 207 SD.1 *They...tomb.*] *This edn; no* SD, Q2–4, F, Q1 207 SD.2 *Enter* MONTAGUE.] Q2–4, F; *Enter olde Montague.* Q1; *Enter* Montague, *and Others.* / *Capell* 209 now] Q2–4, F; more Q1, *Steevens (1778)* 209 early] Q3–4, F, Q1; earling Q2 211] *Following this line, Ritson suggests inserting from* Q1: And yong Benuolio is deceased too: 212 mine] Q2; my Q3–4, F 213] Q2–4, F; First come and see, then speake. Q1; Look in this monument, and thou shalt see. *conj. Steevens;* Look here, and thou shalt see. *Keightley;* Look there, and thou shalt see. *conj. Dyce* 213 SD] *This edn; no* SD, Q2–4, F, Q1; *showing* Romeo. *Capell* 214 is in] Q2–4, Q1; in is F 216 the mouth of outrage] Q2–3, F; the moneth of out-rage Q4; your mouthes of outrage Q1; the mouth of outcry *Collier*[2] 216] *Following this line Capell adds* SD: *comes from the Monument.* 217–21] Q2–4, F; And let vs seeke to finde the Authors out / Of such a hainous and seld seene mischaunce. Q1

203 **mistane** mistaken its proper habitation ('house').

210 **my wife is dead** Spencer suggests that this additional note of pathos may be explained by the necessity of using the actor who played Lady Montague for some other role. Q1 adds the death

of Benvolio, perhaps for the same reason. Neither dies in Brooke or Painter.

216 **outrage** passionate lament. Is there also perhaps a glancing reference to the desecrated entrance of the Montague monument in 'Seal the mouth of outrage'?

And know their spring, their head, their true descent,
And then will I be general of your woes,
And lead you even to death. Mean time forbear,   220
And let mischance be slave to patience.
Bring forth the parties of suspicion.

FRIAR LAWRENCE I am the greatest, able to do least,
Yet most suspected, as the time and place
Doth make against me, of this direful murder;   225
And here I stand both to impeach and purge
Myself condemnèd and myself excused.

PRINCE Then say at once what thou dost know in this.

FRIAR LAWRENCE I will be brief, for my short date of breath
Is not so long as is a tedious tale.   230
Romeo, there dead, was husband to that Juliet,
And she, there dead, that Romeo's faithful wife:
I married them, and their stol'n marriage day
Was Tybalt's doomsday, whose untimely death
Banished the new-made bridegroom from this city,   235
For whom, and not for Tybalt, Juliet pined.
You, to remove that siege of grief from her,
Betrothed and would have married her perforce
To County Paris. Then comes she to me,
And with wild looks bid me devise some mean   240

---

223 greatest,] Q4, F; greatest Q2–3, Q1   224–69] Q2–4, F; Most worthie Prince, heare me but speake the truth, / And
Ile informe you how these things fell out. / *Iuliet* here slaine was married to that *Romeo*, / Without her Fathers or her
Mothers grant: / The Nurse was priuie to the marriage. / The balefull day of this vnhappie marriage, / Was *Tybalts*
doomesday: for which *Romeo* / Was banished from hence to *Mantua*. / He gone, her Father sought by foule constraint
/ To marrie her to *Paris*: But her Soule / (Loathing a second Contract) did refuse / To giue consent; and therefore
did she vrge me / Either to finde a meanes she might auoyd / What so her Father sought to force her too: / Or els
all desperately she threatnd / Euen in my presence to dispatch her selfe. / Then did I giue her, (tutord by mine arte)
/ A potion that should make her seeme as dead: / And told her that I would with all post speed / Send hence to *Mantua*
for her *Romeo*, / That he might come and take her from the Toombe, / But he that had my Letters (Frier *Iohn*) / Seeking
a Brother to associate him, / Whereas the sicke infection remaind, / Was stayed by the Searchers of the Towne, / But
Romeo vnderstanding by his man, / That *Iuliet* was deceasde, returnde in post / Vnto *Verona* for to see his loue. / What
after happened touching *Paris* death, / Or *Romeos* is to me vnknowne at all. / But when I came to take the Lady hence,
/ I found them dead, and she awakt from sleep: / Whom faine I would haue taken from the tombe, / Which she refused
seeing *Romeo* dead. / Anone I heard the watch and then I fled, / What after happened I am ignorant of. / And if in
this ought haue miscaried. / By me, or by my meanes let my old life / Be sacrifĉd some houre before his time. / To
the most strickest rigor of the Law. Q1   228 this.] Q5, *Pope*; this? Q2–4, F   232 that] Q4, Q1; thats Q2–3; that's F
240 mean] Q2; meanes Q3–4, F, Q1

---

218 **spring** source. 'head' simply duplicates 'spring'.

219 **general** leader in your pursuit of justice.

220 **to death** i.e. to the death penalty for those who are guilty.

221 **be slave** be subservient.

222 **parties of suspicion** suspected individuals.

223 **greatest** (1) principal suspect; (2) ? highest in social rank.

226 **impeach and purge** accuse (as guilty) and exonerate (as innocent).

229 **my...breath** the brief time (of life) left me in which to speak.

237 **siege** assault.

238 **perforce** by compulsion.

To rid her from this second marriage,
Or in my cell there would she kill herself.
Then gave I her (so tutored by my art)
A sleeping potion, which so took effect
As I intended, for it wrought on her   245
The form of death. Mean time I writ to Romeo
That he should hither come as this dire night
To help to take her from her borrowed grave,
Being the time the potion's force should cease.
But he which bore my letter, Friar John,   250
Was stayed by accident, and yesternight
Returned my letter back. Then all alone,
At the prefixèd hour of her waking,
Came I to take her from her kindred's vault,
Meaning to keep her closely at my cell,   255
Till I conveniently could send to Romeo.
But when I came, some minute ere the time
Of her awakening, here untimely lay
The noble Paris and true Romeo dead.
She wakes, and I entreated her come forth   260
And bear this work of heaven with patience.
But then a noise did scare me from the tomb,
And she too desperate would not go with me,
But as it seems, did violence on herself.
All this I know, and to the marriage   265
Her nurse is privy; and if ought in this
Miscarried by my fault, let my old life
Be sacrificed, some hour before his time,
Unto the rigour of severest law.
PRINCE We still have known thee for a holy man.   270
        Where's Romeo's man? what can he say to this?
BALTHASAR I brought my master news of Juliet's death,
        And then in post he came from Mantua
        To this same place, to this same monument.

---

248 borrowed] *Capell* (borrow'd); borrowed Q2–4, F   251 stayed] F (stay'd); stayed Q2–4, Q1   253 hour] Q4, F;
hower Q2–3   253 waking] Q2–4, F; awaking *Rowe*³   258 awakening] Q2; awaking Q3–4, F   262 scare] Q2–4; scarre F
263 me,] F; me: Q2–4   265–8] *As Pope; three lines, ending* priuie / ...fault / ...time Q2–4, F   268 his] Q2, Q1; the
Q3–4, F; its *Pope*   271 to this] Q2–4, F; in this Q1, *Capell*   272 SH BALTHASAR] Q2–4, Q1; *Boy.* F   274 place,...
monument.] F; place....monument Q2–4

246 **form** outward appearance.   redundantly with definitions of time (see Abbott
247 **as** Perhaps 'as (he did come)'; used   114). Compare *JC* 5.1.71–2.
                                                    259 **true** faithful to his love (in death).

This letter he early bid me give his father,   275
And threatened me with death, going in the vault,
If I departed not and left him there.
PRINCE Give me the letter, I will look on it.
Where is the County's page that raised the Watch?
Sirrah, what made your master in this place?   280
PAGE He came with flowers to strew his lady's grave,
And bid me stand aloof, and so I did.
Anon comes one with light to ope the tomb,
And by and by my master drew on him,
And then I ran away to call the Watch.   285
PRINCE This letter doth make good the Friar's words,
Their course of love, the tidings of her death;
And here he writes that he did buy a poison
Of a poor pothecary, and therewithal
Came to this vault to die, and lie with Juliet.   290
Where be these enemies? Capulet, Montague?
See what a scourge is laid upon your hate,
That heaven finds means to kill your joys with love!
And I for winking at your discords too
Have lost a brace of kinsmen. All are punished.   295
CAPULET O brother Montague, give me thy hand.
This is my daughter's jointure, for no more
Can I demand.
MONTAGUE   But I can give thee more,
For I will raise her statue in pure gold,
That whiles Verona by that name is known,   300

276–7] *not in* Q1   276 in] Q2–4, F; *to* Pope   281 SH PAGE] F; *Boy.* Q2–4, Q1   281–5] Q2–4, F; I brought my Master
vnto *Iuliets* graue, / But one approaching, straight I calld my Master. / At last they fought, I ran to call the Watch.
/ And this is all that I can say or know. Q1   287–95] Q2–4, F; Come *Capolet*, and come olde *Mountagewe*. / Where
are these enemies? see what hate hath done. Q1   290 vault to die,] F; Vault, to die Q2–4   292 hate,] F; hate? Q2–4
299 raise] Q4, F; raie Q2–3; erect Q1

284 **by and by** immediately, at once.
293 **That** In such a way that.
293 **kill your joys** (1) turn your happiness to
sorrow; (2) kill your children.
293 **with** through.
294 **winking at** closing my eyes to.
295 **brace** pair (Mercutio and Paris).
297 **This…jointure** The handclasp of friendship (ending the feud) is Juliet's jointure (=

marriage settlement made by the bridegroom's
father).
299 ***raise** cause to be set up. Compare Brooke
(3011–14). 'raise' (Q4, F), supported by Brooke
(3014) and Q1's 'erect', is almost universally
preferred to 'raie' (Q2–3), though Hosley defends
'raie' as meaning 'array'.
299 **statue** i.e. recumbent effigy on a tomb;
compare 303.

> There shall no figure at such rate be set
> As that of true and faithful Juliet.

CAPULET As rich shall Romeo's by his lady's lie,
Poor sacrifices of our enmity!

PRINCE A glooming peace this morning with it brings,   305
The sun for sorrow will not show his head.
Go hence to have more talk of these sad things;
Some shall be pardoned, and some punishèd:
For never was a story of more woe
Than this of Juliet and her Romeo.   310

[Exeunt omnes]

---

301 at such rate] Q2; at that rate Q3–4, F; of such price Q1
Q2–4; *Romeo* by his Lady F, Q1; *Romeo*'s by his lady *Theobald*
F (pardon'd); pardoned Q2–4, Q1   310 SD] F; *no SD*, Q2–4, Q1, *but / FINIS. / centred below 310 (also in F)*
303 Romeo's by his lady's] *Cam.*; *Romeos* by his Ladies
305 glooming] Q2–4, F; gloomie Q1, F4   308 pardoned]

---

301 at...set be held in such esteem (with perhaps a suggestion in 'rate' of 'value' or 'cost'). Compare Brooke (3017–20).

304 Poor sacrifices of (1) pitiful victims of; (2) inadequate atonement for (Kermode).

305 glooming peace peace overshadowed by clouds. Compare Spenser, *Faerie Queene*, I, xii, 2: 'Scarsely had *Phoebus* in the glooming East / Yet harnessed his firie-footed teeme'.

306 sun...head Gibbons cites Ovid, *Metamorphoses* (trans. Golding, II, 419): 'A day did pass without the Sunne' (after the fall of Phaëton, a story Shakespeare refers to in 3.2.1–4). Note the possible

link with the quotation from Spenser (who is also using Ovid's story) in the preceding note.

308 Some...punishèd In Brooke (2985–3004) the Nurse is banished, Peter is set free, the Apothecary 'high is hanged', and Friar Lawrence is 'discharged quyte' (i.e. pardoned) for his former services to the commonwealth but chooses to enter a hermitage near Verona, where he dies five years later.

309–10 Compare Brooke's concluding lines (3019–20): 'There is no monument more worthy of the sight: / Then is the tombe of Juliet, and Romeus her knight.'

SUPPLEMENTARY NOTES

The Prologue 6 star-crossed lovers] Compare William Smith, *Chloris* (1596), Sonnet 28: 'What cruel star, or fate, had dominion / When I was born? that thus my love is crossed.'

1.1.0 SD.2 *house of Capulet*] J. J. M. Tobin (*AN&Q* 17 (1979), 154) suggests that Shakespeare ironically named the Capulet servants, whose middle name might be caution, after the great biblical warrior Sampson and the warrior Pope Gregory VII, 'Turk Gregory' as Falstaff calls him (*1H4* 5.3.45).

1.1.63 SD.2–3 *Enter . . . partisans*] The speech heading '*Offi.*' for 64–5 raises a problem, since no Officer (or Officers) is mentioned in the Q2–4, F SD, a good example of the so-called permissive SD ('*three or foure Citizens*', '*Clubs or partysons*'), usually associated with authorial copy. Q1, which omits 52–71 and seems to alter the order of events, also fails to mention Officer(s) but states that '*other Citizens*' help to '*part them*'. At 3.1.127 SD, however, Q1 parallels the situation here exactly: '*Enter Citizens.*', followed by the speech heading '*Watch.*' (128, 130). In view of the speech headings '*Offi.*' and '*Watch.*', each independently associated with '*Citizens*', the present edn treats the Citizens here entering as 'OFFICERS *of the Watch*' and retains '*Offi.*, interpreting it as '*Officers*', since 64–5 are more suitable to several speakers than to a single '*Officer*' (compare *Temp.* 1.1.60–2; *JC* 3.2.204–5). Other editorial solutions may be consulted in the collation. Capell's addition ('*several of both houses, who join the fray*') seems to be called for by 105–6, suggested to Shakespeare perhaps by Brooke's description of the later fight in which Tybalt is killed ('both kinreds thether hye', 984).

1.1.117–21 I . . . me] Compare Montemayor's *Diana* (p. 111): 'it is the property of sorrowfull soules not onely to abhorre comfort, but to flie from them, by whom they thinke by any meanes to receive it'.

1.1.122–31] The remainder of the scene, in Romeo's posturing and oxymoronic excess, continues to fill in this portrait of fashionable love-melancholy. Andreas Laurentius's (trans. R. Surphlet) *A Discourse of the Preservation of the Sight: of Melancholike diseases. . .* (1599; pp. 117–21) and Robert Burton's 'Symptoms of Love' (*Anatomy of Melancholy*, III, 153–217) serve as a valuable comment on the huge store of love doctrine and conventional response (from classic to contemporary) that underlies Shakespeare's handling of both Romeo's Petrarchan 'passion' for Rosaline and Romeo and Juliet's mutual, consuming love. Burton (III, 216–17) refers to Romeo and Juliet (quoting the last two lines of the play) as among those who had suffered in 'this Tragicomedy of love'.

1.1.151–9 (see also 1.1.122–31 and commentary and supplementary notes)] Compare Michael Drayton, *Piers Gaveston* (1593), 455–6 (Edward II lamenting his loss of Gaveston): 'He countes the howers, so sloly how they runne, / Reproves the daye, and blames the loytring sunne.'

1.1.166 Here's. . . love] Line 166, if we substitute Juliet for Rosaline, foreshadows the whole course of the play (almost as an epigraph) and generates a series of paradoxes (167–85) commenting on the extremes of happiness and grief, good and evil, which constitute love. It also significantly looks forward to Friar Lawrence's speech (2.3.15–30) on the fundamental ambiguity of all created things and moral qualities. Such a series of contrarieties (through paradox and oxymoron) was a commonplace of the courtly love and sonnet traditions. Farmer (*Essay on the Learning of Shakespeare*, 1767) compares, among other passages, a section in the pseudo-Chaucerian part of *The Romaunt of the Rose* (4703–50):

> Love, it is an hatefull pees. . .
> Wis woodnesse [madness], and wod resoun. . . [compare 184]
> An hevy birthen, lyght to bere. . . [compare 169]
> It is discordaunce that can accorde,
> And accordaunce to discorde. . . [compare 167]
> It is sike hele [health] and hool seknesse. . . [compare 171]
> Bitter swetnesse and swete errour. . . [compare 185 and Tilley L505a]

Compare also Petrarch, *Rime*, 134, trans. by Wyatt (*Tottel's Miscellany*, ed. Rollins, No. 49) and by Thomas Watson, *Hekatompathia* (1582; ed. Arber, No. 40); Watson's No. 18 ('Love is a sowr delight; a sugred greefe; / A livinge death; an everdying life') and his 'Quid Amor?' (after No. 98); and George Gascoigne's 'The Passion of a Lover' (7–12). Mario Praz ('Shakespeare's Italy', *S.Sur.* 7 (1954), 100–2) discusses other Italian analogues for some of the more extreme conceits in *Rom.*

1.1.193 *Bid . . . *make his will] From Q4, Q1; Q2 reads 'A sicke man in sadnesse makes his will:', which is metrically defective and lacks the necessary referent for 'urged' in 194.

1.1.205 ope. . . gold] Gibbons compares Daniel's *Complaint of Rosamond*:

> Doost thou not see how that thy King thy *Jove*,
> Lightens foorth glory on thy dark estate:
> And showres downe golde and treasure from above,
> Whilst thou doost shutte thy lappe against thy fate. (232–5)

Shakespeare seems to recall this passage in *2H4* 5.5.46: 'My King, my Jove!'

1.1.212–13 She . . . despair] Compare Montemayor's *Diana* (p. 60):

> Who had not any thing, of all
> She had, but was extreme in her.
> For meanely wise none might her call,
> Nor meanely faire, for he did erre,
>   If so he did: but should devise
>   Her name of passing faire and wise.

Compare 'passing fair' in 225, 227 below.

1.2.9 not . . . years] That Brooke's sixteen was not forgotten by Shakespeare is shown by Capulet's excuse (10–11) that 'two more summers' should pass 'Ere we may think her ripe to be a bride'. But this caution seems to have evaporated by 1.3, in which Lady Capulet presses speedy marriage on Juliet. Juliet's age may surprise a modern reader, but brides of fourteen and fifteen, though not the rule, were not unknown among the Elizabethans (see L. E. Pearson, *Elizabethans at Home*, 1957, p. 298). Marriage was legal at fourteen for boys and twelve for girls. Marina in *Per.* is fourteen, Miranda in *Temp.*, fifteen, and Perdita in *WT*, sixteen. Otway, however, makes Lavinia (Juliet) 'bare Sixteen' in his *Caius Marius* (1680); Theophilus Cibber (1744), makes Juliet almost fifteen, and David Garrick (1748), almost eighteen, the last a tradition that continued until the middle of the nineteenth century.

1.2.15 hopeful . . . earth] 'Earth' may also be taken to mean (1) 'body' (compare 2.1.2 and *Sonnets* 146.1), in which sense, as before, 'hopeful' suggests the life-through-posterity theme of *Sonnets* 1–14; or (2) 'wealth', 'worldly possessions', in which case 'hopeful' refers to Juliet as his heir (i.e. a good match for Paris, a 'fille de terre' = heiress (Steevens). It is possible that 'earth' is a compositor's error, caught from 'Earth' in 14; we should expect a word rhyming with 'she' (14), since the rest of the speech is in rhymed couplets. Q1 omits 14–15, followed by Williams, who treats them as two versions of a line Shakespeare finally rejected.

1.2.32–3 Which . . . none] NS offers a paraphrase more flattering to Juliet: 'Among which ladies, on a "closer" view, mine may hold her own, although among a number one is reckoned none.' Brooke (195–6) seems to have suggested the underlying idea.

1.2.38–40] See Tilley c480, who points out the parody here of Lyly's *Euphues* (1578; 1, 180): 'The Shomaker must not go above his latchet, nor the hedger meddle with anye thing but his bill. It is unsemely for the Paynter to feather a shaft, or the Fletcher [= arrowmaker] to handle a pensill.'

1.2.65 *Vitruvio] From F3. 'Vtruuio' (Q1–4, F), i.e. 'Utruvio' (Q5), was accepted for the first time by Gibbons, though without comment. Hosley (in Williams, p. 106) calls attention to two uses of 'Utruvio' in two of Davenant's plays, *The Cruel Brother* (1627; ed. Maidment and Logan, 3.1 ('The Lady Benvolia, or the Lady / Utruvia!')) and *The Just Italian* (1629), 1.1 ('Utruvio, or the rich Pirracco'). The value of the evidence is slight, however, since Davenant in the earlier play was obviously recalling *Rom.* (witness 'Lady Benvolia'). Because the text here depends directly on Q1 and because no other independent uses of 'Utruvio' as an Italian name have been found (names beginning with U are comparatively rare in Italian), the commonly accepted 'Vitruvio' has been retained as an Italian form of Vitruvius.

1.2.78 thee] Since Q1 is the basic copy-text here, 'thee' has been retained in preference to Q2 'you', which may well have been caught up by the compositor from the following line. In addressing a social inferior, 'thee' was the preferred form (see Franz 289a).

1.3.27 laid ... dug] Maynard Mack ('Rescuing Shakespeare', International Shakespeare Association, Occasional Paper No. 1, 1979, pp. 10–11), drawing on data from Lloyd de Mause ('The Evolution of Childhood' in *The History of Childhood*, ed. Lloyd de Mause, 1974, p. 36), points out that by ordinary Elizabethan standards Juliet's weaning just short of three years old was unusually late. E. Roesslin, *The Byrth of Mankynde* (1540; eight editions by 1600), sets it at commonly one year; on the other hand, John Jones, *The Arte and Science of Preserving Bodie and Soule* (1579), allows seven to thirty-six months. That comparatively late weaning was not uncommon, however, is suggested by Bishop Richard Montague, who implies that a child must be weaned by three years (*Acts and Monuments of the Church* (1642), p. 526). Mack also points out (citing De Mause, p. 50) that children seemed to learn to walk later at this period (James I at five years, a child of Anne Clifford's (1617) at thirty-four months). Thus the Nurse's admiration for Juliet's standing 'high-lone' and 'waddl[ing] all about 'just before she became three would not necessarily have surprised an Elizabethan audience.

1.3.67, 68 *honour] From Q1; though Q2 'houre' (retained by Johnson, Capell, and Hoppe) makes sense in 67, it makes little or none in 68 and the two readings obviously must stand together. 'houre' is, moreover, either an easy minim misreading of 'honor' (Q1) in Secretary hand, or of a form like 'hōoure', where the tilde was missed by the compositor (as in 'kisman' for 'kinsman' at 2.4.6 and 3.1.136, 139).

1.4.47 *five wits] Malone's 'five' (from Wilbraham's conj.) for Q2 'fine', which makes a weak kind of sense, is justified by the context set up by 'Five times' and 'once'. 'fine' is an easy minim misreading of 'five' (i.e. 'fiue') or the 'n' in 'fine' may be simply a turned 'u' in Q2.

1.4.53 Queen Mab] Sir Henry Ellis (ed.), Brand's *Popular Antiquities*, III (1842), 218, notes a Warwickshire phrase 'mab-led', meaning misled by an *ignis fatuus*,and *OED* sites a line in the anonymous morality *Jacob and Esau* (1568), 5.6 (MSR, 1571): 'Come out thou mother Mab, out olde rotten witche' – both of which also associate Mab with the supernatural. The name and other details of the speech, mingled with recollections of *MND*, are taken over by Ben Jonson in the *Entertainment at Althrope* (1603) and by Michael Drayton in 'Nimphidia' (1627); in both Mab appears as Queen of the Fairies, in Jonson with marked Puck-like characteristics and in Drayton as the wife of Oberon.

1.4.57 little *atomi] Although Q1 'Atomi' is generally accepted, it may be noted that 'Otimie' (a form close to Q2 'ottamie') occurs in *Look About You* (anon., 1598–1600; MSR, 280).

1.4.59–61] These lines, not in Q1, follow 69 in Q2–4, F. Most eds., as here, follow Lettsom's conj., who argued that Shakespeare would naturally describe Mab's chariot as a whole before giving details of its parts. It seems highly likely that 59–61 were marginal insertions by Shakespeare in his foul papers, the correct point of insertion being unclearly marked so that the compositor inserted them in the wrong place. Otway (*Caius Marius* 1.2.385–6) solves the problem by omitting 61–9.

1.4.64–6 Her ... film] NS conjectures that parts of 64–5 have been interchanged and that Shakespeare actually wrote:

her traces of the moonshines watry beams,

her collors of the smallest spider web

Duthie comments: 'It is difficult to visualize moonbeams as collars round the necks of tiny horses, but the framework of the common spider's web might suggest the shape of a horse's collar' (see Francis Gentleman's objection to this line, *Dramatic Censor*, 1770, 1, 174). Curiously, Duthie does not notice that Q1 supports the reading of 64 ('The traces are the Moone-shine watrie beames'), while wrongly conflating 65 and 66 ('The collers crickets bones, the lash of filmes').

1.4.69 *maid] From Q1; Q2–4, F 'man' makes sense, but 'maid' appears to fit the context better if Nares is to be trusted. Graphically, the misreading of MS. 'maid' as 'man' is not easy to account for.

1.4.77 courtier's nose] The repetition of 'courtier' (see 72) has been considered textually suspicious. Q1 reads 'Lawers [= lawyer's] lap', which fits well with a legal interpretation of 'suit' in 78, but lawyers also have been earlier mentioned in 73.

1.4.113 Direct my *sail] Q1 'saile' seems best to fit the nautical image of God as helmsman in 112 (compare the linking of the sea imagery and fate in 2.2.82–4, 5.3.116–18), but Q2 'sute' (= suit = pursuit of an object or quest) has recently been defended by Williams and Gibbons.

1.5.93 sin] Warburton's conj. 'fine' (= penalty, mulct) for Q2 'sinne' has recently been widely adopted because 'sinne' is an easy 's/f' and minim misreading of 'fine' in Secretary hand; 'paine', adopted by NS, is defended on legal and theological grounds.

1.5.94 ready] From Q1; Q2 'did readie', awkward in tense and metrics, may best be taken as a 'false start' not clearly deleted by Shakespeare (Hosley).

1.5.133–4 If he ... bed] Compare Sir Philip Sidney, *Arcadia* (1593; ed. A. Feuillcrat, 1922, p. 45): 'But first shal *Zelmanes* grave, become her marriage bedd, before my soule shall consent to his owne shame ... ' Basilius is attempting to seduce Zelmane, thinking that Zelmane is a woman.

2.1.10 *pronounce but 'love' and *'dove'] Mercutio's burlesque intention here may have been suggested by Richard Barnfield, *The Affectionate Shepheard* (1594; ed. Montague Summers, n.d., p. 11): 'My Love, my Dove, my Sollace, and my Joy.'

2.1.10 *pronounce] From Q4, Q1. Q2–3, F 'prouaunt' (= to provision), used uniquely as a verb by Nashe in 1599 (see *OED*), makes no sense and may be explained (Williams) as arising from manuscript 'pronounc', a combination of a minim and 't' for 'c' misreading. On the evidence of the scene in *STM*, generally considered to be autograph, Shakespeare tended to drop the 'e' in words ending in 'ce' (98 'offyc', 112 'obedienc'). Q2 'day', in the same line, may be taken as a misreading of manuscript 'doue' or 'dou'.

2.1.36–8 medlars. . . *open-arse] Compare Davies of Hereford, *The Scourge of Folly* [1611], Epig.23 (ed. Grosart, II, 10):

> *Of her exclamation against Busic-bodies.*
> Kate still exclaims against great medlers,
> A busie-body hardly she abides,
> Yet she's well pleased with all bum-fiddlers,
> And her owne body stirring still besides:
> > I muse her stomacke now so much should faile
> > To loath a medlar, being an open-taile.

2.1.38 *open-arse] This edn (like Riverside) takes 'or' in Q2–3 'open, or' to be a compositor's stab at a manuscript 'ars' and not the conjunction 'or', which is disjunctive, where rather 'and', as in Q4, is called for by the context; the present reading, like Q1, implies 'and'. Q1 'open *Et cætera*' is a euphemism for 'open-arse'.

2.2.3 Juliet is the sun] Shakespeare here begins the light-in-darkness imagery associated with Romeo and, particularly, Juliet; compare 19–22 below and 3.2.17 (for Romeo), culminating in 5.3.84–6. In *Sonnets* 21 Shakespeare burlesques lovers 'Who heaven itself for ornament doth use ... / Making a couplement ... With sun and moon, with earth and sea's rich gems'.

2.2.24 O that I were a glove] English examples (two earlier than *Romeo and Juliet*) of the 'glove' conceit: Sir Philip Sidney, *Old Arcadia* (ed. A. Feuillerat, 1926, p. 160); Barnabe Barnes, *Parthenophil and Parthenophe* (1593), Sonnet 63.5–7; Robert Parry, *Sinetes Passions upon his Fortunes* (1597), Sonetto 20.7–10.

2.2.95–106 Or if ... discovered] Juliet's 'apology' for admitting her love for Romeo so readily (not found in Brooke's *Romeus and Juliet*, 1562) may have been influenced by Sir Philip Sidney's *Arcadia* (1590; ed. A. Feuillerat, 1922, pp. 260–1): '[After Zelmane has revealed that he is in fact Pyrocles, Philoclea immediately admits her love for him (even when he was disguised as a woman)] But even sicke with a surfet of joy, and fearefull of she knewe not what ... with a shrugging kinde of tremor through all her principall partes, she gave these affectionate wordes for answere. Alas, how painefull a thing it is to a devided minde to make a wel-joyned answere?. . . Shall I say Prince *Pyrocles*? wretch that I am, your shew [disguised as a woman] is manifest against it. But this, this I may well say; If I had continued as I ought, *Philoclea*, you had either never bene, or ever bene *Zelmane*: you had either never attempted this change, set on with hope, or never discovered it, stopt with despaire. But I feare me, my behaviour ill governed, gave you the first comfort: I feare me, my affection ill hid, hath given you this last assurance: I feare indeed, the weakenesse of my government before, made you thinke such a maske would be gratefull unto me: & my weaker government since, makes you to pull of the visar. What shall I doo then? shal I seeke far-fetched inventions? shall I labour to lay marble coulours over my ruinous thoughts? or rather, though the purenes of my virgin-minde be stained, let me keepe the true simplicitie of my word. True it is, alas, too true it is, ô *Zelmane* ... that even so while thou wert, ... my passions were fitter to desire, then to be desired. . . .

Thou hast then the victorie: use it with vertue. Thy vertue wan me; with vertue preserve me. Doost thou love me? keepe me then still worthy to be beloved. . . . so that with such imbracements, as it seemed their soules desired to meete, and their harts to kisse, as their mouthes did: which faine *Pyrocles* would have sealed with the chiefe armes of his desire, but *Philoclea* commaunded the contrary; and yet they passed the promise of marriage.' With the conclusion of this passage, compare 2.2.125–6 and 142–8.

2.2.158–9 Hist . . . lure] 'Hist' may be a falconer's call, though unattested: 'and alwayes when you call hir or feede hir, you must chirpe with your mouth, or whistle, to the ende she may becomme acquainted with your whistle and come there unto' (Turbervile, *Booke of Faulconrie*, 1575, p. 93).

2.2.163 Romeo's name] Q2 ends the line with '*Romeo*.', but omits the final word of the preceding line ('mine') and both 'name' and 'mine', preserved in Q1, make excellent sense. Perhaps the lines fell at the bottom of a damaged leaf in Shakespeare's MS. (Williams).

2.2.182–3 thy bird . . .. cherishing] Suggested perhaps by ll.12–13 of a sonnet on the problems raised by the extremes of love in Sidney's *Arcadia* (1590; ed. A. Feuillerat, 1922, p. 253): 'Thus children doo the silly birds they finde, / With stroking hurt, and too much cramming kill.'

2.2.184–7] The exact attribution of these lines shows considerable variation in the early texts (see collation). The attribution most commonly adopted (as here) is that of Q1. Q2 is obviously confused, assigning two contiguous speeches to Juliet (182–5, 186) and printing one line (184) as two part-lines. Q3-4, F attempt some redistribution of the dialogue, but eds. now agree (except Hosley) that the Q1 arrangement, apart from its relative authority as representing stage usage, most suitably gives Juliet and Romeo each a farewell rhyming couplet.

2.3.4 Titan's fiery wheels] This synecdoche for the sun god's chariot may have been picked up by Shakespeare from Spenser, *The Faerie Queene* (1590), I, ii, xxix, or from Michael Drayton, *Ideas Mirrour* (1594), Amour 47.

2.4.18–19 captain of compliments] Two duelling manuals detailing the Italian style appeared in England in the 1590s: *Di Grassi His True Art of Defence* (1594) and Vincentio Saviolo, *Practice of the Rapier and Dagger* (1595), the last possibly satirised by Shakespeare in *AYLI* 5.4. Compare Porter, *Two Angry Women* (1598; MSR, 1329–47).

2.4.25 affecting *phantasimes] John Crow's emendation of Q2 'phantacies' postulates only a dropped tilde over 'i' (as in Q2 'kisman' for 'kinsman' in 6 above) and Shakespeare uses 'phantasime' twice in *LLL* (4.1.99; 5.1.18) to describe Don Armado, who is 'too picked, too spruce, too affected, too odd as it were, too peregrinate [i.e. foreign]' (5.1.12–14). Most eds. adopt Q1 'fantasticoes' and cite Nashe's 'new-fangled *Galiardos* and Senior *Fantasticoes*' (*Saffron-Walden, Works*, III, 31), a reading considered tempting because of the numerous other Nashe echoes in the play. This fifth link with *LLL* (see 13–14, 15, 22–3, 23) is worth noting.

2.4.26 new . . . accent] Nashe (*Saffron-Walden, Works*, III, 76) asserts that Gabriel Harvey, who, he claims, had been told by the Queen 'that he lookt something like an Italian', 'quite renounct his naturall English accents and gestures, & wrested himselfe wholy to the Italian *puntilios*, speaking our homely Il-land tongue strangely, as if he were but a raw practitioner in it'.

2.4.29–30 stand . . . bench] Crofts cites Sir John Harington's complaint (*A Treatise on Playe* (c. 1597), in *Nugae Antiquae*, 1779, II, 173) that 'since great breeches were layd asyde, men can skant indewr to sit on' the 'great plank forms' in the Queen's presence chamber; he urges the introduction of 'easye quilted and lyned forms and stools'.

2.4.34–5 numbers that Petrarch . . . kitchen wench] In an anonymous sonnet in *Tottel's Miscellany* (1557; ed. Hyder E. Rollins, 1966, I, 169–70), No. 218, Petrarch is described as having the 'lively gift of flowyng eloquence' ('A praise of Petrarke. . . ', 2). That this sonnet may have influenced Shakespeare's 'the numbers Petrarch flowed in,' is suggested by the fact that the next poem (also anonymous) in *Tottel's Miscellany* (No. 219) is entitled 'That petrarck cannot be passed but notwithstanding that Laura is far surpassed', line 11 of which reads 'If Lawra livde she [i.e., the writer's mistress] would her clene deface', thus tying in closely with Shakespeare's 'Laura to his lady [i.e. Romeo's Rosaline] was a kitchen wench'.

2.4.59 wild-goose chase] Compare, perhaps, 'goose-riding': 'A goose, whose neck is greased, being suspended by the legs to a cord tied to two trees or high posts, a number of men on horseback, riding full speed, attempt to pull off the head; which if they effect, the goose is their prize' (Francis Grose, *Dictionary of the Vulgar Tongue*, 1785).

2.4.68–70 a wit of cheverel. . . word 'broad'] J. J. M. Tobin suggests that Shakespeare is here drawing on Nashe, *Christs Teares*, 'To the Reader' (1594: *Works*, II, 182): 'Infinite number of these phanatical strange hierogliphicks have these new decipherers framed to themselves, & stretcht words on the tenter hooks so miserably, that a man were as good, considering everie circumstance, write on cheverell as on paper.'

2.4.169 lay knife aboard (see also commentary note)] The following quotation from William Warner, *Albions England* (1612 ed., p. 389) suggests that this phrase may also mean to gorge or eat greedily: 'They [the Puritans] of their owne provided are sufficiently no doubt, / Or know to lay their knife aboord, at others Costs, for Fare / And greater Ease than Studie them or Pulpetrie can spare.'

2.5.26 jaunce] This is the only instance in *OED* as a noun before 1875; similarly 'jauncing' (also in *R2* 5.5.94) appears only in Shakespeare before 1792. Some eds. thus consider them misreading of 'iaunt' (Q4, F, Q1) and 'iaunting' (Q4, F). Lower-case 'c' and 't' are easily misread in Secretary hand.

2.5.42 flower of courtesy] To the other suggested borrowings from Nashe's *Have with You to Saffron-Walden*, 1596 (see Introduction, pp. 3–4) should be added (*Works*, III, 49): 'It is a common scoffe amongst us, to call anie foolish prodigall yong gallant, the gentleman or floure of curtesie'. The phrase appears nowhere else in Shakespeare (J. J. M. Tobin).

2.6.16–17 light . . . flint] Dowden's gloss on 'everlasting flint' as referring to 'the hardness and sharpness of the path of life' seems, as Kittredge remarks, 'out of harmony with the context'. Mahood, postulating a play on 'ne'er' and 'near', distinguishes four possible readings of 17: (1) it will never wear away the everlasting flint; (2) it will never last it out; (3) it will nearly outlast it; (4) it will nearly wear it away.

2.6.16–20 O, so light . . . vanity] Compare *Venus and Adonis*, 1027–8: 'As falcons to the lure, away she [Venus] flies, / The grass stoops not, she treads on it so light.' Steevens compares Virgil, *Aeneid*, VII, 808–9: 'Illa vel intactae segetis per summa volaret / gramina nec teneras cursu laesisset aristas.' (She [Camilla] might have flown o'er the topmost blades of unmown corn, nor in her course bruised the tender ears. Loeb). Ovid's lines (*Metamorphoses*, X, 654–5; Golding, 766–8), however, seem as likely to have caught Shakespeare's eye: 'A man would think they able were upon the Sea too go / And never wet theyr feete, and on the ayles of corne also / . . . and never downe them tread.'

3.1.5–26] Mercutio's surprising description of Benvolio as a fiery gallant who will pick a fight on any pretext, no matter how unwarranted or foolish, may have been suggested by Nashe's description of Gabriel Harvey in *Have with You to Saffron-Walden* (1596; *Works*, III, 68): 'Thirdly, he is verie seditious and mutinous in conversation, picking quarrells with everie man that will not magnifie and applaud him, libelling most execrably and inhumanely on *Iacke* of the Falcon, for that he would not lend him a messe of mustard to his red herrings; yea, for a lesser matter than that, on the Colledge dog he libeld, onely because he proudly bare up his taile as he past by him.'

3.1.55–8, 61–5] Painter's account reads (p. 112): '*Thibault* thou maiest know by the pacience which I have had untill this present tyme, that I came not hether to fyght with thee or thyne, but to seeke peace & attonemente betweene us, and if thou thinkest that for default of courage I have fayled myne endevor, thou doest greate wronge to my reputacion. And impute thys my suffrance to some other perticular respecte, rather than to wante of stomacke. Wherfore abuse mee not but be content with this greate effusion of Bloude and murders already committed, And provoke mee not I beseeche thee to passe the boundes of my good will and mynde.'

3.1.98–9] Dyce's arrangement; in Q2 98 is metrically deficient and no useful purpose is served by leaving it as a three- or four-stress line. If it is argued that the Q2 arrangement indicates that Mercutio is running out of breath, the same effect is achieved by making 99 a short line, and with less metrical awkwardness. Textual corruption may be signalled by the Q2 pointing ('I haue it, and soundly, to your houses.') which implies that we should break after 'and soundly', 'to' going with 'your houses', and that something like 'a plague' was accidentally omitted following 'soundly,' (compare Theobald's emendation in collation).

3.1.113 *Again*] A much debated reading. Capell's emendation has been accepted, though doubtfully, on the grounds that 'A' in Secretary hand might have been misread as 'He' (Gibbons), hence Q2 'He gan', the compositor interpreting 'gan' as a form of 'gone' (Q5, F3) or 'gon' (Q3–4, F). Against reading 'He gone' (Q3–4, F subst.) it is objected that Tybalt has just re-entered, a valid but not conclusive objection. Q1 'A liue', either as 'Alive' or as 'A live' (i.e. He live), makes excellent sense but does not help to explain Q2 'He gan' graphically. See Williams's extensive note on the crux.

3.1.138 O Prince! O husband!] The Capell-Dyce arrangement of the unmetrical Q2 'O Prince, O Cozen, husband' supposes that either 'Cozen' was an unclearly deleted 'first shot' (Hosley) or was picked up by the compositor from the line above (NS).

3.2] The first part of this scene (Juliet's impatience for Romeo's promised visit and her interaction with her Nurse) contains elements in common with Hero's strong desire for Leander's return to Sestos as described in Ovid's *Heroides*, Epistle XIX (*The Heroycall Epistles*, trans. George Turbervile, 1567; ed. F. Boas, 1928, p. 268): 'Now I can none of these [i.e. the ways in which Leander, as a man, is able to kill the time of separation] / though lesser were my flame: / Thy Hero can doo nothing els / but cleape her lovers name . . . / Or I with Beldame nurse / doo sit and chat of thee, / And doo not little muse what should / thy cause of lingring be.'

3.2.1–4 Gallop . . . immediately] See Gary McCown, ' "Runnawayes Eyes" and Juliet's epithalamium', *SQ* 28 (1976), 150–70, for a detailed study of Juliet's speech as an adaptation of the classical and Renaissance epithalamium. T. W. Baldwin (*Shakspere's Five Act Structure*, 1947, pp. 765–7) attributes lines 1–4 to two passages in Brooke (821–6, 919–20). Some connection with Marlowe's *Edward II* (4.3.45–7) has long been noted: 'Gallop a pace bright *Phoebus* through the skie, / And duskie night, in rustie iron carre: / Betweene you both, shorten the time I pray'; compare also Lyly, *Woman in the Moon* 4.1.248–9: 'When will the sun go downe? flye *Phoebus* flye! / O, that thy steeds were wingd with my swift thoughts.' But Shakespeare, like Brooke and Marlowe, also seems to have gone to Ovid's story of Phaëton (*Metamorphoses* II) in Golding's translation, from which he borrows 'fiery-footed steeds' (compare 'firiefooted horse' (II, 491) and 'fierifoming Steedes' (II, 160) = the horses of the sun) and 'waggoner' (compare II, 394, referring to Phaëton); he may also have picked up 'whip' (3) from Phoebus's warning to Phaëton: 'Sonne, spare the whip' (II, 169). Shakespeare has already glanced at the story in 2.3.4 (and in *TGV* 3.1.153–5), though there Phoebus is referred to as the Titan Helios. Juliet's reference to Phaëton as the 'waggoner' rather than Phoebus arises from the uncontrolled and fatal speed with which Phaëton drove the chariot of the sun and may perhaps be interpreted as foreshadowing the lovers' career.

3.2.6 That. . . wink] A much discussed crux; Furness devotes twenty-eight pages to it and some forty emendations have been proposed (see collation, where only the most widely considered are cited). All recent eds. except Kittredge retain the Q2–4, F reading (not in Q1), differing only, about equally, in making 'runnawayes' either a possessive plural (as in this edn) or a possessive singular. As a plural, two explanations (as noted above) may be offered: the first links 'runaways' with the 'fiery-footed steeds' and carries on the Ovidian Phoebus-Phaëton myth of lines 1–4, the term being peculiarly applicable to the horses of the sun in the amateur hands of Phaëton; the second, though seriously considered by eds., finds essentially no support in *OED*. As a singular ('runaway's'), it has been interpreted to refer to Phoebus as the sun (Warburton), night, with the stars as eyes (Steevens, comparing *MV* 2.6.47), Romeo (Seymour), Cupid (Halpin, Mitford, McCown), Phaëton (Lunt), Juliet (Massey), the most widely accepted being the sun and Phoebus the sun-god. Dowden suggests taking 'That' as a demonstrative pronoun = yonder) referring to Phoebus and treating 'That . . . eyes' as a parenthetical interjection.

3.2.9 By] 'And by' in Q2; 'And' is considered an undeleted 'false start'.

3.2.19 new snow upon] Most eds. read with F2 'new snow on' for metrical reasons, but slightly hypermetrical lines are not uncommon in Shakespeare; compare 3.5.43. NS treats 'new' as a 'false start', but the emphasis is on 'new' (= pure white, unsullied) snow.

3.2.76 Dove-feathered raven] Q2 'Rauenous douefeatherd rauen' is best explained as Shakespeare's 'false start' on the line, not clearly marked for deletion.

3.2.79 *damnèd] Q2 'dimme' is in part an easy combination minim and final 'e/d' misreading in Secretary hand, though the misreading of 'i' for 'a' is graphically more difficult to justify.

3.2.88 aqua-vitae] Compare Thomas Dekker's *The Whore of Babylon* (1607), 4.1.73: '*Aquavite*, the common drinke of all bawds.' The Nurse's fondness for aqua-vitae may be taken to underline her role as the lovers' personal bawd or go-between.

3.3.15 Here] Although most eds. prefer Q1 'Hence', Q2 'Here' makes good idiomatic sense (i.e. thou art banished from here, Verona). Williams makes a graphically persuasive case that 'Here' is a misreading of 'Hēce' (a missed, or missing, tilde and 'c' misread as 'r') and 'Hence' may be what Shakespeare intended.

3.3.40–3] Globe arrangement (after Steevens); although a few eds. have retained all five Q2 lines, most others agree, though offering different solutions (see collation), that the Q2 passage represents a combination of Shakespeare's first and second thoughts. If we accept the arrangement here adopted, Shakespeare appears to have started with Q2 lines 1 and 2 ('This may flyes do, . . . exile is not death?'), then decided to begin again with Q2 line 3 ('But *Romeo* . . . banished.'), repeated (as Q2 line 4) a slightly revised version of 1 ('Flies may do this, but . . . flie:'), and completed his revision with Q2 line 5 ('They are freemen, . . . banished.'). What he seems to have failed to do was (a) clearly mark Q2 line 1 for deletion and (b) clearly indicate that Q2 line 2 was intended to follow Q2 line 5. See Williams's note for a more extended analysis.

3.5.1–7 Wilt . . . nightingale] Brooke (1703–18) furnishes the situation (the coming of dawn necessitating the parting of the lovers) and perhaps something of the uncertain quality of very early morning light (see 12–13, 19–20). For the nightingale and lark we must look elsewhere. J. W. Lever (*S.Sur.* 6, 82–3) compares 1–7 with a passage in John Eliot's *Ortho-epia Gallica* (1593, p. 149):

Harke, harke, tis some other bird that sings now.
Tis a blacke-bird or a Nightingale.
The Nightingale sings not but evening and morning.
Where is she I pray thee?
Tis a Nightingale I heard her record.
Seest thou not hir sitting on a sprig?
O how sweetly she sings without any stop,
and ceaseth not!

Lever notes that Shakespeare may have received a suggestion for 'vaulty heaven' in 22 from a phrase ('la voute du Ciel') in a quatrain on the lark by Du Bartas quoted earlier by Eliot (*Ortho-epia Gallica*, p. 147), a quatrain that also seems to have influenced *Sonnets* 29.11–12 and *WT* 4.3.9. But the opening lines of a song in Lyly's *Campaspe* (5.1.32–9), which Shakespeare appears to recall in *Sonnets* 29.11–12 and *Cym.* 2.3.20–1, though usually ignored in the present context, deserve consideration as at least a collateral source:

What Bird so sings, yet so dos wayle?
O t'is the ravish'd Nightingale.
Jug, Jug, Jug, Jug, tereu, shee cryes,
And still her woes at Midnight rise.
Brave prick song! who is't now we heare?
None but the Larke so shrill and cleare;
How at heavens gats she claps her wings,
The Morne not waking till she sings.

Here, in Shakespeare's order, is the nightingale as a night singer and the lark as the harbinger of dawn (dawn is only implied, not mentioned, in Du Bartas's quatrain).

3.5.43 ay] The affirmative intensifier 'ay', here meaning 'yes, indeed', raises no difficulty, but the fact that Q2 spells it 'ay' instead of the normal form 'I' (see *OED* Ay) has raised a problem, since no other example of the affirmative spelled 'ay' has hitherto been found in or out of Shakespeare. An example may, however, be found in *Mucedorus* (anon., 1598, Q1; ed. C. F. Tucker Brooke, 4.2.82).

3.5.54-6 ill-divining soul . . . tomb] With Juliet's foreboding, compare the Hero-Leander story in Ovid's *Heroides*, XIX Epistle (*The Heroycall Epistles*, trans. George Turbervile, 1567; ed. F. Boas, 1928, pp. 279-80); 'But I wote nere what colde, / my quaking breast doth nomme, / As oft as to my restless mind / a thought of seas doth come. / . . . What so it be I dread, / have not in scorne my dreames: / Ne (yet unlesse the waters serve) / commit thy corse to streames.'

3.5.106 beseech] 'I beseech of' of Q4 and F2 makes the line metrically regular, but it sacrifices an effective dramatic pause after 'they'. 'Beseech' meaning 'I beseech' is common in Shakespeare.

3.5.176-7 Day . . . company] Recent eds., since Hoppe, are agreed in taking Q2 'houre, tide, time' as an unclearly deleted 'first shot'. It seems likely that 'Day, night' was Shakespeare's second thought, since it more or less subsumes the sequence of 'houre, tide, time'. See collation for other arrangements.

4.1.110] Following this line Q2 adds 'Be borne to buriall in thy kindreds graue:'. Since this line contains the essentials of 111–12, it is generally considered as a 'first shot' that Shakespeare failed to mark clearly for deletion.

4.2.23 tomorrow morning] In Brooke (2072) the marriage is arranged for the 'tenth day of September', but Juliet agrees to meet with Paris on 'wensday next' (2228), when he will be Capulet's guest at a costly feast (2257–8), and they spend many days 'in pleasure and disport' (2278) before the wedding-day arrives. There is, therefore, no sudden change in the wedding date, even though Paris 'with importune sute, the parentes doth he pray, / The wedlocke knot to knit soone up, and hast the mariage day' (2275–6). Compare Paris's comment in 3.4.29 ('My lord, I would that Thursday were tomorrow').

4.2.38 now near night] In Brooke, Juliet claims to have been at St Francis' church 'this morning' (2200); Painter (p. 128) says 'she returned home to hir fathers Pallace about .11. of the clock'.

4.4.13 A jealous hood, a jealous hood!] Because no other example of this exclamatory phrase has been recorded and explanations of it are hypothetical, two examples of a closely related phrase are worth noting, i.e., 'jealous head': Barnabe Googe, *Eglogs* (1563), Egloge septima (ed. Edward Arber, p. 61): 'Who nowe can please these Iealouse heads, / the faute is all in you, / For women never wold change their mind / yf men wold styll be true.'; Ovid, *Heroides* (*The Heroycall Epistles*, trans. George Turbervile, 1567; ed. F. Boas, 1928, p. 316): 'I [Ulysses] could the aged Hecuba had / and used her in her bed, / That thy [Penelope's] mistrustful mind I mought / beguile, and jelous hed, / That would have thought thy husband had / of no such peece been sped.' It is, of course, tempting to suggest that Q2 'hood' is a compositorial misreading of 'head,' but, since Q1 (the 'bad' quarto) also reads 'hood' (representing, as a "memorial reconstruction", presumably, what was spoken on the stage), such a misreading would be very difficult to explain. At least, however, 'jealous head,' by analogy, seems to offer support to G. L. Kittredge's gloss (see commentary note) and to the first definition in *OED*.

4.4.21 *faith] From Q4; Q2 'Father' as a form of address makes no sense in the context and is unlikely as a mild oath'. NS suggests that 'faith' in the copy was misread as 'fath' and interpreted as an abbreviated form of 'father'.

4.5.43–64] Apart from the Nurse's lines (49–54), which contain an element of comic hyperbole proper to her character, it is dangerously unhistorical to view these speeches as intentionally parodic. Many similarly formalised laments may be cited where clearly no parody is intended (see Chaucer, *Troilus and Criseyde*, III, 1450–63; Skelton, *Magnificence*, ed. A. Dyce, I, 292; Seneca, *Thebais*, p. 110 and *Oedipus*, p. 230 (in Newton's *Seneca* (1581)); Kyd, *Cornelia* 5.330–51; *Locrine*, ed. Tucker Brooke, 3.1.43–61; Shakespeare, *R3* 2.2.66–88, 4.4.26–58). That Shakespeare burlesques the style (later?) in *MND* in the Pyramus and Thisbe play need not reflect upon his use of the 'high style' here. The Q1 version of these lines (through 95) is markedly different (see collation) and it introduces a SD (*All at once cry out and wring their hands.*) followed by two lines headed by '*All cry:*'. On the strength of the Q1 SD it has been argued, most recently by Charles Lower (*S.St.* 8 (1975), 177–94) that 41–64 should be delivered chorally, Paris, Lady Capulet, the Nurse and Capulet each speaking six-line speeches simultaneously (*at once*). This has a certain attraction, especially if a comic effect is being sought (as Lower insists), but it runs into textual difficulties (the rearrangement of Paris's lines (41–2, 55–8)) and the obvious fact that the SD in Q1 refers certainly only to the two following lines in which '*All cry:*'. Nor is such an arrangement necessary to explain the Friar's use of 'confusions' in 66 as Lower claims.

4.5.82 *fond] From F2. 'some' of Q2–4, F is generally declared meaningless, probably with justice, though possibly 'some nature' might be interpreted to mean 'some touch of nature'. 'some', however, is an easy minim and final 'e' for 'd' misreading in Secretary hand.

4.5.96 put. . . pipes] NS compares (1) Nashe, *Summer's Last Will* (*Works*, III, 263), where Harvest, disappointed of a 'largesse', says: 'we were as good even put up our pipes, and sing Merry, merry, for we shall get no money'; and (2) Nashe, *Unfortunate Traveller* (*Works*, II, 222): 'This silver-sounding tale made such sugred harmonie in his eares, that . . . he would have found it in his hart to have packt up hys pipes and gone to heaven without a bait.' Note the collocation of 'silver-sounding' (in 125 ff. below) with 'packt up hys pipes' and an associated Nashe echo (*The Unfortunate Traveller*, *Works*, II, 261), 'iron wit', in 118–19.

4.5.126, 129 Prates] To the several other echoes from Nashe (see supplementary note on 4.5.96), may probably be added 'such a prating fellow' from *The Unfortunate Traveller* (*Works*, II, 223), a phrase that occurs on the page immediately following two other Nashe references from *The Unfortunate Traveller* (p. 222). 'Prates!' (126) and 'Prates too!' (129), substantively the readings of Q2 (the only text with authorial authority), have most often, until recently, been displaced by 'Pretty!' and 'Pretty too!' substantively from

Q1, readings which may have led to Q4's 'Pratee' (a variant form of 'pretty') and 'Pratee to' (see collation). Ulrici, however, suggests that 'Pretty' is out of character for Peter, who is not given to ironic praise, and that 'Prates' properly dismisses the answers of the First and Second Musician.

5.1.15 How ... Juliet?] Q2's hypermetrical 'How doth my Lady *Iuliet?*' seems to arise from the compositor's repetition of 'How doth my Lady,' directly above in 14 (Collier). Hosley (p. 154) includes 'doth' as similarly contaminated (following Greg, p. 52) and accepts, perhaps rightly, Q1 'fares'.

5.3.3 *yew trees] From Q1 'Ew-tree'; Q2 'young' for 'yew' is explained (Williams) as a misreading of manuscript 'yeug' or 'yeugh'; see *OED*. The same misreading occurs in 137 below.

5.3.92–115] Compare Daniel's *Rosamond*:

> The poyson soone disperc'd through all my vaines,
> Had dispossess'd my living sences quite:
> When naught respecting death, the last of paines,
> Plac'd his pale collours, th'ensigne of his might,
> Upon hys new-got spoyle before his right ...   (603–7)

> Thus as these passions doe him [Henry II] over-whelme,
> He drawes him neere my bodie to behold it ...   (659–60)

> And as he in hys carefull armes doth hold it,
> Viewing the face that even death commends ...   (663–4)

> O be it lawfull now, that dead thou havest,
> Thys sorrowing farewell of a dying kisse.
> And you fayre eyes, containers of my blisse,
>   Motives of love, borne to be matched never:
>   Entomb'd in your sweet circles sleepe for ever.

> Ah how me thinks I see death dallying seekes,
> To entertaine it selfe in loves sweet place:
> Decayed Roses of discoloured cheekes,
> Doe yet retaine deere notes of former grace:
> And ougly death sits faire within her face;
>   Sweet remnants resting of vermilion red,
>   That death it selfe, doubts whether she be dead.   (668–79)

Compare also *Lucrece* 400–6, and Sidney, *Astrophil and Stella*, Sonnet 85.12 (see supplementary note on 5.3.118). P. B. Bartlett (ed.), *Poems of George Chapman*, 1941, notes Chapman's recollection of 94–6 in the Fifth Sestiad (44–6) of his continuation of *Hero and Leander* (1598).

5.3.102 Shall I believe] Q2 'I will beleeue' preceding 'Shall I beleeue' is generally taken as a 'first shot' that Shakespeare failed to mark clearly for deletion, though Q1 'O I beleeue' might seem to suggest that 'Shall I beleeue' should be taken as the 'first shot' (as Pope apparently interpreted it). However, the position of 'I will beleeue' as the conclusion of a verse line renders such a view unlikely.

5.3.107 *palace] From Q3; Q2 'pallat' is usually explained as a misreading of manuscript 'pallac' (see supplementary note on 2.1.10). Hosley defends 'pallat' (= pallet) as 'an image which supports the theme that Juliet's wedding bed is indeed her grave' (p. 155), and he has been joined by R. Smallwood (*SQ* 26 (1975), 298), who compares *John* 3.4.25–7, in which death is called upon to 'Arise forth from the couch of lasting night'. The argument is tempting, but 'palace' accords better with the description of the tomb as a 'presence' in 86 and, as Williams points out, 'depart from' is 'more appropriate to a palace than a pallet' (p. 140).

5.3.108 Depart again. Here] Q4's arrangement, here adopted, assumes, what is now generally accepted, that the four lines in Q2 following 107 (see collation) are another example of Shakespeare's 'first thoughts', being in part an anticipation of 108–20, particularly of 119–20. No satisfactory explanation of the second of these lines ('Heer's to thy health, where ere thou tumblest in') has been offered, though Gibbons suggests that 'tumblest in' may be 'the germ of the shipwreck metaphor developed in ll. 117–18'.

5.3.118 seasick weary] Sidney's Sonnet 85 reads:

> I see the house, my heart thy selfe containe,
>   Beware full sailes drowne not thy tottring barge:
>   Least joy, by Nature apt sprites to enlarge,
> Thee to thy wracke beyond thy limits straine.
> Nor do like Lords, whose weake confused braine,
>   Not pointing to fit folkes each undercharge,
>   While everie office themselves will discharge,
> With doing all, leave nothing done but paine.
> But give apt servants their due place, let eyes
> See Beautie's totall summe summ'd in her face:
> Let eares heare speech, which wit to wonder ties,
> Let breath sucke up those sweetes, let armes embrace
>   The globe of weale, lips *Love's* indentures make:
>   Thou but of all the kingly Tribute take.

5.3.170 rust] Grant White defends 'rust': 'Her imagination is excited, and, looking beyond her suicidal act, she sees her dead *Romeo's* dagger, which would otherwise rust in its sheath, rusting in her heart; and with fierce and amorous joy, she cries, "*This* is thy sheath; *there* rust and let me die."' The objection that a dagger 'rests', not 'rusts', in its sheath (NS) is beside the point considering the nature of the present 'sheath'. Gibbons suggests a kind of phallic fulfilment in Juliet's action, completing 'the motif of Death as rival to Romeo; Death *lies with* Juliet'.

5.3.190 *shrieked] Q2 'shrike' is another example of final 'd' misread as 'e'; compare 3.5.13 n. and supplementary notes on 3.2.79, 4.5.82, and (in the collation) 2.2.10, 3.3.168, 4.1.7.

5.3.191 O, the people] Hosley (p. 155) treats Q2 'O' as a 'false start' not clearly marked for deletion in Shakespeare's MS., thus accepting (like Pope) the Q1 reading.

TEXTUAL ANALYSIS

The textual situation in *Romeo and Juliet* is fraught with problems, some of them essentially insoluble. There are two substantive editions:[1] Q1 (1597), a 'bad' quarto or memorial reconstruction (i.e. a text put together from memory by one or more actors who had taken part in an earlier production); Q2 (1599), a 'good' quarto, deriving ultimately from Shakespeare's holograph. All seventeenth-century editions derive from Q2: Q3 (1609), a reprint of Q2; Q4 (undated, but probably about 1622), printed, with some intelligent but unauthorised corrections, from Q3 with consultation of Q1; F (the First Folio, 1623), printed from Q3,[2] with almost no attempt at correction apart from the addition of a few obvious stage directions; Q5 (1637), printed from Q4. The later folios (F2, 1632; F3, 1664; F4, 1685) are printed each in turn from the immediately preceding folio. Q2 is thus the only possible copy-text.

Two interrelated problems face the editor: (1) the provenance of the Q2 text; and (2) the extent to which Q2 has been 'contaminated' by Q1. Some discussion of these two editions will help to set the lines of argument.

Quarto One: before H. R. Hoppe's study (1948)[3] of Q1, two related views of its provenance were widely entertained: (1) eighteenth-century editors generally treated Q1 as Shakespeare's first draft, which gave it a false authority; (2) nineteenth-century editors merely refined this view by introducing the intermediary of shorthand reporting to account for the unsatisfactory quality of the Q1 text. The first-draft theory, with or without shorthand reporting, is no longer accepted. Hoppe established that Q1 is a 'bad' quarto, exhibiting all the marks of a memorially reported text: recollection, anticipation, substitution, transposition, vulgarisation of language, repetition, paraphrase, borrowings from other plays (*2* and *3 Henry VI* (the 'bad' quartos), *Richard III*, *Arden of Feversham*), unmetrical verse and patches of 'original' verse (for some examples, see collation at 1.5.124–6; 2.5.29–34; 2.6; 3.1.145–61; 5.3.224–69).

---

[1] Neither Q1 nor Q2 was originally entered in the Stationers' Register, though printing rights were transferred from Cuthbert Burby to Nicholas Ling 22 January 1607 and from Ling to John Smethwick 19 November 1607.

[2] Gibbons (p.2) agrees on Q3 as copy for F1, but adds 'with the exception of a number of passages which follow Q4'. But only in three short stretches (2.6.23, 27, 34, and 3.1.2; 4.2.25, 28; 5.3.189, 201 SD) may the readings common to Q4 and F1 alone be considered comparatively compelling evidence of the use of Q4 (that at 2.6.23 being significantly a common error). Since, however, two different compositors were setting from the same copy (Q3), even these instances do not seem beyond coincidence.

Since this was written, S. W. Reid (*SB* 35 (1982), 43–66) has examined the possible use of Q4 and determined that it does not figure in the printing of the F text. His detailed examination of F leads him to postulate an editor with a knowledge of the play (e.g. Edward Knight, Heminge or Condell) who 'worked through Q3's text with (for his day) considerable care, annotating the printer's copy [of Q3] where it struck him as deficient and relying mainly on the context to do so, though perhaps occasionally – and certainly not often enough – consulting a playhouse manuscript' (p. 66). See also Reid's later article in *The Library*, 6th ser., 5 (1983), 118–25.

[3] *The Bad Quarto of 'Romeo and Juliet': A Bibliographical and Textual Study*, 1948.

Hoppe proposed that the actors playing Romeo and Paris are the most likely 'reporters', since their speeches tend to be more accurately reported. Compared, however, with some other 'bad' quarto texts (*Hamlet*, for example), Q1 is at times comparatively 'good', although the quality of the reporting varies, becoming increasingly erratic after 2.4 (sig. E3^r) and sometimes breaking down completely (see collation at 2.6; 4.5.42–95; 5.3.224–69).[1]

Q1 claims on the title page to have been printed by John Danter, but he printed only sheets A–D. Sheets E–K, in smaller type and with different running-titles, were set by Edward Allde.[2] Danter's establishment was raided by the authorities in 1596/7 and his presses seized. Hoppe argues[3] that Q1 was partially printed (up to and including sheet D) at this point and that Danter employed another printer to complete the volume. He argues further that a date of early 1597 (N.S.) fits well with Danter's claim on the title page that the play 'hath been often... plaid publiquely, by the right Honourable the L. of *Hunsdon* his Seruants', since Shakespeare's company was known by that name only during the short period 22 July 1596 to 17 March 1596/7. More recently, however, the consecutive printing of Q1 has been challenged by J. A. Lavin,[4] who argues that the two parts of Q1 were printed concurrently by Danter and Allde, the copy having been cast off in advance (i.e. the lines counted off so that the break between sheets D and E could be exactly calculated). Thus, Lavin suggests, Q1 was probably 'in the press between 1 January and 17 March 1596/7' and that the 1597 date on Q1 'is no guarantee that it was not printed during the last weeks of 1596'.

Two further bibliographical peculiarities in Q1 should be noticed. (1) Beginning at the bottom of G2^v, the third sheet of Allde's section and the end of 3.4, a row of printer's ornaments has been set across the page to indicate a scene break (a second row has also been inserted in this instance at the top of G3^r, the beginning of 3.5) and the practice was continued thereafter. Such apparent concern with scene division makes Q1 unique among Shakespearean quartos, except for the late 1622 quarto of *Othello*. But this device was only Allde's ploy to stretch his materials to fill out the full six sheets (K4^v being blank) for which he had contracted with Danter.[5] (2) The second peculiarity establishes an important link between Q1 and Q2. In 1.3 (B4^r–C1^r) and 1.5 (C3^v–C4^r) the Nurse's speeches are regularly set in italic type (with roman speech headings). The most likely explanation is that the reporter(s) of Q1 had come into possession of the Nurse's part (or 'side') for these two scenes and that the part was written out in Italian script. In both scenes, even after Q2 abandons its use of Q1 copy at 1.3.36 (see below), the Nurse's lines are mostly verbally close to those in Q2.

Like other 'bad' quarto texts, Q1 represents, filtered through the verbal and visual

---

[1] Hoppe (*Bad Quarto*, p. 220) first suggested Henry Chettle as the 'reporter–versifier' for these sections of Q1. G. Melchiori ('Peter, Balthasar, and Shakespeare's art of doubling', *MLR* 78 (1983), 785–6) proposes that at 5.3.131–4 the individual (? Chettle) responsible for these lines consulted Brooke's *Romeus* (2619–22).

[2] Standish Henning, 'The printer of *Romeo and Juliet*, Q1', *PBSA* 60 (1966), 363–4. Hoppe (*Bad Quarto*, p. 3 n.) had tentatively suggested Allde.

[3] Hoppe, *Bad Quarto*, pp. 38–52.

[4] 'John Danter's ornament stock', *SB* 23 (1970), 29–34.   [5] Hoppe, *Bad Quarto*, p. 45.

memory of the reporter(s), a contemporary stage version of the play. Thus, despite its lack of authority, it carries us beyond Shakespeare's 'literary' text (i.e. Q2) and tells us something of how the play was realised in a contemporary production. Take, for example, the matter of length. Q1 is about one-third shorter (a little over 800 lines) than Q2. The difference can be attributed partly to failure of memory by the reporter(s), but it may also reflect cuts in the production on which the attempted reconstruction was based. Thus, when 3.2.1–33 is found reduced to its first four lines in Q1, we may suspect that the speech had been heavily cut in the earlier stage version and that the reporter(s) had never heard the omitted lines. Q1 also throws light on contemporary stage business through its stage directions, which arise from the recollection of performances seen. A substantial number of Q1's stage directions have been incorporated into the present text.

Quarto Two: Q2, '*Newly corrected, augmented, and amended*', was printed for Cuthbert Burby by Thomas Creed in 1599. The formula '*Newly corrected*', etc., is now considered a publisher's device for asserting the authority of his text and distinguishing it from Danter's Q1. Burby had employed the same formula on the title page of Q1 of *Love's Labour's Lost* (1598), of which a possible earlier 'bad' quarto has not survived. Ironically, Q2 is on the whole less carefully printed than Q1 and reveals no evidence of significant press correction.[1]

There is universal agreement that the printer's copy for Q2 was derived in some way from Shakespeare's rough draft ('foul papers'), except for one section (1.2.50–1.3.35), first identified by Robert Gericke (1879),[2] set from an essentially uncorrected copy of Q1. Elsewhere in Q2 the evidence for the use of 'foul papers' is typical: considerable variation in character names and speech headings (see collation 3.5, and the use of an actor's name, Will Kemp, for Peter at 4.5.99 SD); the appearance of 'permissive' stage directions (1.1.63; 1.4.0 SD; 3.1.29; 4.2.0 SD; 4.4.13); the accidental retention of some lines or part-lines representing Shakespeare's 'first thoughts', followed by his revised version (see collation, 1.2.15; 2.2.184–7 (2.3.1–4); 3.1.138; 3.2.9, 76; 3.3.40–3; 3.5.176–7; 4.1.110; 5.3.102, 108); a small number of special Shakespearean spellings (see collation or text, 1.3.36; 2.4.1; 3.1.93; 5.1.24) and errors attributed to a misreading of a Shakespearean spelling form (2.1.10; 5.3.107). Unlike Q1, Q2 shows no definite evidence of theatrical provenance, though it is possible that a few stage directions were added to the 'foul papers' by the book-keeper preparatory to having a transcript ('fair copy') prepared for the official prompt-book.

The most difficult problem posed by Q2 is the extent of its dependence on Q1. Apart from the single section (1.2.50–1.3.35) admittedly set from Q1, what was the precise nature of the 'copy' used by the printer? Recently, two influential views have been advanced. (1) Q2 was printed from a copy of Q1 corrected and augmented (by inserted slips and marginal notation) by collation with Shakespeare's 'foul papers', thus producing mixed copy, partly printed, partly manuscript transcription. This theory,

---

[1] George W. Williams, *The Most Excellent and Lamentable Tragedie of Romeo and Juliet: A Critical Edition*, 1964, pp. 150–1.
[2] '*Romeo and Juliet* nach Shakespeares Manuscript', *Shakespeare Jahrbuch* 14 (1879), 270–2.

suggested by Greta Hjort in 1926,[1] was supported by G. I. Duthie and Dover Wilson[2] and is the basis of their NS edition (1955). (2) Q2 was printed, apart from the section already excepted, directly from Shakespeare's 'foul papers', with intermittent consultation of Q1 by the two Q2 compositors at certain points where Shakespeare's manuscript was damaged or illegible. This view, supported by E. K. Chambers, Sidney Thomas and W. W. Greg,[3] has been substantiated by Richard Hosley, P. L. Cantrell and G. W. Williams,[4] the first and third of these basing their editions on it. My own analysis favours the second theory, and the present text, like my earlier Riverside text (1974), accepts Q2 as basically derived directly from Shakespeare's 'foul papers'.

Either theory leaves the authority of Q2 ambiguous, the second less so than the first. But even if we accept Q2 as set for the most part directly from Shakespeare's 'foul papers', the bibliographical links with Q1, established in Q2 in addition to 1.2.50–1.3.35, raise the question of how frequent and how pervasive the 'consultation' of Q1 actually was. Identity of punctuation, lineation, spelling, capitalisation or italics show that Q1 influenced the Q2 text at 2.1.13 (Q1, C4^v; Q2, D1^v; see collation), 2.4.25–43 (Q1, E1^v; Q2, E2^v), and 3.5.27–36 (Q1, G3$^{r. v}$; Q2, H3^r). These links are admitted by Hosley; Dover Wilson and Duthie find many more (in 31 out of the 75 pages of Q1), and it is probable that some of these represent sporadic consultation of Q1, if nothing more extensive. And Hosley in 1957 somewhat changed his original view ('the consultation must have been somewhat steadier (that is to say, less "occasional") than I...suggested [in the edition of 1954]'). Thus, although an editor must generally accept a Q2 reading (allowing for compositorial misreading or other error) where it differs from Q1, he is often left with the suspicion in those many lines and passages where Q1 and Q2 are verbally identical that Creede's compositors, particularly Compositor A, who set all but six pages of Q2 (see Cantrell and Williams), seduced by the relative ease of setting from printed copy and the seemingly 'good' quality of the Q1 passage (for example on A3, D3^r, G4^r, H2^r), allowed themselves to drift from their manuscript copy and followed Q1 for one or more lines. Compositor A almost certainly did so on three occasions; but how often he and Compositor B did so, and to what extent, must remain uncertain.

Two further problems in Q2 are best discussed here. In 1.4 (C2^r), lines 54–91 of Mercutio's Queen Mab speech are set as prose, though they appear as verse in Q1's

[1] 'The good and bad quartos of *Romeo and Juliet* and *Love's Labour's Lost*', *MLR* 21 (1926), 140–6.

[2] J. Dover Wilson, 'Recent work on the text of *Romeo and Juliet*', *S.Sur.* 8 (1955), 81–99; J. Dover Wilson and G. I. Duthie, 'The copy for *Romeo and Juliet*, 1599', in NS (1955), pp. 112–18. Duthie had earlier supported a less extreme version of this view in 'The text of Shakespeare's *Romeo and Juliet*', *SB* 4 (1951), 3–29.

[3] E. K. Chambers, *William Shakespeare*, 2 vols., 1930, I, 344; Sidney Thomas, 'The bibliographical links between the first two quartos of *Romeo and Juliet*', *RES* 25 (1949), 110–14; W. W. Greg, *The Editorial Problem in Shakespeare*, 1951 (2nd edn), pp. 61–2, and *The Shakespeare First Folio*, 1955, p. 230.

[4] Richard Hosley, 'Quarto copy for Q2 *Romeo and Juliet*', *SB* 9 (1957), 129–41, and his earlier Yale edition (1954) of *Romeo and Juliet*, pp. 157–67; Paul L. Cantrell and George W. Williams, 'The printing of the second quarto of *Romeo and Juliet* (1599)', *SB* 9 (1957), 107–28, and G. W. Williams in his old-spelling edition (1964) of Q2.

shorter version. The speech begins (line 53) and ends (lines 92–5) as verse in Q2, 92–5 falling at the top of a new page (c2ᵛ). The NS editors suggest, in line with their theory that much of Q2 was set from corrected and expanded Q1 copy, that the compositor, faced with a mass of correction and marginal insertions, was 'baffled by the problem of lineation' and 'would almost inevitably decide that the easiest and quickest solution was to set up the bulk of the speech as prose' (p. 142). But the use of corrected Q1 copy at this point is at best questionable and the explanation does not account for the sudden switch to verse at the top of the following page. Since c2 shows no evidence of being a cancel leaf, two other hypotheses may be considered. (1) Shortly after the printing-off of the inner forme of sheet c (that side of the sheet containing the equivalent of pages 2, 3, 6, 7) was begun, perhaps when the forme was proofread, it was noticed that the compositor (here Compositor A)¹ had failed to include ten lines (perhaps marginal insertions – for example, 59–61) of Shakespeare's 'foul paper' copy. The press was stopped, and since, in seriatim composition (i.e. setting the pages in regular order, 1, 2, 3, etc.), the outer forme was already in type (certainly up to and including c3ʳ) and it would be time-consuming and expensive to reset sheet c (inner and outer formes) beginning with c2ʳ, the problem was solved by resetting the full text of Mercutio's speech (38 lines of verse) as a tightly packed block of prose up to and including line 91. Printing-off of the inner forme would then be resumed. That no copy of the original setting of c2ʳ has survived among the thirteen known copies of Q2 need cause no surprise, particularly if the error were caught early in the press-run.² (2) The second explanation postulates the possibility that the compositor decided to set sheet c by formes (i.e. setting those pages which would fall on either the outer or the inner forme) and that he began with the outer forme, setting c1ʳ, c2ᵛ, c3ʳ and c4ᵛ.³ When he came to set the inner forme, he discovered that, in casting off his copy for the outer forme, he had either miscounted or had failed to allow for marginal additions in the MS. in Mercutio's speech. Since, by the time he recognised his error, the outer forme (containing the last three-and-a-half verse lines of the speech at the top of c2ᵛ) was already printed off, or being printed off, he had either to cut the speech down to the 27 lines remaining to him on c2ʳ or to set the 38 verse lines as prose. To his credit, he chose the second alternative. As should be clear, none of the three explanations suggested above can be proved, unless new evidence can be discovered.⁴

The second problem, one of the most debated cruxes in the play, concerns the near duplication of four lines in Q2 (D4ᵛ), the first version (A) following line 187 of Romeo's final speech in 2.2, the second version (B) forming the opening lines of Friar Lawrence's soliloquy in 2.3, two lines later. Q1 and Q4, the last probably influenced by Q1, omit A, giving the lines to Friar Lawrence; Q3 and F merely reprint Q2's duplicated versions; F2 retains only A, giving the lines to Romeo. The early texts thus run the gamut.

¹ Cantrell and Williams, 'Printing of the second quarto', pp. 107–13.
² See Greg, *Shakespeare First Folio*, pp. 233–4. His discussion is based on a suggestion by Dover Wilson.
³ George W. Williams, 'Setting by formes in quarto printing', *SB* 11 (1958), 39–53.
⁴ Sidney Thomas (*S.Sur.* 25 (1972), 73–80) argues for the superiority of the Q1 version of the Queen Mab speech and tries to show that the Q2 version contains some characteristics of a reported text. His case is interesting but not persuasive.

Pope restored the lines to Friar Lawrence on the authority of Q1 and has been followed by all editors except Hosley, Williams and Gibbons, who argue, echoing Sisson (who nevertheless gives the lines to Friar Lawrence), that the day and night imagery in these lines is consonant with that in 3.5 and is more suitable to Romeo than to the Friar. NS, on the other hand, argues that the lines cannot be Romeo's because they describe his 'blessèd, blessèd night' (139) as 'frowning' and 'like a drunkard'. Neither argument seems conclusive, and other considerations need to be taken into account: (a) Q1's assignment to the Friar, which unquestionably represents a stage tradition (Q1 is generally accurate in its speech assignments); (b) the sententious, rather ponderous pace and tone of the four lines and the moralistic implications of 'darkness' as a 'drunkard', proper to a Friar; (c) the function of these lines as marking some passage of time following, not preceding, Romeo's exit; (d) the close connection of the lines with what immediately follows in the Friar's speech, so that the connective 'Now' tends to dangle without them. These points seem to weight the argument in favour of assigning the lines to Friar Lawrence.

But the question of attribution is only part of the problem. Which version (A or B) should an editor choose? Hosley takes B as Shakespeare's revision of A, on the grounds that 'second thoughts' always follow 'first thoughts' in Q2; Williams, though agreeing on the idea of revision, considers A the revised form; and NS and Gibbons prefer A, the first dismissing B as 'a rather careless reprint' of A by the Q2 compositor. The differences between the A and B versions are slight, except for line 4, which is superior to its counterpart in A, so the NS case for B as a 'careless reprint' of A seems to founder. The present edition accepts B as Shakespeare's rather careless revision (see below), but whichever version is preferred all editors produce an eclectic text of the lines.

How may the duplication in Q2 be explained? Every explanation is hypothetical and influenced by the editor's view of the kind of copy from which Q2 was set at this point. My suggestion, which strongly implies the direct use of Shakespeare's 'foul papers' for Q2 copy, is that Shakespeare entered the Friar and started the Friar's speech immediately after line 187; then, realising the need for lines to prepare for Romeo's visit to the Friar in 2.3, added lines 188–9 below. Deleting the Friar's entry but failing to delete the four lines clearly (as elsewhere with 'first thoughts' in this text), he then re-entered the Friar and hastily recopied the opening lines of his speech, making one or two errors and slight revisions in the process.

The Q2 text affords considerable evidence that the compositors found their copy confused and difficult. As a result, Q2 is frequently in need of emendation. The only other substantive text is Q1, and editors from Pope onward have turned to Q1 for aid or have even preferred Q1 readings. (A list of all the principal editorial borrowings from Q1 is in the collation.) So long as critical opinion accepted Q1 as based on Shakespeare's first draft, a rationale for such dependence might be offered; but since the establishment of Q1 as a 'bad' quarto editors have sought to reduce their dependence on Q1.[1] Even so, the present text, conservative in its adherence to Q2 as

[1] Richard Hosley, 'The corrupting influence of the bad quarto on the received text of *Romeo and Juliet*', *SQ* 4 (1953), 11–33.

copy-text (except for 1.2.50–1.3.35, where Q1 serves as copy-text), accepts three-and-a-half additional lines and eighteen substantive readings on the authority of Q1 and Q4 (a quarto showing evidence of influence from Q1). These figures do not include further debts to Q1 in punctuation and stage directions or its occasional agreements with readings in Q3 and F which have been adopted here.

Although basically a modern-spelling edition, the present text retains a few characteristic Elizabethan variant spellings indicating a difference in pronunciation from other contemporary forms of the same words, the forms which have survived in modern English usage. All such variant forms are glossed in the Commentary and other less distinctive variant forms, here modernised, are recorded in the collation. Internal *th/d* variants (e.g. *burthen/burden*) and forms with variant *en-/in-* prefixes have been silently modernised.

The regular Elizabethan orthographic distinction between the past tense in *-'d* (non-syllabic) and *-ed* (syllabic) has been levelled to *-ed*, the syllabic form being indicated by a grave accent (e.g. *despisèd*) in verse (for examples see the collation at 1.1.78, 120). Metrically ambiguous cases, in which modern usage favours the unstressed form even though the stressed form of the Q2 copy-text is metrically possible, are recorded in the collation.

APPENDIX

The following excerpts from Arthur Brooke's (or Broke's) *The Tragicall Historye of Romeus and Juliet* offer a newly edited text based on the first edition (1562), with consultation (apparently for the first time) of the second (1567) and third (1587) editions (each printed from the preceding edition), any of which Shakespeare could have used for *Romeo and Juliet*. Long-*s*, *i* and *j*, and *u* and *v* have been modernised, and some obvious verbal corrections and adjustments of the punctuation have been admitted, partly on the authority of the second and third editions. Following Edmond Malone's edition (1780), the poem was re-edited by J. P. Collier (1844) and W. C. Hazlitt (1875), but the best old-spelling edition is P. A. Daniel's (New Shakspere Society, 1875). The texts edited by J. J. Munro (1908), a modern-spelling edition, and by Geoffrey Bullough (I, 1957) are based on Daniel and generally repeat his occasional errors.

THE TRAGICALL HISTORYE OF
ROMEUS AND JULIET,
written first in Italian by Bandell, and nowe in Englishe by Ar. Br.

In aedibus Richardi Tottelli. Cum Privilegio.

To the Reader.
The God of all glorye created universallye all creatures, to sette forth his prayse, both those whiche we esteme profitable in use and pleasure, and also those, whiche we accompte noysome, and lothsome. But principally he hath appointed man, the chiefest instrument of his honour, not onely, for ministryng matter thereof in man himselfe: but aswell in gatheryng out of other, the occasions of publishing Gods goodnes, wisdome, & power. And in like sort, everye dooyng of man hath by Goddes dyspensacion some thynge, whereby God may, and ought to be honored. So the good doynges of the good, & the evill actes of the wicked, the happy successe of the blessed, and the wofull procedinges of the miserable, doe in divers sorte sound one prayse of God. And as eche flower yeldeth hony to the bee: so every exaumple ministreth good lessons, to the well disposed mynde. The glorious triumphe of the continent man upon the lustes of wanton fleshe, incourageth men to honest restraynt of wyld affections, the shamefull and wretched endes of such, as have yelded their libertie thrall to fowle desires, teache men to witholde them selves from the hedlong fall of loose dishonestie. So, to lyke effect, by sundry meanes, the good mans exaumple byddeth men to be good, and the evill mans mischefe, warneth men not to be evyll. To this good ende, serve all ill endes, of yll begynnynges. And to this ende (good Reader) is this tragicall matter written, to describe unto thee a couple of unfortunate lovers, thralling themselves to unhonest desire, neglecting the authoritie and advise of parents and frendes, conferring their principall counsels with dronken gossyppes, and superstitious friers (the naturally

fitte instrumentes of unchastitie) attemptyng all adventures of peryll, for thattaynyng of their wished lust, usyng auriculer confession (the kay of whoredome, and treason) for furtheraunce of theyr purpose, abusyng the honorable name of lawefull mariage, to cloke the shame of stolne contractes, finallye, by all meanes of unhonest lyfe, hastyng to most unhappye deathe. This president (good Reader) shalbe to thee, as the slaves of Lacedemon, oppressed with excesse of drinke, deformed and altered from likenes of men, both in mynde, and use of body, were to the free borne children, so shewed to them by their parentes, to thintent to rayse in them an hatefull lothyng of so filthy beastlynes. Hereunto if you applye it, ye shall deliver my dooing from offence, and profit your selves. Though I saw the same argument lately set foorth on stage with more commendation, then I can looke for: (being there much better set forth then I have or can dooe) yet the same matter penned as it is, may serve to lyke good effect, if the readers do brynge with them lyke good myndes, to consider it. which hath the more incouraged me to publishe it, suche as it is.   Ar. Br.

[Brooke's two sonnets 'To the Reader' are omitted.]

The Argument.

Love hath inflamed twayne by sodayn sight.
  And both do graunt the thing that both desyre.
  They wed in shrift by counsell of a frier.
  Yong Romeus clymes fayre Juliets bower by night.
Three monthes he doth enjoy his cheefe delight.
  By Tybalts rage, provoked unto yre,
  He payeth death to Tybalt for his hyre.
  A banisht man he scapes by secret flight.
New mariage is offred to his wyfe.
  She drinkes a drinke that seemes to reve her breath.
  They bury her, that sleping yet hath lyfe.
Her husband heares the tydinges of her death.
  He drinkes his bane. And she with Romeus knyfe,
When she awakes, her selfe (alas) she sleath.

The Tragicall History of Romeus and Juliet.

There is beyonde the Alps, a towne of auncient fame,
Whose bright renoune yet shineth cleare, Verona men it name.
Bylt in an happy time, bylt on a fertile soyle:
Maynteined by the heavenly fates, and by the townish toyle.   4

There were two auncient stockes, which Fortune high dyd place   25
Above the rest, indewd with welth, and nobler of their race.
Loved of the common sort, loved of the Prince alike:
And like unhappy were they both, when Fortune list to strike.
Whose prayse with equall blast, fame in her trumpet blew:
The one was cliped Capelet, and thother Montagew.   30
A wonted use it is, that men of likely sorte
(I wot not by what furye forsd) envye eche others porte.

So these, whose egall state bred envye pale of hew,
And then of grudging envyes roote, blacke hate and rancor grewe.
As of a little sparke, oft ryseth mighty fyre,
So of a kyndled sparke of grudge, in flames flashe out theyr yre.
And then theyr deadly foode, first hatchd of trifling stryfe,
Did bathe in bloud of smarting woundes, it reved breth and lyfe.
No legend lye I tell, scarce yet theyr eyes be drye:
That did behold the grisly sight, with wet and weping eye.   40
But when the prudent prince, who there the scepter helde,
So great a new disorder in his common weale behelde:
By jentyl meane he sought, their choler to asswage:
And by perswasion to appease, their blameful furious rage.
But both his woords and tyme, the prince hath spent in vayne:
So rooted was the inward hate, he lost his buysy payne.
When frendly sage advise, ne jentyll woords avayle:
By thondring threats, and princely powre their courage gan he quayle,
In hope that when he had the wasting flame supprest,
In time he should quyte quench the sparks that boornd within their brest.   50
Now whilst these kyndreds do remayne in this estate,
And eche with outward frendly shew dooth hyde his inward hate:
One Romeus, who was of race a Montague,
Upon whose tender chyn, as yet, no manlyke beard there grewe,
Whose beauty and whose shape so farre the rest did stayne:
That from the cheefe of Veron youth he greatest fame dyd gayne,
Hath founde a mayde so fayre (he found so foule his happe)
Whose beauty, shape, and comely grace, did so his heart entrappe,
That from his owne affayres, his thought she did remove:
Onely he sought to honor her, to serve her, and to love.   60
To her he writeth oft, oft messengers are sent:
At length (in hope of better spede) himselfe the lover went
Present to pleade for grace, which absent was not founde:
And to discover to her eye his new receaved wounde.
But she that from her youth was fostred evermore
With vertues foode, and taught in schole of wisdomes skilfull lore:
By aunswere did cutte of thaffections of his love,
That he no more occasion had so vayne a sute to move.
So sterne she was of chere, (for all the payne he tooke)
That in reward of toyle, she would not geve a frendly looke.   70
And yet how much she did with constant mind retyre:
So much the more his fervent minde was prickt fourth by desyre.
But when he many monthes, hopelesse of his recure,
Had served her, who forced not what paynes he did endure:
At length he thought to leave Verona, and to prove,
If chaunge of place might chaunge awaye his ill bestowed love.

In sighs, in teares, in plainte, in care, in sorow and unrest,   92
He mones the daye, he wakes the long and wery night,
So deepe hath love with pearcing hand, ygravd her bewty bright
Within his brest, and hath so mastred quite his hart:
That he of force must yeld as thrall, no way is left to start.

But one emong the rest, the trustiest of his feeres, 101
Farre more then he with counsel fild, and ryper of his yeeres,
Gan sharply him rebuke, suche love to him he bare:
That he was felow of his smart, and partner of his care.
What meanst thou Romeus (quoth he) what doting rage
Dooth make thee thus consume away, the best parte of thine age,
In seking her that scornes, and hydes her from thy sight?
Not forsing all thy great expence, ne yet thy honor bright:
Thy teares, thy wretched lyfe, ne thine unspotted truth:
Which are of force (I weene) to move the hardest hart to ruthe. 110
Now for our frendships sake, and for thy health I pray:
That thou hencefoorth become thyne owne: O geve no more away
Unto a thankeles wight, thy precious free estate:
In that thou lovest such a one, thou seemst thy selfe to hate.
For she doth love els where, (and then thy time is lorne)
Or els (what booteth thee to sue) loves court she hath forsworne.

Remove the veale of love, that keepes thine eyes so blynde: 129
That thou ne canst the ready path of thy forefathers fynde.
But if unto thy will so much in thrall thou art:
Yet in some other place bestowe thy witles wandring hart.

The yong mans lystning eare receivde the holesome sounde, 141
And reasons truth yplanted so, within his head had grounde:
That now with healthy coole ytempred is the heate:
And piecemeale weares away the greefe that erst his heart dyd freate.
To his approved frend, a solemne othe he plight:
At every feast ykept by day, and banquet made by night:
At pardons in the churche, at games in open streate:
And every where he would resort where Ladies wont to meete.
Eke should his savage heart lyke all indifferently:
For he would view and judge them all with unallured eye. 150

The wery winter nightes restore the Christmas games: 155
And now the season doth invite to banquet townish dames.
And fyrst in Capels house, the chiefe of all the kyn,
Sparth for no cost, the wonted use of banquets to begyn.
No Lady fayre or fowle, was in Verona towne:
No knight or gentleman of high or lowe renowne: 160
But Capilet himselfe hath byd unto his feast:
Or by his name in paper sent, appoynted as a geast.
Yong damsels thether flocke, of bachelers a rowte:
Not so much for the banquets sake, as bewties to searche out.
But not a Montagew would enter at his gate:
For as you heard, the Capilets, and they were at debate:
Save Romeus, and he in maske with hidden face,
The supper done, with other five dyd prease into the place.
When they had maskd a whyle, with dames in courtly wise,
All dyd unmaske, the rest dyd shew them to theyr ladies eyes. 170
But bashfull Romeus, with shamefast face forsooke
The open prease, and him withdrew into the chambers nooke.

The Capilets disdayne the presence of theyr foe: 183
Yet they suppresse theyr styrred yre, the cause I do not knowe.
Perhaps toffend theyr gestes the courteous knights are loth,
Perhaps they stay from sharpe revenge, dreadyng the Princes wroth,
Perhaps for that they shamd to exercise theyr rage
Within their house, gainst one alone and him of tender age.
They use no taunting talke, ne harme him by theyr deede:
They neyther say, what makst thou here, ne yet they say God speede.   190
So that he freely might the Ladies view at ease:
And they also beholding him, their chaunge of fansies please.
Which nature had him taught to doe with such a grace,
That there was none but joyed at his being there in place.
With upright beame he wayd the bewty of eche dame,
And judgd who best, and who next her, was wrought in natures frame.
At length he saw a mayd, right fayre of perfect shape:
Which Theseus, or Paris would have chosen to their rape.
Whom erst he never sawe, of all she pleasde him most:
Within himselfe he said to her, thou justly mayst thee boste,   200
Of perfit shapes renoune, and Beauties sounding prayse:
Whose like ne hath, ne shalbe seene, ne liveth in our dayes.
And whilest he fixd on her his partiall perced eye,
His former love, for which of late he ready was to dye,
Is nowe as quite forgotte, as it had never been:
The proverbe saith, unminded oft are they that are unseene.
And as out of a planke a nayle a nayle doth drive,
So novell love out of the minde the auncient love doth rive.
This sodain kindled fyre in time is wox so great:
That onely death, and both theyr blouds might quench the fiery heate.   210
When Romeus saw himselfe in this new tempest tost:
Where both was hope of pleasant port, and daunger to be lost:
He doubtefull, skasely knew what countenance to keepe:
In Lethies floud his wonted flames were quenchd and drenched deepe.
Yea he forgets himselfe, ne is the wretch so bolde
To aske her name, that without force hath him in bondage folde.
Ne how tunloose his bondes doth the poore foole devise,
But onely seeketh by her sight to feede his houngry eyes.
Through them he swalloweth downe loves sweete empoysonde baite,
How surely are the wareles wrapt by those that lye in wayte?   220
So is the poyson spred throughout his bones and vaines:
That in a while (alas the while) it hasteth deadly paines.
Whilst Juliet (for so this gentle damsell hight)
From syde to syde on every one dyd cast about her sight:
At last her floting eyes were ancored fast on him,
Who for her sake dyd banishe health and fredome from eche limme.
He in her sight did seeme to passe the rest as farre
As Phoebus shining beames do passe the brightnes of a starre.

Eche of these lovers gan by others lookes to knowe: 241
That frendship in their brest had roote, and both would have it grow.
When thus in both theyr harts had Cupide made his breache:

And eche of them had sought the meane to end the warre by speache:
Dame Fortune did assent theyr purpose to advaunce:
With torche in hand a comly knight did fetch her foorth to daunce.
She quit her selfe so well, and with so trim a grace:
That she the cheefe prayse wan that night from all Verona race.
The whilst our Romeus, a place had warely wonne
Nye to the seate where she must sit, the daunce once beyng donne.   250
Fayre Juliet tourned to, her chayre with pleasant cheere:
And glad she was her Romeus approched was so neere.
At thone side of her chayre, her lover Romeo:
And on the other side there sat one cald Mercutio,
A courtier that eche where was highly had in pryce:
For he was coorteous of his speche, and pleasant of devise.
Even as a Lyon would emong the lambes be bolde:
Such was emong the bashfull maydes, Mercutio to beholde.
With frendly gripe he ceasd fayre Juliets snowish hand:
A gyft he had that nature gave him in his swathing band,   260
That frosen mountayne yse was never halfe so cold
As were his handes, though nere so neer the fire he dyd them holde.
As soone as had the knight the vyrgins right hand raught:
Within his trembling hand her left hath loving Romeus caught.
For he wist well himselfe for her abode most payne:
And well he wist she loved him best, unles she list to fayne.
Then she with tender hand his tender palme hath prest:
What joy trow you was graffed so in Romeus cloven brest?
The soodain sweete delight hath stopped quite his tong:

[The lovers exchange vows of mutual love 'so long as lyfe shall last' (298).]

Lo, here the lucky lot that sild true lovers finde: 315
Eche takes away the others hart, and leaves the owne behinde.
A happy life is love if God graunt from above,
That hart with hart by even waight doo make exchaunge of love.
But Romeus gone from her, his heart for care is colde:
He hath forgot to aske her name that hath his hart in holde.   320
With forged careles cheere, of one he seekes to knowe,
Both how she hight, and whence she camme, that him enchaunted so.
So hath he learnd her name, and knowth she is no geast.
Her father was a Capilet, and master of the feast.
Thus hath his foe in choyse to geve him lyfe or death:

As carefull was the mayde what way were best devise   341
To learne his name, that intertaind her in so gentle wise,
Of whome her hart received so deepe, so wyde a wounde.
An auncient dame she calde to her, and in her eare gan rounde.
This olde dame in her youth, had nurst her with her mylke,
With slender nedle taught her sow, and how to spin with silke.
What twayne are those (quoth she) which prease unto the doore,
Whose pages in theyr hand doe beare, two toorches light before?
And then as eche of them had of his houshold name,
So she him namde yet once agayne, the yong and wyly dame.   350

And tell me who is he with vysor in his hand
That yender doth in masking weede besyde the window stand?
His name is Romeus (said she) a Montegewe,
Whose fathers pryde first styrd the strife which both your housholdes rewe.
The woord of Montegew, her joyes did overthrow,
And straight in steade of happy hope, dyspayre began to growe.
What hap have I quoth she, to love my fathers foe?
What, am I wery of my wele? what, doe I wishe my woe?
But though her grievous paynes distraind her tender hart,
Yet with an outward shewe of joye she cloked inward smart.   360
And of the courtlyke dames her leave so courtly tooke,
That none dyd gesse the sodain change by changing of her looke.

[Juliet debates at length Romeus's intentions.]

No no by God above, I wot it well quoth shee,   405
Although I rashely spake before, in no wise can it bee:
That where such perfet shape, with pleasant bewty restes,
There crooked craft and trayson blacke, should be appoynted gestes.
Sage writers say, the thoughts are dwelling in the eyne:
Then sure I am as Cupid raignes that Romeus is myne.   410

These doo suffise, and stedfast I will love and serve him still,   424
Till Attropos shall cut my fatall thread of lyfe:
So that he mynde to make of me his lawfull wedded wyfe.
For so perchaunce this new aliance may procure
Unto our houses suche a peace as ever shall endure.

The mayde had scarsely yet ended the wery warre,   433
Kept in her heart by striving thoughtes, when every shining starre
Had payd his borowed light, and Phebus spred in skies
His golden rayes, which seemd to say: now time it is to rise.
And Romeus had by this forsaken his wery bed:
Where restles he a thousand thoughts had forged in his hed.
And while with lingring step by Juliets house he past:
And upward to her windowes high his gredy eyes did cast: 440
His love that looked for him, there gan he straight espie.
With pleasant cheere eche greeted is: she followeth with her eye
His parting steppes, and he oft looketh backe againe:
But not so oft as he desyres: warely he doth refraine.
What life were lyke to love, if dred of jeopardy,
Ysowred not the sweete, if love were free from jelosy.
But she more sure within, unseene of any wight,
When so he comes, lookes after him, till he be out of sight.
In often passing so, his busy eyes he threw,
That every pane and tooting hole the wily lover knew.   450
In happy houre he doth a garden plot espye:
From which except he warely walke, men may his love descrye.
For lo, it fronted full, upon her leaning place:
Where she is woont to shew her heart by cheerefull frendly face.

And lest the arbors might theyr secret love bewraye:
He doth keepe backe his forward foote from passing there by daye.
But when on earth the night her mantel blacke hath spred:
Well armd he walketh foorth alone, ne dreadfull foes doth dred.
Whom maketh love not bold, naye whom makes he not blynde?
He reveth daungers dread oft times out of the lovers minde.
By night he passeth here, a weeke or two in vayne:
And for the missing of his marke, his griefe hath him nye slaine.
And Juliet that now doth lacke her hearts releefe:
Her Romeus pleasant eyen (I meene) is almost dead for greefe.
Eche day she chaungeth howres, (for lovers keepe an howre,
When they are sure to see theyr love, in passing by their bowre).
Impacient of her woe, she hapt to leane one night
Within her window, and anon the Moone did shine so bright,
That she espyde her love, her hart revived, sprang,
And now for joy she clappes her handes, which erst for woe she wrang. 470

460

What woonder then if he were wrapt in lesse annoye? 483
What marvell if by sodain sight she fed of greater joye?
His smaller greefe or joy, no smaller love doo prove:
Ne for she passed him in both, did she him passe in love.
But eche of them alike dyd burne in equall flame:
The welbeloving knight, and eke the welbeloved dame.
Now whilst with bitter teares her eyes as fountaynes ronne:
With whispering voyce ybroke with sobs, thus is her tale begonne. 490
Oh Romeus (of your lyfe) too lavas sure you are:
That in this place, and at thys tyme to hasard it you dare.
What if your dedly foes my kynsmen, saw you here?
Lyke Lyons wylde, your tender partes asonder would they teare.
In ruth and in disdayne, I weary of my lyfe:
With cruell hand by moorning hart would perce with bloudy knyfe.
For you myne owne once dead, what joy should I have heare?
And eke my honor staynde which I then lyfe doe holde more deare.
Fayre lady myne dame Juliet my lyfe (quod he)
Even from my byrth committed was to fatall sisters three. 500
They may in spyte of foes, draw foorth my lively threed:
And they also, who so sayth nay, a sonder may it shreed.
But who to reave my lyfe, his rage and force would bende:
Perhaps should trye unto his payne how I it could defende.
Ne yet I love it so, but alwayes for your sake,
A sacrifice to death I would my wounded corps betake.

Now love and pitty boyle, in Juliets ruthfull brest, 517
In windowe on her leaning arme, her weary hed doth rest.
Her bosome bathd in teares, to witnes inward payne:
With dreary chere to Romeus, thus aunswerd she agayne.

But these thinges overpast, if of your health and myne 529
You have respect, or pitty ought my teary weping eyen:
In few unfained woords, your hidden mynd unfolde,
That as I see your pleasant face, your heart I may beholde.

For if you doe intende my honor to defile:
In error shall you wander still as you have done this whyle,
But if your thought be chaste, and have on vertue ground,
If wedlocke be the ende and marke which your desire hath found:
Obedience set aside, unto my parentes dewe:
The quarell eke that long agoe betwene our housholdes grewe:
Both me and myne I will all whole to you betake:
And following you where so you goe, my fathers house forsake.   540
But if by wanton love, and by unlawfull sute,
You thinke in ripest yeres to plucke my maydenhods dainty frute:
You are begylde, and now your Juliet you be seekes
To cease your sute, and suffer her to live emong her likes.
Then Romeus, whose thought was free from fowle desyre:
And to the top of vertues haight, did worthely aspyre:
Was fild with greater joy, then can my pen expresse:
Or till they have enjoyd the like the hearers hart can gesse.
And then with joyned hands heavd up into the skies,
He thankes the Gods, and from the heavens for vengeance downe he cries,   550
If he have other thought, but as his lady spake:

To morow eke betimes, before the sunne arise,   557
To fryer Lawrence will I wende, to learne his sage advise.
He is my gostly syre, and oft he hath me taught
What I should doe in things of wayght, when I his ayde have sought.

This barefoote fryer gyrt, with cord his grayish weede,   565
For he of Frauncis order was, a fryer as I reede,
Not as the most was he, a grosse unlearned foole:
But doctor of divinitie proceded he in schoole.
The secretes eke he knew, in natures woorkes that loorke:
By magiks arte most men supposd that he could wonders woorke.   570
Ne doth it ill beseeme devines those skils to know
If on no harmefull deede they do such skilfulnes bestow.

Betwixt the Capilets and him great frendship grew: 581
A secret and assured frend unto the Montegue.
Loved of this yong man more then any other gest,
The frier eke of Verone youth, aye liked Romeus best.
For whom he ever hath, in time of his distres,
(As erst you heard) by skilfull lore, found out his harmes redresse.
To him is Romeus gonne, ne stayth he till the morowe:
To him he paynteth all his case, his passed joy and sorow.
How he hath her espyde with other dames in daunce,
And how that first to talke with her, himselfe he did advaunce.   590
Their talke and change of lookes he gan to him declare:
And how so fast by fayth and troth they both ycoupled are:
That neither hope of lyfe, nor dreed of cruel death,
Shall make him false his fayth to her while lyfe shall lend him breath.
And then with weping eyes he prayes his gostly syre
To further and accomplish all theyr honest hartes desire.

A thousand doutes and moe in thold mans hed arose:
A thousand daungers like to come, the olde man doth disclose.
And from the spousall rites he readeth him refrayne:
Perhaps he shalbe bet advisde within a weeke or twayne.   600
Advise is banishd quite from those that followe love,
Except advise to what they like theyr bending mynde do move.
As well the father might have counseld him to stay
That from a mountaines top thrown downe, is falling halfe the way:
As warne his frend to stop, amyd his race begonne,
Whom Cupid with his smarting whip enforceth foorth to ronne.
Part wonne by earnest sute, the fryer doth graunt at last:
And part, because he thinkes the stormes so lately overpast,
Of both the housholdes wrath, this mariage might apease,
So that they should not rage agayne, but quite for ever cease.   610

The nurce of whom I spake within her chaumber laye: 623
Upon the mayde she wayteth still: to her she doth bewray
Her new received wound, and then her ayde doth crave:
In her she saith it lyes to spill, in her her life to save.
Not easely she made the froward nurce to bowe:
But wonne at length, with promest hyre she made a solemne vowe,
To do what she commaundes, as handmayd of her hest:
Her mistres secrets hide she will, within her covert brest.   630
To Romeus she goes: of him she doth desyre,
To know the meane of mariage, by councell of the fryre.
On Saterday quod he, if Juliet come to shrift,
She shalbe shrived and maried, how lyke you noorse this drift?

And then she sweares to him, the mother loves her well: 651
And how she gave her sucke in youth she leaveth not to tell.
A prety babe (quod she) it was when it was yong:
Lord how it could full pretely have prated with it tong.
A thousand times and more I laid her on my lappe,
And clapt her on the buttocke soft and kist where I did clappe.
And gladder then was I of such a kisse forsooth,
Then I had been to have a kisse of some olde lechers mouth.
And thus of Juliets youth began this prating noorse,
And of her present state to make a tedious long discoorse.   660
For though he pleasure tooke in hearing of his love,
The message aunswer seemed him to be of more behove.
But when these Beldams sit at ease upon theyr tayle,
The day and eke the candle light before theyr talke shall fayle.
And part they say is true, and part they do devise:
Yet boldly do they chat of both when no man checkes theyr lyes.
Then he .vi. crownes of gold out of his pocket drew:
And gave them her, a slight reward (quod he) and so adiew.
In seven yeres twise tolde she had not bowd so lowe,
Her crooked knees, as now they bowe, she sweares she will bestowe   670
Her crafty wit, her time, and all her busy payne,
To helpe him to his hoped blisse, and cowring downe agayne:
She takes her leave, and home she hyes with spedy pace:

The chaumber doore she shuts, and then she saith with smyling face.
Good newes for thee, my gyrle, good tidinges I thee bring:
Leave of thy woonted song of care and now of pleasure sing.
For thou mayst hold thy selfe the happiest under sonne:
That in so little while, so well so worthy a knight hast wonne.
The best yshapde is he, and hath the fayrest face,
Of all this towne, and there is none hath halfe so good a grace,   680
So gentle of his speche, and of his counsell wise:
And still with many prayses more she heaved him to the skies.
Tell me els what (quod she) this evermore I thought:
But of our mariage say at once, what aunswer have you brought?
Nay soft quoth she, I feare, your hurt by sodain joye.
I list not play quoth Juliet, although thou list to toye.

There is no losse quod she, (sweete wench) to losse of time: 693
Ne in thine age shalt thou repent so much of any crime.
For when I call to mynde, my former passed youth:
One thing there is which most of all doth cause my endles ruth.
At sixtene yeres I first did choose my loving feere:
And I was fully ripe before, (I dare well say) a yere.
The pleasure that I lost, that yere so overpast,
A thousand times I have bewept, and shall while lyfe doth last.   700
In fayth it were a shame, yea sinne it were ywisse,
When thou mayst live in happy joy to set light by thy blisse.
She that this mornyng could her mistres mynde disswade,
Is now becomme an Oratresse, her lady to perswade.

[Juliet receives permission to go to shrift, where she meets with Romeus.]

I dare well say there is in all Verona none   741
But Romeus, with whom she would so gladly be alone.
Thus to the fryers cell, they both foorth walked bin:
He shuts the doore as soone as he and Juliet were in.
But Romeus her frend was entred in before,
And there had wayted for his love, two howers large and more.
Eche minute seemde an howre, and every howre a day:
Twixt hope he lived and despayre, of cumming or of stay.

Fayre lady Juliet, my gostly doughter deere,   755
As farre as I of Romeus learne who by you standeth here,
Twixt you it is agreed that you shalbe his wyfe:
And he your spouse in steady truth till death shall end your life.
Are you both fully bent to kepe this great behest?
And both the lovers said it was theyr onely harts request.

Then Romeus said to her, (both loth to part so soone:)   773
Fayre lady send to me agayne your nurce this after noone.
Of corde I will bespeake, a ladder by that time,
By which, this night, while other sleepe, I will your window clime.
Then will we talke of love, and of our olde dispayres:
And then with longer laysure had, dispose our great affaires.

Thy stearles ship (O Romeus) hath been long while betost.   800
The seas are now appeasd, and thou by happy starre
Art comme in sight of quiet haven, and now the wrackfull barre
Is hid with swelling tyde, boldly thou mayst resort
Unto thy wedded ladies bed, thy long desyred port.
God graunt no follies mist so dymme thy inward sight,
That thou do misse the chanell, that doth leade to thy delight.
God graunt no daungers rocke, ylurking in the darke,
Before thou win the happy port wracke thy sea beaten barke.
A servant Romeus had, of woord and deede so just,
That with his life (if nede requierd) his master would him trust.   810
His faithfulnes had oft our Romeus proved of olde
And therfore all that yet was done unto his man he tolde.
Who straight as he was charged, a corden ladder lookes:
To which he hath made fast two strong and crooked yron hookes.
The bryde to send the nurce at twylight fayleth not:
To whom the bridegroome yeven hath, the ladder that he got.

How long these lovers thought the lasting of the day,   821
Let other judge that woonted are lyke passions to assay.
For my part, I do gesse eche howre seemes twenty yere:
So that I deeme if they might have (as of Alcume we heare)
The sunne bond to theyr will, if they the heavens might gyde:
Black shade of night and doubled darke should straight all over hyde.
Thappointed howre is comme, he clad in riche araye,
Walkes toward his desyred home, good Fortune gyde his way.
Approching nere the place from whence his hart had life:
So light he wox, he lept the wall, and there he spyde his wife,   830
Who in the windowe watcht the cumming of her lorde:
Where she so surely had made fast the ladder made of corde:
That daungerles her spouse the chaumber window climes,
Where he ere then had wisht himselfe above ten thousand times.

[The lovers discuss their perilous situation.]

O Romeus quoth she, in whome all vertues shyne: 853
Welcome thou art into this place where from these eyes of myne,
Such teary streames dyd flowe, that I suppose welny
The source of all my bitter teares is altogether drye.
Absence so pynde my heart, which on thy presence fed:
And of thy safetie and thy health so much I stood in dred.
But now what is decreed by fatall desteny:
I force it not, let Fortune do and death their woorst to me.   860
Full recompensd am I for all my passed harmes,
In that the Gods have graunted me to claspe thee in myne armes.

Fayre Juliet began to aunswere what he sayde: 889
But foorth in hast the olde nurce stept, and so her aunswere stayde.
Who takes not time (quoth she) when time well offred is,
An other time shall seeke for time, and yet of time shall misse.

And when occasion serves, who so doth let it slippe,
Is woorthy sure (if I might judge) of lashes with a whippe.
Wherfore, if eche of you hath harmde the other so,
And eche of you hath been the cause of others wayled woe,
Loe here a fielde, (she shewd a fieeldbed ready dight)
Where you may, if you list, in armes, revenge your selfe by fight.
Wherto these lovers both gan easely assent,
And to the place of mylde revenge with pleasant cheere they went.   900

Thus passe they foorth the night in sport, in joly game: 919
The hastines of Phoebus steeds in great despyte they blame.
And now the virgins fort hath warlike Romeus got,
In which as yet no breache was made by force of canon shot.
And now in ease he doth possesse the hoped place:
How glad was he, speake you that may your lovers parts embrace?
The mariage thus made up, and both the parties pleasd:
The nigh approche of dayes retoorne these seely foles diseasd.

So wavering Fortunes whele her chaunges be so straunge.   935
And every wight ythralled is by fate unto her chaunge.
Who raignes so over all, that eche man hath his part:
(Although not aye perchaunce alike) of pleasure and of smart.
For after many joyes, some feele but little payne:
And from that little greefe they toorne to happy joy againe.   940
But other somme there are, that living long in woe,
At length they be in quiet ease, but long abide not so.
Whose greefe is much increast by myrth that went before:
Because the sodayne chaunge of thinges doth make it seeme the more.
Of this unlucky sorte our Romeus is one
For all his hap turnes to mishap, and all his myrth to mone.

[The open quarrel between the Capilets and Montagewes begins.]

The prince could never cause those housholds so agree,   955
But that some sparcles of their wrath, as yet remaining bee:
Which lye this while raakd up, in ashes pale and ded,
Till tyme do serve that they agayne in wasting flame may spred.
At holiest times men say most heynous crimes are donne:
The morowe after Easter day the mischiefe new begonne.   960
A band of Capilets did meete (my hart it rewes)
Within the walles by Pursers gate, a band of Montagewes.
The Capilets as cheefe, a yong man have chose out:
Best exercisd in feates of armes, and noblest of the rowte:
Our Juliets unkles sonne that cliped was Tibalt.
He was of body tall and strong, and of his courage halt.
They neede no trumpet sounde to byd them geve the charge,
So lowde he cryde with strayned voyce and mouth out stretched large.
Now, now, (quod he) my frends, our selfe so let us wreake,
That of this dayes revenge, and us, our childrens heyres may speake.   970

And whilst this noyse is ryfe in every townes mans eare,   993
Eke walking with his frendes, the noyse doth wofull Romeus heare.
With spedy foote he ronnes unto the fray apace:
With him those fewe that were with him he leadeth to the place.
They pittie much to see the slaughter made so greate:
That wetshod they might stand in blood on eyther side the streate.
Part frendes (sayd he) part frendes, helpe frendes to part the fray:
And to the rest, enough (he cryes) now time it is to staye.   1000
Gods farther wrath you styrre, beside the hurt you feele:
And with this new uprore confounde all this our common wele.
But they so busy are in fight so egar and feerce,
That through theyr eares his sage advise no leysure had to pearce.
Then lept he in the throng, to part, and barre the blowes,
As well of those that were his frendes as of his dedly foes.
As soone as Tybalt had our Romeus espyde:
He threw a thrust at him that would have past from side to side.
But Romeus ever went (douting his foes) well armde:
So that the swerd (kept out by mayle) hath nothing Romeus harmde.   1010
Thou doest me wrong (quoth he) for I but part the fraye,
Not dread, but other waighty cause my hasty hand doth stay.
Thou art the cheefe of thine, the noblest eke thou art:
Wherfore leave of thy malice now, and helpe these folke to parte.
Many are hurt, some slayne, and some are like to dye.
No, coward traytor boy (quoth he) straight way I mynd to trye
Whether thy sugred talke, and tong so smoothely fylde,
Against the force of this my swerd shall serve thee for a shylde.
And then at Romeus hed, a blow he strake so hard,
That might have clove him to the brayne but for his cunning ward.   1020

Even as two thunderboltes, throwne downe out of the skye,   1031
That through the ayre the massy earth and seas have power to flye:
So met these two, and while they chaunge a blowe or twayne,
Our Romeus thrust him through the throte and so is Tybalt slayne.

[Juliet laments Romeus's banishment and Tybalt's death.]

The fray hath end, the Capilets do bring the brethles corce,   1040
Before the prince: and crave, that cruell dedly payne
May be the guerdon of his falt, that hath their kinsman slaine.
The Montagewes do pleade, theyr Romeus voyde of falt:
The lookers on do say, the fight begonne was by Tybalt.
The prince doth pawse, and then geves sentence in a while,
That Romeus, for sleying him should goe into exyle.

But how doth moorne emong the moorners Juliet?   1075
How doth she bathe her brest in teares? what depe sighes doth she fet?
How doth she tear her heare? her weede how doth she rent?
How fares the lover hearing of her lovers banishment?
How wayles she Tibalts death, whom she had loved so well?

Then rapt out of her selfe, whilst she on every side   1095
Did cast her restles eye, at length the windowe she espide,
Through which she had with joy seene Romeus many a time:
Which oft the ventrous knight was wont for Juliets sake to clyme.
She cryde O cursed windowe, acurst be every pane,
Through which (alas) to sone I raught the cause of life and bane.   1100

O Romeus, when first we both acquainted were,   1113
When to thy paynted promises I lent my listning eare:
Which to the brinkes you fild with many a solemne othe,
And I them judgde empty of gyle, and fraughted full of troth:
I thought you rather would continue our good will,
And seeke tappease our fathers strife which daily groweth still.
I little wend you would have sought occasion how
By such an heynous act to breake the peace, and eke your vowe   1120
Wherby your bright renoune, all whole yclipsed is,
And I unhappy husbandles, of cumfort robde, and blisse.

And then agayne, wroth with her selfe, with feble voyce gan say.   1144
Ah cruell murthering tong, murthrer of others fame:
How durst thou once attempt to tooch the honor of his name?
Whose dedly foes doe yelde him dewe and earned prayse:
For though his fredome be bereft, his honor not decayes.
Why blamst thou Romeus for sleying of Tybalt,
Since he is gyltles quite of all, and Tybalt beares the falt?   1150
Whether shall he (alas) poore banishd man now flye?
What place of succor shall he seeke beneth the starry skye?
Synce she pursueth him, and him defames by wrong:
That in distres should be his fort, and onely rampier strong.
Receive the recompence, O Romeus of thy wife,
Who for she was unkind her selfe, doth offer up her lyfe,
In flames of yre, in sighes, in sorow and in ruth:
So to revenge the crime she did commit against thy truth.

[The Nurse finds Juliet in a faint and revives her.]

You are accounted wise, a foole am I your nurce: 1209
But I see not how in like case I could be have me wurse.
Tibalt your frend is ded: what, weene you by your teares,
To call him backe againe? thinke you that he your crying heares?
You shall perceve the falt, (if it be justly tryde)
Of his so sodayn death, was in his rashnes and his pryde.
Would you that Romeus, him selfe had wronged so,
To suffer himselfe causeles to be outraged of his foe?
To whom in no respect, he ought a place to geve?
Let it suffise to thee fayre dame, that Romeus doth live.
And that there is good hope that he within a while,
With greater glory shalbe calde home from his hard exile.   1220

[The Nurse goes to find Romeus at the Friar's cell.]

In doutfull happe ay best, a trusty frend is tride,   1265
The frendly fryer in this distresse, doth graunt his frend to hyde.
A secret place he hath, well seeled round about,
The mouth of which, so close is shut, that none may finde it out.
Both roome there is to walke, and place to sitte and rest,
Beside, a bed to sleape upon, full soft and trimly drest.   1270
The flowre is planked so with mattes, it is so warme,
That neither wind, nor smoky damps have powre him ought to harme.
Where he was wont in youth, his fayre frendes to bestowe,
There now he hydeth Romeus whilst forth he goeth to knowe
Both what is sayd and donne, and what appoynted payne,
Is published by trumpets sound: then home he hyes agayne.

These heavy tydinges heard, his golden lockes he tare: 1291
And like a frantike man hath torne the garmentes that he ware.
And as the smitten deere, in brakes is waltring found,
So waltreth he, and with his brest doth beate the troden grounde.
He riseth eft, and strikes his head against the wals,
He falleth downe againe, and lowde for hasty death he cals.

Fyrst, nature did he blame, the author of his lyfe,   1325
In which his joyes had been so scant, and sorowes aye so ryfe:
The time and place of byrth, he fiersly did reprove,
He cryed out (with open mouth) against the starres above:
The fatall sisters three, he said, had done him wrong,
The threed that should not have been sponne they had drawne foorth too long.   1330
He wished that he had before this time been borne,
Or that as soone as he wan light, his life he had forlorne.
His nurce he cursed, and the hand that gave him pappe,
The midwife eke with tender grype that held him in her lappe:
And then did he complaine, on Venus cruel sonne
Who led him first unto the rockes, which he should warely shonne,
By meane wherof he lost, both lyfe and libertie,
And dyed a hundred times a day, and yet could never dye.
Loves troubles lasten long, the joyes he geves are short:
He forceth not a lovers payne, theyr ernest is his sport.   1340
A thousand thinges and more, I here let passe to write,
Which unto love this wofull man, dyd speake in great despite.
On Fortune eke he raylde, he calde her deafe, and blynde,
Unconstant, fond, deceitfull, rashe, unruthfull, and unkynd.
And to him self he layd a great part of the falt:
For that he slewe, and was not slayne, in fighting with Tibalt.
He blamed all the world, and all he did defye
But Juliet, for whom he lived, for whom eke would he dye.
When after raging fits, appeased was his rage,
And when his passions (powred forth) gan partly to asswage: 1350
So wisely did the fryre, unto his tale replye,
That he straight cared for his life, that erst had care to dye.

Art thou quoth he a man? thy shape saith so thou art:
Thy crying and thy weping eyes, denote a womans hart,
For manly reason is quite from of thy mynd outchased,
And in her stead affections lewd, and fansies highly placed.
So that I stoode in doute this howre (at the least)
If thou a man, or woman wert, or els a brutish beast.
A wise man in the midst of troubles and distres,
Still standes not wayling present harme, but seeks his harmes redres,   1360
As when the winter flawes, with dredfull noyse arise,
And heave the fomy swelling waves up to the starry skies,
So that the broosed barke in cruell seas betost,
Dispayreth of the happy haven in daunger to be lost.
The pylate bold at helme, cryes, mates strike now your sayle:
And tornes her stemme into the waves, that strongly her assayle.
Then driven hard upon the bare and wrackfull shore,
In greater daunger to be wract, then he had been before:
He seeth his ship full right against the rocke to ronne,
But yet he dooth what lyeth in him the perilous rocke to shonne.   1370
Sometimes the beaten boate, by cunning government,
The ancors lost, the cables broke, and all the tackle spent,
The roder smitten of, and over boord the mast,
Doth win the long desyred porte, the stormy daunger past.
But if the master dread, and overprest with woe,
Begin to wring his handes, and lets the gyding rodder goe,
The ship rents on the rocke, or sinketh in the deepe,
And eke the coward drenched is: So if thou still be weepe
And seke not how to helpe the chaunges that do chaunce,
Thy cause of sorow shall increase, thou cause of thy mischaunce.   1380
Other account thee wise, proove not thy selfe a foole,
Now put in practise lessons learnd, of old in wisdomes schoole.

Vertue is alwayes thrall, to troubles and annoye,   1393
But wisdome in adversitie, findes cause of quiet joye.
And they most wretched are, that know no wretchednes:
And after great extremity, mishaps ay waxen lesse.
Like as there is no weale, but wastes away somtime,
So every kind of wayled woe, will weare away in time.
If thou wilt master quite, the troubles that the spill,
Endevor first by reasons help, to master witles will.   1400
A sondry medson hath, eche sondry faynt disease,
But pacience, a common salve, to every wound geves ease.
The world is alway full of chaunces and of chaunge,
Wherfore the chaunge of chaunce must not seeme to a wise man straunge.
For tickel Fortune doth, in chaunging but her kind:
But all her chaunges cannot chaunge, a steady constant minde.
Though wavering Fortune toorne from thee her smyling face,
And sorow seeke to set him selfe, in banishd pleasures place,
Yet may thy marred state, be mended in a while,
And she eftsones that frowneth now, with pleasant cheere shall smyle.   1410
For as her happy state, no long whyle standeth sure,
Even so the heavy plight she brings, not alwayes doth endure.

What nede so many woordes, to thee that art so wyse?
Thou better canst advise thy selfe, then I can thee advyse.
Wisdome I see is vayne, if thus in time of neede,
A wise mans wit unpractised, doth stand him in no steede.
I know thou hast some cause, of sorow and of care:
But well I wot thou hast no cause thus frantikly to fare.
Affections foggy mist, thy febled sight doth blynde,
But if that reasons beames agayne, might shine into thy mynde: 1420
If thou wouldst view thy state with an indifferent eye,
I thinke thou wouldst condemne thy plaint, thy sighing and thy crye.
With valiant hand thou madest thy foe yeld up his breth,
Thou hast escapd his swerd, and eke the lawes that threatten death.
By thy escape, thy frendes, are fraughted full of joy,
And by his death thy deadly foes are laden with annoy.
Wilt thou, with trusty frendes, of pleasure take some part?
Or els to please thy hatefull foes, be partner of theyr smart?
Why cryest thou out on love, why doest thou blame thy fate?
Why dost thou so crye after death? thy life why dost thou hate?   1430
Dost thou repent the choyce, that thou so late didst choose?
Love is thy Lord, thou oughtest obay, and not thy prince accuse.
For thou hast found (thou knowst) great favour in his sight:
He graunted thee at thy request, thy onely hartes delight:
So that the Gods envyde the blisse thou livedst in:
To geve to such unthankefull men, is folly and a sin.
Me thinkes I heare thee say the cruell banishment,
Is onely cause of thy unrest: onely thou dost lament,
That from thy natife land, and frendes thou must depart,
Enforsd to flye from her that hath the keping of thy hart.   1440
And so opprest with waight of smart that thou dost feele,
Thou dost complaine of Cupides brand, and Fortunes turning wheele.
Unto a valiant hart, there is no banishment:
All countreys are his native soyle beneath the firmament.
As to the fishe, the sea: as to the fowle, the ayre:
So is like pleasant to the wise, eche place of his repayre.
Though froward Fortune chase thee hence into exyle:
With doubled honor shall she call thee home within a whyle.
Admyt thou shouldst abyde abrode a yere or twayne:
Should so short absence cause so long, and eke so greevous payne?   1450
Though thou ne mayst thy frendes, here in Verona see,
They are not banishd Mantua, where safely thou mast be.
Thether they may resort, though thou resort not hether,
And there in suretie may you talke, of your affayres together.
Yea, but this whyle (alas) thy Juliet must thou misse,
The onely piller of thy helth, and ancor of thy blisse.
Thy hart thou leavest with her, when thou dost hence depart:
And in thy brest inclosed bearst, her tender frendly hart.
But if thou rew so much, to leave the rest behinde,
With thought of passed joyes, content thy uncontented mynde.   1460
So shall the mone decrease, wherwith thy mynd doth melt,
Compared to the heavenly joyes which thou hast often felt.

He is too nyse a weakeling, that shrinketh at a showre,
And he unworthy of the sweete, that tasteth not the sowre.
Call now againe to mynde, thy first consuming flame,
How didst thou vainely burne in love of an unloving dame.
Hadst thou not welnigh wept, quite out thy swelling eyne?
Did not thy parts fordoon with payne, languishe away and pyne?
Those greefes and others like, were happly overpast:
And thou in haight of Fortunes wheele, well placed at the last: 1470
From whence thou art now falne, that raysed up agayne,
With greater joy a greater while in pleasure mayst thou raygne.
Compare the present while, with times ypast before,
And thinke that Fortune hath for thee, great pleasure yet in store.
The whilst, this little wrong, receive thou paciently,
And what of force must nedes be done, that doe thou willingly.
Foly it is to feare that thou canst not avoyde
And madnes to desire it much, that can not be enjoyde.
To geve to Fortune place, not ay deserveth blame:
But skill it is, according to the times, thy selfe to frame.   1480
Whilst to this skilfull lore, he lent his listning eares:
His sighes are stopt, and stopped are the conduits of his teares.

The old mans woords have fild with joy, our Romeus brest: 1511
And eke the olde wives talke, hath set our Juliets hart at rest.
Whereto may I compare, (O lovers) this your day?
Like dayes the painefull mariners, are woonted to assay.
For beat with tempest great, when they at length espye
Some little beame of Phoebus light, that perceth through the skie,
To cleare the shadowde earth, by clearenes of his face:
They hope that dreadles, they shall ronne the remnant of their race.
Yea, they assure them selfe, and quite behynd theyr backe,
They cast all doute, and thanke the Gods for scaping of the wracke.   1520
But straight the boysterous windes, with greater fury blowe,
And over boord the broken mast, the stormy blastes doe throwe.
The heavens large, are clad with cloudes, as darke as hell:
And twise as hye, the striving waves begin to roare, and swell.
With greater daungers dred, the men are vexed more:
In greater perill of their lyfe, then they had been before.

[Romeus and Juliet spend a last night together, lamenting his exile.]

Nay Romeus, nay, thou mayst of two thinges choose the one: 1601
Either to see thy castaway as soone as thou art gone,
Hedlong to throw her selfe downe from the windowes haight,
And so to breake her slender necke, with all the bodies waight:
Or suffer her to be companion of thy payne,
Where so thou goe (Fortune thee gyde) till thou retoorne agayne.

Receave me as thy servant, and the fellow of thy smart.   1616
Thy absence is my death, thy sight shall geve me life.

[Romeus refuses to allow Juliet to accompany him.]

If thou be bend tobay the lore of reasons skill,   1657
And wisely by her princely powre suppresse rebelling will:
If thou our safetie seeke, more then thine owne delight,
Since suerty standes in parting, and thy pleasures growe of sight: 1660
For beare the cause of joy, and suffer for a while,
So shall I safely live abrode, and safe torne from exile.
So shall no slaunders blot, thy spotles life destayne,
So shall thy kinsmen be unstyrd, and I exempt from payne.

But if I be condemd to wander still in thrall,   1677
I will returne to you (mine owne) befall what may befall.
And then by strength of frendes, and with a mighty hand,
From Verone will I cary thee, into a forein lande.
Not in mans weede disguisd, or as one scarcely knowne,
But as my wife and onely feere, in garment of thyne owne.

Thus these two lovers passe away the wery night,   1701
In payne and plaint, not (as they wont) in pleasure and delight.
But now (somewhat too soone) in farthest East arose
Fayre Lucifer, the golden starre, that Lady Venus chose:
Whose course appoynted is, with spedy race to ronne,
A messenger of dawning daye, and of the rysing sonne.
Then freshe Aurora, with her pale and silver glade
Did clear the skyes, and from the earth, had chased ougly shade.
When thou ne lookest wide, ne closely dost thou winke,
When Phoebus from our hemysphere, in westerne wave doth sinke: 1710
What cooller then the heavens do shew unto thine eyes,
The same, (or like) saw Romeus in farthest Esterne skyes.
As yet, he saw no day: ne could he call it night,
With equall force, decreasing darke, fought with increasing light.
Then Romeus in armes his lady gan to folde,
With frendly kisse: and ruthfully she gan her knight beholde.
With solemne othe they both theyr sorowfull leave do take:
They sweare no stormy troubles shall theyr steady frendship shake.

The wery watch discharged, did hye them home to slepe,   1729
The warders, and the skowtes were chargde theyr place and coorse to keepe:
And Verone gates awyde, the porters had set open.
When Romeus had of his affayres with frier Lawrence spoken,
Warely he walked forth, unknowne of frend or foe:
Clad like a merchant venterer, from top even to the toe.

[Romeus suffers in exile in Mantua.]

Then doth he wet with teares, the cowche wheron he lyes,   1751
And then his sighes the chamber fill, and out aloude he cryes
Against the restles starres, in rolling skyes that raunge,
Against the fatall sisters three, and Fortune full of chaunge.

When he doth heare abrode, the praise of ladies blowne,   1767
Within his thought he scorneth them and doth preferre his owne.
When pleasant songes he heares wheile others do rejoyce
The melody of Musike doth styrre up his mourning voyce.   1770
But if in secret place he walke some where alone,
The place it self, and secretnes redoubleth all his mone.

[In Verona, Juliet is counselled to forget the death of Tybalt.]

For time it is that now you should our Tybalts death forget.   1794
Of whom, since God hath claymd the lyfe, that was but lent,
He is in blisse, ne is there cause why you should thus lament.
You can not call him backe with teares, and shrikinges shrill:
It is a falt thus still to grudge at Gods appoynted will.

[Juliet's mother reports Juliet's sad state to Capilet and urges marriage as a remedy.
Capilet approaches Paris.]

Some greater thing, not Tybalts death, this chaunge in her hath wrought.   1838
Her selfe assured me, that many dayes a goe,
She shed the last of Tybalts teares, which woord amasd me so,   1840
That I then could not gesse what thing els might her greeve,
But now at length I have bethought me. And I doe beleve
The onely crop and roote of all my daughters payne,
Is grudgeing envies faynt disease: perhaps she doth disdayne
To see in wedlocke yoke the most part of her feeres,
Whilst onely she unmaried, doth lose so many yeres.
And more perchaunce she thinkes you mynd to kepe her so,
Wherfore dispayring doth she weare her selfe away with woe.
Therfore (deere syr) in time, take on your daughter ruth,
For why, a brickel thing is glasse, and frayle is frayllesse youth.   1850
Joyne her at once to somme, in linke of mariage,
That may be meete for our degree, and much about her age.
So shall you banish care out of your daughters brest:

Emong the rest was one inflamde with her desire,   1881
Who County Paris cliped was, an Earle he had to syre.
Of all the suters, him the father liketh best,
And easely unto the Earle he maketh his behest,
Both of his owne good will, and of his frendly ayde,
To win his wife unto his will, and to perswade the mayde.
The wife did joy to heare the joyfull husband say,
How happy hap, how meete a match, he had found out that day.
Ne did she seeke to hyde her joyes within her hart,
But straight she hyeth to Juliet: to her she telles apart,   1890
What happy talke (by meane of her) was past no rather
Betwene the woing Paris, and her carefull loving father.
The person of the man, the fewters of his face,
His youthfull yeres, his fayrenes, and his port and semely grace,
With curious wordes she payntes before her daughters eyes,
And then with store of vertues prayse, she heaves him to the skyes.

She vauntes his race, and gyftes, that Fortune did him geve:
Wherby (she saith) both she and hers, in great delight shall live.
When Juliet conceived her parentes whole entent,
Wherto, both love, and reasons right, forbod her to assent: 1900
Within her selfe she thought, rather then be forsworne,
With horses wilde, her tender partes a sonder should be torne.
Not now with bashfull brow (in wonted wise) she spake,
But with unwonted boldnes, straight into these woordes she brake.
Madame, I marvell much, that you so lavasse are,
Of me your childe, (your jewel once, your onely joy and care,)
As thus to yelde me up, at pleasure of another,
Before you know if I doe like, or els mislike my lover.
Doo what you list, but yet of this assure you still,
If you do as you say you will, I yelde not there untill. 1910
For had I choyse of twayne, farre rather would I choose,
My part of all your goodes, and eke my breath and lyfe to lose:
Then graunt that he possesse of me the smallest part.
First, weary of my painefull life, my cares shall kill my hart.
Els will I perce my brest, with sharpe and bloody knife,
And you my mother shall becomme the murdresse of my life:
In geving me to him, whom I ne can ne may,
Ne ought to love. Wherfore on knees, deere mother I you pray
To let me live henceforth, as I have lived tofore:

The syre, whose swelling wroth her teares could not asswage, 1945
With fiery eyen, and skarlet cheekes, thus spake her in his rage:
Whilst ruthfully stood by the maydens mother mylde:
Listen (quoth he) unthankfull and thou disobedient childe.
Hast thou so soone let slip out of thy mynde the woord,
That thou so often times hast heard rehearsed at my boord? 1950
How much the Romayne youth of parentes stood in awe,
And eke what powre upon theyr seede the fathers had by lawe?

Such care thy mother had, so deere thou wert to me, 1961
That I with long and earnest sute, provided have for thee
One of the greatest lordes, that wonnes about this towne,
And for his many vertues sake, a man of great renowne.
Of whom, both thou and I, unworthy are too much,
So riche ere long he shalbe left, his fathers welth is such.
Such is the noblenes, and honor of the race,
From whence his father came, and yet thou playest in this case,
The dainty foole, and stubberne gyrle, for want of skill,
Thou dost refuse thy offred weale, and disobay my will. 1970
Even by his strength I sweare, that fyrst did geve me lyfe
And gave me in my youth the strength, to get thee on my wyfe,
On lesse by wensday next, thou bende as I am bent,
And at our castle cald free towne, thou freely doe assent
To Counte Paris sute, and promise to agree
To whatsoever then shall passe, twixt him, my wife, and me:

Not onely will I geve all that I have away,
From thee, to those that shall me love, me honor, and obay:
But also too so close, and to so hard a gayle,
I shall thee wed for all thy life, that sure thou shalt not fayle,   1980
A thousand times a day to wishe for sodayn death:
And curse the day, and howre when first thy lunges did geve thee breath.

[Juliet visits the Friar for comfort and aid.]

Her voyce with piteous plaint was made already horce,   2013
And hasty sobs, when she would speake, brake of her woordes parforce.
But as she may peece meale, she powreth in his lappe,
The mariage newes, a mischief newe, prepared by mishappe.
Her parentes promisse erst to Counte Paris past,
Her fathers threats she telleth him, and thus concludes at last.
Once was I wedded well, ne will I wed agayne,
For since I know I may not be the wedded wyfe of twayne,   2020
For I am bound to have one God, one fayth, one make,
My purpose is as soone as I shall hence my jorney take
With these two handes which joynde unto the heavens I stretch,
The hasty death which I desire unto my selfe to reache.
This day (O Romeus) this day thy wofull wife
Will bring the end of all her cares by ending carefull lyfe.
So my departed sprite shall witnes to the skye,
And eke my blood unto the earth beare record how that I
Have kept my fayth unbroke, stedfast unto my frende.

Whereat, the fryer astonde, and gastfully afrayde,   2033
Lest she by dede perfourme her woord, thus much to her he sayde.
Ah lady Juliet, what nede the wordes you spake?

So holesome salve will I for your afflictions finde,   2041
That you shall hence depart agayne with well contented mynde.
His wordes have chased straight out of her hart despayre:
Her blacke and ougly dredfull thoughts by hope are waxen fayre.
So fryer Lawrence now hath left her there alone,
And he out of the church in hast is to his chaumber gone.
Where sundry thoughtes within his carefull head arise:
The old mans foresight divers doutes hath set before his eyes.
His conscience one while condems it for a sinne,
To let her take Paris to spouse, since he himselfe had byn   2050
The chefest cause, that she unknowne to father or mother,
Not five monthes past in that selfe place was wedded to another.
An other while an hugy heape of daungers dred,
His restles thought hath heaped up, within his troubled hed.

Deere daughter (quoth the fryer) of good chere see thou be,   2073
For loe, sainct Frauncis of his grace hath shewde a way to me,
By which I may both thee, and Romeus together,
Out of the bondage which you feare assuredly deliver.

Wherfore my daughter geve good eare, unto my counsels sounde.   2090
Forget not what I say, ne tell it any wight,
Not to the nurce thou trustest so, as Romeus is thy knight.
For on this threed doth hang thy death and eke thy lyfe,
My fame, or shame, his weale or woe, that chose thee to his wyfe.

But not in vayne (my childe) hath all my wandring byn,   2105
Beside the great contentednes my sprete abydeth in.
That by the pleasant thought of passed thinges doth grow
One private frute more have I pluckd which thou shalt shortly know:
What force the stones, the plants, and metals have to woorke,
And divers other things that in the bowels of earth do loorke,   2110
With care I have sought out, with payne I did them prove,
With them eke can I helpe my selfe, at times of my behove,...

Knowe therfore (daughter) that with other gyftes which I   2125
Have well attained to by grace and favour of the skye,
Long since I did finde out, and yet the way I knowe
Of certain rootes and savory herbes, to make a kinde of dowe,
Which baked hard, and bet into a powder fine,
And dronke with conduite water, or with any kynd of wine,   2130
It doth in halfe an howre astonne the taker so,
And mastreth all his sences, that he feeleth weale nor woe,
And so it burieth up the sprite and living breath,
That even the skilfull leche would say, that he is slayne by death.
Receive this vyoll small, and keepe it as thine eye,   2149
And on thy mariage day before the sunne doe cleare the skye,
Fill it with water full, up to the very brim.
Then drinke it of, and thou shalt feele, throughout eche vayne and lim
A pleasant slumber slide, and quite dispred at length,
On all thy partes, from every part reve all thy kindly strength.
Withouten moving thus thy ydle parts shall rest,
No pulse shall goe, ne hart once beate within thy hollow brest.
But thou shalt lye as she that dyeth in a traunce:
Thy kinsmen, and thy trusty frendes shall wayle the sodain chaunce:
Thy corps then will they bring to grave in this church yarde,
Where thy forefathers long agoe a costly tombe preparde,   2160
Both for themselfe, and eke for those that should come after,
Both deepe it is, and long and large, where thou shalt rest my daughter,
Till I to Mantua sende for Romeus thy knight.

Her fainting hart was comforted, with hope and pleasant thought.   2176
And then to him she said, doubte not but that I will
With stoute and unappauled hart, your happy hest fulfill.
Yea, if I wist it were a venemous dedly drinke:
Rather would I that through my throte the certaine bane should sinke, 2180
Then I (not drinking it) into his handes should fall,
That hath no part of me as yet, ne ought to have at all.

A thousand thankes and more, our Juliet gave the fryer,   2191
And homeward to her fathers house joyfull she doth retyre.
And as with stately gate she passed through the streete,
She saw her mother in the doore, that with her there would meete:
In mynd to aske if she her purpose yet did holde,
In mynd also a part twixt them, her duety to have tolde:
Wherfore with pleasant face, and with unwonted chere,
As soone as she was unto her approched sumwhat nere,
Before the mother spake, thus did she fyrst begin:
Madame, at sainct Frauncis churche have I this morning byn,   2200
Where I did make abode, a longer while (percase)
Then dewty would, yet have I not been absent from this place,
So long a while, whithout a great and just cause why:
This frute have I receaved there, my hart erst lyke to dye,
Is now revived agayne, and my afflicted brest,
Released from affliction, restored is to rest.
For lo, my troubled gost (alas too sore diseasde,)
By gostly counsell and advise, hath fryer Lawrence easde,
To whome I did at large discourse my former lyfe,
And in confession did I tell of all our passed strife: 2210
Of Counte Paris sute, and how my lord my syre,
By my ungrate and stubborne stryfe, I styrred unto yre.
But lo, the holy fryer hath by his gostly lore,
Made me another woman now, then I had been before.

Yet mother now behold, your daughter at your will,   2221
Ready (if you commaunde her ought) your pleasure to fulfill.
Wherfore in humble wise dere madam I you pray
To goe unto my lord and syre, withouten long delay:
Of him fyrst pardon crave of faultes already past,
And shew him (if it pleaseth you) his child is now at last
Obedient to his lust and to his skilfull hest.
And that I will (god lending life) on wensday next be prest,
To wayte on him and you, unto thappoynted place,
Where I will in your hearing and before my fathers face,   2230
Unto the Counte geve my fayth and whole assent,
To take him for my lord and spouse: thus fully am I bent.
And that out of your mynde I may remove all doute,
Unto my closet fare I now, to searche and to choose out
The bravest garmentes and the richest jewels there,
Which (better him to please) I mynd on wensday next to weare.

These said, the glad old man, from home, goeth straight abrode,   2255
And to the stately palace hyeth, where Paris made abode.
Whom he desyres to be on wensday next his geast,
At Freetowne, where he myndes to make for him a costly feast.
But loe, the Earle saith such feasting were but lost,
And counsels him till mariage time to spare so great a cost.   2260
For then he knoweth well the charges wilbe great,
The whilst his hart desyreth still her sight, and not his meate.

He craves of Capilet, that he may straight go see
Fayre Juliet, wher to he doth right willingly agree.
The mother warnde before, her daughter doth prepare:
She warneth and she chargeth her that in no wyse she spare
Her curteous speche, her pleasant lookes, and commely grace,
But liberally to geve them forth when Paris commes in place.
Which she as cunningly could set forth to the shewe,
As cunning craftesmen to the sale do set theire wares on rew: 2270
That ere the County did out of her sight depart,
So secretly unwares to him, she stale away his hart,
That of his lyfe and death the wyly wench hath powre:
And now his longing hart thinkes long for theyr appoynted howre.
And with importune sute, the parentes doth he pray,
The wedlocke knot to knit soone up, and hast the mariage day.

The flattring nurce did prayse the fryer for his skill, 2295
And said that she had done right well by wit to order will.
She setteth foorth at large the fathers furious rage,
And eke she prayseth much to her, the second mariage.
And County Paris now she praiseth ten times more,
By wrong, then she her selfe by right, had Romeus praysde before. 2300
Paris shall dwell there still, Romeus shall not retourne,
What shall it boote her life, to languish still and mourne.
The pleasures past before, she must account as gayne,
But if he doe retorne, what then? for one she shall have twayne.
The one shall use her as his lawfull wedded wyfe,
In wanton love, with equall joy the other leade his lyfe:
And best shall she be sped of any townish dame,
Of husband and of paramour, to fynde her chaunge of game.
These wordes and like, the nurce did speake, in hope to please,
But greatly did these wicked wordes the ladies mynde disease: 2310
But ay she hid her wrath, and seemed well content,
When dayly dyd the naughty nurce new argumentes invent:

Unto her chaumber doth the pensive wight repayre, 2317
And in her hand a percher light the nurce beares up the stayre.
In Juliets chamber was her wonted use to lye,
Wherfore her mistres dreading that she should her work descrye 2320
As sone as she began her pallet to unfold,
Thinking to lye that night, where she was wont to lye of olde:
Doth gently pray her seeke, her lodgeing some where els.
And lest the crafty should suspect, a ready reason telles.
Dere frend (quoth she) you knowe, to morow is the day
Of new contract, wherfore this night, my purpose is to pray,
Unto the heavenly myndes, that dwell above the skyes,
And order all the course of thinges, as they can best devyse,
That they so smyle upon the doynges of to morow,
That all the remnant of my lyfe, may be exempt from sorow: 2330
Wherfore I pray you leave me here alone this night,
But see that you to morow comme before the dawning light,

For you must coorle my heare, and set on my attyre.
And easely the loving nurse, dyd yelde to her desire.
For she within her hed dyd cast before no doute,
She little knew the close attempt, her nurce childe went about.
The nurce departed once, the chamber doore shut close,
Assured that no living wight, her doing myght disclose,
She powred forth into the vyole of the fryer,
Water out of a silver ewer, that on the boord stoode by her.   2340
The slepy mixture made, fayre Juliet doth it hyde,
Under her bolster soft, and so unto her bed she hyed:
Where divers novel thoughts arise within her hed,
And she is so invironed about with deadly dred,
That what before she had resolved undoutedly,
That same she calleth into doute, and lying doutfully,
Whilst honest love did strive with dred of dedly payne,
With handes ywrong, and weping eyes, thus gan she to complaine.
What, is there any one beneth the heavens hye,
So much unfortunate as I, so much past hope as I?   2350
What, am not I my selfe of all that yet were borne,
The depest drenched in dispayre, and most in Fortunes skorne?
For loe the world for me, hath nothing els to finde,
Beside mishap and wretchednes, and anguish of the mynde,
Since that the cruel cause of my unhappines,
Hath put me to this sodaine plonge, and brought to such distres,
As (to the end I may my name and conscience save,)
I must devowre the mixed drinke, that by me here I have.
Whose woorking and whose force as yet I doe not know.
And of this piteous plaint began another doute to growe.   2360
What doe I knowe (quoth she) if that this powder shall
Sooner or later then it should or els not woorke at all?
And then my craft descride, as open as the day,
The peoples tale and laughing stocke, shall I remayne for aye.
And what know I (quoth she) if serpentes odious,
And other beastes and wormes that are of nature venemous,
That wonted are to lurke, in darke caves under grounde,
And commonly as I have heard in dead mens tombes are found,
Shall harme me yea or nay, where I shall lye as ded,
Or how shall I that alway have in so freshe ayre been bred   2370
Endure the lothsome stinke of such an heaped store
Of carkases, not yet consumde and bones that long before
Intombed were, where I my sleping place shall have,
Where all my auncesters doe rest, my kindreds common grave?
Shall not the fryer and my Romeus, when they come,
Fynd me (if I awake before) ystifled in the tombe?
And whilst she in these thoughtes doth dwell somwhat to long,
The force of her ymagining, anon dyd waxe so strong,
That she surmysde she saw out of the hollow vaulte,
(A griesly thing to looke upon,) the carkas of Tybalt,   2380
Right in the selfe same sort, that she few dayes before
Had seene him in his blood embrewde, to death eke wounded sore.
And then, when she agayne within her selfe had wayde,

That quicke she should be buried there, and by his side be layde
All comfortles, for she shall living feere have none
But many a rotten carkas, and full many a naked bone:
Her dainty tender partes gan shever all for dred,
Her golden heares did stand upright, upon her chillish hed.
Then pressed with the feare that she there lived in,
A sweat as colde as mountaine yse, pearst through her tender skin, 2390
That with the moysture hath wet every part of hers,
And more besides, she vainely thinkes, whilst vainely thus she feares,
A thousand bodies dead have compast her about,
And lest they will dismember her, she greatly standes in dout.
But when she felt her strength began to weare away,
By little and little, and in her hart her feare increased ay:
Dreading that weakenes might, or foolish cowardise,
Hinder the execution of the purposde enterprise,
As she had frantike been, in hast the glasse she cought,
And up she dranke the mixture quite, withouten farther thought. 2400
Then on her brest she crost her armes long and small,
And so, her senses fayling her, into a traunce did fall.
And when that Phoebus bright heaved up his seemely hed,
And from the East in open skies his glistring rayes dispred,
The nurce unshut the doore, for she the key did keepe,
And douting she had slept to long, she thought to breake her slepe.
Fyrst, softly dyd she call, then lowder thus did crye,
Lady, you slepe to long, (the Earle) will rayse you by and by.
But wele away, in vayne unto the deafe she calles,
She thinkes to speake to Juliet, but speaketh to the walles. 2410

She thought to daw her now as she had donne of olde, 2417
But loe, she found her parts were stiffe, and more then marble colde.
Neither at mouth nor nose, found she recourse of breth:
Two certaine argumentes were these, of her untimely death. 2420
Wherfore as one distraught, she to her mother ranne,
With scratched face, and heare betorne, but no woord speake she can.
At last (with much a doe) dead (quoth she) is my childe.
Now, out alas (the mother cryde) and as a Tyger wilde,
Whose whelpes whilst she is gonne out of her denne to pray,
The hunter gredy of his game, doth kill or cary away:
So, rageing forth she ranne, unto her Juliets bed,
And there she found her derling, and her onely comfort ded.

[All lament the supposed death of Juliet.]

That day the day of wrath, and eke of pity to have beene. 2450
But more then all the rest the fathers hart was so
Smit with the heavy newes, and so shut up with sodain woe,
That he ne had the powre his daughter to bewepe,
Ne yet to speake, but long is forsd, his teares and plaint to kepe.

If ever there hath been a lamentable day, 2459
A day ruthfull, unfortunate, and fatall, then I say,

The same was it in which, through Veron towne was spred,
The wofull newes how Juliet was sterved in her bed.

Whilst Juliet slept, and whilst the other wepen thus: 2473
Our fryer Lawrence hath by this, sent one to Romeus.
A frier of his house, there never was a better,
He trusted him even as himselfe, to whom he gave a letter:

Thys letter closde he sendes to Romeus by his brother: 2485
He chargeth him that in no case he geve it any other.
Apace our frier John to Mantua him hyes,
And for because in Italy it is a wonted gyse,
That friers in the towne should seeldome walke alone,
But of theyr covent ay should be accompanide with one   2490
Of his profession, straight a house he fyndth out,
In mynde to take some frier with him, to walke the towne about.
But entred once, he might not issue out agayne,
For that a brother of the house, a day before or twayne,
Dyed of the plague (a sickenes which they greatly feare and hate)
So were the brethren charged to kepe within theyr covent gate,
Bard of theyr felowship, that in the towne do wonne:

The fryer by this restraint, beset with dred and sorow,   2501
Not knowing what the letters held, differd untill the morowe:
And then he thought in tyme to send to Romeus,
But whilst at Mantua where he was, these dooinges framed thus,
The towne of Juliets byrth was wholy busied,
About her obsequies, to see theyr darlyng buried.
Now is the parentes myrth quite chaunged into mone,
And now to sorow is retornde the joy of every one.
And now the wedding weedes for mourning weedes they chaunge,
And Hymene into a Dyrge, alas it seemeth straunge.   2510
In steade of mariage gloves, now funerall gloves they have,
And whom they should see maried, they follow to the grave.
The feast that should have been of pleasure and of joy,
Hath every dish, and cup, fild full of sorow and annoye.
Now throughout Italy this common use they have,
That all the best of every stocke are earthed in one grave:
For every houshold, if it be of any fame,
Doth bylde a tombe, or digge a vault that beares the housholdes name.
Wherein (if any of that kindred hap to dye)
They are bestowde, els in the same no other corps may lye.   2520
The Capilets, her corps in such a one dyd lay,
Where Tybalt slayne of Romeus, was layde the other day:
An other use there is, that whosoever dyes,
Borne to their church with open face, upon the beere he lyes
In wonted weede attyrde, not wrapt in winding sheete:
So, as by chaunce he walked abrode, our Romeus man dyd meete
His maisters wyfe: the sight with sorow straight dyd wounde
His honest hart: with teares he sawe her lodged under ground.

And for he had been sent to Verone for a spye,
The doynges of the Capilets by wisdome to descrye, 2530
And for he knew her death dyd tooch his maister most,
(Alas) too soone, with heavy newes he hyed away in post:
And in his house he found his maister Romeus,
Where he besprent with many teares, began to speake him thus.

[Romeus receives the fatal news and seeks out an Apothecary.]

· Wherfore, when he his face hath washt with water cleene, 2557
Lest that the staynes of dryed teares, might on his cheekes be seene,
And so his sorow should of every one be spyde,
Which he with all his care dyd seeke from every one to hyde: 2560
Straight, wery of the house, he walketh forth abrode:
His servaunt at the maisters hest in chamber styll abode:
And then fro streate to streate, he wandreth up and downe,
To see if he in any place may fynde in all the towne,
A salve meete for his sore, an oyle fitte for his wounde,
And seeking long (alack too soone) the thing he sought, he founde.
An Apothecary sate unbusied at his doore,
Whom by his heavy countenaunce he gessed to be poore,
And in his shop he saw his boxes were but fewe,
And in his window (of his wares) there was so small a shew, 2570
Wherfore our Romeus assuredly hath thought,
What by no frendship could be got, with money should be bought.
For nedy lacke is lyke the poore man to compell,
To sell that which the cities lawe forbiddeth him to sell.
Then by the hand he drew the nedy man apart,
And with the sight of glittring gold inflamed hath his hart.
Take fiftie crownes of gold (quoth he) I geve them thee,
So that before I part from hence thou straight deliver me
Somme poyson strong, that may in lesse then halfe an howre,
Kill him whose wretched hap shalbe the potion to devowre. 2580
The wretch by covetise is wonne, and doth assent,
To sell the thing, whose sale ere long too late he doth repent.
In hast he poyson sought, and closely he it bounde,
And then began with whispering voyce thus in his eare to rounde:
Fayre syr (quoth he) be sure, this is the speeding gere,
And more there is then you shall nede, for halfe of that is there
Will serve, I under take, in lesse then half an howre,
To kill the strongest man alive, such is the poysons power.

But Romeus, the whyle, with many a dedly thought, 2603
Provoked much, hath caused ynke and paper to be brought,
And in few lynes he dyd of all his love dyscoorse,...

The letters closd and seald, directed to his syre, 2611
He locketh in his purse, and then, a post hors doth he hyre.
When he approched nere, he warely lighted downe,
And even with the shade of night, he entred Verone towne,

Where he hath found his man, wayting when he should comme,
With lanterne, and with instruments, to open Juliets toomme.
Helpe Peter, helpe quod he, helpe to remove the stone,
And straight when I am gone fro thee my Juliet to bemone,
See that thou get thee hence, and on the payne of death,
I charge thee that thou comme not nere, whyle I abyde beneath,   2620
Ne seeke thou not to let thy masters enterprise,
Which he hath fully purposed to doe in any wise.
Take there a letter, which as soone as he shall ryse,
Present it in the morning to my loving fathers eyes.
Which unto him perhaps farre pleasanter shall seeme,
Then eyther I do mynd to say, or thy grose head can deeme.
Now Peter that knew not the purpose of his hart,
Obediently a little way withdrew himselfe apart,
And then our Romeus, (the vault stone set upright)
Descended downe, and in his hand, he bare the candle light.   2630
And then with piteous eye, the body of his wyfe
He gan beholde, who surely was the organ of his lyfe.
For whom unhappy now he is, but erst was blyst:
He watred her with teares, and then an hundred times her kyst.
And in his folded armes, full straightly he her plight,
But no way could his greedy eyes be filled with her sight.
His fearfull handes he layd upon her stomacke colde,
And them on divers parts besyde, the wofull wight did hold.
But when he could not fynd the signes of lyfe he sought,
Out of his cursed box he drewe the poyson that he bought.   2640
Wherof, he gredely devowrde the greater part,
And then he cryde with dedly sigh, fetcht from his mourning hart:
Oh Juliet, of whom the world unwoorthy was,
From which, for worldes unworthines thy worthy gost dyd passe:
What death more pleasant could my hart wish to abyde,
Then that which here it suffreth now, so nere thy frendly syde?
Or els so glorious tombe, how could my youth have craved,
As in one selfe same vaulte with thee haply to be ingraved?
What Epitaph more worth, or halfe so excellent,
To consecrate my memorye, could any man invente   2650
As this, our mutuell, and our piteous sacrifice
Of lyfe, set light for love: but while he talketh in this wise,
And thought as yet a while his dolors to enforce,
His tender hart began to faynt, prest with the venoms force:
Which little and little gan to overcomme hys hart:
And whilst his busy eyne he threwe about to every part,
He saw hard by the corce of sleping Juliet,
Bold Tybalts carkas dead, which was not all consumed yet,
To whom (as having life) in this sort speaketh he:
Ah cosin dere Tybalt, whereso thy restles sprite now be,   2660
With stretched handes to thee for mercy now I crye,
For that before thy kindly howre I forced thee to dye.
But if with quenched lyfe, not quenched be thine yre,
But with revengeing lust as yet thy hart be set on fyre:

What more amendes, or cruell wreke desyrest thou
To see on me, then this which here is shewd forth to thee now?
Who reft by force of armes from thee thy living breath,
The same with his owne hand (thou seest) doth poyson himselfe to death.
And for he caused thee in tombe too soone to lye,
Too soone also, yonger then thou himselfe he layeth by.   2670
These said, when he gan feele, the poysons force prevayle,
And little and little mastred lyfe, for aye beganne to fayle,
Kneeling upon his knees, he said with voyce full lowe.
Lord Christ that so to raunsome me descendedst long agoe,
Out of thy fathers bosome, and in the virgins wombe,
Didst put on fleshe, Oh let my plaint out of this hollow toombe,
Perce through the ayre, and graunt my sute may favour finde.
Take pity on my sinnefull and my poore afflicted mynde.
For well enough I know, this body is but clay,
Nought but a masse of sinne, to frayle, and subject to decay.   2680
Then pressed with extreme greefe, he threw with so great force,
His overpressed parts upon his ladies wayled corps,
That now his wekened hart, weakened with tormentes past,
Unable to abyde this pang, the sharpest and the last,
Remayned quite deprived, of sense and kindly strength,
And so the long imprisond soule, hath freedome wonne at length.

[The Friar goes to the tomb at the appointed time.]

Approching nigh the place, and seeing there the lyght,   2695
Great horror felt he in his hart, by straunge and sodaine sight,
Tyll Peter (Romeus man) his coward hart made bolde,
When of his masters being there, the certain newes he tolde.
There hath he been (quoth he) this halfe howre at the least,
And in this time I dare well say his plaint hath still increast.   2700
Then both they entred in, where they (alas) dyd fynde,
The bretheles corps of Romeus, forsaken of the mynde.
Where they have made such mone, as they may best conceve,
That have with perfect frendship loved, whose frend, feerce death dyd reve.
But whilst with piteous playnt, they Romeus fate bewepe,
An howre too late fayre Juliet awaked out of slepe.
And much amasde to see in tombe so great a light,
She wist not if she saw a dreame, or sprite that walkd by night.
But cumming to her selfe, she knew them, and said thus:
What fryer Lawrence, is it you? where is my Romeus?   2710
And then the auncient frier, that greatly stoode in feare,
Lest if they lingred over long, they should be taken theare,
In few plaine woordes, the whole that was betyde he tolde,
And with his fingar shewd his corps out stretched, stiffe, and colde,
And then perswaded her with pacience to abyde
This sodain great mischaunce, and sayth that he will soone provyde
In somme religious house for her a quiet place,
Where she may spend the rest of lyfe, and where in time percase
She may with wisdomes meane, measure her mourning brest,
And unto her tormented soule call backe exiled rest.   2720

[Juliet laments Romeus's death.]

Ah thou most fortunate and most unhappy tombe,   2755
For thou shalt beare from age to age, witnes in time to comme,
Of the most perfect leage, betwixt a payre of lovers,
That were the most unfortunate, and fortunate of others:
Receave the latter sigh, receave the latter pang,
Of the most cruell of cruell slaves, that wrath and death ay wrang.   2760
And when our Juliet would continue still her mone,
The fryer and the servant fled, and left her there alone.
For they a sodayne noyse, fast by the place did heare,
And lest they might be taken there, greatly they stoode in feare.
When Juliet saw her selfe left in the vaulte alone,
That freely she might worke her will, for let or stay was none:
Then once for all, she tooke the cause of all her harmes,
The body dead of Romeus, and claspd it in her armes:
Then she with earnest kisse, sufficiently did prove,
That more then by the feare of death, she was attaint by love.   2770
And then past deadly feare, for lyfe ne had she care,
With hasty hand she did draw out, the dagger that he ware.
O welcome death (quoth she) end of unhappines,
That also art beginning of assured happines:
Feare not to darte me nowe, thy stripe no longer stay,
Prolong no longer now my lyfe, I hate this long delaye.
For straight my parting sprite, out of this carkas fled,
At ease shall finde my Romeus sprite, emong so many ded.
And thou my loving lord, Romeus my trusty feer,
If knowledge yet doe rest in thee, if thou these woordes dost heer: 2780
Receve thou her whom thou didst love so lawfully,
That causd (alas) thy violent death although unwillingly.
And therfore willingly offers to thee her gost,
To thend that no wight els but thou, might have just cause to boste
Thinjoying of my love, which ay I have reserved,
Free from the rest, bound unto thee, that hast it well deserved.
That so our parted sprites, from light that we see here,
In place of endlesse light and blisse, may ever live yfere.
These said, her ruthlesse hand through gyrt her valiant hart.

The watchemen of the towne, the whilst are passed by,   2793
And through the grates the candel light within the tombe they spye:
Wherby they did suppose, inchaunters to be comme,
That with prepared instrumentes had opend wide the tombe,
In purpose to abuse the bodies of the ded,
Which by theyr science ayde abusde do stand them oft in sted.
Theyr curious harts desire, the trueth herof to know,...

Then here and there so long with carefull eye they sought,   2805
That at the length hidden they found the murthrers, so they thought.
In dongeon depe that night they lodgde them under grounde,
The next day do they tell the prince the mischefe that they found.

The prince did straight ordaine, the corses that wer founde   2817
Should be set forth upon a stage, hye raysed from the grounde,
Right in the selfe same fourme, (shewde forth to all mens sight)
That in the hollow valt they had been found that other night.   2820
And eke that Romeus man, and fryer Lawrence should
Be openly examined, for els the people would
Have murmured, or faynd there were some wayghty cause,
Why openly they were not calde, and so convict by lawes.

[The Friar, with philosophical embellishments and at great length, recounts the whole course of events.]

But at all times men have the choyce of dooing good or bad: 2872
Even as the sprite of God, the hartes of men doth guyde,
Or as it leaveth them to stray from Vertues path asyde.
As for the yrons that were taken in my hand,
As now I deeme, I neede not seeke, to make ye understande,
To what use yron first was made, when it began:
How of it selfe it helpeth not, ne yet can helpe a man.
The thing that hurteth, is the malice of his will,
That such indifferent thinges is wont to use and order yll.   2880

The wyser sort to councell called by Escalus,   2985
Have geven advyse, and Escalus sagely decreeth thus.
The nurse of Juliet, is banisht in her age,
Because that from the parentes she dyd hyde the mariage.
Which might have wrought much good, had it in time been knowne,
Where now by her concealing it, a mischeefe great is growne.   2990
And Peter, for he dyd obey his masters hest,
In woonted freedome had good leave to leade his lyfe in rest.
Thapothecary, high is hanged by the throte,
And for the paynes he tooke with him, the hangman had his cote.
But now what shall betyde of this gray bearded syre?
Of fryer Lawrence thus araynde, that good barefooted fryre.
Because that many times he woorthely did serve
The commen welth, and in his lyfe was never found to swerve:
He was discharged quyte, and no marke of defame,
Did seeme to blot, or touch at all, the honor of his name.   3000
But of him selfe he went into an Hermitage,
Two myles from Veron towne, where he in prayers past forth his age.
Tyll that from earth to heaven, his heavenly sprite dyd flye,
Fyve yeres he lived an Hermite, and an Hermite dyd he dye.
The straungenes of the chaunce, when tryed was the truth
The Montagewes and Capelets hath moved so to ruth,
That with their emptyed teares, theyr choler and theyr rage,
Was emptied quite, and they whose wrath no wisdom could asswage,
Nor threatning of the prince, ne mynd of murthers donne:
At length (so mighty Jove it would) by pitye they are wonne.   3010

And lest that length of time might from our myndes remove,
The memory of so perfect, sound, and so approved love:
The bodies dead removed from vaulte where they did dye,
In stately tombe, on pillers great, of marble rayse they hye.
On every syde above, were set and eke beneath,
Great store of cunning Epitaphes, in honor of theyr death.
And even at this day the tombe is to be seene.
So that among the monumentes that in Verona been,
There is no monument more worthy of the sight:
Then is the tombe of Juliet, and Romeus her knight.   3020

¶ Imprinted at London in
Flete strete within Temble barre, at
the signe of the hand and starre, by
Richard Tottill the .xix. day of
November. An. do. 1562.

READING LIST

This list includes details of books and articles referred to in the Introduction or Commentary, and may serve as a guide to those who wish to undertake further study of the play.

Andrews, J. F. (ed.). *'Romeo and Juliet': Critical Essays*, 1993
Appelbaum, Robert. '"Standing to the Wall": The Pressures of Masculinity in *Romeo and Juliet*', *SQ* 48 (1997), 251–72
Brooke, Nicholas. *Shakespeare's Early Tragedies*, 1968
Brown, John R. *Shakespeare's Dramatic Style*, 1970
Buhler, Stephen M. 'Reviving Juliet, Repackaging Romeo: Transformations of Character in Pop and Post-Pop Music', *Shakespeare After Mass Media*, ed. Richard Burt, 2002, 243–64
Callaghan, Dympna. 'The Ideology of Romantic Love: The Case of *Romeo and Juliet*', Callaghan, Lorraine Helms and Jyotsna Singh. *The Wayward Sisters*, 1994, 59–101
Carroll, W. C. '"We were born to die": *Romeo and Juliet*', *Comparative Drama* 15 (1981), 54–71
Charlton, H. B. *Shakespearian Tragedy*, 1948
Clemen, W. H. *The Development of Shakespeare's Imagery*, 1951
Colaco, Jill. *'Lovers' tongues by night'. The Window Scenes in 'Romeo and Juliet'*, Winthrop Sargent Prize, Harvard, 1981
Colie, Rosalie L. *Shakespeare's Living Art*, 1974
Cribb, T. J. 'The Unity of *Romeo and Juliet*', *S.Sur.* 34 (1981), 93–104
Dickey, Franklin M. *Not Wisely But Too Well: Shakespeare's Love Tragedies*, 1957
Doran, Madeleine. *Shakespeare's Dramatic Language*, 1976
Evans, Bertrand. *Shakespeare's Tragic Practice*, 1979
Garber, Marjorie. *Coming of Age in Shakespeare*, 1981
Gibbons, Brian. Introduction to the New Arden *Romeo and Juliet*, 1980
Goddard, H. C. *The Meaning of Shakespeare*, 1951
Granville-Barker, H. *Prefaces to Shakespeare*, 1951 (vol. II)
Halio, J. L. (ed.). *Shakespeare's 'Romeo and Juliet' Texts, Contexts, and Interpretation*, 1995
Hodgdon, Barbara. '*William Shakespeare's Romeo + Juliet*: Everything's Nice in America?', *S.Sur.* 52 (1999), 88–98
Holmer, Joan Ozark. '"Myself Condemned and Myself Excused": Tragic Effects in *Romeo and Juliet*', *Studies in Philology* 88 (1991), 345–62
Hunt, Maurice (ed.). *Approaches to Teaching Romeo and Juliet*, 2000

Kiefer, Frederick. *Fortune and Elizabethan Tragedy*, 1983

Kirsch, Arthur. *The Passions of Shakespeare's Tragic Heroes*, 1990

Lawlor, John. 'Romeo and Juliet', in J. R. Brown and B. Harris (eds.), *Early Shakespeare*, 1961

Levenson, J. L. 'Romeo and Juliet'. *Shakespeare In Performance*, 1987

Levin, Harry. 'Form and formality in *Romeo and Juliet*', in his *Shakespeare and the Revolution of the Times*, 1976

Mason, Harold A. *Shakespeare's Tragedies of Love*, 1970

Moisan, Thomas. 'Chaucer's Pandarus and the sententious Friar Lawrence', *Publications of the Arkansas Philological Association* 8 (1982), 38–48

   'Rhetoric and rehearsal of death: the Lamentations' scene in *Romeo and Juliet*', *SQ* 34 (1983), 389–404

Shakespeare's Chaucerian allegory: the quest for death in *Romeo and Juliet* and the Pardoner's Tale', in E. T. Donaldson, et al. (eds.), *Chaucerian Shakespeare: Adaptation and Transformation*, 1983

   '"O anything of nothing first create": gender, patriarchy, and the tragedy of *Romeo and Juliet*', in Dorothea Kehler and Susan Baker (eds.), *Another Country: Feminist Perspectives on Renaissance Drama*, 1991

Moore, Olin H. *The Legend of Romeo and Juliet*, 1950

Muir, Kenneth. *Shakespeare's Tragic Sequence*, 1972

Nevo, Ruth. *Tragic Form in Shakespeare*, 1972

Peterson, D. L. 'Romeo and Juliet and the art of moral navigation', in W. F. McNeir and T. N. Greenfield (eds.), *Pacific Coast Studies in Shakespeare*, 1966

Porter, J. A. *Shakespeare's Mercutio. His History in Drama*, 1988

Porter, Joseph (ed.). *Critical Essays on Shakespeare's Romeo and Juliet*, 1997

Quinones, Ricardo J. *The Renaissance Discovery of Time*, 1972

Rabkin, Norman. *Shakespeare and the Common Understanding*, 1967

Seward, J. H. *Tragic Vision in 'Romeo and Juliet'*, 1973

Shakespeare Survey 47, 1996 (devoted largely to *Romeo and Juliet*)

Siegel, Paul. 'Christianity and the religion of love in *Romeo and Juliet*', *SQ* 12 (1961), 371–92

Stamm, Rudolf. 'The first meeting of the lovers in Shakespeare's *Romeo and Juliet*', *English Studies* 67 (1986), 2–13

   Shakespeare's Theatrical Notation: The Early Tragedies, 1989

Stavig, Mark. *The Forms of Things Unknown; Renaissance Metaphor in 'Romeo and Juliet' and 'A Midsummer Night's Dream'*, 1995

Stewart, Stanley. 'Romeo and necessity', in W. F. McNeir and T. N. Greenfield (eds.), *Pacific Coast Studies in Shakespeare*, 1966

Wallace, Nathaniel. 'Cultural Tropology in *Romeo and Juliet*', *Studies in Philology* 88 (1991), 329–44

Wells, Stanley. 'Juliet's Nurse: the uses of inconsequentiality', in Philip Edwards, Inga-Stina Ewbank and G. K. Hunter (eds.), *Shakespeare's Styles. Essays in Honour of Kenneth Muir*, 1980

Wells, Stanley (ed.). *Romeo and Juliet and its Afterlife: S.Sur.* 49 (1996)

Whitaker, Virgil. *The Mirror up to Nature. The Technique of Shakespeare's Tragedies*, 1965

Wilson, H. S. *On the Design of Shakespearian Tragedy*, 1957

Wright, K. L. *Shakespeare's 'Romeo and Juliet' in Performance*, 1997

Young, B. W. 'Haste, consent, and age at marriage: some implications of social History for *Romeo and Juliet*', *Iowa State Journal of Research* 62 (1988), 459–74.